Regional Governance in Post-NAFTA North America

Twenty years after NAFTA, the consensus seems to be that the regional project in North America is dead. The trade agreement was never followed up by new institutions that might cement a more ambitious regional community. The Security and Prosperity Partnership (SPP), launched with some fanfare in 2005, was quietly discontinued in 2009. And new cooperative ventures like the US-Canada Beyond the Border talks and the US-Mexico Merida Initiative suggest that the three governments have reverted to the familiar, pre-NAFTA pattern of informal, incremental bilateralism. One could argue, however, that while NAFTA itself has been buried, the region somehow lives on, albeit in a form very different from regional integration in other parts of the world.

A diverse group of contributors, from the US, Canada, and Mexico, with experience in academia, government service, think tanks, and the private sector bring to bear a sophisticated and much-needed examination of regional governance in North America, its historical origins, its connection to the regional distribution of power and the respective governments' domestic institutions, and the variance of its forms and function across different issue areas. The editors begin by surveying the literature on North American regional politics, matching up developments there with parallel debates and controversies in the broader literatures on comparative regional integration and international policy coordination more generally. Six contributors later explore the mechanisms of policy coordination in specific issue-areas, each with an emphasis on a particular set of actors, and with its own way of characterizing the relevant political and diplomatic dynamics. Chapters on the political context for regional policy coordination follow, leading to concluding remarks on the future of North America.

At a time when scholarly interest in North America seems to be waning, even while important and interesting political and economic developments are taking place, this volume will reinvigorate the study of North America as a region, to better understand its past, present, and future.

Brian Bow is Associate Professor of Political Science at Dalhousie University. He is the author of *The Politics of Linkage: Power, Interdependence and Ideas in Canada-US Relations* (2009), which was awarded the Donner Prize as the best public policy book published in Canada that year. He has also published a number of articles and chapters on US-Canada relations, Canadian foreign policy, and regional integration, and has co-edited volumes on North American security cooperation and Canadian foreign policy.

Greg Anderson is Associate Professor of Political Science at the University of Alberta. He is the author of numerous articles on North American integration, international political economy, and US foreign economic policy. He was co-editor, with Christopher Sands, of *Forgotten Partnership Redux: Canada-US Relations in the 21st Century* (2012).

Routledge Studies in North American Politics

1 **Political Institutions and Lesbian and Gay Rights in the United States and Canada**
Miriam Smith

2 **Black Women, Cultural Images and Social Policy**
Julia S. Jordan-Zachery

3 **How Courts Impact Federal Administrative Behavior**
Robert J. Hume

4 **State Failure, Underdevelopment, and Foreign Intervention in Haiti**
Jean-Germain Gros

5 **Mexico-United States Relations**
The Semantics of Sovereignty
Arturo Santa-Cruz

6 **Federalism, Secession, and the American State**
Divided, We Secede
Lawrence M. Anderson

7 **The State and Security in Mexico**
Transformation and Crisis in Regional Perspective
Edited by Brian Bow and Arturo Santa-Cruz

8 **North American Integration**
An Institutional Void in Migration, Security and Development
Edited by Gaspare M. Genna and David A. Mayer-Foulkes

9 **Regional Governance in Post-NAFTA North America**
Building without Architecture
Edited by Brian Bow and Greg Anderson

Regional Governance in Post-NAFTA North America

Building without Architecture

Edited by Brian Bow and Greg Anderson

Routledge
Taylor & Francis Group
NEW YORK AND LONDON

First published 2015
by Routledge
711 Third Avenue, New York, NY 10017

and by Routledge
2 Park Square, Milton Park, Abingdon, Oxon OX14 4RN

Routledge is an imprint of the Taylor & Francis Group, an informa business

Library of Congress Cataloging-in-Publication Data
Regional governance in post-NAFTA North America : building without architecture / edited by Brian Bow and Greg Anderson.
pages cm. — (Routledge studies in North American politics ; 9)
Includes bibliographical references and index.
1. Regionalism—Political aspects—North America. 2. North America—Politics and government—21st century. 3. North America—Foreign relations. 4. North America—Foreign economic relations. 5. North America—Economic integration—Political aspects. 6. North American Free Trade Agreement (1992 October 7). I. Bow, Brian J., author, editor of compilation. II. Anderson, Greg, 1969– author, editor of compilation.
JJ1010.R45 2014
382'.917—dc23
2014021207

ISBN: 978-1-138-77687-6 (hbk)
ISBN: 978-1-315-77299-8 (ebk)

Typeset in Sabon
by Apex CoVantage, LLC

Contents

Figures and Tables

FIGURES

TABLES

Acknowledgments

This volume is dedicated to the memory of a great colleague and mentor, Robert A. Pastor, the founding director of the Center for North American Studies at American University. Bob was an extraordinary role model and friend, having played the game at the highest level—in public service, in academia, and in the service of great causes he believed in—but still generous with his time and energies with those just starting out on their own paths. He could be combative and inflexible, but right behind that sharp edge, there was always openness and warmth, an infectious delight in problem solving and debate, and an irrepressible sense of humor. Bob's doctors told him in 2010 that he had stage 4 cancer, and only a few months to live, but that hardly seemed to slow him down. When we first approached him about contributing to this volume, we were a little hesitant, but Bob jumped in with both feet, and immediately set about challenging (and thereby improving) the core premises and structure of the project itself. We deeply regret that he was not able to complete his contribution to this volume, which built on ideas and evidence from his last book, *The North American Idea* (Oxford 2011). Bob's passing leaves a big hole in the community of scholars working on regional issues in North America, and he will be sorely missed.

We think, however, that Bob would be pleased by the way this volume has renewed and expanded personal and professional connections among varied scholars with an interest in North American issues, and with the forward-looking approach taken by our contributors. We would like to extend sincere thanks to all of our contributors, who stuck with this project over two years, through many changes. We would also like to thank our editor at Routledge, Natalja Mortenson, who was unfailingly patient and supportive throughout the process.

The project began with a workshop in Edmonton, and we would like to thank all of the workshop's participants, whose comments and support helped to solidify the rationale and framework for the resulting volume. That workshop was hosted by the now-defunct Alberta Institute for American Studies (AIAS), and we would like to acknowledge the AIAS, the University of Alberta, and the Canadian Political Science Association for logistical support, and the US Consulate in Calgary for facilitating financial support from the US Embassy in Ottawa.

Bow would like to acknowledge financial support (in the form of a Standard Research Grant) from the Social Sciences and Humanities Research Council of Canada, which made possible a cluster of closely related research projects, bolstering the theoretical and empirical foundations of this volume.

Both authors greatly appreciate the dedicated and skillful research assistance of some of Bow's students over the last few years, particularly John Mitton and Ben O'Bright.

Finally, a word of thanks to our families, for their love, support, and patience.

Brian Bow, Halifax
Greg Anderson, Edmonton

1 Building without Architecture
Regional Governance in Post-NAFTA North America

Brian Bow and Greg Anderson

In the early 1990s, there was some optimism—at least among some pro-market academics—that the North American Free Trade Agreement (NAFTA) might be the first step in the consolidation of North America as a dynamic new world region, following in the wake of the newly resurgent European Community.[1] Twenty years later, the North American regional integration project—if there ever was such a thing—seems to have foundered. And the academic project of studying North America as a region, after a brief revival in the mid-2000s, might be seen to have lost momentum as well.[2]

In retrospect, however, it is clear that the conventional story of North America's foundation and failure is ultimately based on a misreading of the region's dynamics, which came from looking in the wrong places and expecting the wrong things. In the 1990s, perceptions of North America and its prospects were too much influenced by the general dynamics of twentieth-century trade negotiations and by the long shadow of the Maastricht Treaty and newly consolidated European Union. Since then, the wider academic study of regional cooperation has come to recognize more of the complexity and diversity within and between world regions, generating new concepts and theories—i.e., "new regionalism" and "multilevel governance"—which are more relevant to the practice of regional politics in North America, but which have so far only lightly brushed against the specialist literature on North America.

Now that these newer theoretical approaches are starting to run out of steam themselves, and there are calls for the development of a synthetic framework that would reconcile "old" and "new" models of regional cooperation, there is an opportunity to move the study of North America to the forefront of academic and policy debates about regional policy coordination. The purpose of this chapter is to try to gather up some of the threads from past debates and set the stage for a new one. The purpose of this volume as a whole is to try to spur that new debate, by exploring the complex relationship between intergovernmental negotiation, transnational and transgovernmental networks, and domestic institutional constraints, as facets of an already-established but still-evolving complex of regional governance.

ONE STEP BEHIND? A BRIEF REVIEW OF THE NORTH AMERICA DEBATES

The 1992 NAFTA deal followed on the heels of the 1987 Canada-US Free Trade Agreement (CUSFTA), and both were, after all, trade agreements, so our thinking about what they were—and what they could lead to—was unavoidably shaped by the way we think about trade negotiations. Unlike many other issues, international trade has, since the 1950s, been managed by an essentially permanent multilateral process, which has progressed through a series of (more or less productive) bargaining "rounds," and therefore naturally gets us thinking in terms of convergence and tension, stasis and movement, crisis and breakthrough.[3] NAFTA was also a *regional* agreement, and one conceived and crafted during a time when participants and observers agreed that the global multilateral order was giving way to "a world of regions," and the new European Union was boldly blazing a new trail to regional stability, prosperity, and community.[4] No one argued that North America would be, could be, or should be like Europe; but those that hoped North America could be more than just a preferential trade agreement—and even some that hoped otherwise—could not help but be influenced in their thinking by the European "model" and European-inspired ideas about regions and regionalism.[5]

At that time the study of regions was essentially the study of regional integration, the process of integration was seen to play out through the negotiation of ever more ambitious treaties and more robust supranational institutions (or at least intergovernmental agreements that could effectively channel and constrain policy choices), and progress was measured in terms of ratcheting up through sequential steps or stages.[6] There was of course recognition that different regions would follow their own pathways—as seen in Southeast Asia, Latin America, Africa, and the Persian Gulf—but the basic purposes and stages would be similar, and in all cases the observers' focus was on centralized state-to-state negotiations, aimed at identifying common principles and practices, and the development of formal or informal structures for intergovernmental decision making.[7]

NAFTA seemed to fit those patterns, in design if not in intention. But what followed NAFTA did not fit those patterns—or did so only negatively. Some called for leaders to try to maintain regional momentum, by pursuing a "deepening" agenda that would go beyond trade and investment.[8] But this led only to the creation of low-key interbureaucratic working groups and occasional summit meetings.[9] The terrorist attacks of September 11, 2001, were seen at first by some as an opportunity to jump-start the flagging intergovernmental process and move to a new stage,[10] but then very quickly recognized by most as a catastrophe for North American integration, as the new US obsession with border control and homeland security threatened to fatally disrupt the push for a more "streamlined" regional economy.[11] The three countries' political leaders renewed trilateral talks in 2005, by launching the Security and Prosperity Partnership (SPP), but again no new regional institutions were built, and again, the three governments fell back on interbureaucratic working groups, with some input from private-sector stakeholders, and backed up by summit meetings. After the SPP was quietly terminated in 2009, the US began new bilateral talks with Canada and with Mexico, on border management and regulatory coordination, which essentially followed the same basic "working group" format as the much-maligned SPP.[12] Twenty years after NAFTA, no new treaties had been negotiated, no new regional institutions were being built, and there was still no sense of regional identification or any spirit of regionalism to move things forward. In terms of the "old" NAFTA-era regional integration studies, nothing was happening in North America.[13]

But of course we see in retrospect that quite a bit has been happening over the last twenty years, across a wide variety of policy fields. It is not so much that scholars did not take note of these developments, but rather that most dismissed them as unimportant because they did not fit the pattern of formal institutionalization through stages they were looking for. The removal of trade barriers and the new global mobility of capital catalyzed the formation of broad and complex transnational corporate alliances, intrafirm trade complexes, and a new regionalized economy in which—as Stephen Blank put it—the three countries no longer traded with one another, but rather "made things together."[14] Even the severe dislocations to intraregional trade set off by 9/11 effectively reinforced some of these transnational connections, by creating a sense of common purpose in trying to shape policy outcomes in a complex, unpredictable, and sometimes threatening bureaucratic and legal environment. And, as the regional agenda shifted from tariff reduction to more demanding forms of policy coordination, the management of frictions over issues like subsidies, taxes, and regulation increasingly involved subfederal governments and the courts.

Equally importantly, the working groups of bureaucrats dismissed after NAFTA as a poor substitute for formal institution building have become an increasingly prominent and important part of the emergent regional governance structure. The complex array of post–9/11 security challenges put some strain on Cold War-era transgovernmental connections, but also catalyzed the formation of dozens of new networks, particularly with respect to border control, policing, immigration, and infrastructure. Rather than serving as default-option placeholders when formal policy coordination is blocked by the weakness of regional institutions or the inflexibility of domestic institutions, these transgovernmental networks have often been the political leaderships' first-choice option for managing difficult policy frictions. And, rather than simply "caretaking" issues on a day-to-day basis, these transgovernmental networks have—at least in some cases—been actively shaping political outcomes, by identifying policy frictions and then devising instruments to contain or even remedy these frictions. Thus we have seen the consolidation of a new mode of regional governance in North

America, which takes forms unanticipated by, and poorly explained by, the regional integration literature that shaped our collective expectations back in the early 1990s.

However, these developments are not unique to North America, and in fact have been widely recognized—though not always well understood—in the academic and political-practitioner literatures on international policy coordination, regional politics, public policy and international law over the last fifteen to twenty years. Two bodies of new theoretical work emerged in the 1990s, which rejected the core premises of traditional regional integration theory, and directed attention toward new aspects of regional policy coordination. The first of these is often called "new regionalism," and is usually associated with the work of Björn Hettne and Henrik Söderbaum.[15] It called for new attention to regional politics outside of Europe, focusing on the variety of regional purposes and practices, the links between global and regional dynamics, the social construction of "region-ness," and the multiplicity of levels and actors in contemporary regional politics. The second branch, coming directly from post-Maastricht work on European integration, is a more complex cluster of related theories, often associated with the phrase "multi-level governance" (MLG), and with theory and research by Fritz Scharpf, Gary Marks, and Liesbit Hooghe. It includes research on transgovernmental networks, transnational coalition politics in the context of supranational and subnational institutions, regulatory coordination, and "soft law."[16] It also includes greater attention to the institutions of federalism, and the interaction between supranational, national, and subfederal actors.

The "new regionalism" approach was predicated on the recognition that regionalism outside of Europe had been conceived for and directed toward purposes other than those which fueled the Cold War-era European integration agenda, and that the post-Cold War European project was in fact being driven by new goals and through new mechanisms. Hettne, Söderbaum, and their collaborators sought to understand the variety of different ways that regions were conceived and the political purposes to which they were directed.[17] To that end, they emphasized the social construction of "regionness," the importance of political power within and between regions, and the way in which various regional projects were defined with reference to overarching global tensions and alignments. In keeping with these theoretical and methodological commitments, proponents of the new regionalism approach tended to de-emphasize formal institutions and legal structures, and focus instead on political agendas, diplomatic and policy-making practices, and rhetorical struggles over the framing (and re-framing) of contested concepts, values, and identities.[18]

The new regionalism approach recognized that regional politics involved a multiplicity of different levels and actors but did not tend to put much emphasis on understanding the way these different actors interacted with one another, or the broader political and theoretical implications of this more complex political ecosystem. After the passing of the Maastricht Treaty in 1992, theory and research on European politics began to shift away from intergovernmental negotiation and toward what Gary Marks called "multi-level governance"—the formation of new networks of political actors (including transnational groups and subfederal governments) within the context of supranational institutions like the EU.[19] Anne-Marie Slaughter later redeployed some of these concepts on a global scale, and shifted the focus to transgovernmental networks, identifying this new, network-driven mode of governance as the foundation for the post–Cold War world's "real new world order."[20] Slaughter argued that the state had effectively been "disaggregated"—at least with respect to some issues and contexts—and networks of government officials were increasingly free to work closely with their counterparts from other governments and from various global or regional institutions, to reconcile national policy differences and manage pressing political challenges.

With Liesbet Hooghe, Marks would later develop a basic distinction between "Type I" and "Type II" governance models, which informed much of the research on regional politics and policy coordination during the 2000s.[21] Type I referred to the traditional concept of regional integration, in which states negotiated formal agreements on common rules and procedures, and then adjusted their own national policies to bring them into compliance with the regional agreement. It tended to see policy coordination as centralized, authoritative/hierarchical, territorially delimited, general-purpose, and intensely political. Type II, on the other hand, referred to a new model in which networks of government agencies worked out informal understandings about common practices and standards, which could bring national policies into alignment without formal intergovernmental agreements. It tended to see policy coordination as network-driven, fragmented, specialized/functional, and "technical" (rather than political). This distinction between these two governance models also resonated with a parallel distinction between the traditional concept of "hard law" and increasingly important forms of "soft law," which involved governance without formal legislation, through the coordination of reciprocal executive commitments and negotiated common practices.[22]

These elements came together in post-Maastricht Europe, in the principle of subsidiarity and the "open method of coordination" (OMC). Following the principle of subsidiarity, the EU has attempted not only to bolster the overarching EU bargain by reaffirming national sovereignty in specific policy domains, but also to use supranational agreements to try to manage member states' subnational rivalries, by devolving responsibilities to lower levels.[23] The OMC concept has allowed for progress in policy coordination without building new formal institutions or agreements, by permitting individual member states to chart their own paths toward a common policy standard or effect. Initially dismissed by some observers as a reflection of the EU's weakness after the crises of the late 1990s, OMC is now recognized by many as a useful hedging option, which opens the door for "soft law" solutions to otherwise intractable intergovernmental impasses.[24]

In much of this new theory and research, the perceived impetus for transgovernmental network making was the inadequacy of global or regional institutions to effectively reconcile member state policies and/or the weight of entrenched national interests or inflexible institutions as an obstacle to participation or compliance.[25] Christer Jönsson and his collaborators, for example, explain the formation of transgovernmental networks in Europe in functional terms: when EU decision-making rules make it too difficult to negotiate a formal agreement, but policy frictions are creating urgent political problems, governments are compelled to rely on transgovernmental networks to work out mutually acceptable commitments and practices.[26] Much of the early work in this vein tended to see the shift from Type I to Type II modes of governance as a thoroughly positive development, based on the resolution of otherwise intractable policy problems (and in some cases, based on a general enthusiasm for "progress" in regional integration). Critics of these approaches—and, later, some of the original advocates themselves—eventually recognized that Type II, network-driven governance could often be politically and normatively problematic, however, in terms of challenges to national sovereignty and democratic accountability.[27]

Equally importantly, there was a growing recognition in the late 2000s that the real world rarely approximates either of Hooghe and Marks's two ideal-type modes of governance, but rather tends to gray areas in between.[28] The same kinds of regional and domestic political constraints that drive policymakers to pursue network solutions will often set strict limits on what can be achieved and with what policy instruments. More generally, it is clear that formal structures and legal rules enable, limit, and direct transgovernmental and transnational network interactions, and in turn network processes and outcomes may sometimes effectively reshape overall government priorities and practices.[29] Thus there has been some cooling of the initial enthusiasm for new regionalism and multi-level governance frameworks, replaced by a new interest in bridging the Type I and Type II models, and for developing some kind of synthetic approach that captures both sets of phenomena (and the interactions between them).[30] This would most likely involve continuing attention to the multiplicity of actors and contexts in "multi-level governance," but with renewed attention to the "old" regionalism's focus on intergovernmental negotiation, formal decision-making structures, and competitive coalition building.

It is surprising that the new regionalism approach did not have more of an impact on the study of North America over the last twenty years, given the degree to which its core research concerns matched up with features usually seen to be most distinctive about the North American experience. While each of the three governments had their own "local" rationales for participating in regional free trade agreements, those were powerfully reinforced and made urgent by the perceived regionalization of the world economy in the 1990s, and the need to create a viable regional market to ensure economic competitiveness in the face of challenges from China, Brazil, and other rising economies.[31] After NAFTA and beyond trade issues, the three governments continue to look to regional policy coordination as a vehicle for building up distinctive and effective policy "models," which can be used either to create the option to opt out of global regimes or as a way to get leverage in competition with rival regional economies. Both of these latter rationales can be seen, for example, in recent debates about the creation of a North American energy and climate policy accord.[32]

While there has been extensive regionalization since NAFTA, moreover, North America's "region-ness" remains highly contested. Indeed, political elites in all three countries—and particularly in Canada—have actively challenged the idea of trilateral North America, and pushed for a return to disconnected bilateral relationships.[33] And finally, regional relations in North America have evolved their own set of distinctive pathways and practices, which shape the process and outcomes of policy coordination. We have seen, for example, a marked tendency to prefer coordinated executive commitments over formal legislation (i.e., "soft law" over "hard law"), "market-driven" over "state-driven" policy solutions, problem-driven working groups of bureaucratic specialists over permanent councils, and some experimentation with regularized private stakeholder consultations.

It is even more surprising that the multi-level governance literature has been only weakly reflected in theory and research on North America over the last twenty years because some of the core themes from this body of work had actually been very prominent in classic work on what made the US-Canada relationship distinctive and important to the study of world politics. Robert Keohane and Joseph Nye's work on the US-Canada relationship, published in the 1970s, cited the importance of transnational and transgovernmental relations in shaping a uniquely cooperative set of diplomatic processes and outcomes.[34] Allied arguments were made in Roger Frank Swanson's work on the "United States Canadiana constellation," and—in a slightly more skeptical way—in Kal Holsti's early work on the bilateral relationship.[35] Each of these anticipated Slaughter's argument about the "disaggregation" of the state and the broader debates about multi-level governance; in fact the aspects of the US-Canada bilateral relationship highlighted by Keohane and Nye were strikingly similar to those brought out by Hooghe and Marks's distinction between Type I and Type II modes of governance.

The US-Mexico relationship, on the other hand, was remarkable in the degree to which it had remained virtually untouched by these new patterns of diplomacy. In a much less well-known piece, Donald Wyman applied Keohane and Nye's "complex interdependence" concepts to the US-Mexico relationship and found that the much more centralized and hierarchical Mexican state had prevented the formation of substantial transgovernmental links between the US and Mexico, which had in turn prevented the building up of trust between the two governments and derailed opportunities for bilateral cooperation.[36] John Cope and Roderic Camp found that this was particularly true of defense and security cooperation, where transgovernmental ties had been stifled on the Mexican side by political centralization and entrenched anti-Americanism, and on the US side by disinterest and mistrust.[37] Thus trilateral North America, as set in place by NAFTA, has until quite recently represented a kind of "split-personality" region, with one bilateral relationship (US-Canada) characterized by exceptionally deep and well-established openness to Type II governance and the other (US-Mexico) characterized mainly by a reliance on formal, Type I governance.[38]

Some important work on US-Canada relations in the 1980s and early 1990s recognized the continuing importance of the disaggregated state and transnational or transgovernmental relations, but most of this work was primarily concerned with the way this complicated or disrupted traditional diplomacy.[39] The academic tilt toward statist, structuralist models during the 1980s, and the overshadowing effects of the CUSFTA and NAFTA negotiations, shifted the focus in academic work on North America more decisively toward intergovernmental negotiation and formal institution building.[40] Thus during the late 1990s and early 2000s the study of regional politics in North America was not well prepared to recognize the growing importance of network-driven governance after NAFTA, or to integrate insights from the new regionalism and multi-level governance schools. (Conversely, these broader comparative research programs were diminished by the lack of supporting research on the evolving North American case.)

There have been some important exceptions, however, particularly in the last five years. Questions and concepts from the multi-level governance literature have found their way into recent studies on North American politics, although much of this has been in studies on policy coordination in particular issue-areas, rather than in broad surveys of the region as a whole. Jeffrey Ayres and Laura Macdonald, for example, explored the dynamics of transnational civil society and organized labor in North America and attempted to explain when and how these groups influence regional and national policy outcomes.[41] The contributors to Monica Gattinger and Geoffrey Hale's 2010 volume, *Borders and Bridges*, variously touched on transnational coalitions, transgovernmental networks, federal-subfederal relations, regulatory coordination, and soft law.[42]

There has also been some attention to the concepts and methods associated with Hettne and Soderbaum's new regionalism approach, although these have only been very recent and often combine the approach's premises with those of other theoretical frameworks. Some of the contributions to Finn Laursen's 2010 volume on comparative regional integration (e.g., Warleigh-Lack, Morales) apply new regionalism concepts in comparing North America with Europe, highlighting the importance of the broader, global context in shaping policymakers' ideas about the regional agenda, and the nature and importance of the region itself.[43] More recently, Laura Macdonald has explicitly and directly applied new regionalism's core ideas to post-NAFTA North America.[44] She finds that the approach is generally useful in illuminating key aspects of the North American experience but focuses most of her attention on struggles over the social construction of the regional context itself, arguing that proponents of further economic integration failed to develop a compelling narrative that would secure the support of a broader political coalition.[45]

Some recent work on North America has explicitly recognized the limits of these approaches, and pointed toward some kind of synthesis of "old" and "new" regionalisms. In *So Near Yet So Far*, for example, Hale maps out several different layers of multi-level governance but also highlights the way that domestic interest-group configurations and government institutions can constrain, enable, or redirect transgovernmental or transnational network activity.[46] Neil Craik and Debora VanNijnatten have developed the concept of "bundled transgovernmental networks," to describe the way that various networks may be deliberately grouped together by political leaders, in order to give them greater momentum and to increase executive oversight and control.[47] Craik's earlier work in this area (with Joseph DiMento) identified the SPP initiative as a prototype for "bundled" networks in the North American context, and VanNijnatten and Craik's more recent research has shifted the empirical focus to ongoing environmental policy coordination (further developed in their contribution to this volume).[48]

Thus we are seeing an effort, in this most recent wave of theory and research, to try to build a bridge between Hooghe and Marks's two ideal-type models of governance and provide a more complete picture of policy coordination in North America, in bilateral or trilateral contexts. As always, though, where analysts tilt toward broader and more nuanced descriptions of political phenomena, they tend to lose some explanatory leverage in the process. Thus we still do not have theoretical tools to help us answer some fairly fundamental questions: When and how do political leaders seek to more actively direct transgovernmental or transnational networks, when and how do they do so through structured, multi-issue initiatives, and when and how does this lead to more effective centralization and/or more productive forms of policy coordination? When and how do existing regional agreements and institutions and/or domestic laws and institutions enable, constrain, or direct transgovernmental or transnational relations, and what effects does this have on regional policy coordination? Once we have made progress in sorting out each of these two dynamics, the next challenge will be to connect them together: that is, to try to understand how political leaders' decisions about how to "manage" transgovernmental and transnational networks are affected by the overarching institutional context, and how that institutional context is shaped by the transgovernmental and transnational connections that are continuously flowing through and around it. Our aim in this volume is to try to move forward on these questions, by explicitly bringing together Type I and Type II concerns, and by connecting studies of particular issue-areas and initiatives to broader theoretical propositions.

CORE PROBLEMS AND CONTRIBUTIONS

Although this volume covers a wide variety of puzzles and problems, there are two main concerns that hold it together: The main aim is to try to identify a predominant or characteristic mode of regional governance in post-NAFTA North America, and to map out some of the variation across bilateral relationships and issue-areas. The secondary aim is to try to explain how this particular mode of regional governance was created and has been sustained, with attention to the prevailing global context, domestic political institutions, the configuration of domestic and transnational coalitions, and the worldviews and attitudes of the general public, in each of the three countries. The early chapters of the volume are generally more concerned with the former question, and the later chapters with the latter question, but all chapters have something to say about both questions.

Regional Governance in North America: Variations on a Theme

In trying to define and understand the predominant mode of regional governance in North America, this volume is not built on systematic cross-regional comparisons, although most of the chapters refer to insights from the comparative regionalism literature, and several either make explicit comparisons or try to place the North American experience in a broader cross-regional or global context. Our approach here is rather to identify specific modes of policy coordination we find within and across policy domains (e.g., security, environment, trade, investment, energy), and then try to relate those to some of the distinctive structural and institutional features of North America as a region (e.g., power asymmetry, weak regional institutions, limited regional identification).

There are a variety of different dimensions that could be considered in characterizing the predominant mode of governance in a given region.[49] We outline three such dimensions here, to set the stage for the chapters to follow. First, how *regional* is it? That is, to what extent do policy coordination outcomes impact all regional states, and to what extent are all regional states involved in the process of policy coordination? Of course, in the North American case, where there are only three states, this essentially boils down to asking whether policy issues impact all three states, and whether there is genuinely trilateral (as opposed to bilateral) coordination. NAFTA was followed by the creation of regionally oriented offices within each of the three governments, but not by any new formal intergovernmental institution building in trilateral context. The SPP and the "Three Amigos" summits were originally framed as a renewal of regional diplomacy, but were recognized by most observers as a trilateral shell covering the "dual-bilateral" reality underneath.[50] After the SPP was discontinued in 2009, trilateral summits were held from time to time, but the region could be more readily seen as three interlocking bilateral relationships. It is clear, however, that while the three bilateral pairs are very different from one another, they are not *separate* from one another, and the interdependence of policy effects sustains a deeper regional reality—at least in some issue-areas—even in the absence of meaningfully trilateral cooperation.[51] It is not the purpose of this volume to revisit the well-rehearsed debate over whether or not a renewal of trilateral engagement is desirable and/or likely. We do, however, want to be attentive to the degree to which policy coordination in particular issue-areas tends to be trilateral in process and effects, and to connect that to the particular mode of decision making reflected in those issue-areas.

Second, *what types of actors* are involved in the policy coordination process? To what extent do we see evidence of genuinely "multi-level" governance, as opposed to more conventional intergovernmental negotiation? The original theory and research on multi-level governance in the European context was concerned with the way that national governments might be circumvented by new connections between supranational institutions and various component agencies at the national or subfederal levels. There is no supranational layer in North America, of course—except perhaps, in very dilute form, with the NAFTA trade-dispute resolution mechanism. The question in the North American context is whether and how national-level government agencies, subfederal governments, business associations, labor unions, or other public sector or civil society actors might be seen as more or less autonomous players in the policy coordination process, with their own goals and strategies, and their own independent effects on policy coordination outcomes. Given that the formal institutional structure of North American regional governance is very thin, these actors would be most likely to become important through their ability to direct central government policymaking either in their own, "home" countries or across borders in other regional partner countries. Thus theoretical insights from the core literature on multi-level governance, as developed in Europe, are likely to be less useful to us in the North American context than are those from the more traditional international relations literatures on transgovernmental networks and/or on transnational advocacy networks and contentious politics.[52]

A closely related consideration, raised by the theoretical literature on multi-level governance in Europe, is the role played by federal systems. To this point, federal institutions and subfederal actors have generally been seen as an impediment to regional integration in North America.[53] We are now, however, beginning to see a de facto recognition of (and active negotiation of the terms for) something like European-style subsidiarity in North America, with subfederal actors taking responsibility for a wide variety of issues, and coordinating those policies more or less effectively with their cross-border counterparts and national capitals. Examples include trade subsidies (lumber stumpage fees), procurement ("Buy American"), and immigration (Arizona's SB 1070, "smart" driver's licenses).

In post-NAFTA North America, there have been very few formal intergovernmental agreements, and even nominally intergovernmental processes like the SPP tend to reinforce the primacy of informal, network-driven coordination.[54] Thus we seem to be seeing a general and enduring preference for this latter mode of governance, which in itself calls for some explanation. However, while there seems to be a general preference for informalism in North America, there is clearly significant variation in the amount of political control over the process of coordination from one issue area to another.[55] Our expectation is that trilateral or bilateral coordination in some areas will look more like Hooghe and Marks's Type I governance, with central political actors keeping tight control over the policy agenda, and focusing on working out formal agreements, while in other areas we will find something more like Type II governance, with bureaucrats and private stakeholders forming networks in an ad hoc way, to manage specific policy frictions, and little or no formal institution or law making. In virtually all areas, however, we expect to see some kind of hybrid form, which combines Type I and Type II elements.

Last but not least, what is the nature of the political relationship between the actors, and *what is the mode of agenda setting and decision making* by which policy coordination is carried out? Are participants organized into more or less horizontal networks, or are they compartmentalized and vertically organized? What are the mechanisms for input and accountability between public and private actors? How are policy frictions identified and reconciled? Is policy coordination cemented through formal agreements translated into national legislation (i.e., hard law) or through informal reciprocal commitments to make complementary adjustments (i.e., soft law)? Are participating states required to adopt the same policies, or—following the logic of Europe's OMC—are they given space to follow different policies with complementary effects?

The Origins and Foundations of North American Regional Governance

We have already noted the continuity between the distinctive features of US-Canada cooperation observed during the 1970s and those observed in post-NAFTA North America—i.e., the (partial) disaggregation of the state, the lack of hierarchy between issue-areas, the salience of transnational coalition building and transgovernmental networks, and the preference for informal executive commitments. This, in combination with the paucity of new regional institutions after 1994, suggests that that CUSFTA and NAFTA were not harbingers for a much more institutionalized North America, but rather striking exceptions to the broader pattern in US-Canada relations, and perhaps North American regional politics more broadly.[56]

Broad continuities direct our attention to durable, structural variables, like the overall asymmetry of power among the three states. The most distinctive features of North America as a regional complex are the small number of states within the region and the overwhelming power of the US.

One could argue that these factors together tend to drive all three states away from trilateralism and formal institution building. The US, as the preponderant power, would generally be expected to prefer a hub-and-spokes arrangement, in order to avoid entanglement in robust multilateral institutions and to prevent counterbalancing coalitions.[57] Canada and Mexico, on the other hand, as the much weaker, more dependent neighbors, would be—and indeed historically have been—anxious to avoid US-dominated regional institutions that might undermine their sovereignty. These structural features have obviously had a deep impact on the region, but there are at least three reasons to think that they do not constitute a sufficient explanation for the pattern of regional governance: the striking differences between the US-Canada and US-Mexico relationships, especially, but not only, before NAFTA; the previously noted "exceptions" represented by CUSFTA and NAFTA; and the significant variation in forms of governance across issue-areas, in both bilateral relationships. We pause here to consider the CUSFTA and NAFTA exceptions, leaving the other two considerations for later chapters.

Proponents of the new regionalism approach have emphasized the way that regions are created to serve political purposes, and those purposes are often shaped by developments outside of the region itself. CUSFTA and NAFTA were made possible by a specific alignment of common perceptions and priorities among the three governments in the late 1980s and early 1990s. Canada and Mexico had historically been profoundly anxious about "deep" economic integration with the United States, but in the 1980s, both suddenly became much more anxious about influencing US policy than they were about protecting their own autonomy. Falling oil prices, declining growth rates, and a rising tide of protectionism in Washington convinced both Canada and Mexico that they had no choice but to try to expand and protect their access to US markets and investment, and the only way to do so—particularly given recent Congressional belligerence—was to negotiate ambitious free trade agreements that would "lock in" US commitments.

Canada's and Mexico's new openness to economic integration happened to resonate with a new American interest in region building. As the world's only genuinely global power, the US has incentives to encourage regionalization in other parts of the world but has historically been disinterested in regionalism "at home."[58] In the 1980s, however, America's perceived decline as a global power and the rise of dynamic regional economies in Europe and Asia convinced many observers that the world was becoming regionalized, and the US would need to pursue its own "regional option" in order to maintain its bargaining position and competitive edge within the global economy. These arguments were not prevalent in the public debate over CUSFTA and NAFTA, but they were pivotal in the building of an elite consensus, and sustaining it through the difficult NAFTA ratification battle.[59] However, this region-building impulse melted away almost immediately after NAFTA came into effect, partly because of the new intensity of the domestic antiglobalization movement, but mostly because of the derailment of the regionalization process in the wider world economy, after Germany was overwhelmed by the costs of reunification and Japan by a catastrophic financial crisis.

Since then, the resurgence of the US as a global economic power in the late 1990s, the rise of China, and the post–9/11 "global war on terrorism" have further reinforced US planners' tendency to focus on the global-multilateral order and have drawn their attention far away from North America. Canada and Mexico have of course continued to seek US attention, but since the mid-2000s, each, for its own reasons, has usually preferred to frame its engagement with Washington in bilateral rather than regional/trilateral terms. Some observers have warned that inattention to North American "neighborhood" issues has undermined the NAFTA partners' global competitiveness, but these arguments have so far had little traction in any of the three capitals.[60] The one set of genuinely regional policy challenges that has captured high-level political attention over the last decade has been border control and homeland security issues, but these have generally been tackled bilaterally, especially since the closing of the SPP process in 2009. The new momentum behind transregional trade and investment pacts—i.e., transatlantic free trade and the Trans-Pacific Partnership negotiations—has drawn some attention to NAFTA, even in Washington, but mostly as a set of "extra" diplomatic and legal hurdles that have to be navigated in addition to the core negotiations with European and Asian partners.

Thus the late 1980s and early 1990s represent an awkward and half-hearted tilt toward regionalism in North America, which quickly lost political momentum, but raised the political stakes for subsequent policy coordination efforts, by uncovering the latent potential for regional integration, in the eyes of both proponents and opponents. Whatever political momentum remained after NAFTA was wiped away—as many observers have noted—by the terrorist attacks of 9/11. In fact, there never was very much political momentum behind regionalism in North America, even in the immediate afterglow of NAFTA ratification, and that had much to do with the kinds of structural constraints outlined above. These were further reinforced, moreover, by two additional factors not specific to the region: a new set of "post-trade" policy coordination challenges, and America's post–Cold War inclination to soft law diplomacy.

The growth of the global-multilateral and regional trade regimes has resolved most conventional trade and investment issues among the advanced economies, shifting the policy coordination agenda toward more complex economic issues like fiscal policy and regulation, and noneconomic issues like border security, organized crime, and migration.[61] These "post-trade" issues seem by nature to be especially difficult ones for traditional intergovernmental negotiation and hard law solutions because they impinge more directly on national sovereignty, are more likely to create conflicts between federal and subfederal governments, and raise more contentious questions about the proper relationship between the state and its citizens. Thus, following Jönsson et al's functionalist logic, these issues have been identified as important contexts and drivers for transgovernmental network coordination and soft law diplomacy.[62]

As in Europe and elsewhere, it was this cluster of issues that came to the forefront of the regional agenda after NAFTA, creating demand for further coordination, but making it less likely that that coordination would look anything like NAFTA. Because the new issues were more "sensitive," political leaders were inclined to *informal* coordination—which, at least in the US-Canada context, could be seen as a "return" to past practices. Because there were already strong diplomatic and legal foundations for close, informal coordination between the US and Canada, but not between the US and Mexico, political leaders were inclined to return to bilateral coordination.[63]

At the same time, these tendencies seem to have been reinforced—in North America and elsewhere—by the US's general ambivalence about international institution building in the post–Cold War context. The end of the Cold War was heralded as the dawn of a "new world order," built on strengthened multilateral institutions, but in practice the US has become more unilateralist with respect to security and environmental politics, and has shown a marked preference for bilateralism and informal agreements in trade and investment. The US has also shown a marked preference for soft law arrangements in many issue-areas, often relying on executive orders, signing statements, and other forms of informal policy adjustment, rather than treaties or other formal agreements. This reflects not only the powerful state's impulse to avoid being tied down, but also a more distinctively American aversion to supranationalism and the White House's clear desire to shelter foreign policy from Congressional oversight and interference.[64]

Thus the evident preference for informal bilateralism in North America seems to be consistent with a broader tendency in the post–Cold War world, and reinforced by the particular strategic, cultural, and political predispositions of the US as a global and regional leader. Moreover, as Geoffrey Hale has noted in previous research, these inclinations seem to be especially pronounced in the context of the North American "neighborhood," in which the American public is especially anxious about threats to national sovereignty and identity, and in which Congress may feel particularly entitled to intervene in the policymaking process.[65]

Another continuity that has reinforced the overall tendency toward informal coordination in North America is the basic configuration of domestic institutions and interests. In their pioneering work on US-Canada relations, Keohane and Nye anticipated the way that the disaggregation of the state could have important implications for diplomacy between highly interdependent states but paid little attention to the way that domestic institutions might affect transgovernmental and transnational relations.[66] Later research on these phenomena tackled this problem head-on, and found that domestic political structures often functioned as a "switch," which enabled or constrained transgovernmental and transnational relations.[67]

This was borne out in the North American context, as domestic political structures—especially the separation of powers in the US, the federal structure in Canada, and entrenched interest-group associations in Mexico—were later seen to be major obstacles to CUSFTA and NAFTA negotiations, and then to the post-NAFTA "deepening" agenda.[68] The US Congress, in particular, was seen to be a major barrier to successful regional policy coordination because the incentive structure for individual members drove the institution as a whole to unpredictable and self-defeating bouts of parochialism and paternalism. Particularly after the bruising political battles leading up to the NAFTA ratification vote in the US, it was not surprising that political leaders in all three countries were thinking about ways to pursue policy coordination that could effectively circumnavigate Congressional oversight and approval. After 9/11, most observers focused on divergent priorities—i.e., the US's preoccupation with security, while Canada and Mexico focused on trade and investment—as major obstacles to further regional coordination. But later reflection on the SPP process highlighted the way that the form it took, and its overall weaknesses, were heavily influenced by (the anticipation of) fixed institutional constraints like legislative gridlock and federalism.[69]

Political leaders in all three countries thus had strong political incentives to avoid public debate, binding agreements, and formal ratification processes. This, as noted above, has often been a key rationale for shifting from Type I to Type II modes of governance, in Europe and elsewhere. However, these same political risk-avoidance impulses also work against "pure" Type II forms of governance, and political leaders in North America have therefore attempted to direct and limit transgovernmental relations, through the creation and oversight of working groups and/or the "bundling" of these groups described by Craik and VanNijnatten. A number of observers have described the SPP process, launched in 2005 and quietly suspended in 2009, in these terms.

One could therefore argue that this mode of regional governance took root after NAFTA because it serves five important political "needs" simultaneously: it creates opportunities for network-driven policy coordination and management; it preserves a measure of executive control over the transgovernmental process and its public profile; it creates rituals for demonstrating political "commitment" and "momentum" (e.g., summit meetings, timetables); it avoids formal legislative and other domestic ratification processes; and it generally minimizes public scrutiny and criticism. Thus, while the SPP process was roundly criticized from virtually all sides, there are good (political) reasons to expect that this basic form is likely to persist, and to be applied to future policy problems and contexts. Indeed, it has been carried on—albeit on a bilateral basis only—in the form of the US-Canada Beyond the Border (BTB) and the US-Canada Regulatory Cooperation

Council (RCC), and US-Mexico High-Level Regulatory Cooperation Council (HLRCC) processes, all of which rely on politically managed, network-driven coordination.[70]

There are a variety of circumstances in which informal policy coordination is seen to be inadequate and/or is disallowed by existing agreements, laws, or mandates. (That is, the scope and nature of soft law coordination is limited and shaped by the prevailing body of hard law.) There are also some gray areas where the division of authority between branches, levels, or agencies is ambiguous. National political institutions not only define times and places where there is latent demand for network-driven governance, but they may also affect the supply, by setting up legal requirements for budgeting, oversight, or ratification. The existing theory and research on hard and soft law has developed a number of propositions and findings on when and how formal institutions affect the form and results of informal coordination.[71] However, this work has not yet been well integrated into the new theory and research on transgovernmental and transnational network relations in the North American regional context, or in the Canadian and Mexican national contexts.

The final dimension outlined here is the effect of popular attitudes and beliefs, in all three countries, with particular attention to the social construction of "region-ness." Until quite recently, this was often seen as the pivotal dimension in identifying and explaining what was distinctive about the North American experience. NAFTA had paved the way for extensive regional*ization*, it was often said, but this had not brought about much meaningful regional integration because—in sharp contrast to Europe and other parts of the world—in North America there was a glaring absence of regional*ism*.[72] In fact, each of the three countries was seen to derive so much of its own sense of national identity from its differentness and separation from its regional neighbors that North America was seen to be a distinctively—perhaps uniquely—antiregional region. Even the signing and ratifications of NAFTA reinforced this reading because of the breadth and intensity of popular opposition to it, and the final product's limitations as a mechanism of regional governance.

Thus the conventional wisdom about regional governance in North America today is that political elites have made a strategic choice to rely on networks and soft law in order to avoid a political backlash like that triggered by CUSFTA in Canada in 1988 and by NAFTA in the US in 1993.[73] On one level, this is about avoiding national legislatures and subfederal governments, but the underlying challenge comes from deep-seated public opposition to regionalism per se. In his final major work, Robert Pastor directly challenged this conventional wisdom, by using poll numbers to show that public opposition to regional cooperation was much more limited than is often assumed, and in fact there are signs of a growing openness to regionalism, in all three countries.[74] Yet there are clear problems with Pastor's poll evidence, and many would argue that there is still a significant pool of latent opposition to regional integration in North America, although it is not always clear whether that opposition is grounded in interests, ideology, identity, or some combination of these three.

Overview of the Volume

In Chapter 2, Debora VanNijnatten and Neil Craik further develop and apply their concept of "bundled" transgovernmental networks, with particular attention to the governance of environmental regulation in North America. They are most directly focused on characterizing the organization and function of transgovernmental working groups, such as those developed under the aegis of the SPP and the RCC, and the political relationship between political leaders, bureaucrats, and civil society stakeholders within the working group process. VanNijnatten and Craik argue that bundled transgovernmental networks represent a political balancing strategy, which provides a measure of autonomy to technical specialists, but also maintains a measure of indirect accountability through the political leadership's "orchestration" of the agenda and outcomes.

In Chapter 3, Jason Ackleson and Yosef Lapid argue that, contrary to conventional wisdom, transgovernmental networks have important agenda-setting and policy-shaping effects, even in the security domain. They challenge the prevailing assumption that states are too rigid to respond to more flexible "network threats" like drug smuggling and human trafficking, arguing instead that states have been able to develop their own form of network-like flexibility, through the development of transgovernmental networks. Ackleson and Lapid highlight the relative autonomy and impact of bureaucrats and law enforcement agents through their accounts of two exemplar initiatives—the Border Enforcement Security Task Force (BEST) teams and the Shiprider program. Their account of these initiatives makes it clear that there are two different sets of policy challenges at the two borders, but they also highlight the political, legal, and administrative pressures on the US government to deliver more or less "standardized" border control and law-enforcement policies, and other kinds of interdependencies linking the two bilateral agendas.

In Chapter 4, Ruben Zaiotti looks at border control and homeland security coordination from another angle. The conventional wisdom about homeland security in North America, he argues, is that it is underdeveloped, particularly by contrast with Europe, which is supposed to have achieved a much more robust and effective institutional structure for ongoing policy coordination in this area. However, Zaiotti makes the case that in fact the two regions are much more similar than we recognize, in terms of both their approach to homeland security issues and the "depth" of their coordination. Like Ackleson and Lapid, Zaiotti is primarily concerned with transgovernmental networks. He recognizes the way that central political authorities set the general direction of policy but emphasizes the way bureaucrats and law-enforcement officials play an important role in shaping specific policies through implementation, and the ongoing need to try to make new policies consistent with existing policies, across international relationships and issue-areas. This cumulative, adaptive process leads to the emergence of "communities of practice," which may have important, semi-autonomous effects on subsequent agenda-setting and policy outcomes. Thus the political relationship between politicians, bureaucrats, and relevant civil society actors may be more complex and less hierarchical in practice than it is supposed to be, "on paper," according to the formal organization of any given policy coordination initiative.

Stephen Clarkson, in his discussion of the three North American countries' trade policies (Chapter 5), offers a very different view of the region. Indeed, he sees little evidence of regionalism in any of three governments' trade policies, but rather consistent tendencies to unilateralism and opportunism. More importantly, unlike some of our other contributors, Clarkson finds relatively little meaningful autonomy for bureaucratic actors or subfederal governments, as political leaders in each of the three governments have found ways to defeat or elide formal political constraints on trade policymaking, and have pursued relatively coherent and consistent national strategies. If there is an important pattern of fragmentation and network building in Clarkson's account, then it is not within the state, but rather within society, and in the connections between certain state and society actors. Rather than a shift from conventional "hard law" to informal "soft law" arrangements, moreover, Clarkson argues that there has been a sustained effort to reorganize political and legal prerogatives to suit the interests of powerful nongovernment interests, with some national prerogatives reinforced and others deliberately handed over to global-level, quasi-judicial authorities like the WTO.

In Chapter 6, Christopher Kukucha looks at the role played by subfederal governments (i.e., provinces in Canada, states in the US and Mexico) in trade policymaking, and—more particularly—at the impact that civil society actors have on subfederal governments' priorities and strategies. He begins by noting that subfederal governments have been becoming increasingly active in engaging with national trade policymaking since NAFTA came into effect in 1994, and—as expected by proponents of the multi-level governance approach—this has encouraged various civil society actors to try to influence trade and closely related policies through lobbying and other forms of influence at the subfederal level. However, Kukucha's review of these lobbying efforts finds that, while there is a significant amount of civil society activity at the subfederal level in the US and Canada, overall these actors seem to have had little or no effect on national trade policy outcomes. In Mexico, on the other hand, civil society actors operating at the state level have tended to focus on other kinds of economic policy issues, and there has been relatively little engagement with subfederal governments on trade policy specifically.

In his analysis of the politics of Mexico's oil and gas policy (Chapter 7), Isidro Morales makes the case that this national policy debate cannot be properly understood without putting it into the context of broader economic and political developments at the broader regional level, but he also raises questions about the importance of transgovernmental relations in shaping national and regional policy outcomes. He finds that the evolution of energy policy in Mexico has had relatively little to do with network-driven coordination, and much more to do with national institutions and national political struggles, which in turn are following behind fast-moving technological and market developments at the regional and global levels. Morales argues that the Peña government's recent energy reform represents a major political turning point for the oil, gas, and electricity sectors in Mexico, which could have significant effects on the country's economic development, but also on its diplomatic and political relationships with the US and Canada.

In Chapter 8, Geoffrey Hale argues that Congress is still the "controversial pivot" for North American regional politics, but he rejects the conventional wisdom that Congress is naturally or necessarily an obstacle to all regional policy coordination. Congress represents a core feature of the overarching institutional context, by which various interests seek to promote or prevent specific policy concepts or outcomes. It is therefore essential—in trying to explain or anticipate policy coordination outcomes—to understand the inner workings of Congress, as an enabler and constraint on political coalition building, but also to recognize that it is the underlying configurations of interests and ideas that ultimately drive the broader patterns we observe.

In Chapter 9, Brian Bow and Arturo Santa Cruz take another look at the role of public attitudes and public opinion in North American regional politics, and link it to the general theoretical literature on the politicization of regional integration. They make three main arguments: First, that popular opposition in the immediate aftermath of NAFTA did discourage policymakers, particularly in the US, from pursuing more ambitious forms of region building, but they were already inclined to a more informal approach for other reasons, so public opposition merely reinforced an established tendency. Second, recent survey research supports neither the conventional wisdom that there is widespread opposition to regional integration nor Robert Pastor's counterargument that the public is actually receptive to further integration. And third, the depoliticization of regional affairs after NAFTA was probably reinforced by the predominant electoral system in North America. Europe's proportional representation systems encourage small parties to adopt explicitly pro- or anti-Europe platforms, and sometimes make those parties politically important through interparty coalition building. The single-member plurality systems in the US and Canada, on the other hand, discourage small parties from forming, and force advocates of minority positions to pursue leverage *within* the major parties, where they are often effectively marginalized. (Mexico has a hybrid electoral system, and the pattern of politicization there shares features with both the US and European experiences.)

In Chapter 10, Stephen Blank picks up on this debate, and on Pastor's broader arguments about how "deeper" forms of regional cooperation could be moved forward. Blank is generally supportive of Pastor's call for more extensive and intensive regional cooperation, but he rejects the argument made by Pastor and others, that it can only be moved forward effectively through a highly politicized trilateral negotiation toward an across-the-board agreement.[75] He tries to map out a middle ground between Pastor's call for a grand bargain and a more passive muddling through. One part of this effort would be to build a broad constituency for regional cooperation, but it would have to be counterbalanced by a focus on working through strategically chosen elite-level initiatives, which could create momentum for further coordination. Blank's approach therefore relies mainly on the kind of bureaucrat-and-stakeholder networks emphasized in Hooghe and Marks's Type II model but recognizes the importance of the kind of political direction and popular support that are crucial in conventional Type I governance. Because Blank's approach brings together many different kinds of actors and involves both top-down and bottom-up dynamics, it could be appealing to proponents of many different visions of North American regionalism.

In the concluding chapter, Greg Anderson and Brian Bow seek to bring together these varied strands and provide an overview of the volume's overall findings. The chapter begins by collecting and comparing the various chapters' insights into the volume's two core questions: how can we characterize the predominant mode of regional governance in North America, and how can we explain the origins and bases for this distinctive regional structure? We find that in fact there is no "predominant" mode of regional governance in North America, except in the very limited sense that the varied issue-specific and sectoral governance structures we have observed all involve some distinctive mixture of elements from the Type I and Type II models. And, just as the modes of governance vary across different issue-areas, so do their political and historical sources. Thus the focus shifts in the concluding chapter to searching for a framework to describe and explain the pattern of variation across issue-areas. Based in part on inductive assessment of the pattern revealed in the issue-specific empirical chapters, and their recognition of the theoretical framework's inattention to "bottom-up" patterns of private activity, we attempt to refine and extend the political science framework developed here, by grafting on concepts and questions from economics. More specifically, they borrow from the New Institutional Economics approach, with particular attention to the question of institutional forms as mechanisms for the optimization of transactions costs. Attention to the pursuit of efficiency gains, and the search for policy autonomy in the context of asymmetrical interdependence, helps explain some of the variation in institutional forms across cases in the preceding empirical chapters. It therefore seems like a promising approach to the further development of a more versatile and encompassing theoretical template, to explain variation of governance structures across bilateral relationships, issue-areas, and time periods.

Thus the concluding section of the volume—like the volume as a whole—is not so much a "wrapping up" of questions that have been answered, but rather a starting place for tackling questions that we are only just starting to wrap our heads around. Twenty years after NAFTA, we are just beginning to understand the region that the agreement created, both through what it did and what it did not do. Looking again at North America with fresh eyes, we can see that it did not turn out to be what some hoped it would become, nor what others feared. It is in fact much more complex, more varied, and more interesting than either of those two visions. We are therefore optimistic that the third decade of exploring North America will be even more exciting and fruitful than the first two.

NOTES

1. Hart 1990; Baer 1991; Weintraub 1992; O'Brien 1995; Weintraub 1996; Doran 1996; Courchene and Harris 1999. For reviews of the politics surrounding NAFTA in the 1990s, see, e.g.: Cooper 1999; Pastor 2001; Hufbauer and Schott 2005.
2. Capling and Nossal 2009; Clarkson 2008; Ayres and Macdonald 2012; see also Studer and Wise 2007a.
3. Destler and Balint 1999; Wilkinson 2009.
4. Mattli 1999; Milner 1995; Tornell and Esquivel 1997.
5. E.g., Pastor 2001; Pastor 2002; Clarkson 2008. See also Goldfarb 2003a.
6. Thus, as Farrell (2005, 13)—among others—has argued, the European experience became "the benchmark against which all other forms of regionalism [were] judged." Many at the time were powerfully influenced by economists' arguments about a natural sequence of stages for economic integration, from free trade agreement through customs union to deep economic and monetary union: e.g., Balassa 1962.
7. Neofunctionalism in the 1950s and 1960s, popularized by Ernst Haas, Karl Deutsch, and others, recognized that networks of like-minded bureaucrats could shape the policy coordination agenda, sometimes by short-circuiting state-to-state negotiations. By the 1980s, however, neofunctionalist ideas had been substantially displaced by approaches that emphasized intergovernmental negotiations, as popularized by Andrew Moravcsik (1993 and 1998), among others. For a good review of these debates, see Wiener and Diez 2009.
8. Doran and Drischler 1996; Doran 1996; Courchene and Harris 1999; Pastor 2001; see also the review in Goldfarb 2003b.
9. Pastor 2004; Goldfarb 2003b; Clarkson 2008.
10. E.g., Dobson 2002.
11. Pastor 2004; Pastor 2008.
12. Sands 2011b. See VanNijnatten and Craik's contribution to this volume.
13. See, especially, Capling and Nossal 2009; Clarkson 2008.
14. See Blank and Prentice 2010. Blank picks up again on the implications of these trends in his contribution to this volume.
15. Mittelman 1996; Hettne et al 1999; Hettne and Soderbaum 2000; Hettne 2005.

16. Marks et al 1996; Scharpf 1997; Scharpf 1999a; Peters and Pierre 2001; Hooghe and Marks 2003.
17. Hettne et al 1999; Hettne 2005.
18. Hettne and Soderbaum 2000; Kelly 2007; Warleigh-Lack and Rosamond 2010.
19. Marks 1993.
20. Slaughter 1997; Slaughter 2004.
21. Hooghe and Marks 2003; see also Raustiala 2002.
22. Abbott and Snidal 2000; Eberlein and Grande 2005.
23. Keesbergen and Verbeek 1994.
24. Borrás and Jacobsson 2004; Eberlein and Grande 2005.
25. See, for example, Schafer 2006.
26. Jönsson et al 1998.
27. Scharpf 1999b; Slaughter 2000; for a counterargument, see Moravcsik 2002.
28. Abbott and Snidal 2000; Warleigh-Lack 2007; Warleigh-Lack and Rosamond 2010; Warleigh-Lack et al 2011.
29. Jacobsson 2004; Eberlein and Newman 2008.
30. Hettne 2005; Warleigh-Lack 2006; Trubek and Trubek 2005; Newman 2010; Warleigh-Lack et al 2011.
31. Studer and Wise eds. 2007b; Pastor 2001.
32. Fickling and Schott 2011; Selin and VanDeveer 2011; VanNijnatten 2011.
33. Golob 2012.
34. Keohane and Nye 1974; Keohane and Nye 1977.
35. Swanson 1972; Holsti 1971; Holsti and Levy 1974.
36. Wyman 1978.
37. Cope 1996; Camp 1992; Camp 2007, esp. pp. 139–144, 244–253.
38. Bow 2006.
39. E.g., Holmes 1981; Gotlieb 1982; Pastor and Fernandez de Castro 1998.
40. Milner 1995; Cameron 1997; Haggard 1997; Cameron and Tomlin 2000; Winham and DeBoer-Ashworth 2000. For an interesting early effort to bridge these different "levels of analysis," see Mayer 1998.
41. Ayres and Macdonald 2009.
42. Gattinger and Hale 2010. See also Brunet-Jailly 2004; Morales 2008.
43. Laursen 2010.
44. Macdonald 2011.
45. Macdonald 2011; see also Ayres and Macdonald 2012.
46. Hale 2012a.
47. Craik and VanNijnatten 2012.
48. Craik and DiMento 2008; Craik and VanNijnatten 2012. See also Craik and VanNijnatten's contribution to this volume.
49. For a much more elaborate typological framework (which served as a starting point for the simple one laid out here), see Acharya and Johnston 2009.
50. Clarkson 2008; Sands 2011a; Pastor 2011. See also Sands 2002.
51. Morales 2011.
52. On North America's lack of institutional depth (in absolute and relative terms) and its implications for transgovernmental and transnational relations, see Ayres and Macdonald 2006; Belanger 2007.
53. For example, see Hülsemeyer 2004.
54. There have been a small number of policy frictions that have been worked out through formal agreements, such as the 2006 US-Canada softwood lumber agreement. However, these seem to be exceptions that prove the rule, as they have come about only in situations where policymakers are compelled to undertake them by previous international agreements, domestic laws, or agency mandates.

55. This is consistent with the general findings of recent research on policy coordination in Europe and within global multilateral institutions—e.g., Raustiala 2002; Eberlein and Newman 2008.
56. On the pivotal dispute-resolution mechanism component of CUSFTA and NAFTA as a pragmatic solution to a domestic political problem in the United States (i.e., politicized overuse of "unfair" trade remedy laws), see Goldstein 1994.
57. Pastor 2005; Hurrell 2006.
58. Other regions—such as Europe, Latin America, and Southeast Asia—were originally constituted as such, at least in part, as a way of managing the power of the US as an "extra-regional" interloper; local powers formed together to resist US power, the US encouraged regionalization as a way to create manageable administrative units, and a few regional powers (especially Germany and Japan) took leading roles in order to set themselves up as mediators between the US and their respective regional communities. See Katzenstein 2005; Acharya 2007.
59. Mayer 1998; Destler and Balint 1999; Cameron and Tomlin 2000.
60. For a general overview, see Bow 2012.
61. On the nature and implications of the "new trade agenda," in general terms, see Destler and Balint 1999; with respect to North America, see Studer and Wise 2007b.
62. Abbott and Snidal 2000; Trubek and Trubek 2005.
63. Both of these impulses were most pronounced in Ottawa, where the preference for informal bilateralism was often seen in unabashedly nostalgic terms, as a return to the Cold War–era "special relationship."
64. Pildes 2003–2004; Murphy 2004; Aggarwal 2009.
65. Hale 2012b; see also Clarkson 2008.
66. Keohane and Nye 1987. See also Bow 2009.
67. E.g., Risse-Kappen 1995.
68. Hülsemeyer 2004; Doran and Drischler 1996; Pastor and Fernandez de Castro 1998; Pastor 2001; Studer 2007.
69. Anderson and Sands 2007.
70. On the basic parallel, see Sands 2011a. On the BTB and RCC/HLRC processes, see US Embassy 2011a; US Embassy 2011b; US International Trade Administration 2011.
71. Abbott and Snidal 2000; Mosher and Trubek 2003; Pennings 2006; Burbank 2006; Schafer 2006; Gerson and Posner 2008.
72. Capling and Nossal 2009.
73. Two examples, from very different viewpoints: Ayres and Macdonald 2006; Anderson and Sands 2007.
74. Pastor 2011.
75. Other versions of the "grand bargain" argument include Dobson 2002; Rozental 2002; Gotlieb 2003.

REFERENCES

Abbott, Kenneth W., and Duncan Snidal. 2000. "Hard and Soft Law in International Governance," *International Organization* 54 (3): 421–456.

Acharya, Amitav. 2007. "The Emerging Regional Architecture of World Politics," *World Politics* 59 (4): 629–652.

Acharya, Amitav, and Alistair Iain Johnston. 2009. *Crafting Cooperation: Regional International Institutions in Comparative Perspectives.* Cambridge UK: Cambridge University Press.

Aggarwal, Vinod K. 2009. "Reluctance to Lead: US Trade Policy in Flux," *Business and Politics* 11 (3): 1–21.

Anderson, Greg, and Christopher Sands. 2007. "Negotiating North America: The Security and Prosperity Partnership," *Hudson Institute White Paper* (Fall).

Ayres, Jeffrey, and Laura Macdonald. 2006. "Deep Integration and Shallow Governance: The Limits of Civil Society Engagement across North America," *Politics and Society* 25 (3): 23–42.

Ayres, Jeffrey, and Laura Macdonald, eds. 2009. *Contentious Politics in North America: National Protest and Transnational Collaboration under Continental Integration.* New York: Palgrave Macmillan.

Ayres, Jeffrey, and Laura Macdonald. 2012. "Introduction: North America in Question," in Ayres and Macdonald, eds., *North America in Question: Regional Integration in an Era of Economic Turbulence.* Toronto: University of Toronto Press.

Baer, M. Delal. 1991. "North American Free Trade," *Foreign Affairs* 70 (4): 132–149.

Balassa, Bela. 1962. *The Theory of Economic Integration.* London: Allen & Unwin.

Bélanger, Louis. 2007. "An Unsustainable Institutional Design: Incompleteness and Delegation Deficit in NAFTA," in Gordon Mace, J.P. Thérien and Paul Haslam, eds. *Governing the Americas: Assessing Multilateral Institutions.* Boulder, CO: Lynne Rienner.

Blank, Stephen, and Barry Prentice. 2010. "Canada-US Transportation and Corridor Policies," in Monica Gattinger and Geoffrey Hale, eds., *Borders and Bridges; Canada's Policy Relations in North America.* Don Mills ON: Oxford University Press.

Borrás, Susana, and Kerstin Jacobsson. 2004. "The Open Method of Co-ordination and New Governance Patterns in the EU," *Journal of European Public Policy* 11:2 (April): 185–208.

Bow, Brian. 2006. "'When in Rome . . .': Comparing Canadian and Mexican Strategies for Influencing Policy Outcomes in the United States," *Canadian-American Public Policy* 65 (January).

Bow, Brian. 2009. *The Politics of Linkage: Power, Interdependence, and Ideas in Canada-US Relations.* Vancouver: UBC Press.

Bow, Brian. 2012. "Immovable Object or Unstoppable Force? Crisis and the Social Construction of North America," in Jeffrey Ayres and Laura MacDonald, eds., *North America in Question.* Toronto: University of Toronto Press.

Brunet-Jailly, Emmanuel. 2004. "NAFTA, Economic Integration, and the Canadian-American Security Regime in the Post-September 11, 2001 Era: Multi-Level Governance and Transparent Border?" *Journal of Borderlands Studies* 19 (1): 123–142.

Burbank, Stephen B. 2006. "Federalism and Private International Law: Implementing the Hague Choice of Court Convention in the United States," *Journal of Private International Law* 2 (2): 287–309.

Cameron, Maxwell A. 1997. "North American Trade Negotiations: Liberalization Games Between Asymmetric Players," *European Journal of International Relations* 3 (1): 105–139.

Cameron Maxwell A., and Brian W. Tomlin. 2000. *The Making of NAFTA: How the Deal Was Done.* Ithaca NY: Cornell University Press.

Camp, Roderic Ai. 1992. *Generals in the Palacio: The Modern Military in Mexico.* New York: Oxford University Press.

Camp, Roderic Ai. 2007. *Politics in Mexico.* 5th ed., New York: Oxford University Press.

Capling, Ann, and Kim Richard Nossal. 2009. "The Contradictions of Regionalism in North America," *Review of International Studies* 35 (1): 147–167.

Clarkson, Stephen. 2008. *Does North America Exist?: Governing the Continent after NAFTA and 9/11.* Toronto: University of Toronto Press.

Cooper, Andrew F. 1999. "NAFTA and the Politics of Regional Trade," in Brian Hocking and Stephen McGuire, eds., *Trade Politics: International, Domestic and Regional Perspectives*. New York: Routledge.

Cope, John A. 1996. "In Search of Convergence: US-Mexican Military Relations into the 21st Century," in John Bailey and Sergio Aguayo, eds., *Strategy and Security in US-Mexican Relations: Beyond the Cold War*. San Diego: UC San Diego Press.

Courchene, Thomas J., and Richard G. Harris. 1999. "From Fixing to Monetary Union: Options for North American Currency Integration" *CD Howe Commentary* 127 (June).

Craik, Neil, and Joseph DiMento. 2008. "Environmental Cooperation in the (Partially) Disaggregated State: Lessons from the Security and Prosperity Partnership of North America," *Chicago Journal of International Law* 8 (2): 479–512.

Craik, Neil, and Debora VanNijnatten. 2012. "Bundled Transgovernmental Networks in North America," paper presented to the Canadian Political Science Association conference, Edmonton AB.

Destler, I.M., and Peter J. Balint. 1999. *The New Politics of American Trade: Trade, Labor and the Environment*. Washington DC: Institute for International Economics.

Dobson, Wendy. 2002. "Shaping the Future of the North American Economic Space: A Framework for Action," *CD Howe Border Papers* 162 (April).

Doran, Charles F. 1996. "When Building North America, Deepen Before Widening," in Charles F. Doran and Alvin P. Drischler, eds., *A New North America: Cooperation and Enhanced Interdependence*. Westport CT: Praeger.

Doran, Charles F., and Alvin P. Drischler, eds. 1996. *A New North America: Cooperation and Enhanced Interdependence*. Westport CT: Praeger.

Eberlein, Burkard, and Edgar Grande. 2005. "Beyond Delegation: Transnational Regulatory Regimes and the EU Regulatory State," *Journal of European Public Policy* 12 (1): 89–112.

Eberlein, Burkard, and Abraham L. Newman. 2008. "Escaping the International Governance Dilemma?: Incorporated Transgovernmental Networks in the European Union," *Governance* 21 (1): 25–52.

Farrell, Mary. 2005. "The Global Politics of Regionalism: An Introduction," in Mary Farrell, Bjorn Hettne, and Luk Van Langenhove, eds., *The Global Politics of Regionalism: Theory and Practice*. Ann Arbor MI: Pluto Press.

Fickling, Mary, and Jeffrey Schott. 2011. *NAFTA and Climate Change*. Washington DC: Peterson Institute for International Economics.

Gattinger, Monica, and Geoffrey Hale, eds. 2010. *Borders and Bridges: Canada's Policy Relations in North America*. Don Mills ON: Oxford University Press.

Gerson, Jacob E., and Eric A. Posner. 2008. "Soft Law: Lessons from Congressional Practice," *Stanford Law Review* 61 (3): 573–627.

Goldfarb, Danielle. 2003a. "The Road to a Canada-US Customs Union: Step-by-Step or in a Single Bound?" *CD Howe Institute Border Papers: Commentary* 184 (June).

Goldfarb, Danielle. 2003b. "Beyond Labels: Comparing Proposals for Closer Canada-US Economic Relations," *CD Howe Institute Border Papers: Backgrounder* 76 (October).

Goldstein, Judith. 1994. "International Law and Domestic Institutions: Reconciling North American 'Unfair' Trade Laws," *International Organization* 50 (4): 541–562.

Golob, Stephanie R. 2012. "*Plus Ça Change:* Double-Bilateralism and the Demise of Trilateralism," in Jeffrey Ayres and Laura Macdonald, eds., *North America in Question*. Toronto: University of Toronto Press.

Gotlieb, Allan. 1982. "Canada-US Relations: The Rules of the Game," *SAIS Review* 2 (4): 177–187.

Gotlieb, Allan. 2003. "A North American Community of Law," *The Quarterly: Ideas that Matter* 2 (4): 25–30.
Haggard, Stephan. 1997. "The Political Economy of Regionalism in Asia and the Americas," in Edward D. Mansfield and Helen V. Milner, eds., *The Political Economy of Regionalism*. New York: Columbia University Press.
Hale, Geoffrey. 2012a. *So Near Yet So Far: The Public and Hidden Worlds of Canada-US Relations*. Vancouver: UBC Press.
Hale, Geoffrey E. 2012b. "In Pursuit of Leverage: The Evolution of Canadian Trade and Investment Policies in an Increasingly Multipolar World," *Canadian Foreign Policy Journal* 18 (1): 106–119.
Hart, Michael. 1990. "The Future on the Table: The Continuing Negotiating Agenda under the Canada-United States Free-Trade Agreement," in Richard Dearden, Michael Hart, and Debra Steger, eds., *Living With Free Trade: Canada, the Free Trade Agreement and the GATT*. Ottawa: Centre for Trade Policy and Law and Institute for Research on Public Policy.
Hettne, Bjorn. 2005. "Beyond the 'New' Regionalism," *New Political Economy* 10 (4): 543–571.
Hettne, Bjorn, Andras Inotai, and Osvaldo Sunkel, eds. 1999. *Globalism and the New Regionalism*. Basingstoke UK: Macmillan.
Hettne, Bjorn, and Fredrik Soderbaum. 2000. "Theorising the Rise of Regionness," *New Political Economy* 5 (3): 457–472.
Holmes, John W. 1981. *Life with Uncle: The Canadian-American Relationship*. Toronto: University of Toronto Press.
Holsti, Kal J. 1971. "Canada and the United States," in Steven Spiegel and Kenneth Waltz, eds., *Conflict in World Politics*. Boston: Winthrop.
Holsti, Kal J., and Thomas Allen Levy. 1974. "Bilateral Institutions and Transgovernmental Relations between Canada and the United States," *International Organization* 28 (4): 875–901.
Hooghe, Liesbit, and Gary Marks. 2003. "Unraveling the Central State, but How?: Types of Multi-Level Governance," *American Political Science Review* 97 (2): 233–243.
Hufbauer, Gary Clyde, and Jeffrey J. Schott. 2005. *NAFTA Revisited: Achievements and Challenges*. Washington DC: Peterson Institute.
Hülsemeyer, Axel. 2004. *Globalization and Institutional Adjustment: Federalism as an Obstacle?* Aldershot UK: Ashgate.
Hurrell, Andrew. 2006. "Hegemony in a Region that Dares not Speak its Name," *International Journal* 61 (2): 545–566.
Jacobsson, Kerstin. 2004. "Soft Regulation and the Subtle Transformation of States: The Case of EU Employment Policy," *Journal of European Social Policy* 14 (4): 355–370.
Jönsson, Christer, et al. 1998. "Negotiations in Networks in the European Union," *International Negotiation* 3 (3): 319–344.
Katzenstein, Peter J. 2005. *A World of Regions*. Ithaca NY: Cornell University Press.
Keesbergen, Kees van, and Bertjan Verbeek. 1994. "The Politics of Subsidiarity in the European Union," *Journal of Common Market Studies* 32 (2): 215–236.
Kelly, Robert E. 2007. "Security Theory in the 'New Regionalism,'" *International Studies Review* 9 (2): 197–229.
Keohane, Robert O., and Joseph S. Nye, Jr. 1974. "The Complex Politics of Canadian-American Interdependence," *International Organization* 28 (4): 595–607.
Keohane, Robert O., and Joseph S. Nye, Jr. 1977. *Power and Interdependence: World Politics in Transition*. Boston: Little, Brown.
Keohane, Robert O., and Joseph S. Nye, Jr. 1987. "Power and Interdependence Revisited," *International Organization* 41 (4): 725–753.
Laursen, Finn. 2010. *Comparative Regional Integration: Europe and Beyond*. Farnham UK: Ashgate.

Macdonald, Laura. 2011. "Regionalism in Flux: Politics, Economics, and Security in the North American Region," in Timothy M. Shaw, J. Andrew Grant, and Scarlett Cornelisson, eds., *The Ashgate Research Companion to Regionalisms*. Farnham UK: Ashgate.

Marks, Gary. 1993. "Structural Policy and Multilevel Governance in the EC" (pp. 391–410), in Alan Cafruny and Glenda Rosenthal, eds., *The State of the European Community*. New York: Lynne Rienner.

Marks, Gary, Liesbit Hooghe, and Kermit Blank. 1996. "European Integration from the 1980s: State-Centric vs Multi-Level Governance," *Journal of Common Market Studies* 34 (3): 341–378.

Mattli, Walter. 1999. *The Logic of Regional Integration: Europe and Beyond*. Cambridge UK: Cambridge University Press.

Mayer, Frederick W. 1998. *Interpreting NAFTA: The Science and Art of Political Analysis*. New York: Columbia University Press.

Milner, Helen. 1995. "Regional Economic Co-operation, Global Markets and Domestic Politics: A Comparison of NAFTA and the Maastricht Treaty," *Journal of European Public Policy* 2 (3): 337–360.

Mittelman, James H. 1996. "Rethinking the 'New Regionalism' in the Context of Globalization," *Global Governance* 2: 189–213.

Morales, Isidro. 2008. *Post NAFTA North America: Reshaping the Economic and Political Governance of a Changing Region*. Houndsmill UK: Palgrave Macmillan.

Morales, Isidro. 2011. *National Solutions to Trans-Border Problems?: The Governance of Security and Risk in a Post-NAFTA North America*. London: Ashgate.

Moravcsik, Andrew. 1993. "Preferences and Power in the European Community: A Liberal Intergovernmentalist Approach," *Journal of Common Market Studies* 31 (4): 473–524.

Moravcsik, Andrew. 1998. *The Choice for Europe: Social Purpose and State Power from Messina to Maastricht*. Ithaca NY: Cornell University Press.

Moravcsik, Andrew. 2002. "In Defence of the 'Democratic Deficit': Reassessing Legitimacy in the European Union," *Journal of Common Market Studies* 40 (4): 603–624.

Mosher, James S., and David M. Trubek. 2003. "Alternative Approaches to Governance in the EU: EU Social Policy and the European Employment Strategy," *Journal of Common Market Studies* 41 (1): 63–88.

Murphy, John L. 2004. *The United States and International Law*. Cambridge UK: Cambridge University Press.

Newman, Abraham L. 2010. "International Organization Control under Conditions of Dual Delegation: A Transgovernmental Politics Approach," in Deborah D. Avant, Martha Finnemore, and Susan K. Sell, eds., *Who Governs the Globe?* Cambridge UK: Cambridge University Press.

O'Brien, Robert. 1995. "North American Integration and International Relations Theory," *Canadian Journal of Political Science* 28 (4): 693–724.

Pastor, Robert A. 2001. *Toward a North American Community: Lessons from the Old World for the New*. Washington DC: Institute for International Economics.

Pastor, Robert A. 2002. "NAFTA is Not Enough: Steps toward a North American Community," in Peter Hakim and Robert I. Litan, eds., *The Future of North American Integration: Beyond NAFTA*. Washington DC: Brookings Institution Press.

Pastor, Robert A. 2004. "North America's Second Decade," *Foreign Affairs* 83 (1): 124–135.

Pastor, Robert A. 2005. "North America and the Americas: Integration among Unequal Partners," in Mary Farrell, Bjorn Hettne, and Luk Van Langenhove, eds., *Global Politics of Regionalism: Theory and Practice*. Ann Arbor MI: Pluto Press.

Pastor, Robert A. 2008. "The Future of North America: Replacing a Bad Neighbor Policy," *Foreign Affairs* 87 (3): 84–98.

Pastor, Robert A. 2011. *The North American Idea: A Vision of a Continental Future.* New York: Oxford University Press.

Pastor, Robert A., and Rafael Fernandez de Castro. 1998. "Replacing Paternalism with Partnership," in Pastor and Fernandez de Castro, eds., *The Controversial Pivot: The US Congress and North America.* Washington DC: Brookings Institution Press.

Pennings, Frans, ed. 2006. *Between Soft and Hard Law: The Impact of International Social Security Standards on National Social Security Law.* The Hague: Kluwer Law International.

Peters, B. Guy, and Pierre, Jon. 2001. "Developments in Intergovernmental Relations: Towards Multi-Level Governance," *Policy and Politics* 29 (2): 131–135.

Pildes, Richard H. 2003–2004. "Conflicts Between American and European Views of Law," *Virginia Journal of International Law* 44 (2): 142–180.

Risse-Kappen, Thomas. 1995. *Bringing Transnational Relations Back In: Non-State Actors, Domestic Structures and International Institutions.* Cambridge: Cambridge University Press.

Rozental, Andrés. 2002. "Integrating North America: A Mexican Perspective," in Peter Hakim and Robert I. Litan, eds., *The Future of North American Integration: Beyond NAFTA.* Washington DC: Brookings Institution Press.

Raustiala, Kal. 2002. "Architecture of International Cooperation: Transgovernmental Networks and the Future of International Law," *Virginia Journal of International Law* 43 (1).

Sands, Christopher. 2002. "North America at Two Speeds," *CSIS Integration Monitor* 1 (2).

Sands, Christopher. 2011a. "Who Killed North America?" *CSIS Simon Chair Blog*, May 4. http://csis.org/blog/who-killed-north-america

Sands, Christopher. 2011b. "The Canada Gambit: Will It Revive North America?" *Hudson Institute Briefing Paper*, March. www.hudson.org/files/publications/Canada%20Gambit%20Web.pdf

Schafer, Armin. 2006. "Resolving Deadlock: Why International Organizations Introduce Soft Law," *European Law Journal* 12 (2): 194–208.

Scharpf, Fritz W. 1997. "Introduction: The Problem-Solving Capacity of Multi-Level Governance," *Journal of European Public Policy* 4 (4): 520–538.

Scharpf, Fritz W. 1999a. "Community and Autonomy: Multi-Level Policy-Making in the European Union," *Journal of European Public Policy* 1 (2): 219–242.

Scharpf, Fritz W. 1999b. *Governing in Europe: Effective and Democratic?* Oxford UK: Oxford University Press.

Selin, Henrik, and Stacey VanDeveer. 2011. "Climate Change Regionalism in North America," *Review of Policy Research* 28 (3): 295–304.

Slaughter, Anne-Marie. 1997. "The Real New World Order," *Foreign Affairs* 76 (5): 183–197.

Slaughter, Anne-Marie. 2000. "Agencies on the Loose?: Holding Government Networks Accountable," in George A. Bermann, Matthias Herdegen, and Peter Lindseth, eds., *Transatlantic Regulatory Cooperation: Legal Problems and Political Prospects.* Oxford: Oxford University Press.

Slaughter, Anne-Marie. 2004. *A New World Order.* Princeton: Princeton University Press.

Studer, Isabel, and Carol Wise, eds. 2007a. *Requiem or Revival?: The Promise of North American Integration.* Washington DC: Brookings Institution Press.

Studer, Isabel. 2007b. "Obstacles to Integration: North America's Institutional Weakness," in Isabel Studer and Carol Wise, eds. 2007. *Requiem or Revival?: The Promise of North American Integration.* Washington DC: Brookings Institution Press.

Swanson, Roger F. 1972. "The United States Canadiana Constellation, I: Washington, DC," *International Journal* 27 (2): 185–218.

Tornell, Aaron, and Gerardo Esquivel. 1997. "The Political Economy of Mexico's Entry into NAFTA," in Takatoshi Ito and Anne O. Krueger, eds., *Regionalism versus Multilateral Trade Arrangements*. Chicago: University of Chicago Press.

Trubek, David M., and Louise G. Trubek. 2005. "Hard and Soft Law in the Construction of Social Europe: The Role of the Open Method of Co-ordination," *European Law Journal* 11 (3): 343–364.

US Embassy. 2011a. "Beyond the Border: A Shared Vision for Perimeter Security and Economic Competitiveness," February 4. http://canada.usembassy.gov/canada-us-relations/border-issues/beyond-the-border-a-new-strategy/declaration-by-president-obama-and-prime-minister-harper-of-canada---beyond-the-border.html

US Embassy. 2011b. "Terms of Reference for the United States-Canada Regulatory Cooperation Council," June 3. http://canada.usembassy.gov/canada-us-relations/trade/terms-of-reference-for-the-united-states-canada-regulatory-cooperation-council.html

US International Trade Administration. 2011. "High-Level Regulatory Council Terms of Reference." www.whitehouse.gov/sites/default/files/omb/oira/irc/high-level_regulatory_cooperation_council-terms_of_reference_final.pdf

VanNijnatten, Debora L. 2011. "North American Environmental Regionalism: Multi-Level, Bottom-Heavy, and Policy-Led," in Lorraine Elliot and Shaun Breslin, eds., *Comparative Environmental Regionalism*. New York: Routledge.

Warleigh-Lack, Alex. 2006. "Towards a Conceptual Framework for Regionalisation: Bridging 'New Regionalism' and 'Integration Theory,'" *Review of International Political Economy* 13 (5): 750–771.

Warleigh-Lack, Alex. 2007. "Studying Regionalisation Comparatively," in Andrew Cooper, et al., eds., *Regionalism and Global Governance: The Taming of Globalisation?* New York: Routledge.

Warleigh-Lack, Alex, and Ben Rosamond. 2010. "Across the EU Studies-New Regionalism Frontier: Invitation to a Dialogue," *Journal of Common Market Studies* 48 (4): 993–1013.

Warleigh-Lack, Alex, et al., eds. 2011. *New Regionalism and the European Union: Dialogues, Comparisons and New Research Directions*. New York: Routledge.

Weintraub, Sidney. 1992. "US-Mexico Free Trade: Implications for the United States," *Journal of Interamerican Studies and World Affairs* 34 (2): 29–52.

Weintraub, Sidney. 1996. "Next Steps: Policy Options after NAFTA," in Charles F. Doran and Alvin P. Drischler, eds., *A New North America: Cooperation and Enhanced Interdependence*. Westport CT: Praeger.

Wiener, Antje, and Thomas Diez. 2009. *European Integration Theory*. 2nd ed., Oxford: Oxford University Press.

Wilkinson, Rorden. 2009. "Language, Power, and Multilateral Trade Negotiations," *Review of International Political Economy* 16 (4): 597–619.

Winham, Gilbert R., and Elizabeth DeBoer-Ashworth. 2000. "Asymmetry in Negotiating the Canada-US Free Trade Agreement, 1985–1987," in I. William Zartman and Jeffrey Z. Rubin, eds., *Power and Negotiation*. Ann Arbor: University of Michigan Press.

Wyman, Donald L. 1978. "Dependence and Conflict: US Relations with Mexico, 1920–1975," in Robert L. Paarlberg, Eul Y. Park, and Donald L. Wyman, *Diplomatic Dispute: US Conflict with Iran, Japan and Mexico*. Cambridge MA: Harvard University Press.

2 "Bundled Transgovernmentalism" and Environmental Governance in North America

Debora VanNijnatten and Neil Craik

Rising awareness of mounting environmental threats in the post-NAFTA era, propelled by concerns about trade and economic impacts but also climate change, have focused attention to an even greater extent on degradation in the continental space and on the governance architecture necessary for responding to this degradation. In keeping with the metaphor of architecture that animates this volume, we are interested in the interplay between federal executive actors and transgovernmental networks in addressing common environmental concerns. The environment provides an interesting and important example of the evolution of regional cooperation in North America because of the divided jurisdictional responsibilities for environmental regulation in each North American state, and the high degree of regulatory complexity that issues such as climate change and biodiversity engender. This necessitates coordination at multiple levels, but also horizontal coordination with energy, resource, and trade regulators. As suggested in the introductory chapter, these characteristics push the regulatory architecture toward decentralized configurations, but the impetus toward decentralization is constrained by institutional and political requirements for national orchestration. The result, which we describe as a tendency toward "bundled transgovernmentalism," shows how these tensions do not necessarily pull governance arrangements toward one pole or another, but can result in a managed compromise between top-down hierarchical governance, on the one hand, and more dispersed and less formal forms of governance, on the other.

The chapter begins by tracing the evolution of the predominant modes of regional environmental governance in North America. We show that, whereas the three governments conducted their environmental interactions prior to the mid-1990s primarily through the lenses of binationalism, diplomacy, and territorial maintenance, interactions have since become more multi-scalar and network-driven over the past decades.[1] We argue, however, that network interactions in North America have been leavened and shaped by the continued force of formal institutions within and beyond the state. We also link these dynamics to the portrayals of those multilevel governance analysts who see policy networks as nested within formal institutions rather than as functioning in alternate, autonomous arenas. We then illustrate how formal institutional constraints, particularly political executive dominance and federal systems, have influenced network potential for contributing to environmental policy coordination and implementation effectiveness. In particular, we trace this potential through the emergence of "bundled" transgovernmental networks, which gather multiple transgovernmental networks under the banner of national executive institutions that operate beyond national borders and have been particularly prominent in the environment-climate change sphere.[2]

THE EVOLUTION OF THE TRANSNATIONAL ENVIRONMENTAL GOVERNANCE ARCHITECTURE IN NORTH AMERICA

Earlier perspectives on environmental governance in North America from the 1970s through to the 1990s emphasized the ways in which national governments related to one another, primarily bilaterally and with an overriding concern for territoriality. As Maxwell Cohen noted in 1983, "Canada and the United States occupy and inevitably have to jointly manage a vast continental region—some five thousand miles of boundary [that] are the major fact of sovereign life for both countries."[3] John Carroll, in setting out the framework for the first comprehensive, cross-case analysis of Canadian-American environmental relations, aptly entitled *Environmental Diplomacy*—explained that he would deal with "bilateral issues," by which he meant "any project or undertaking representing a benefit to one country and a cost to another and concerning which the latter raises objection."[4] The cases examined in Carroll's book were in fact chosen due to their "diplomatic importance and relevance to the overall bilateral relationship." Other analyses at the time focused on the seemingly inevitable tension between national, political, and legal sovereignty on the one hand, and the emerging bilateral environmental regime on the other.[5]

In a similar manner, the literature on the US-Mexico environmental relationship highlighted themes of binationality and, in particular, territorial integrity. Given the history of annexation on the southern border, with the US taking significant portions of what had been Mexican territory, subsequent management of the border was extremely sensitive. Certainly, the relationship has often been acrimonious. In Pastor and Castañada's book, *The Limits to Friendship*, the authors portray two governments mired in misperception, who consequently view each other with suspicion.[6] Environmental interactions, however, revealed a different side to the relationship; despite the sheer magnitude of degradation along the shared border, including depletion of water resources, high levels of air and water pollution, as well as hazardous wastes, analysts saw joint action bear fruit. Sánchez notes that the environment was often the *only* issue on which any agreement between the two governments could be reached during the diplomatically sensitive bilateral context of the 1980s.[7] Belausteguigoitia and Guadarrama also depict bilateral environmental interactions as quite successful, despite a context characterized by "the persistence of sovereignty as a goal unto itself."[8]

Such analyses necessarily privileged national-level actors, and particularly those constitutionally authorized to negotiate. By the same token, they downplayed the role of subnational governments who were seen as being of minor constitutional significance to the resolution of cross-border issues[9] as having little expertise[10] and as secondary actors in a two-level game where all roads led through federal officials.[11] Given the weaker constitutional position of Mexican states, subnational governments elicited almost no comment in analyses of the US-Mexico environmental relationship. Moreover, this earlier literature also downplayed engagement by nongovernmental organizations, which were seen as bit-players left outside a high-stakes diplomatic game where the border was a clear demarcation line for political sovereignty and policy autonomy.

The institutional framework supporting these environmental interactions consisted of a mix of (mostly) quiet, behind-the-scenes diplomacy and administrative management on the backdrop of a relatively well-articulated system of treaties and agreements.[12] Canada-US examples include the Boundary Waters Treaty (1909), the Migratory Bird Treaty (1918), the Great Lakes Water Quality Agreement (1972, revised in 1978, 1987, and 2012), the Pacific Salmon Treaty (1985) and the Canada-US Air Quality Agreement (1991). On the US-Mexico border, the 1889 International Border Convention, the 1944 Water Utilization Treaty, and the 1983 Agreement on Cooperation for the Protection and Improvement of the Environment in the Border Area ("La Paz" Agreement) framed cooperation. Trilateralism was almost nonexistent. In one rare exception, Mexico became party to the (Canada-US) Migratory Bird Treaty. Other efforts to undertake trilateral cooperation on conservation issues, however, were rebuffed by successive US administrations.[13]

Several changes occurred over the course of the 1990s that altered the nature of environmental cooperation across borders in North America. At the same time that national governments backed off environmental policymaking beginning in the mid-1990s, for budgetary, ideological, and political-constitutional reasons, transboundary environmental engagement flourished at other levels.[14] Looking "downward," this decade saw the buildup of increasingly dense subnational and cross-border regional organizational linkages along the Canada-US border, and to a somewhat lesser extent the US-Mexico border. This mirrored developments in other countries, as subnational governments became more assertive in shaping their economic and policy futures.[15] On the northern border, the focus shifted to US state and Canadian provincial governments, whose capacity to address environmental challenges grew rapidly after the late 1980s, who exhibited a willingness to undertake innovations in environmental policy approaches and instruments,[16] and who began interacting in a much more direct manner on the shared border.[17] National governments, less fiscally able than in earlier decades, seemed content to take on supporting roles in this lower level transboundary activism.[18] Even in the more centralized Mexican context, successive legislative amendments over the 1990s and into the 2000s expanded the role of the states in environmental protection, and they enacted legislation in an increasing range of environmental areas.[19] In keeping with this, Mexican states also became more active in terms of cooperating with their US state counterparts across the southern border, although not as aggressively as US states and Canadian provinces. Because subnational governments have no formal authority to engage in treaty making, the form of these arrangements was necessarily informal, resulting in cooperation agreements, as opposed to hard commitments.

The 1990s also brought renewed attempts at environmental trilateralism. With the signing of the North American Agreement on Environmental Cooperation (NAAEC) and creation of a new institution—the Commission for Environmental Cooperation (CEC)—continent-wide collaboration on and tracking of environmental policy activities intensified. NAAEC was the result of intense lobbying by US environmental and labor groups, which sought assurances that freer trade would not result in an environmental race to the bottom. Thus the focus of the NAAEC was not on transboundary pollution, the traditional focus of bilateral cooperation, but on avoiding trade distortions or trade barriers and environmental cooperation measures, such as the development of common indicators, data sharing, and research and technology cooperation (NAAEC Articles 1 and 10). Other initiatives, also continental in scope, gained firmer traction, including the Canada/US/Mexico Trilateral Committee for Wildlife and Ecosystem Conservation and Management and the North American Research Strategy for Tropospheric Ozone. Again, both of these initiatives focus on soft cooperation, not regulatory standards.

By the early 2000s, then, transboundary environmental cooperation had been "rescaled." Bilateral interactions continued under the existing hard law, diplomatic, and administrative framework, although progress on many fronts had stalled and very little was added to the existing transboundary architecture.[20] But considerable activity was now taking place at lower (subnational) levels, some at higher (trilateral) scales, and some even in diagonal fashion—i.e., between subnational and trilateral actors.[21]

Moreover, the nature of interaction had also altered. From the 1970s into the 1990s, policy officials engaging in bilateral cooperation were quite closely tied to the hard law framework, their roles defined in the first instance by agency mandates and the division of responsibilities under the federal systems of the three countries and then by the provisions of bilateral agreements, which were carefully constructed on these mandates and responsibilities. For example, the Air Quality Committee and its subcommittees, populated by federal policy and science officials, were utilized to implement the narrow aims of the Canada-US Air Quality Agreement on an ongoing basis.[22] On the US-Mexico border, the issue-specific provisions of the La Paz Agreement (e.g., hazardous waste and air pollution) were attended to by committees of national officials, resourced disproportionately by the US EPA. At the subnational level, though, governments simply did not possess the constitutional authority to conclude formal binding agreements with their counterparts across the border—the authority to engage in foreign relations being reserved to the federal governments in all three North American states—and they needed to work around this constraint. As a consequence, the interactions that emerged at the subnational and trinational levels possessed more informal bases, such as statements of intent or "resolutions" to cooperate rather than treaties or formal agreements, and they needed to operate through softer channels utilizing peer deliberation and persuasion. Similarly, at the trinational level, the long-standing reluctance to cede sovereign authority to supranational organizations meant that little in the way of hard law or formal structures existed and the mode of cooperation was quite similar to that practiced at the subnational level. The obvious exception here is the North American Commission for Environmental Cooperation, which we discuss in more detail below.

A simultaneous development was the pressing need to direct transboundary environmental governance in North America toward addressing the myriad problems associated with climate change policy—and to do so in a context where climate-specific institutions and agreements were almost completely lacking at the bilateral and continental levels; where domestic policy competencies and tools were dispersed awkwardly across national and subnational levels; and where the political pay-off for action was uncertain, at best, given prevailing political and economic conditions.[23] Unlike transboundary pollution, climate change is an issue of common concern at a global scale, requiring greenhouse gas (GHG) emission reduction commitments to be negotiated in a global forum. However, the economic and technological transformations required to address the move to a less carbon-intensive economy pushes downward into land use, energy, and transportation systems, many of which operate and are regulated on subnational scales. Climate cooperation in North America also needs to operate alongside and in conjunction with a highly differentiated system of cross-border and continental ties for energy production and trade, if the transboundary system is to have any effectiveness in terms of mitigation. Here, too, the lack of a hard law framework meant that informal institutions would need to provide the backbone for climate cooperation across borders.[24]

TRANSGOVERNMENTAL NETWORKS AND FORMAL INSTITUTIONS IN NORTH AMERICA: THE LEAVENING EFFECT

North American environmental transboundary structures, then, seemed to conform quite nicely to the shift from "government" to "governance" being observed across states, whereby public decision making was occurring in a less hierarchical manner than government, with the participation of a wider range of actors, and within institutional arrangements that were more informal and decentralized.[25] The literature on networks, particularly of the "transgovernmental" variety, seemed to aptly describe the evolution of interactions across borders in the North American context. Transgovernmental networking, as explained by Slaughter in 2004, occurs among "separate, functionally distinct parts" of the state and is operationalized through peer-to-peer, horizontal relations between discrete, specialized agencies or departments.[26] Significantly, these networks tend not to have a distinct legal personality, any permanent supporting infrastructure, nor any ability to bind members; rather, cooperative results are arrived at through peer communication and persuasion. All of these descriptors seemed to fit the more recent institutional configurations emerging at the subnational and trinational levels, as well as some recent bilateral activity. By 2010, Kirton and Guebert were observing that, despite the presence of a considerable framework of hard law in the form of bilateral and (a few) trilateral treaties, North America had "a rich sub-stratum of voluntary standards and informal institutions that have promoted regulatory cooperation and convergence."[27]

Policy network theory has proven useful in showing us what more informal institutions actually look like: how different groups of actors can engage in decision making outside of formal channels and instead create normative expectations through peer interaction.[28] Transgovernmental networks, as originally described by Keohane and Nye, highlight the ways in which government agency officials form close relationships with their counterparts in neighboring jurisdictions and, through continuing communication, work together on common environmental policy programming.[29] For Slaughter and others, transgovernmental networks offer much promise for international governance, as they provide a means to harmonize standards, share information, and cooperate on enforcement outside of state structures, creating flexible solutions to global governance problems.[30]

But how might we envisage dynamics at the interface of formal institutions and informal entities such as networks, given that the former do not simply cease to exist when the latter come into being?

In this regard, the multi-level governance (MLG) literature has been useful in drawing our attention to the increasingly complex vertical and horizontal relations between policy actors. The concept of MLG implies spatial distinctions and geographical separation, but, at the same time, its most vital feature is the focus on linkages that connect political arenas.[31] In their early works, Hooghe and Marks identified two types of MLG. Type I rests on the fundamental assumptions of federalism theory, whereby a limited number of territorial jurisdictions bundle together multiple policy functions under their individual umbrellas.[32] The primary concern is the relationship between the central government and a tier of nonintersecting subnational governments; the unit of analysis is the individual government, rather than any specific policy or policy domain. Type II, by contrast, sees jurisdictions as fragmented into functionally specific pieces, grouping together to provide a particular local service or solve a common resource problem.[33] Within these jurisdictions subnational actors have become more assertive vis-à-vis national governments, "wearing away executive control in many policy areas."[34] In these situations, where jurisdictions are problem driven, more flexible and ad-hoc forms of governance have been created, such as networks.[35]

Among the main claims of MLG analysts, and important for this analysis, is the contention that "decision making competences are shared by actors at different levels rather than monopolized by state [national] executives" and, correspondingly, that state executives do lose some control.[36] For our purposes, how much control is lost, and how do we judge the tipping point beyond central state control where critical decisions are being taken in alternate arenas? Type I theorists argue that national governments maintain their ability to orchestrate from above. Type II theorists, on the other hand, believe that the "growth of MLG at the subnational level is a way of capturing and integrating regions' policy makers towards a new center"—to networks, for example.[37]

This debate should not be understood as a binary choice between two alternate conceptions, but rather a critical question is how institutional arrangements configure the demands for central orchestration with the need for greater flexibility and autonomy among cooperating actors that must engage one another both vertically (between levels) and horizontally (across sectors and policy domains) in the transnational sphere. These developments, while functional in nature, are influenced by the broader institutional context in which they have evolved. Informal arrangements, such as networks, interact with, and consequently, are affected by, formal institutions.[38]

A critical attribute of the formal institutional framework vis-à-vis transgovernmental networks is the degree of autonomy possessed by participating agencies. Clearly, transgovernmental networks (TGN) could not operate where agencies have *no* freedom to engage in cooperative interactions across borders. The existence of TGNs presupposes that, while the legislative branch in both parliamentary and presidential systems sets broad policy direction, much of the details of regulation are delegated to administrative agencies, who are then in a position to coordinate implementation with their counterparts across the border. The exercise of this discretion is subject to domestic procedural safeguards, judicial oversight, and some legislative oversight through parliamentary and (considerably more thorough) Congressional committees. But the "hard edge" to the power of transgovernmental networks is that network participants are assumed to exercise power at home to implement network decisions, without frequent recourse to the legislature or to senior executive approval.

Yet, the ability of agencies to actually do this varies considerably. In Slaughter's analysis of transgovernmental networks, she focuses primarily on "strong" bureaucratic entities, such as financial regulators, judges, and central bankers, as well as law enforcement and intelligence officials, all of which have higher levels of independence from national executives than line agencies.[39] Similarly, Eberlein and Newman, in their analysis of inter-agency networking, isolate out "independent agencies . . . typically found in economic sectors" whose autonomy is "more substantial," as "their very institutional design explicitly buffers them from direct political control."[40] Specifically, they argue that these agencies have "long-term leadership tenure, guaranteed budgets, and control over personnel appointments," attributes that differentiate them from "street level bureaucrats."[41] The extent of statutory authority—to make rules under the terms of legislation and enforce them—is also significant here, i.e., to what degree and under what conditions must draft regulations be vetted by political officials, or what are the reporting requirements to the legislature? More generally, what degree of discretion has accrued to an agency under the primary legislation governing its rule-making and administrative functions? As Eberlein and Newman note, transgovernmental networks "critically depend on the extent of domestic delegation of authority" such that they are able to implement and enforce agreements reached at the international level.[42] These authors empirically demonstrate the relationship, linking variable delegation across agencies to variations in outcomes using two case studies of energy regulation and data privacy. Eberlein and Grande further explain that the success of informal regulatory coordination through networks is tied to a key "external" condition, namely that agency participants have "*de facto* room for manoeuvre in their decisions."[43] They explain that, "[a] national regulatory authority that has no significant powers within its respective national regime, for instance, will find it hard to become effectively involved in transnational networks, because it will lack the capacity for making credible commitments to its partners."[44]

Across all of these measures, it might be argued that environmental agencies in North America tend to have less autonomy, and retain less room for maneuver in terms of international collaboration. It is telling that, after producing a long list of examples involving finance and intelligence officials who are *making policy* independently in their transboundary networks, one of the few environmental references—to the US EPA and its work in the International Network for Environmental Compliance and Enforcement (INECE)—focuses on considerably less intensive activities including provision of "technical assistance," and holding "global conferences at which environmental regulators learn and exchange information."[45]

If we were to designate as a primary indicator of the robustness of networks the ability of the network to withstand executive tampering, then environmental transgovernmental networks would be considered quite weak. We illustrate this in the next section, in a discussion of "bundled" transgovernmental networks (TGN), through which political leaders gather multiple networks under the banner of a single executive initiative. We also argue, however, that this is not necessarily "bad" for the environment; in fact, bundled TGNs may offer some benefits in terms of policy coordination, capacity building, and implementation effectiveness.

BUNDLED TGNs AND ENVIRONMENTAL GOVERNANCE IN NORTH AMERICA

In earlier work, we have traced the emergence in the North American context of "bundled" transgovernmental networks.[46] Bundled TGNs differ from the conventional understanding of transgovernmental networks, in that they gather multiple network activities under the banner of a single executive initiative, thereby providing enhanced executive direction over interagency cooperation. Like conventional transgovernmental networks, bundled TGNs generally have no foundational treaty or permanent secretariat, and each participating state retains its sovereign authority over regulatory matters. But unlike traditional networks, which tend to be focused on specific policy areas, and engage bureaucratic counterparts within those policy areas, bundled TGNs provide a vehicle for multiple initiatives to be considered within a common framework and provide a coordinating role for central executive officials. Bundled TGNs can take the form of an agenda with an accompanying process; the agenda is assembled and negotiated centrally, with regulatory coordination activities specified and then the actual coordination delegated to sector- or policy-specific working groups made up of regulatory officials from each country. Timeframes for completion are also identified centrally, and working groups are expected to report back to political leaders. TGNs are typically understood as operating autonomously from the cabinet or chief executives of governments,[47] and as such they rely on an extension of their domestic authority to coordination activities beyond the state. Bundled TGNs, which receive their mandate from central authorities, are expressly authorized by those authorities to engage in transnational activity. At the same time, bundled TGNs are constrained by that mandate, which often identifies quite specific deliverables, and are subject to established oversight mechanisms. In essence, bundled TGNs represent a deliberate attempt by executive authorities to harness the power of transgovernmental networks to achieve more encompassing collective ends.

As a means of further describing the primary attributes of bundled TGNs, we can trace its rise in North American environmental governance. An early form of bundled transgovernmentalism can be seen in the design and operation of the North American Commission for Environmental Cooperation (CEC). Established under the North American Agreement for Environmental Cooperation, the CEC is intended as the principal vehicle for promoting environmental cooperation between the three NAFTA partners. While the CEC is structured as a formal international organization—it has a permanent secretariat and is formally constituted under the North American

Agreement for Environmental Cooperation—it functions on a day-to-day basis as a multi-tiered and bundled collection of networks. The CEC has no authority to bind its members, but rather provides policy recommendations to a council made up of the political executives of each member's respective federal environment agency. Thus, the principal interactions within the CEC are agency-to-agency, and high level. The executive-led Council provides firm direction to the CEC both through Joint Ministerial Statements, issued annually (or whenever an issue comes to their attention) and via more detailed direction through the approval of five-year strategic plans and annual operating plans. At an operational level, the work of the CEC is carried out by numerous working groups made up of midlevel bureaucrats from each country.

Viewed through the lens of bundled TGNs, the CEC creates two tiers of networks. A high-level transgovernmental forum sets the agenda for a constellation of administrative-level working groups. The centrally controlled work plans are quite specific in nature and often include timelines and identified budgets. The political level direction generates political lift given the clear mandate—although it is possible that the efficacy of these bundled networks comes at the cost of innovation. By tightly conscribing network activities, the CEC may allow less room for entrepreneurial activity among regulators.

Successive US-Mexico border environmental plans have increasingly functioned as examples of bundled TGNs. In 1992, the two national governments released the first US-Mexico Border Environmental Plan, which endeavored to bring a wide range of previously disparate environmental management efforts under a comprehensive program of network building managed by EPA and the Mexican environmental agency, SEMARNAT. Over the course of renewals of the Plan—Border XXI (1996), Border 2012 (2002) and Border 2020 (2012), all named for the date by which environmental objectives were to be met—these border frameworks have become increasingly differentiated, establishing three types of coordinating bodies—regional workgroups (for California-Baja California, Arizona-Sonora, New Mexico-Texas-Chihuahua, and Texas-Coahuila-Nuevo León-Tamaulipas), border-wide workgroups focusing on broad topics (e.g., cooperative enforcement and compliance) and policy fora centered on pollution to particular media (e.g., air, water, and land/waste). Besides the two national agencies, state and local governments have played significant roles in the Border Plans, a role that has increased over time. All of the workgroups and policy fora function as transgovernmental networks, with some participation from NGO and private sector representatives, but executive direction is provided through five central environmental policy goals, five guiding principles, and two-year Action Plans which set priorities and allocate resources.

Another recent example of bundling can be found in the US-Canada Clean Energy Dialogue. In early 2009, both the Canadian and Mexican leaders, recognizing that climate change and energy would be a priority for the recently elected Barack Obama, and fearing that they might be disadvantaged by a new American regulatory regime, wasted no time in attempting to forge tighter links with the new administration. Rather than adopting a trilateral approach, however, separate negotiations were conducted between the US and Canada, and the US and Mexico with respect to climate-energy cooperative frameworks. In February of 2009, the US-Canada Clean Energy Dialogue (CED) was established, following a series of high-level meetings at the ministerial/secretary level and deputy level, as well as more substantive roundtable discussions considering potential areas for cooperation.[48] The roundtables were "by invitation only." The co-chairs of the Dialogue are the US Energy Secretary but in Canada—perhaps surprisingly—the Minister of Environment.

Of interest here is that the CED's mandate is not focused on developing or coordinating regulatory regimes; instead, its aim is "to enhance joint collaboration on the development of clean energy science and technologies to reduce greenhouse gases and combat climate change."[49] The rationale is quite minimalist; joint activities under the Dialogue are intended to reinforce domestic climate policy efforts and further "our ongoing efforts toward building a low carbon economy."[50]

The work of the CED is being conducted by means of a "network of networks." There are three working groups focusing on Clean Energy Research and Development, Carbon Capture and Storage, and the Electricity Grid. Membership is primarily interagency but there is also participation from universities, scientific organizations, think tanks, and private industry.[51] Each of these working groups was instructed to delineate "priority areas" for collaboration, arrived at after broader consultations with a variety of policy actors. Each priority area then formed its own set of partners, including both governmental and nongovernmental members. Some networks are clearly overlapping, particularly in terms of governmental membership.

The reporting structure is two stages, hierarchical, and high level; agency leads on priority tasks report to their senior executive officials, who then report to the President and Prime Minister. The entire structure is guided by the Clean Energy Action Plan, which contains all of the priority tasks and was endorsed by the two leaders during their first meeting in the fall of 2009. Each priority area has a timeline attached, and designated at least one lead agency in each country responsible for implementation.

In each of these examples, multiple network activities are bundled together by political executive leaders who designate priorities, assign tasks, and allocate resources. In addition, all incorporate clear timelines and reporting requirements. Border 2020, the most recent iteration of the US-Mexico environmental plan, also provides a clear assessment framework with the release of regular Border Environmental Indicators reports, which show whether environmental conditions along a range of media are improving or not.[52]

BUNDLED TGNs AND POLICY IMPACTS

Understanding the actual policy impacts of bundled TGNs is critical, given the role they currently play in North American environmental policy, and the role that they are likely to play in the future. We would argue that two aspects are central here. First, policy coherence is increasingly important in the context of complex environmental problems, such as climate change, where there is a need to integrate policy across multiple sectors and multiple scales. Second, achieving implementation effectiveness is an enduring concern, and this includes the ability to promote and mobilize policy capacity. This is critical in a context where participants come to the table with asymmetrical resources, as in North America.[53]

Contrary to the picture drawn in the broader literature on TGNs, bundled TGNs offer considerable potential in terms of enabling higher levels of environmental policy coordination. While there is an active debate about the degree to which TGNs are issue specific, they are generally seen as promoting a lack of coherence.[54] Considerable emphasis is placed on the technocratic nature of the regulatory issues being addressed and, perhaps not surprisingly, much of the literature on TGNs consists of specific policy case studies. Here, the concern is with networks viewing their problems narrowly and without regard for broader governmental (and, in this case, environmental) concerns. The concern is also structural in the sense that networks tend to inculcate a shared understanding of particular transnational problems based on the common professional and technical backgrounds of their members—and these are necessarily viewed from a narrow perspective.

Bundled TGNs may to some extent overcome this limitation, as executive control over the agenda offers opportunities for promoting coherence among separate initiatives, given that the cooperative exercise is treated like a package. Achieving coherent policy across sectors and scales is a function both of having clearly stated goals and agendas, but also of fashioning a structure that can facilitate their implementation, by integrating policy activities in such a way that they are mutually reinforcing. The ability of the CEC to coordinate regional environmental issues cross-sectorally is evident in the creation of working groups along functional lines; for example, its work on air pollution and electricity privatization has enabled it to provide some policy intelligence on climate change–related instruments such as emissions trading. The US-Mexico Border 2020, by synchronizing the efforts of media-specific policy groups with regional working groups that are explicitly cross-media and multi-issue, promotes a broader perspective on what the policy priorities should be and where resources should be directed. The Clean Energy Dialogue has provided the clearest bilateral linkage yet of the environmental and energy infrastructures, in such a way that cross-cutting issues would be visible.

It might be noted, however, that both the CEC and Border 2020 are somewhat hampered in their ability to promote coherence given their inability to reach across agencies. For example, on trade and environment issues, the CEC has been unsuccessful in engaging the Free Trade Commission, while Border 2020 has failed to engage the Departments of Energy or Transportation, both important stakeholders in border pollution. In this respect, the Clean Energy Dialogue may offer more potential; given the political direction provided at the highest levels, it would presumably be easy to incorporate other departments and agencies.

Even where there is a consensus on what should be done to address an environmental problem, implementation may be hindered by resource and capacity inequalities across policy actors and institutions. Given the varying levels of environmental capacity within North America, making sure that adequate resources are available to support the initiatives being undertaken is challenging. In many ways, this is the real test of the strength and likely durability of the network because resources need to come from domestic coffers—there is not usually an international "budget" in North America for environmental cooperation. Resources to support transboundary environmental cooperation, as well as the implementation at the domestic level of any agreements reached, may come in the tangible form of domestic (likely agency) budgetary outlays for such things as training workshops, technical support, technology transfer, or equipment, and to pay for implementing collaborative projects, such as reducing hazardous waste or building sewage treatment plants. Alternatively, resources may involve in-kind contributions from participating agencies, including personnel time, technical support, or even travel funding so that policy actors from different jurisdictions can meet and learn from each other.

The informality of transgovernmental networks is likely to make resources difficult to marshal. For example, the North American Energy Working Group, a network made up of energy regulators, produced some prominent reports on continental energy supplies in 2002 and 2006, but by 2009 it had simply ceased to meet. Bundling, however, by designating priorities and tasking officials with meeting specified goals, can increase the resources that are drawn from departments for the purposes of the network. The CEC is somewhat of an exception here, as it has its own budget, but the amount is small and it tends to leverage the bureaucratic resources of the three environment agencies—as well as NGO resources—to increase its capacity. Those participating in Border 2020 benefit in a general way from the treaty infrastructure that exists at arm's length in terms of designating border environmental protection as a priority, but perhaps more important is the constant engagement of executive heads, particularly on the EPA side.

In a general sense, we might ask how effective TGNs can be, given their reliance on primarily "soft" instruments of influence. Kenneth Anderson has forcefully questioned whether networks are able to effect real change: "Networks held meetings, wrote papers, made recommendations, and drafted statements. To be sure, this is what networks must do in order to create successful outcomes in which network members go back to their own operations and implement now-coordinated policies. Yet unfortunately this is also precisely the procedure followed when networks create unsuccessful outcomes."[55] This criticism may be overstated; there are now numerous examples of tangible network outcomes, such the Trilateral Energy, Science and Technology Agreement and the *Memorandum of Understanding on Cooperation for Wilderness Conservation.* But even these outcomes do not contain clear standards or deliverables, and their actual impact is thus hard to assess. Unlike most supranational environmental agreements, which have clearly identified goals and purposes, network expectations are often undefined.

Bundling, however, has implications for network effectiveness, the most important being that executive attention to networks mobilizes bureaucratic resources toward network activities. Bundling, particularly where there is an expectation of regular reporting, provides a mechanism for overcoming bureaucratic inertia. The clear identification and prioritization of issues at political levels provided a form of "political lift" for network activities. This is particularly important, in our view, for regulatory areas, such as environment and climate change, where there is not a high degree of structural independence from ministerial levels of government, as discussed above. Certainly, meaningful cooperation is much more likely to emerge where network members have a clearly defined mandate to arrive at cooperative solutions, one that is endorsed at the very highest levels. From this perspective, executive "interference" might be regarded as having positive policy impacts.

CONCLUSIONS

While TGNs have certainly shown their utility, it is far from clear that the grander aspirations of a "new world order," as contemplated by Slaughter, where TGNs play a dominant role in North American environmental governance, has come to fruition. Instead, there is ample evidence that national governments are able to mold and direct transgovernmental interactions, and harness them in such a way as to achieve their own ends. Interestingly, Slaughter also contends that "states have evolved and will continue to evolve mechanisms for reaggregating the interests of their distinct institutions when necessary."[56] Inherent in our conceptualization of bundled TGNs is a clear and direct form of executive oversight of network activities; networks are nested within formal domestic frameworks with attendant impacts on how networks operate. We also indicate in the discussion above, however, that bundled TGNs bring with them considerable advantages. Indeed, Eberlein and Newman argue that the effectiveness of "'new' functional governance arrangements," or transgovernmental networks, actually depends on "the shadow of governmental hierarchy";[57] here, formal domestic authority is viewed as a *resource* that, when mobilized and leveraged, can be harnessed to support transboundary ends.

NOTES

1. Craik and DiMento 2009; VanNijnatten 2006, 2009a, 2009b, 2011; VanNijnatten and Craik 2012; Craik, Studer, and VanNijnatten 2013; Healy, VanNijnatten, and Vallejo 2014.
2. VanNijnatten and Craik 2012; Craik and VanNijnatten 2013.
3. Cohen 1983, ix.
4. Carroll 1983, 5.
5. See, for example: Doran 1984; Munton and Castle 1992.
6. Pastor and Casteñeda 1989; see, for example Doran 1984; Munton and Castle 1992.
7. Sánchez 1998.
8. Belausteguigoitia and Guadarrama, 1997, 105.
9. Schmandt and Roderick 1985, 232, 240.
10. Carroll 1983, 17.
11. Munton and Castle 1992, 316–17.
12. VanNijnatten 2003.
13. Healy, VanNijnatten, and Vallejo 2014, 49–50.
14. VanNijnatten 2006.
15. Peters and Pierre 2001, 132.
16. Rabe 2002.
17. VanNijnatten 2006, 5.
18. VanNijnatten 2009, 44.
19. Hogenboom 1998.
20. One exception here was the 2000 Ozone Annex to the 1991 Canada-United States Air Quality Agreement.
21. Osofsky 2008; VanNijnatten and Craik 2013.
22. VanNijnatten and Lambright 2001.
23. VanNijnatten and Craik 2013, 5–6.
24. Underdal 2010.
25. Pierre and Peters 2000.
26. Slaughter 2004.
27. Kirton and Guebert 2010, 61.
28. Helmke and Levitsky 2003, 7–8.
29. Keohane and Nye, 1974.
30. Slaughter 2004.
31. Bache and Flinders 2004, 3; Stephenson 2013, 817.
32. Hooghe and Marks 2003, 236.
33. Ibid, 237.
34. Eilstrup-Sangiovanni 2006, 331.
35. Hooghe and Marks 2004, 25.
36. Bache 2008, 25.
37. Gore and Webber 2004, 55.
38. Farrell and Heritier 2003.
39. Slaughter 2004.
40. Eberlein and Newman 2008, 29–30.
41. Ibid.
42. Ibid, 45.
43. Eberlein and Grande 2005, 103.
44. Ibid, 103.
45. Slaughter 2004, 3.
46. VanNijnatten and Craik 2012; Craik and VanNijnatten 2013.
47. Keohane and Nye 1974; Slaughter 2004.

48. Government of Canada 2012.
49. Environment Canada 2012.
50. Ibid.
51. Ibid.
52. US Environmental Protection Agency and SEMARNAT 2012.
53. Healy, VanNijnatten, and Vallejo 2014.
54. See, for example, Slaughter and Zaring 2006 versus Pollack and Schaffer 2001.
55. Anderson 2005, 1277–1278.
56. Slaughter, 2004, 18.
57. Eberlein and Newman 2008, 46.

REFERENCES

Anderson, Kenneth. 2005. "Squaring the Circle: Reconciling Sovereignty and Global Governance through Global Government Networks (Review of Anne-Marie Slaughter, a New World Order)," *Harvard Law Review* 118 (3): 1255–1312.

Bache, Ian. 2008. *Europeanization and Multi-Level Governance: Cohesion Policy in the European Union and Britain.* Lanham MD: Rowman & Littlefield.

Bache, Ian, and Matthew Flinders. 2004. *Multi-Level Governance.* New York: Oxford University Press.

Belausteguigoitia, Juan Carlos, and Luis F. Guadarrama. 1997. "United States-Mexico Relations: Environmental Issues," in B. Bosworth, Susan M. Collins, and Nora Claudia Lustig, eds., *Coming Together: Mexico-United States Relations.* Washington DC: Brookings Institution Press.

Carroll, John E. 1983. *Environmental Diplomacy: An Examination and a Prospective of Canadian-US Transboundary Environmental Relations.* Ann Arbor: University of Michigan Press.

Cohen, Maxwell. 1983. "Preface," in John E. Carroll, ed., *Environmental Diplomacy: An Examination and a Prospective of Canadian-US Transboundary Environmental Relations.* Ann Arbor: University of Michigan Press.

Craik, Neil, and Joseph DiMento. 2009. "Climate Law and Policy in North America: Prospects for Regionalism," *San Diego Journal of Climate and Energy Law* 1: 195–257.

Craik, Neil, Isabel Studer, and Debora VanNijnatten, eds. 2013. *Climate Policy in North America: Designing Integration in a Regional System.* Toronto: University of Toronto Press.

Craik, Neil and Debora VanNijnatten. 2013. "'Bundled' Transgovernmental Networks in North America," unpublished manuscript.

Doran, Charles F. 1984. *Forgotten Partnership: US-Canada Relations Today.* Baltimore MD: Johns Hopkins University Press.

Eberlein, Burkhard, and Edgar Grande. 2005. "Beyond Delegation: Transnational Regulatory Regimes and the EU Regulatory State," *Journal of European Public Policy* 12 (1): 89–112.

Eberlein, Burkhard, and Abraham L. Newman. 2008. "Escaping the International Governance Dilemma? Incorporated Transgovernmental Networks in the European Union," *Governance* 21 (1): 25–52.

Eilstrup-Sangiovanni, Mette. 2006. *Debates on European Integration.* Hampshire UK: Palgrave MacMillan.

Environment Canada. 2012. "Action on Climate Change: US-Canada Clean Energy Dialogue." www.climatechange.gc.ca/Dialogue/default.asp?lang=En&n=E47AAD1C-1

Farrell, Henry, and Adrienne Hèritier. 2003. "Formal and Informal Institutions under Codecision: Continuous Constitution-Building in Europe," *Governance* 16 (4): 577–600.

Gore, Tony and Webber, Don 2004. "Dematerialising Economies and Local Growth: The Case for ad hoc Governance." in Walzenbach, G. (Ed.) *European Governance: Policy making between Politicization and Control (53-67).* Ashgate, Aldershot, Hampshire.

Government of Canada. 2012. *US-Canada Clean Energy Dialogue Action Plan.* www.climatechange.gc.ca/Dialogue/default.asp?lang=En&n=3E0E8E12-1

Healy, Robert G., Debora L. VanNijnatten, and Marcela López Vallejo. 2014. *North American Environmental Policy: Capacity, Approaches and Transboundary Issue Management.* Toronto: University of Toronto Press.

Helmke, Gretchen, and Steven Levitsky. 2003. "Informal Institutions and Comparative Politics: A Research Agenda," Working Paper 307, Kellogg Institute. http://kellogg.nd.edu/publications/workingpapers/WPS/307.pdf

Hogenboom, Barbara. 1998. *Mexico and the NAFTA Environment Debate: The Transnational Politics of Economic Integration.* Utrecht NL: International Books.

Hooghe, Lisbet, and Gary Marks. 2003. "Unraveling the Central State, but How? Types of Multi-Level Governance," *American Political Science Review* 97 (2): 233–243.

Keohane, Robert, and Joseph Nye. 1974. "Introduction: The Complex Politics of Canadian-American Interdependence," *International Organization* 28 (4): 595–607.

Kirton, John, and Jenilee Guebert. 2010. "Soft Law, Regulatory Coordination, and Convergence in North America," in Monica Gattinger and Geoffrey Hale, eds., *Borders and Bridges: Canada's Policy Relations in North America.* Don Mills ON: Oxford University Press.

Munton, Don, and Geoffrey Castle. 1992. "Air, Water and Political Fire: Building a North American Environmental Regime," in A. Claire Cutler and Mark W. Zacher, eds., *Canadian Foreign Policy and International Economic Regimes.* Vancouver: UBC Press.

Osofsky, Hari M. 2008. "Is Climate Change 'International'? Litigation's Diagonal Regulatory Role." http://works.bepress.com/hari_osofsky/3

Pastor, Robert A., and Jorge G. Castañeda. 1989. *The Limits to Friendship: The United States and Mexico.* New York: Vintage Books.

Peters, B. Guy, and Jon Pierre. 2001. "Developments in Intergovernmental Relations: Towards Multi-Level Governance," *Policy & Politics* 29 (2): 131–135.

Pierre, Jon, and B. Guy Peters. 2000. *Governance, Politics and the State.* London: Macmillan.

Pollack, Mark A., and Gregory Schaffer. 2001. *Transatlantic Governance in the Global Economy.* Lanham MD: Rowman and Littlefield.

Rabe, Barry G. 2002. *Statehouse and Greenhouse: The Emerging Politics of American Climate Change Policy.* Washington, DC: Brookings Institution Press.

Sánchez, Roberto. 1998. *Conflictos ambientales y Negociaci en Binacional entre Mexico y Los Estadoes Unidos. El Media Ambiente como de conflicto en had ralaci en binacional Mexico Estado Unidos.* Mexico City: *Cuadernos de Trabajo. Fundacion Friederich Ebert,* Schmandt, Jurgen, and Hilliard Roderick. 1985. *Acid Rain and Friendly Neighbours: The Policy Dispute between Canada and the United States.* Durham NC: Duke University Press.

Slaughter, Anne-Marie. 2004. *A New World Order.* New Jersey: Princeton University Press.

Slaughter, Anne-Marie and David Zaring. 2006. "Networking Goes International: An Update," *Annual Review of Law and Social Sciences* 2: 211–229.

Stephenson, Paul J. 2013. "20 Years of Multi-Level Governance: Where Does It Come From? What Is It? Where Is It Going?" *Journal of European Public Policy* 20 (6): 817–837.

Underdal, Arild. 2010. "Complexity and Challenges of Long-Term Environmental Governance," *Global Environmental Change* 20: 386–393.

United States Environmental Protection Agency and Secretaria de medio ambiente et recursos naturales. 2012. *Border 2020: US-Mexico Environmental Program.* www2.epa.gov/sites/production/files/documents/border2020-factsheet.pdf

VanNijnatten, Debora L. 2003. "Analyzing the Canada-United States Environmental Relationship: A Multi-Faceted Approach," *The American Review of Canadian Studies* 33 (1): 93–120.

———. 2006. "Towards Cross-Border Environmental Policy Spaces in North America: Province-State Linkages on the Canada-US Border," *AmeriQuests* 3. http://ejournals.library.vanderbilt.edu/ojs/index.php/ameriquests/article/viewArticle/54/49

———. 2009a. "The North American Context: Canadian Environmental Policy and the Continental Push," in Debora L. VanNijnatten and Robert Boardman, eds., *Canadian Environmental Policy: Prospects for Leadership and Innovation.* 3rd ed., Oxford: Oxford University Press.

———. 2009b. "Environmental Cross-Border Regions and the Canada-US Relationship: Building from the Bottom-Up in the Second Century," in Barry G. Rabe and Stephen Brooks, eds., *Transborder Environmental Governance in Canada and the United States.* Washington DC: Woodrow Wilson International Center for Scholars.

VanNijnatten, Debora, and Neil Craik. 2012. "Environment and Energy: Prospects for New Forms of Continental Governance," in Jeffrey Ayres and Laura Macdonald, eds., *North America in Question: Regional Integration in an Era of Political Economic Turbulence.* Toronto: University of Toronto Press.

———. 2013. "Designing Integration: The System of Climate Change Governance in North America," in Neil Craik, Isabel Studer, and Debora VanNijnatten, eds., *Climate Change Policy in North America: Designing Integration in a Regional System.* Toronto: University of Toronto Press.

VanNijnatten, Debora L., and W. Henry Lambright. 2001. "North American Smog Policy: Science-Policy Linkages Across Multiple Boundaries," *Canadian-American Public Policy* 45: 1–42.

3 New Directions in North American Border Security Governance

Jason Ackleson and Yosef Lapid

In the aftermath of 9/11, scholars and policymakers alike have been forced to acknowledge that many contemporary security threats have become inherently *global* in nature; they blur the traditional distinction between domestic and international security, involve state and nonstate actors, originate within rather than between states, and are typically transnational in nature.[1] Not surprisingly, this changing security landscape has also led to a general recognition that new threats and risks demand new forms of international cooperation and new kinds of domestic and global security governance. As the Council on Foreign Relations points out, the international architecture to deal with new security threats has "not kept pace with fundamental changes in the international system" and "largely reflects the world as it existed in 1945."[2] This is also true in the North American context; while the US, Canada, and Mexico have built a free trade framework, progress on institutionalized border security architectures has historically been far less robust.

Border security policy, in particular, is a key area in which scholarly innovations and policy practices have failed to catch up with contemporary transformations. Under conditions of globalization, borders have not become irrelevant. Rather, they have increased in number and complexity. Growing mobility and deepened interdependence—and the need to effectively respond to problems such as terrorism, international crime, and unauthorized migration—have elevated border security concerns to the very heart of national security policy. Mette Eilstrup Sangiovanni has aptly categorized these concerns as "networked threats," which prompt a set of unique challenges to states in the post–9/11 period.[3] Some scholars have argued, in this context, that large, bureaucratic, and vertically organized states are ill equipped to adequately cope with the smaller, agile, horizontally organized, "dark" networked threats that increasingly dominate today's security environment. This chapter takes this problem as a starting point, focusing on a central question: can state structures reconfigure themselves to deal more effectively with networked security threats?

To explore this question, we focus on international collaboration as a key dimension of US homeland security policy. Our premise is that, in an era of globalized risks and threats, the international dimension of border security policy must be recognized as a critical prerequisite for the effective provision of homeland security. Indeed, the urgent need for international cooperation has been a recurrent theme in recent US security policy statements, including in former US Department of Homeland Security (DHS) Secretary Janet Napolitano's approach. DHS's strategic vision includes increasing cooperation with state and local law enforcement, international allies, the private sector, and other federal departments. Key organizational components of DHS, such as US Customs and Border Protection (CBP), which is the lead central agency charged with securing US frontiers, have adopted similar strategic positions. CBP's recently released 2012–2016 National Strategy, for example, focuses on an intelligence-driven "whole of government approach" that highlights interagency and international collaboration.[4,5] With this emphasis, DHS has embraced the idea of *governance* as a key component of national and international border security policy. However, while promising in some respects, this new approach may be limited due to constraints in resources devoted to intergovernmental and international policy development at DHS.

The US Department of Homeland Security is not alone in reorienting its thinking toward the governance dimensions of border security. One common thread around the world in recent years has been the desire of many states to "export" borders: i.e., transferring some border procedures and controls to sites and practices in other countries. North American observers, for instance, have long argued for a "perimeter" approach to continental security. Adopting such an approach in their February 2011 *Beyond the Border* declaration, President Obama and Canadian Prime Minister Stephen Harper outlined a perimeter security framework in which the US and Canada share responsibility for the security and resilience of both countries, including operating away from their shared land border to achieve those goals. Compatible strategic concepts for US border policy in recent years include a number of similar security objectives such as the provision of layered security; the reduction of screening pressures at domestic land, air, and sea ports; and the extension of threat warning times to allow for more adequate enforcement responses.

For our present purposes, it is noteworthy that the implementation of this new strategic approach requires extensive and sustained international cooperation with foreign governments and other relevant actors. Due in part to a set of key structural constraints, including asymmetric power relations and the absence of a formal, binding, and institutionalized North American border security architecture, we propose an *alternative* form of security governance—namely transgovernmental networks (TGNs)—which may have the potential to advance common border security interests of the US, Canada, and Mexico. And, as we will argue here, this form of security governance requires a new research framework to inform and evaluate its implementation.

In the following analysis, we focus on selected international aspects of border security policy using a *governance-oriented* conceptual and theoretical framework. We define border security governance as a pluricentric process that involves a mix of individual, public sector, and private sector actors operating at different geographic and functional levels. Our premise is that such border security–related processes in North America and many other global settings have important domestic and international dimensions. However, whereas the domestic dimensions of post–9/11 national security policy reforms in the US, Canada, the EU, and elsewhere have been extensively researched, the international dimensions of border security policy have not received equivalent attention. There is therefore a problematic gap in the fund of knowledge that informs some border security practices in the post–9/11 strategic landscape. In this paper, we attempt to narrow this gap by showing how the US and other North American actors can more effectively secure and manage their borders through new international governance arrangements. In this context, we posit that unilateral efforts to provide border security will need to be augmented by multilateral cooperative measures involving judiciously selected tools of border security governance.

We begin our analysis by exploring key literatures related to international security governance, risk assessment, and border security policy. Next, we highlight the central role that a unique governance mechanism—transgovernmental networks (TGNs)—can play in the provision of more effective border security policies in a globalized environment. To illuminate the TGN concept in practice, we present illustrative case studies of TGNs in the North American (US-Mexico and US-Canada) border contexts. These cases illustrate both the limits and opportunities of TGN-oriented cooperation for border security governance. The chapter concludes by sketching the outlines of a research framework that might enhance additional interdisciplinary work in this domain.

EMERGING ISSUES AND TRENDS IN SECURITY AND GOVERNANCE ANALYSIS

How to make sense of an increasingly complex and fast-changing security landscape and how to realign defense efforts with present threats and future risks are key challenges faced by all Western security agencies. This is illustrative of a more generalized shift in international affairs: symmetrical and clear monolithic threats from other sovereign states have been overshadowed by asymmetrical, amorphous, and frequently hard-to-quantify security "risks." Thus, the actors of most concern today are mobile individuals, groups, and de-territorialized networks that can easily cross international boundaries and take advantage of new technologies to advance their political, religious, and illicit market agendas.[6] As pointed out by Hoffman, the security landscape now also entails "hybrid" threats, which may involve interlinking operational methods of activity, such as smuggling people, weapons, and drugs across international borders.[7] Hybrid threats "incorporate a range of different modes of warfare including conventional capabilities, irregular tactics and formations, terrorist acts (including indiscriminate violence and coercion), and criminal disorder. Hybrid wars can be also multi-nodal—conducted by both states and a variety of non-state actors."[8] To date, hybrid threats have received relatively little attention in the literature. We posit, however, that in the context of contemporary border security, governance of such hybrid threats will acquire greater centrality in the near future.

Five trends have been listed as contributing to the rising importance of hybrid threats in the current security environment: (1) the increased density of cross-border interactions and transactions under globalization; (2) fragile political institutions and weak civil society in the underdeveloped world; (3) the multiplication of poorly governed and poorly policed global spaces; (4) the rise of new interlinking information technologies and cyber-vulnerabilities; and (5) the dispersion and growing availability of weapons of mass destruction/disruption. This last factor is particularly important in the case of transnational terrorism; actors who gain access and utilize such destructive technologies pose a serious challenge to traditional security architectures. For obvious reasons, all of these factors have important ramifications for effective border management and national security.[9]

Terrorist and Criminal Networks

Of particular importance in the North American context are discrete and hybrid threats originating from terrorism and transnational organized crime. This is consistent with key US homeland security strategic concerns.[10] The rise of global terrorist organizations and "dark" criminal networks that exploit the opportunities created by global mobility, weak and failing states, and the rising worldwide demand for illicit goods and services are noteworthy in this context.[11] In our formulation (which concurs with Tussing's analysis), such border "safety" and border "security" threats require new and properly applied border governance tools and mechanisms.

Terrorist and criminal organizations are not new, but current geopolitical changes and new technological revolutions have given birth to a new social morphology—the network—that has been embraced by increasingly adept terrorist and criminal groups.[12] As aptly put by US Principal Deputy Assistant Secretary of State Brian Nichols at a recent international meeting on the subject in Vienna:

> We have . . . witnessed the impressive *adaptability* of criminal organizations to both law enforcement actions and to new opportunities for profit. Today, most criminal organizations bear no resemblance to the hierarchical organized crime family groups of the past. Instead, they consist of *loose and informal networks* that often converge when it is convenient and engage in a diverse array of criminal activities.[13]

These nonhierarchical networks are more flexible and fluid than traditional economic markets or bureaucratic states. They rely on trust, redundancy, and decentralization to render themselves highly resilient. They do not operate under legal or territorial constraints. In the words of one analyst, networks give criminals and terrorists a "competitive edge."[14] The new security environment, according to Duffield, is thus increasingly "shaped by the advent of network war."[15] It follows that the challenge for security agencies engaged in such conflicts is to reconstitute themselves in a more *network-like* fashion, allowing nimble and effective policy responses to changing domestic and global threat environments.

Hybrid Threats: The Terrorism-Crime Nexus

The terrorism-crime nexus—possible alliances of terrorist organizations with illicit criminal networks—is one particular domain where sovereign states have been called upon to develop innovative responses. Evidence for such collaboration is available in different parts of the world, including Taliban activities in Afghanistan and terrorists and criminals operating in the Tri-Border Area of Paraguay, Brazil, and Argentina. Some have mentioned the potential for such activities also on the US-Mexico border.[16] Needless to say, if validated in the North American context, such activities would be instantaneously catapulted to the top of continental border security agendas.

Scholars differ in their assessments of the seriousness of the threats posed by the putative terrorism-crime nexus. In her important work, Shelley has provocatively referred to the nexus as "The Unholy Trinity: Transnational Crime, Corruption, and Terrorism."[17] Other scholars disagree, but we argue that at least three sets of factors may lend preliminary support to Shelley's hypothesis: (1) the relative decline in state sponsorship of terrorism; (2) the rise of ungoverned spaces; and (3) new relationships between criminal groups and the state.

In terms of financing, in the aftermath of the Cold War, we have witnessed a significant decrease in the level of traditional state support for political terrorism. As noted by Hutchinson and O'Malley, this may have important ramifications for the terrorist-criminal network linkages; terrorist organizations now must locate alternative financial streams. Indeed groups such as the FARC, LTTE, and al-Qaeda have developed their own "in-house" criminal and financial capabilities.[18] As David Luna, Director for Anti-Crime Programs at the US State Department points out, nineteen of the forty-four groups designated by the US government as Foreign Terrorist Organizations are currently using criminal operations to self-finance.[19] This includes drug trade transactions and other criminal activities such as smuggling. The open source literature on this issue confirms that these illicit activities are increasingly sophisticated, nimble, and widespread.

In addition to the financing issue, the rise of ungoverned or poorly policed global spaces and conflict zones adds a new dimension to the convergence thesis. Concurring with Shelley's "unholy trinity" concept, Luna asserts that such areas are amenable safe havens for criminal and terrorist organizations as well as breeding grounds for corruption.[20] Applicable examples are readily available, including Somalia, Lebanon, Afghanistan, and Yemen.

Finally, regarding relationships with the state, it is noteworthy that traditional organized crime was typically tied to the state in a collusion-driven, parasitic fashion. The Italian Mafia is perhaps the most infamous example of such collusion. Such groups tended to reject association with terrorist networks.[21] However, Shelley points out that "new" transnational crime networks may have a different relationship with the state. Today, the interests of these new criminal networks may not coincide with state and may in fact collide with it, leading to network efforts to weaken governance (as illustrated by narco-violence in Mexico). In certain cases, this may also lead to new forms of full or partial collaboration with certain terrorist organizations.

On the other side of the debate, Forrest asserts that while terrorist-criminal cooperation may occasionally be forged, "the linkages between criminals and terrorists tend to dissolve once their transactional reason for collaboration has been completed."[22] In particular, when trust dissolves, alignment becomes increasingly problematic. However, while full, systematic, and symbiotic cooperation may rarely emerge between organized criminal and terrorist groups, even a partial or ad hoc collaboration may pose a serious threat for border security policymakers. As Shelley puts it, "the milieu into which transnational crime, terrorism, and corruption merge is extremely threatening to the international order."[23] This challenge, in our view, requires robust domestic and international-oriented policy responses.

CATCHING UP WITH THE NEW ENVIRONMENT: BORDER SECURITY GOVERNANCE

The previous section of this chapter explored emerging threats to states in the currently evolving security environment. As we will discuss later, the traditional view of these agile "dark networks" is that they pose a severe challenge to "clumsy," unitary states. Consistent with our argument for new forms of collaboration on border security, we propose a variant on this idea, suggesting a more nuanced approach, which recognizes the ability of states to reconfigure in response to dark network challenges. To further explicate this argument, we next explore the notion of *governance*.

At the most general level, the term *governance* connotes "any form of coordination of interdependent social relations."[24] Hänggi, for instance, defines governance in a wide-ranging way: "the structures and processes whereby a social organization—from the family to corporate business to international institution—steers itself, ranging from centralized control to self-regulation."[25] Thus there is an important distinction to be made between "governance" and the more familiar concept of "government." Whereas government suggests unified and authoritative political control by a centralized state, governance has a more expansive definition, which encompasses the totality, both formal and informal, of all governing processes.[26] Early notions of governance emphasized: (1) the *fragmentation* of political authority (between public and private actors) and (2) activity at *different levels* (international, national, regional, and local).[27] Padovani and Tuzzi have moved the definitional effort further down the road, offering the following clarifications:

- Governance involves *different actors* of institutional, public, and private nature, at different levels of authority;[28]
- Governance should not be considered as a set of rules of an activity, but as a *process*;
- Governance is not based on authoritative allocation of resources but on *negotiation* and *consensus* building among divergent interests;
- Governance is *not a formalized concept*, but the development of continuous interactions.[29]

Based on this discussion, we define governance as a *process* that involves both formal and informal actions, coordination, and management by *different* political, economic, and social actors—in addition to governments. These actions occur on multiple levels, such as the international, national, regional, and local.[30]

As Hooghe and Marks (2003) make clear, governance can further be represented in two broad types: Type I (intergovernmental, formal, hierarchical) and Type II (networked, informal, and more fragmented). As we argue about a shift from Type I to Type II in the North American context, we also concur with Rhodes, who argues that, "for clarity's sake, it is best if the word [governance] always has a qualifying adjective."[31] In this chapter, we will focus on two such qualifying adjectives, referring to different levels of specificity within the security policy domain: *security* governance and *border security* governance.

Security Governance

Given the traditional preeminence and exclusive monopoly of the sovereign state on security affairs, one might have expected that the concept of governance would encounter significant resistance in the security sector. However, as Hänggi (2005) points out, this has not been the case because states increasingly face security challenges that are difficult to manage with traditional government approaches.[32]

To capture this more complex reality, Abrahamsen and Williams propose the concept of *global security assemblages*. Global security assemblages are "settings where a range of different global and local, public and private security agents . . . interact, cooperate, and compete to produce new institutions, practices, and forms of security governance."[33] Such assemblages, they argue, emerge from the "disassembling" of traditional nation-state functions (including the provision of security) and its repackaging/reassembly within a governance context. [34]

As with our general concept of governance, security governance can also be systemically examined through four levels of analysis: international, regional, state, and local. At the international level, security governance takes the form of "rule-based cooperation" between governments, international institutions (such as the United Nations and NATO), as well as transnational actors, including businesses and nongovernment organizations. At this level, "governance is more encompassing than government; it helps to grapple with the complex reality of the contemporary world in which governments are still the central actors in domestic and international affairs though they increasingly are seen to share authority with non-state actors on multiple levels of interaction."[35]

At the regional level, security governance refers to security arrangements in a given geographic area.[36] To date, the most advanced example of regional security governance is the European Union (EU). However, as Brunet-Jailly has pointed out, similar dynamics may be observed in other world regions, including North America.[37] In the next section of this chapter, we will focus on the North American region in the context of border-related emerging security governance practices.

At the state level, security governance includes "all the main bodies whose main responsibilities are the protection of the state and its constituent communities."[38] This includes the military forces, police, intelligence agencies, border agencies, and policymakers in control of formulating and implementing security policy. Since 9/11, the US has witnessed significant reorientation and reconfiguration of its state-level security governance architectures (e.g., the Homeland Security Act of 2002).

Finally, at local level, security governance involves domestic security arrangements, which may include national forces, local and county police, and, in some situations, militant nonstate actors such as guerrilla groups or militia organizations.

Another parallel trend has involved the transition from *state-centric* security approaches to *network-centric* governance. This network-centric approach involves the following four interrelated elements:

- Multiple and diverse security sector actors (ministries, security forces, nonstate actors, corporate sector);
- Multi-level decision making and action (global, regional, state, local);
- Diverse security instruments (military, civilian, economic, and diplomatic incentives and coercion);
- Clearly articulated tasks to be accomplished (such as conflict prevention, crisis management, risk assessment, etc.).[39]

Security governance thus becomes something that transcends the sovereign state and involves a mix of actors both *within* and *without* the state. As Garland points out, this involves "[c]omplementing and extending the formal controls of the . . . state. Instead of imagining that they can monopolize . . . control[,] . . . state agencies now adopt a strategic relation to other forces of social control. They seek to build broader alliances, enlisting the 'governmental' powers of private actors and shaping them to the ends of . . . control."[40]

In sum, states are arguably exploring new kinds of security governance strategy that rely on their own capabilities *mixed* with multilateral action, nongovernmental organizations, and private security providers.[41]

Border Security Governance

As noted above, in the aftermath of 9/11, scholars and policymakers alike have come to recognize that borders deserve special attention in the emerging security agenda. Surprisingly, however, the concept of governance has yet to be fully applied in the specific context of border security. This is startling because at the empirical level, the developments that have triggered such interest in governance in other sectors are also manifest in the border domain. In the following, we propose such an exploration, centered on the concept of "border security governance."

The empirical evidence suggests that border security governance increasingly describes new types of border management practices that invoke network structure. For instance, private actors have played an important role in the implementation of newly launched border management programs in the US, such as the Container Security Initiative (CSI) and the Visa Waiver Program (VWP). DHS has new mandates to engage private stakeholders. Public-private partnerships to expand and revamp border security infrastructures (such as bridges and ports of entry), for example, have been accelerated. And, as demonstrated by the current strategic orientation of DHS, international collaborations are now considered increasingly vital if not indispensable for effective border control. However, despite the fact that the same dynamics that have triggered rethinking in terms of governance in other areas are also evident in border contexts, governance-related conceptualizations are typically missing in border-related scholarly work. In the following, we engage the conceptual and theoretical literatures offered by the governance perspective.[42] We will do so by discussing a particular form of border security governance, namely transgovernmental networks, or TGNs.

TRANSGOVERNMENTAL NETWORKS

In the context of border security governance, transgovernmental networks represent a relatively new type of international cooperation. Here, we define

TGNs as innovative groups of state and substate actors working across both agency lines and international borders to solve common security problems. TGNs are based on direct links among substate officials who operate without close supervision by either cabinets or state chief executives. The concept of TGNs can be traced back to work on transgovernmental relations conducted by Keohane and Nye in their seminal piece, "Transnational Relations and International Organizations."[43] In it, they describe transgovernmental relations as "sets of direct interactions among sub-units of different governments that are not controlled or closely guided by the policies of the cabinets or chief executives of those governments."[44] Transgovernmental relations may manifest themselves through policy coordination or coalition building, but in both cases, they involve networks of actors at the subunit level who interact, forming bonds based on common interests and relations. The range of activity for these groups, according to Keohane and Nye, may be correlated with the degree of control central policymakers exercise.

Building on this work and adapting it to contemporary developments and conditions, scholars such as Anne-Marie Slaughter developed the related notion of "transgovernmental networks," positing their important contemporary role in "the real world order."[45] TGNs, according to Slaughter, are "a dense web of relations" created by "functionally distinct parts" of "states, courts, regulatory agencies, executives, and even legislatures" networked with foreign counterparts. TGNs, Slaughter suggests, signal that the state is "not disappearing, [but is] disaggregating."[46] Importantly, TGNs have value in the international order because they are "more flexible than international institutions [and] expand the regulatory reach of all participating nations."[47] This notion is reinforced in recent work by Eilstrup-Sangiovanni, who argues that "due to their flexibility, speed and low sovereignty costs, many predict that government networks will be the primary vehicles for international cooperation in the twenty-first century."[48] Hollis, Eberlein and Newman, Lavenex and Wichmann, and others have also written about the importance of TGNs in multi-level governance (including in the security arena), particularly in the European context.[49]

With this concept of TGNs in mind, we can now outline two distinct types of security cooperation (see Table 3.1, below), corresponding with the Type I/Type II distinction developed by Hooghe and Marks, and outlined in the introduction to this volume. The "traditional" form, derived largely from the concept of "government," is built on a centralized, state-based system and on the long-standing practice of formal government-to-government cooperation in rule-based bilateral or multilateral forums.

In contrast, TGNs represent a new form of security cooperation, one that is directly in line with *governance* frameworks. In TGNs, member units are networked actors at the substate level, operating in a decentralized or "flat" structure with low political visibility and sovereignty costs. Rather than rule-based unit relations, TGN relations and interactions tend to be

Table 3.1 Varieties of security cooperation

	Traditional	New Forms: *Transgovernmental Networks* (TGNs)
Membership	Unitary states, Multilateral IGOs	Substate units/agency officials who share information and coordinate policies across borders
Structure	Centralized/Hierarchical/Vertical	Decentralized/Flat/Horizontal
Political Visibility and Sovereignty Costs	High	Low
Scope	Broad, Slow	Narrow, Adaptable
Unit Relations	Rule based	Trust based (capacity-building key)
Examples	UN; US-Mexico bilateral relationship	Proliferation Security Initiative
General Trend → Movement from Traditional State Forms to TGNs		

trust based. TGNs may be narrower in scope, but they have the advantage of being potentially more agile and more responsive to the type of actors and threats common in the current security environment. An example of a TGN in practice is the Proliferation Security Initiative (PSI) for WMD materials. PSI is not a treaty, has no legal authority, nor an organizational framework, but rather is an ad hoc, interagency process with meetings of experts across borders. Other TGNs have begun to manifest themselves in other security situations, including, for instance, intensified information sharing among intelligence agencies, interior ministry officials, and police forces such as Interpol.

TGNs IN PRACTICE ON THE BORDER: ILLUSTRATIVE NORTH AMERICAN CASES

We now turn to brief illustrative case studies that demonstrate the growing salience of TGNs in border security governance in North America. These cases are drawn from the US-Mexico and the US-Canada border regions. While in some ways emblematic of the unavailability of a larger, more ambitious supranational institutional architecture for the region, the cases under examination here demonstrate new opportunities for TGN-based cooperation in border security governance to advance shared national interests. They also signify the limits of such TGN-based cooperation due to issues of trust, culture, competition, and other obstacles.

Border Security Governance: The US-Mexico Context

Recent years have witnessed a growing recognition in both Mexico and the US of the importance of security cooperation along the 2,000 mile US-Mexico frontier. At the traditional level of state-based security, the broad bilateral agreement on security between the US and Mexico, known as the Mérida Initiative, has played an important role. In response to elevated threats of drug trafficking, transnational crime, and money laundering, the US has provided Mexico with nearly $1 billion for law enforcement training, equipment, and intelligence support.[50] Mérida II, the next iteration of the initiative, explicitly includes a pillar to "create a twenty-first century border that advances commerce and security." Other high-level bilateral activities, such as the Declaration for 21st Century Border Management signed between the two countries, also represent traditional cooperative efforts to bolster security in Mexico and the US while facilitating the flow of legal travelers and goods.

To some degree, these policy initiatives have been launched in response to recommendations made by think tanks, scholars, and policymakers who have promoted better border management practices. In October 2009, for instance, the Binational Task Force on the United States-Mexico Border, convened by the Los Angeles–based Pacific Council for International Policy and the Mexican Council on Foreign Relations, released the results of a yearlong study of US-Mexico border.[51] The blue-ribbon panel of scholars, diplomats, and others recommended a number of changes to US-Mexico border policy that fall squarely within the governance domain, including public-private partnerships for economic development and cooperative US-Mexican police patrols along the frontier. This effort reflects the growing concern with finding cooperative solutions to difficult border management issues.

According to this panel, "Taken as a whole, however, cooperation along the border remains spotty and imperfect. Many of these efforts remain unsystematic and ad hoc; they are not guided by any broader vision of how the shared boundary between Mexico and the United States should be managed." The panel goes on to note that "the most effective institutions that operate along the border share certain features. First, they are bi-national in character. Second, they can act with power in their domains or (as a second-best alternative) include delegates from government bodies that can act with power. Third, they have permanent, skilled staffs that can devise long-terms plans; base their decisions on expert, technical assessments; and ensure follow-up on decisions reached by policy-makers. Fourth, they are open to input from a range of concerned parties, especially state and local governments, regional business associations, and civic groups."[52] We submit that the abovementioned characteristics reflect the characteristics of TGN forms of cooperation discussed in this chapter.

Acknowledging these new challenges and operational needs, the US Border Patrol, the chief American security agency charged with securing the country's frontier between legal ports of entry, has recently signaled a strategic shift, moving toward a targeted enforcement posture with the goal of preventing and disrupting terrorist and transnational threats. Its 2012–2016 Strategic Plan explicitly calls for the organization to reconstitute itself in a more network-like fashion. As the report explains, "Given the dynamic nature of cross-border threats, we must ensure that our organization becomes more mobile in order to appropriately respond to the changing threat."[53] Although launched in 2005, Border Enforcement Security Task Force (BEST) Teams appear to be a reinforcement and manifestation of this new strategic orientation.

Border Enforcement Security Task Force (BEST) Teams

As of 2013, there were thirty-five BEST teams on both the US-Mexico and US-Canada borders.[54] Teams are active in sixteen US states. Led by the US Department of Homeland Security's Immigration and Customs Enforcement (ICE) component (specifically ICE's Homeland Security Investigations unit), BESTs are multiagency, binational task forces created to identify, disrupt, and dismantle criminal organizations posing significant threats to border security. BEST teams began to be set up in 2005. More recently, in December 2012 they were formally codified into law through an amendment to Homeland Security Act of 2002, Jaime Zapata Border Enforcement Security Task Force (BEST) Act.[55] The law enables the Secretary of Homeland security to establish BEST units; direct the assignment of federal personnel to the program; and assist multi-level governance through collaborations with federal, state, local, and tribal law enforcement agencies.

Over eighty participating federal, state, local, and international partners work in BEST teams, including several international law enforcement agencies such as Mexico's *Secretaria de Seguridad Publica* (SSP).[56] BEST teams have included international participation from the very beginning, including support from Canadian law enforcement agencies such as the Canada Border Services Agency, the Royal Canadian Mounted Police, the Ontario Provincial Police, the Niagara Regional Police Service, the Toronto Metropolitan Police, the Windsor Police Service and others. One BEST team is now located within the US Embassy in Mexico City; the Argentinean Customs Agency is part of the Miami BEST team and the Colombian National Police is part of both the Miami and New York-New Jersey BEST teams. BEST teams are also active in Puerto Rico.[57] This international component, as well as their organizational framework and operation style, in general, justifies their classification as applied TGNs.

The main thrust of the BEST model, according to Carr, is in sharing intelligence and information between organizations that can then be used to support operations against criminal threats on North American borders.[58] BEST teams have operated in a variety of enforcement efforts such as dismantling drug smuggling tunnels under the US-Mexico border, intercepting ultra-light aircraft, and countering arms trafficking.

To date, BEST teams have not been rigorously evaluated despite the fact that such a study has been called for by the US Government Accountability Office (GAO). However, based on limited analysis and anecdotal evidence, it is apparent that BEST teams have achieved some impressive successes. In fiscal year 2012, BESTs made 2,676 criminal arrests and 809 administrative arrests, and federal prosecutors obtained 1,419 indictments and 1,335 convictions in BEST-investigated cases.[59] From their inception through August 2013, BEST teams have initiated more than 10,654 cases resulting in 12,718 criminal arrests, large seizures of illegal drugs and weapons, and over $130 million in currency.[60] In its one existing (but narrow) study of interagency forums like BEST on the Northern Border, GAO reported that (TGN-like) "[i]nteragency forums improved coordination of border intelligence information, resources, and operations between US federal agencies and their law enforcement partners in Canada, according to the majority of the representatives of these entities [GAO] interviewed across four northern border sectors."[61] As a result, BEST teams have been granted modest additional resources in the context of deep federal budgetary cuts. In 2009, for example, former DHS Secretary Napolitano indicated that the number of agents assigned to BEST teams has doubled during her tenure.[62] Other officials have heralded the BEST team model as well.[63] Law enforcement officials point to three specific benefits: (1) facilitating the sharing of border security intelligence information; (2) facilitating the sharing of resources such as equipment and personnel; and in some cases, (3) serving as a tool for de-confliction—or as a means to inform partners of special border security operations.[64]

While information sharing may have increased through these TGNs, detractors of the BEST initiative have pointed to an "inability to resource the increasing number of interagency forums," insinuating "that some efforts were overlapping."[65] In addition, BEST teams—like US-Canada Integrated Border Enforcement Teams (IBETs)—do not have discrete geographic boundaries of operation. Further, difficult problems of governance—particularly issues of joint-command and cross-designation of each country's law enforcement officers—remain. Finally, because BESTs and IBETs are TGNs, they retain a relatively high degree of autonomy, operating under relatively loose rules; thus cooperation can weaken at any time. Table 3.2 provides a summary description of BESTs and IBETs as border security TGNs.

Border Security Governance: The US-Canada Context

Security cooperation between the US and Canada extends back over decades. Border issues, in particular, were advanced through cooperative bilateral agreements such as the Smart Border Accord, the Security and Prosperity Partnership (SPP) initiative, and the Cross Border Crime Forum (CBCF), a framework for law enforcement collaboration that dates to 1997. Even outside these frameworks, informal, localized, cross-border

Table 3.2 Selected North American border security TGNs

	TGN	
	Border Enforcement Security Task Force (BEST)	**Integrated Border Enforcement Team (IBET)**
Purpose and Structure	Permanent binational fora developed and facilitated by ICE to enhance border security, investigate transnational smuggling organizations, and combat violence related to smuggling occurring at the nation's borders through coordinated, co-located efforts.	Charter-established, permanent binational fora for coordinated, multidisciplinary, binational intelligence and enforcement efforts between the ports of entry. IBET teams and committees meet periodically to exchange pertinent information and, at times, facilitate joint operations that bring together federal, state, local, and US and Canadian resources.
Number	35 (32 US-Mexico; 3 US-Canada).	15 IBET regions with individual IBET units established (US-Canada).
Partners	US components include DHS [ICE, Intelligence and Analysis, CBP, and USCG], FBI, and DEA. Canadian components include CBSA and RCMP. Mexican components include *Secretaria de Seguridad Publica* (SSP). BEST teams also include other key federal, state, and local law enforcement agencies.	Core agencies: Canada's RCMP and CBSA, CBP's Border Patrol, ICE, USCG. Other stakeholders include federal, state, local, tribal, and other enforcement agencies.
Characteristics	Intelligence and information sharing for operational support; investigational.	Operational; planning and coordinating joint enforcement initiatives; sharing of intelligence; routinized border security governance relationships.

Source: Adapted from GAO 2011; Carr 2011.

networks of law enforcement collaboration have long existed. However, currently, the most comprehensive high-level framework for extensive and innovative US-Canada border security cooperation is the Beyond the Border (BTB) initiative. On February 4, 2011, President Obama and Canadian Prime Minister Stephen Harper announced this shared security declaration. BTB describes a perimeter and layered approach to security whereby both the US and Canada share responsibility for effective security and trade requirements both at and beyond the shared frontier. Beyond the Border identifies four key areas of cooperation: (1) addressing threats early; (2) trade facilitation, economic growth, and jobs; (3) *integrated cross-border law enforcement*; and (4) critical infrastructure and cybersecurity.[66]

The US and Canadian governments released a BTB Action Plan in December 2011, which is built on the premise "that working together significantly increases our ability to combat crime at the international border."[67] The specific models of collaboration highlighted are TGN-like: the previously discussed BEST teams initiative; a related program known as Integrated Border Enforcement Teams (IBETs); and finally, the Shiprider initiative, an integrated security program that provides cross-designated officers to patrol the maritime US-Canada border.

Integrated Border Enforcement Teams (IBETs)

IBETs are multiagency, joint US-Canada law enforcement teams that target cross-border criminal activity. For our present purposes, it is noteworthy that IBETS rely extensively on TGN-type coordination practices, which exist in the absence of a larger supranational institutional structure. IBET teams are typically made up of US and Canadian federal, state/provincial, and local law enforcement personnel, including representatives from six agencies: the Royal Canadian Mounted Police, the Canada Border Services Agency (CBSA), the US Border Patrol, the US Coast Guard, the US Bureau of Immigration and Customs Enforcement, and US Customs and Border Protection. IBETs were originally set up as a result of the 1995 Our Shared Borders agreement to target cross-border narcotics crimes. However, as pointed out by Carr, "the IBETs operations were so successful—seizing an average of $1 million worth of drugs, weapons, alcohol, tobacco, and vehicles per month—that it led to the formation of 6 more IBETS across the northern border."[68] Currently fourteen such IBETs operate on the US-Canada border.[69]

The 2001 Smart Border Accord expanded the IBET initiative to new designated areas across the northern border and broadened its focus to include counterterrorism measures. The goal of the teams is to integrate intelligence and tactical approaches to counter terrorism and criminal networks along the border. IBETs also offer integrated mobile response capability (air, land, marine) to augment border enforcement efforts. In his review, Carr goes on to indicate that "from all accounts . . . IBETs have been very successful and are models for international border collaboration for security operations."[70] Despite this strong record of success, it is important to note that, as with other TGN arrangements, the structure and success of IBETs depends largely on each agency/component's will to participate, its resources to do so, and, in particular, its level of trust in its informal relations with other units participating in the TGN network. As Carr points out, the loose network structure means that "the willingness of the component to participate and share . . . can shift at any time depending on the situation."[71]

Shiprider

The base model for new TGN initiatives on the US-Canada frontier is the Shiprider program (officially called "Cross-Border Maritime Law Enforcement Operations (CMLEO)." Shiprider is (for now) a pilot arrangement to patrol cross-border waterways with the legal authority to enforce both US and Canadian law. Officers from both countries who are onboard Shiprider vessels can apply either country's law in a maritime setting. As the Royal Canadian Mounted Police describe it, "Shiprider removes the international maritime boundary as a barrier to law enforcement by enabling seamless continuity of enforcement and security operations across the border, facilitating cross-border surveillance and interdiction, and serving as both a force multiplier and, potentially, as a model for other US/Canadian cross-border (integrated) enforcement and security initiatives."[72] Shiprider pilots began in 2005 in the Detroit-Windsor area and have been used at major public events such as the 2006 Super Bowl, the 2010 Olympics in Vancouver, and the G8/G20 Summits in Toronto. In June 2012, the Canadian government passed legislation to expand and fully authorize this program. One year later, both the US and Canada signed final policy agreements to facilitate the initiative.

Next Generation of Integrated Law Enforcement on the US/Canada Border (NxtGen)

Based loosely on the BTB framework and lessons learned from the abovementioned TGNs (BEST, IBET, and particularly Shiprider), the US and Canada are now pursuing another iteration of cooperative border security governance through the "Next Generation of Integrated Law Enforcement on the US/Canada border (NxtGen)" initiative. The BTB *Action Plan for Perimeter Security and Economic Competitiveness* details the goal to "deepen cooperative investigation and prosecution efforts to identify and stop serious offenders and violent criminals," envisioning that "Canada and the United States will develop integrated cross-border law enforcement operations, including deploying regularized Shiprider teams."[73]

In addition, in summer 2012, the US and Canada planned to

> . . . [i]mplement two Next-Generation pilot projects to create integrated teams in areas such as intelligence and criminal investigations, and an intelligence-led uniformed presence between ports of entry. This model draws on the proven cross-border policing approaches that were introduced by Shiprider, while incorporating the best practices and successes of other existing border law enforcement programs such as the

> Integrated Border Enforcement Teams and the Border Enforcement Security Task Forces.[74]

It appears that these pilots were put on hold because key political, legal (particularly sovereignty and privacy), and operational issues emerged, which will require resolution in this process. In particular, disputes have emerged regarding the potential applicability of Canadian law to US police. If successful, however, the application of the maritime TGN to the US-Canada land border would represent a major extension of the TGN model. Further evaluation of this yet-to-be implemented TGN application will be required.

CONCLUSIONS

Observers of the evolving international security environment have outlined a set of emerging "dark network" security threats such as cyber-attacks, transnational terrorists, drug trafficking organizations, and so on. This security environment suggests a paradigmatic shift from a geopolitics of "states versus states" to a geopolitics of "states versus networks." In thinking about this change, some analysts have gone so far as to suggest that states are structurally incapable of adequately responding to this new environment, citing the weaknesses of vertically oriented, bureaucratic organizations, which are bound by formal rules that can frustrate and slow international cooperation to deal with these challenges.

This chapter posited an alternative hypothesis: that new forms of cooperation, in the form of TGNs, are occurring at the subnational level, outside or underneath standard institutional frameworks and traditional authorities. Our preliminary analysis confirms this hypothesis, indicating that, around the world, vertically and hierarchically structured governments are reshaping themselves through TGNs in a more horizontal, networked fashion to cope in the post–9/11 threat spectrum. This is particularly the case in Europe, where TGNs have been successfully applied in a variety of policy settings. Overall, TGNs offer a variety of structural and operational advantages that can harness state power and redeploy it in a more nimble, network-like fashion that may have "staying power."

We suggest that this can also be the case in the specific context of border security governance in North America. Taking North America as a region of focus, we argued that while bilateral cooperation continues along vertical dimensions through long-standing traditional intergovernmental relationships, cooperation is increasingly organized horizontally, in a network fashion across the international frontier. TGNs such as BEST teams, IBETs, and other existing and proposed initiatives that build on these models are clear manifestations of this trend in practice.[75]

As pointed out by the 2009 Pacific Council report, a number of obstacles to sustain and/or enhance US-Mexico border cooperation exist, including domestic political considerations, differences in priorities, existing laws, weakness in Mexican institutions, and a lack of parallel structures. Generally these obstacles are all relevant to successful deployment of TGN forms of security cooperation. Thus, despite the promise of TGNs as a mechanism to enhance border security governance, challenges to their successful implementation remain, particularly those that are structural and quite difficult to address. For example, while the TGN design of noninstitutionalized, informal, narrow, and adaptable mechanisms offers some important advantages, this very design can also be detrimental to the stability and scope of TGN work.

In addition, at the organizational level, North American border security TGNs have been subjected to larger competitive pressures, such as rivalries and resource games, that exist between participating partner organizations (on both sides of the border). Moreover, component-oriented TGN participation strategies have frequently sought narrow organizational gains instead of wider team (TGN-wide) outcomes. And, problems of mission overlap and duplication between TGNs have continued to hinder such operations. Such problems have been identified, for instance, by the DHS Inspector General, who, in April 2007, pointed out that duplication of efforts was a serious concern because it was not entirely clear how BEST teams would operate differently from IBETs.[76]

Furthermore, because TGNs operate across borders, cultural differences inherent in any form of international collaboration can be highly problematic. Cultural differences may manifest themselves in terms of linguistic barriers, and also in terms of culturally influenced styles and methods of law enforcement. And, while border security TGNs in North America have received modest resource increments, compared to the volume of overall spending directed to traditional homeland security enterprises, their funding remains very limited.

Finally, and perhaps most importantly, typically there is a serious problem of trust in most TGNs operations. In view of the fact that TGNs rely heavily on informal, personal relationships in order to forge common goals and methods, trust may indeed be the most critical ingredient for success in TGN relationships. Fostering trust is especially important in the sensitive TGN law enforcement realm. Research suggests that trust is particularly hard to forge in asymmetrical power situations (such as the US-Canada relationship) or in cases where state governance may be weak (such as in elements of the US-Mexico security relationship given the ongoing narco-trafficking violence). Therefore, the problem of trust in border-related TGN cooperation deserves additional exploration, particularly through the evaluation of TGN practices, which may both forge and fray trust in an international context.[77]

As new forms of international collaboration on border security deepen and expand, there is a need for extensive interdisciplinary research to analyze and evaluate developments in theory and practice. In addition to explorations of the dimensions of trust in TGNs in border contexts, there is a need for further empirical validation of the above outlined TGN framework, using both qualitative and quantitative analysis of relevant benchmarks, metrics, best practices, and standards. In the US, while DHS has been reportedly working on mechanisms to identify and report on the cost and benefits of IBET and BEST teams, it is not yet in a position to do so in an authoritative manner. In addition, there is an urgent need to distill common risk assessment frameworks for TGNs. In order for TGNs to work effectively, partners must operate under similar definitions of risks and threats, including common conceptions and methods to address them. Finally, there is a strong requirement for comparative studies of security-oriented TGNs—including in the European Union and elsewhere globally—in order to illuminate best practices and advance new empirical, conceptual, and theoretical findings in this important and emerging area.[78]

NOTES

1. Borchert and Oriesek 2004.
2. Indeed it was in response to this problem that the Council on Foreign Relations (CFR) launched its major new five-year initiative, entitled "International Intuitions and Global Governance Program." Council on Foreign Relations 2008, 1.
3. Eilstrup Sangiovanni 2009.
4. See the special issue of *European Security*, "Putting Security Governance to the Test" (volume 22, issue 3, 2014).
5. US Border Patrol 2012. The document outlines a "comprehensive approach. . . . Border Patrol builds coalitions with local, state, tribal and international law enforcement agencies, public service entities and other identified stakeholders to develop a common operational strategy in the border environment to ensure unity of effort and maximum enforcement benefits from combined resources."
6. Ó Tuathail 1998; Adamson and Grossman 2004.
7. Hoffman 2009, 5.
8. Ibid, 5.
9. A significant literature on the emerging security environment exists. In his extensive survey, Moisés Naím (2003) characterizes the challenges facing us as "five wars of globalization": struggles against the illegal international trade in drugs, arms, intellectual property, people, and money. These conflicts have been fought by nation-states for centuries but have taken on new significance, expansiveness, and impact given the contemporary global economy.
10. On this, see DHS 2007.
11. Gerspacher and Dupont 2007, 347.
12. Ibid, 348.
13. Nichols 2012 (emphasis added).
14. Williams 1994.
15. Duffield 2002, 153.
16. Carter 2009.
17. Shelley 2004; see also Shelley 2007.
18. Hutchinson and O'Malley 2007.
19. Luna 2009.
20. Ibid.

21. Shelley 2004.
22. Forest, 3.
23. Shelley 2004, 102.
24. Jessop 1999, 351.
25. Hänggi 2005, 7. In a seminal work, John Ruggie (2004, 9) offers another general definition, arguing that governance "refers to conducting the public's business: to the constellation of authoritative rules, institutions, and practices by means of which any collectivity manages its affairs." In James Rosenau and Ernst-Otto Czempiel's (1992, 13) view, governance denotes more than formal institutions of control, but rather "systems of rule at all levels of human activity." Finally, Krahmann (2005, 11) offers this account: "Governance denotes the structures and processes which enable a set of public and private actors to coordinate their interdependent needs and interests through the making and implementation of binding policy decisions in the absence of a central political authority."
26. Seven dimensions can be used as a typology to distinguish between "government" and "governance": (1) geographical scope, (2) functional scope, (3) distribution of resources, (4) interests, (5) norms, (6) decision making, and (7) policy implementation. Krahmann 2005; see also Kooiman 2003, 4; Majone 1997; Ruggie 2004.
27. Rhodes 1996.
28. Such functions are consistent with our understanding of security governance, as states increasingly rely on a spectrum of actors to provide security and security-related functions—for instance, in the customs clearance domain. As Abrahamsen and Williams (2009) note, private police now outnumber public police two to one. As evidence of the rise of the privatization of security, prominent accounts of private military companies ("mercenaries") fighting Third World wars and supporting US military operations abroad in the Iraq and Afghanistan conflicts have arisen. More common, however, is the large array of private security providers (guarding, screening, surveillance, etc.) that constitute an estimated $165 billion global market.
29. Padovani and Tuzzi 2003, 7 (emphasis added).
30. Elements of this definition are drawn from Pierre 2000.
31. Rhodes 2000, 7.
32. Hänggi, 9.
33. Abrahamsen and Williams 2009, 3.
34. Similar to Krahmann, Abrahamsen and Williams suggest that the development of global security assemblages is due to three factors: (1) neoliberal economics and concepts of "networked governance" in public policy and security provision, (2) shifting norms of security, and (3) the commodification of security and the increasing salience of risk-based security thinking and technology. Ibid, 3. See also Hall 2014.
35. Ibid, 7.
36. Hänggi 2005, 9.
37. See Brunet-Jailly 2004 and Brunet-Jailly 2006.
38. Ibid.
39. Borchert 2004, 2.
40. Garland 2001, 125.
41. Krahman 2005.
42. Brunet-Jailly 2004.
43. Keohane and Nye 1974.
44. Ibid, 43.
45. Slaughter 1997; 2004.
46. Slaughter 1997, 184.

47. Ibid, 185.
48. Eilstrup-Sangiovanni 2007.
49. See Hollis 2010; Eberlein and Newman 2008; Lavenex and Wichmann 2009.
50. Congressional Research Service 2012.
51. Binational Task Force on the United States-Mexico Border 2009.
52. Ibid.
53. US Border Patrol 2012–2016.
54. According to US Immigration and Custom Enforcement, as of October 2013, BEST teams were located Arizona (Phoenix, Tucson, Nogales, Yuma, and Casa Grande); California (Imperial Valley, Los Angeles Seaport, San Diego Seaport, San Ysidro, and San Francisco Seaport); Florida (Miami Seaport, Fort Lauderdale Seaport); Michigan (Detroit); New Mexico (Albuquerque, Deming, and Las Cruces); New York (Buffalo, Massena, and New York Seaport); New Jersey (Newark Seaport); Texas (El Paso, Laredo, Rio Grande Valley, Houston Seaport, and Big Bend); Washington (Blaine, Seattle Seaport); Louisiana (New Orleans Seaport); Alabama (Mobile Seaport); Mississippi (Gulfport Seaport); South Carolina (Charleston Seaport); Georgia (Savannah Seaport); Virginia (Hampton Roads); Puerto Rico (San Juan Seaport); and Hawaii (Honolulu Seaport). US ICE 2013.
55. US Public Law 112-205. The law recalls Jaime Zapata, an ICE special agent assigned to a BEST unit, who was shot and killed during service in Mexico on February 15, 2011.
56. US ICE 2013.
57. Ibid.
58. Carr 2009, 37.
59. Beers 2013.
60. US ICE 2013.
61. US GAO 2010, 4.
62. Napolitano 2009.
63. As one US official was quoted in the *Globe and Mail*, "We think the model is good . . . BEST works—and it's really hard to put the genie back in the bottle." Sher 2011.
64. US GAO 2010.
65. Ibid, 14.
66. Department of State 2011 (emphasis added).
67. Anonymous 2012, 10.
68. Carr 2009, 35.
69. US CBP 2013.
70. Carr 2009, 35.
71. Ibid, 36.
72. RCMP 2010.
73. Foreign Affairs and International Trade Canada 2011, 25.
74. Department of State 2011, 25.
75. The Arizona Alliance to Combat Transnational Threats (ACTT), for example, is a TGN which utilizes over sixty federal, state, local, and tribal agencies in Arizona and in Mexico to combat transnational crime.
76. GAO 2011. Other working groups have been periodically established to examine interactions between border TGNs, but the outcome of these evaluations is unclear.
77. Hollis, among others, asserts "an area of [TGN] research that is currently underdeveloped is the importance of the notion of trust on governance." See Hollis 2010, 325.
78. See, for example, Baert et al forthcoming.

REFERENCES

Abrahamsen, Rita, and Michael Williams, 2009. "Security Beyond the State: Global Security Assemblages in International Politics," *International Political Sociology* 3 (1): 1–17.

Adamson, Fiona, and Andrew Grossman. 2004. "Framing 'Security' in a Post-9/11 Context," paper prepared for the Program on Global Security and Cooperation, Social Science Research Council, October.

Baert, Francis, Iziana Scaramagli, and Fredrik Soderbaum, eds. *Intersecting Interregionalism: New Regionalism, Multilateralism, and the EU*. London: United Nations University Series on Regionalism, 2014.

Beers, Rand. 2013. Written testimony before the Senate Homeland Security and Government Affairs Committee, October 3.

Binational Task Force on the United States-Mexico Border. 2009. *Managing the United States-Mexico Border: Cooperative Solutions to Common Problems*. San Diego: Pacific Council on International Policy.

Borchert, Heiko. 2004. "Network Security Policy and the Transformation of the Security Sector," *Europaische Sicherheit* 53 (6): 1–33.

Borchert, Heiko, and Daniel Oriesek. 2004. "Security Sector Transformation: Why New Risks Demand a New Kind of Security Governance," Booz Allen Hamilton Study Report, May 25. www.boozallen.com/publications/article/658460

Brunet-Jailly, Emmanuel. 2004. "NAFTA, Economic Integration, and the Canadian-American Security Regime in the Post-September 11, 2001 Era: Multi-Level Governance and Transparent Border?" *Journal of Borderlands Studies* 19 (1): 123–142.

Brunet-Jailly, Emmanuel. 2006. "Security and Border Security Policies: Perimeter or Smart Border? A Comparison of the European Union and Canadian-American Border Security Regimes," *Journal of Borderlands Studies* 21 (1): 3–21.

Carr, Alan. 2009. "Regional Joint Border Commands: A Pathway to Improving Collaboration and Effectiveness for Border Control," Master's thesis, Naval Postgraduate School.

Carter, Sara A. 2009. "Al Qaeda Eyes Bio Attack from Mexico," *Washington Times*, June 3. http://washingtontimes.com/news/2009/jun/03/al-qaeda-eyes-bio-attack-via-mexico-border/

Congressional Research Service. 2012. "US-Mexican Security Cooperation: The Mérida Initiative and Beyond," CRSE Report R1349, February 13.

Council on Foreign Relations. 2008. "International Institutions and Governance Program: World Order in the 21st Century," May 1. www.cfr.org/content/thinktank/CFR_Global%20_Governance_%20Program.pdf

Department of Homeland Security. 2007. "National Strategy for Homeland Security." www.dhs.gov/xlibrary/assets/nat_strat_homelandsecurity_2007.pdf

Department of State. 2011. "Beyond the Border: A Shared Vision for Perimeter Security and Economic Competitiveness," Action Plan, December. http://photos.state.gov/libraries/canada/303578/pdfs/us-canada-btb_action_plan.pdf

Duffield, Mark. 2002. "War as Network Enterprise: The New Security Terrain and Its Implications," *Cultural Values* 6 (1–2): 153–165.

Eberlein, Burkard, and Abraham Newman. 2008. "Escaping the International Governance Dilemma? Incorporated Transgovernmental Networks in the European Union," *Governance* 21 (1): 24–52.

Eilstrup-Sangiovanni, Mette. 2007. "Changing Patterns of International Security Provision: From Interstate Cooperation to Transgovernmental Networks," paper presented at the annual meeting of the International Studies Association Annual Convention, Chicago, February 28.

Eilstrup Sangiovanni, Mette. 2009. "Varieties of Cooperation: Government Networks in International Security," in Miles Kahler, ed., *Networked Politics: Agency, Power, and Governance*. Ithaca: Cornell University Press.

Foreign Affairs and International Trade Canada. 2011. *Beyond the Border: A Shared Vision for Perimeter Security and Economic Competitiveness*. Ottawa: Public Works and Government Services Canada. http://actionplan.gc.ca/grfx/psec-scep/pdfs/bap_report-paf_rapport-eng-dec2011.pdf

Forrest, James J. F. 2007. "Countering Linkages between Criminal and Terrorist Networks," paper prepared for the EAPC/PfP Workshop on Threat Convergence, Zurich, Switzerland, March 5.

Garland, David. 2001. *The Culture of Control*. Oxford: Oxford University Press.

Gerspacher, Nadia, and Benoit Dupont. 2007. "The Nodal Structure of International Police Cooperation: An Exploration of Transnational Security Networks," *Global Governance* 13 (3): 347–364.

Hall, Ian. 2014. "The Rise of Security Governance,," Mark Bevir, Oliver Daddow, and Ian Hall, eds., *Interpreting Global Security*. London: Routledge.

Hänggi, Heiner. 2005. "Approaching Peacebuilding from a Security Governance Perspective," (pp. xx), in Alan Bryden and Heiner Hänggi, eds., *Security Governance in Post-Conflict Peacebuilding*. Geneva: Geneva Centre for the Democratic Control of Armed Forces.

Hoffman, Frank G. 2009. "Hybrid Threats: Reconceptualizing the Evolving Character of Modern Conflict," *Strategic Forum* 240 (April): 1–8.

Hollis, Simon. 2010. "The Necessity of Protection: Transgovernmental Networks and EU Security Governance," *Cooperation and Conflict* 45 (3): 312–330.

Hooghe, Liesbit, and Gary Marks. 2003. "Unraveling the Central State, but How?: Types of Multi-Level Governance," *American Political Science Review* 97 (2): 233–243.

Hutchinson, Steven, and Pat O'Malley. 2007. "A Crime-Terror Nexus? Thinking on Some of the Links between Terrorism and Criminality," *Studies in Conflict & Terrorism* 30 (12): 1095–1107.

Jessop, Bob. 1999. "The Changing Governance of Welfare: Recent Trends in Its Primary Function, Scale, and Modes of Coordinator," *Social Policy and Administration* 33 (4): 348–359.

Keohane, Robert O., and Joseph S. Nye Jr. 1974. "Transgovernmental Relations and International Organization," *World Politics* 27 (1): 39–62.

Kooiman, Jan. 2003. *Governing as Governance*. London: Sage.

Krahmann, Elke. 2005. "Security Governance and Networks: New Theoretical Perspectives in Transatlantic Security," *Cambridge Review of International Affairs* 18 (1): 15–30.

Lavenex, Sandra, and Nicole Wichmann. 2009. "The External Governance of EU Internal Security," *European Integration* 31 (1): 13–102.

Luna, David. 2009. "Threat Convergence: Subversion, Destabilization, and Insecurity," presentation at George Mason University School of Public Policy, Arlington, VA, May 4.

Majone, Giandomenico. 1997. "From the Positive to the Regulatory State: Causes and Consequences of Changes in the Mode of Governance," *Journal of Public Policy* 17 (2): 139–67.

Naím, Moisés. 2003. "The Five Wars of Globalization," *Foreign Policy* (January/February): 29–37.

Napolitano, Janet. 2009. Remarks at the Border Security Conference, El Paso, Texas, August 11.

Nichols, Brian A. 2012. Opening Statement to the 21st UN Commission on Crime Prevention and Criminal Justice, Vienna, April 23. www.state.gov/j/inl/rls/rm/188272.htm

Ó Tuathail, Gearóid. 1998. "Postmodern Geopolitics: States, Space-Time, and Security at the End of the Twentieth Century," paper presented at the "Geopolitics and Globalization in a Postmodern World" conference, Haifa, Israel, January 25–30.

Padovani, Claudia, and Arjuna Tuzzi. 2003. "Changing Modes of Participation and Communication in an International Political Environment," paper presented to the International Political Science Association Congress, Durban, South Africa, July.

Pierre, Jon. 2000. *Debating Governance: Authority, Steering, and Democracy*. Oxford: Oxford University Press.

Public Safety Canada. 2012. "Canada and the United States Discuss Border and Law Enforcement-Related Issues at the 12th Cross-Border Crime Forum in Ottawa," March 2. www.publicsafety.gc.ca/cnt/nws/nws-rlss/2012/20120302-eng.aspx

Rhodes, R.A.W. 1996. "The New Governance: Governing without Government," *Political Studies* 44 (4): 652–667.

Rhodes, R.A.W. 2000. "Understanding Governance: Ten Years On," Australian National University, Canberra, Australia. http://rsss.anu.edu.au/discussion/wp/understandinggov.pdf

Rosenau, James, and Ernst-Otto Czempiel, eds. 1992. *Governance without Government: Order and Change in World Politics*. Cambridge: Cambridge University Press.

Royal Canadian Mountain Police (RCMP). 2010. "Canada-US Shiprider," *Fact Sheet*, June. www.rcmp-grc.gc.ca/ibet-eipf/shiprider-eng.htm

Ruggie, John Gerard. 2004. "Reconstituting the Global Public Domain: Issues, Actors, and Practices," Working Paper for the Corporate Social Responsibility Initiative, John F. Kennedy School of Government, Harvard University.

Sher, Julian. 2011. "With Cross-Border Policing Set to Expand, Mounties Fret over Who Calls Shots," *Globe and Mail,* December 7. www.theglobeandmail.com/news/politics/with-cross-border-policing-set-to-expand-mounties-fret-over-who-calls-shots/article4180408/

Shelley, Louise. 2004. "Unholy Trinity: Transnational Crime, Corruption, and Terrorism," *The Brown Journal of World Affairs* 11 (2): 101–111.

Shelley, Louise. 2007. *Growing Together: Ideological and Operational Linkages Between Terrorist and Criminal Networks*. Washington DC: Fund for Peace.

Slaughter, Ann Marie. 1997. "The Real New World Order," Foreign Affairs (September/October): 183–197.

Slaughter, Ann Marie. 2004. *A New World Order*. Princeton: Princeton University Press.

US Border Patrol. 2012. *2012–2016 Border Patrol National Strategy*. Washington DC: US Customs and Border Protection.

US Customs and Border Protection (CBP). 2013. "Protecting Our Borders—This is CBP," July 25. www.cbp.gov/xp/cgov/about/mission/cbp.xml

US Government Accountability Office (GAO). 2010. "Border Security: Enhanced DHS Oversight and Assessment of Interagency Coordination Is Needed for the Northern Border," GAO Report 11–97 (December 17).

US Government Accountability Office (GAO). 2011. "DHS Oversight Could Help Eliminate Potential Duplicating Efforts of Interagency Forums in Securing the Northern Border," GAO Report 11–318SP.

US Immigration and Customs Enforcement (ICE). 2013. "Border Enforcement Security Task Force (BEST)," *Fact Sheet*, October. www.ice.gov/best/

Williams, Phil. 1994. "Transnational Criminal Organizations and International Security," *Survival* 36 (1): 96–113.

4 Faraway So Close
Territorial Security and Regionalism in North America and Europe

Ruben Zaiotti

Since 9/11, territorial security in North America has undergone substantial transformations that have affected the strategic vision, governance, and practices defining this policy field. The key component of these transformations has been the quest to "push borders out"—that is, to expand the geographical and functional scope of security measures closer to potential sources of threat and to engage other regional and international partners to achieve this goal. As the main target of international terrorism, the United States' government has been the most resolute in fostering these changes. Canada and Mexico, however, have also embraced this new vision of territorial security, partly because of the recognition of the common threats and challenges affecting the continent, and partly to please their powerful neighbor. The three North American governments have pursued this new approach to territorial security through an overhaul of their internal security apparatuses, and the elaboration of new policy initiatives both within the region (e.g., the North American security perimeter project) and with overseas partners (e.g., various bilateral agreements concerning the exchange of inbound passengers' personal data).

Territorial security in North America is certainly different from what it was at the beginning of the millennium, but how radical have the changes in this policy field been? Have they challenged traditional state-centric assumptions about territorial security in the region? Has a distinctive *regional* system in this policy area emerged, or is territorial security in North America still the sum of national approaches? Scholars and practitioners who have weighed in on these questions, while recognizing the range and scope of new policies and institutional arrangements introduced in the last decade, are generally skeptical about their impact on North America's quest for greater integration in territorial security matters.[1] The lack of formal regional institutions to govern this policy area, and the persistence—in some cases, even thickening—of national border controls, are evidence that a truly "post-national" dimension is missing from these transformations. This pessimistic view is put into sharper relief when the North American experiment with territorial security is compared with Europe's.[2] Although they share similar security challenges with their partners across the Atlantic (*in primis*, the threat of international terrorism), European governments have, in fact, been more daring in reshaping the way that national security is managed within their borders and beyond. The most spectacular example of this approach is represented by the creation a continent-wide border control regime—known as "Schengen"—operating under a regional institutional umbrella, the European Union. North American governments have not only failed to match Europe's alleged post-national achievements in this policy area, but also have no plans to follow its path in the foreseeable future.

When observed through a European prism, the experiment with territorial security in North America therefore seems limited in scope and impact—but is that really the case? In this chapter I argue that existing comparative accounts tend to overstate the differences between the two regions and that this assessment is based on a superficial (mis)reading of the European model. This model is not as coherent, integrated, and institutionalized as is often assumed. Despite its formal inclusion in the EU institutional framework and the increased competence in this area allocated to supranational actors such the European Commission, territorial security in the Old Continent still maintains a strong intergovernmental and informal orientation, with national governments and their bureaucracies holding crucial responsibilities, and a pragmatic approach to policymaking.[3] This *practical continentalism* is not a fully-fledged doctrine, in the sense of being planned and premised on a common vision. Instead it refers to a set of shared practices among an ever-growing network of policy practitioners, which over time has led to the creation of a distinctive regional policy field.[4]

This rereading of the European experience with territorial security can shed new light on the comparison with North America, and, in turn, provide a novel interpretation of the latter's accomplishments. North America's recent experiments with territorial security are, in fact, not as removed from its transatlantic counterpart as is often claimed. Albeit not as advanced, a kind of practical continentalism is transpiring in relations between the US and Canada, and Mexico as well. This emerging system of governance has not completely displaced the state-centric model upon which the modern approach to territorial security is based. It has, however, reformulated some of its core principles, such as the emphasis on a clear distinction between a territory's "inside" and "outside," on well protected national borders, and on limited interaction with the external world, resulting in a more complex and regionalized model of territorial security.

To illustrate this argument, this chapter first presents the key principles underlying the territorial security model that has emerged in North America after 9/11, highlighting the parallels with the European experience. It then considers some of this model's most relevant policy applications and compares them to initiatives proposed on the other side of the Atlantic. Given its regional dimension, special attention is devoted to the parallels between, on one hand, the project for a "North American Security Perimeter" as it has been elaborated in projects such as the Smart Border initiative, the

Security and Prosperity Partnership (SPP) and, more recently, the Beyond the Border agreement and, on the other hand, Europe's Schengen border control regime. The chapter concludes by exploring possible future scenarios characterizing relations between North America and Europe over territorial security, and, in particular, the prospect for further transatlantic convergence in this policy field.

REFRAMING TERRITORIAL SECURITY IN NORTH AMERICA AND EUROPE AFTER 9/11

In its final report, the 9/11 Commission listed a series of damning shortcomings of existing US policies in the homeland security field, from lax borders and poor communication among agencies, to lack of adequate funding, and it called for a fundamental reformulation of the entire approach to domestic and international security in the US.[5] The Canadian and Mexican governments followed the American example and launched internal reviews of their security policies, although these were narrower in scope. This policy review process led to the drafting of new legislation (e.g., the US Patriot Act, and Canada's Antiterrorism Act and Immigration and Refugee Protection Act), as well as strategic action plans for Homeland Security (the 2002 National Homeland Security Strategy in the US, and the 2004 National Security Policy in Canada).

Taken together, these documents outline a relatively coherent set of new assumptions and practices that should regulate North American borders, and guide policymakers in the everyday management of territorial security in the post–9/11 era. In this policy model the state as sovereign territorial unit remains the main point of reference. The object to be protected and the means to guarantee its security are, however, substantially reformulated. A rarely used term has been resumed in North American political discourse: "homeland."[6] The term has an explicit territorial connotation. The protection of the "land," however, is not restricted to the national territory proper. While homeland security "is a concerted national effort to prevent terrorist attacks *within* the United States, reduce America's vulnerability to terrorism, and minimize the damage and recover from attacks that do occur,"[7] if necessary, the homeland's boundaries can be stretched beyond their physical location. Indeed, the US National Homeland Security Strategy is largely based on policy proposals to "push US borders out" beyond US territorial boundaries.[8] The goal is to "extend our zone of security outward so that American borders are the last line of defense, not the first."[9] These "extraterritorial" borders are the homeland's outer limits and coexist with national borders; they are not linear, but "a continuum framed by land, sea, and air dimensions."[10] In the US, these changes, especially the extraterritorial dimension of border control, are a more central component of the border strategy and their implications more wide ranging. Canada and Mexico, however, have also embraced this new vision of territoriality. Despite having some reservations over the new policies and their impact, especially in the economic realm, the Canadian and Mexican governments' policy agendas have been more in tune with those of the US than their official positions would suggest. One feature of Canada's "comprehensive approach" to border control, for instance, is "applying the smart borders principles internationally."[11] Pragmatically, the Canadian and Mexican governments have also realized that pursuing the new initiatives would help maintain a working relationship with their powerful neighbor.

One of the implications of the externalization of territorial security is that foreign affairs would become a central component of a policy field that hitherto had been focused mainly on "internal" matters. International cooperation is actively encouraged, even in countries where unilateralism is deeply rooted, such as the US.[12] The areas indicated for this cooperation include emergency preparedness; intelligence; law enforcement; and land, sea, and air border security, and it should involve neighboring and overseas countries, and international organizations.[13]

The call for a new vision of territorial security has also led to a substantial overhaul of the policy field's governance. Before 9/11, the US and Canada did not have a dedicated governmental agency dealing with internal security. The organization of the security apparatus was a legacy of the Cold War and was ill equipped to address the challenge of transnational terrorism.[14] The proposed solution was that of creating a department that would put under a unique institutional umbrella the hitherto scattered agencies dealing with territorial security issues. The new departments of "Homeland Security" in the US and "Public Safety and Emergency Preparedness" in Canada would be working side by side with other governmental actors traditionally responsible for border-related issues (e.g., ministries of foreign affairs, transportation, and finance).

The reorganization of North America's approach to territorial security that has taken place since 9/11 is echoed in developments across the Atlantic. Since the late 1990s, European policymakers have tried to advance a comprehensive approach to territorial security that relies on bi- and multilateral cooperation with third countries and that addresses the structural factors causing poverty and instability. Relations with third countries, however, have remained mostly intergovernmental and asymmetric, and over time they have become more antagonistic and security oriented.[15] These trends were reinforced with the terrorist attacks on European soil in Madrid and London (in 2004 and 2005, respectively). In the aftermath of these events, a more proactive territorial security policy was, in fact, seen as a central aspect of the fight against terrorism. The securitization of Europe's external action in territorial security matters was apparent in the policies that European governments formulated during the period. As in North America, what we witness in this phase is an intensification of a set of practices directed toward the prevention of potential threats at their source. These practices have taken different forms (e.g., visa regimes, carrier sanctions, interdiction policies) and have involved a multiplicity of policy actors (e.g., consulates, airlines, security agencies, immigration officers).

The parallels with Europe do not end with the internationalization of territorial security; although less visible, North America shares with its partners across the Atlantic relevant features of its territorial security governance. As noted, in North America there is no equivalent of the regional supranational institutional framework developed in Europe.[16] The governance of North American territorial security remains mainly a transgovernmental affair. At a closer look, however, Europe presents similar characteristics. The European regional model of territorial security and its evolution are, in fact, not as coherent or as linear as it might appear in official accounts. On one hand, since the late 1990s, the European Union has acquired greater responsibilities in this policy area, resulting in the expansion of policymaking occurring at regional level. On the other hand, national governments maintain a prominent role in territorial security matters. Governmental representatives—from heads of state to cabinet ministers and ministry officials—are the main players in the Council of the European Union, the EU institution where key decisions regarding territorial security are taken. Despite the formal powers acquired, the European Commission, the more supranational of EU institutions, is often relegated to the margins, having to follow the lead of member states.[17] Even the European model of territorial security governance is therefore still characterized by a strong intergovernmental component, despite its "communitarian" credentials.

The European approach to territorial security is also characterized by flexible arrangements devised to push the policy process forward when unanimity among member states cannot be achieved. One of the most controversial of these arrangements is what in EU jargon is called "variable geometry."[18] Variable geometry entails that initiatives that foster greater regional integration do not have to include all EU member states, but can be based only on a limited number of "willing" partners who are eager to go ahead without having to wait for the "laggards." The most notorious example of this policymaking method has to do with territorial security. The Schengen regime was, in fact, originally conceived (in the mid-1980s) outside the European Union's (then European Community) institutional framework, and based on a series of ad hoc bi- and multi-lateral forums where national policymakers and experts regularly met to discuss and negotiate the terms of the emerging border security arrangement. Initially this initiative involved only a small group of participants (Germany, France, the Benelux countries). Over the years, its membership has expanded—today it includes twenty-seven countries—but it was only with the 1997 Amsterdam Treaty that the regime was formally incorporated in the EU. The regime's complexity is compounded by the fact that not all EU countries are Schengen members (some, such as the United Kingdom and Ireland, out of choice, and others, such as Bulgaria, Romania, and Cyprus, because they have not yet been deemed ready to join), while not all Schengen members belong to the EU (e.g., Norway, Iceland, and Switzerland). The flexible institutional arrangement and pragmatic method of policymaking that characterize the Schengen regime is still popular today among European policymakers, as evidenced in the experience of the new intergovernmental initiatives dealing with internal security in Europe launched since the turn of the millennium.[19]

This "practical" characterization of the key principles underlying the European model of territorial security echoes approaches taken in North America. The parallels between the two models are also reflected in the content of the policy initiatives undertaken across the Atlantic in the last decade. It is to these parallels that I now turn.

TERRITORIAL SECURITY IN PRACTICE: COMPARING NORTH AMERICA AND EUROPE'S "PERIMETERS"

From early 2002, the US administration began to address some of the requests made by Congress to increase the security of the country's land, sea, and air borders. The first measures included the Container Security Initiative (CSI), which entailed a series of agreements between American and foreign port authorities permitting the prescreening by American inspectors of shipping containers destined for the US; the collection of Passenger Name Records (PNR) on US-bound flights; and the application of a rule that foreigners entering the US hold biometric passports. Because of their geographical proximity and high level of interdependence with the US, Canada and Mexico are the countries that more directly felt the effects of their neighbor's new border policies. The US administration's drive to tighten its borders indeed seriously hampered the movement of people and goods across their common frontiers, becoming a source of contention in the relations between the three North American governments. It is in this context that the idea of a North America security perimeter was put on the table. Presented as a way to strike a balance between the often-clashing requirements of security and freedom of movement, a security perimeter entails the coordination of entry controls for visitors arriving in the region so that less scrutiny would be needed at land borders. Initially, the debate focused primarily on a perimeter around Canada and the US because Mexico was deemed unsuitable for such a project.

Although the idea of a common security perimeter had been flagged in the past,[20] it was only after 9/11 that it gained political traction and landed on the political agendas of governments in the region. The institutional framework that formalized and gave coherence and political direction to this project was the Smart Border initiative, which was officially launched in December 2001 with a joint declaration by Canada's Foreign Minister John Manley and US Secretary of Homeland Security Tom Ridge. As its name suggests, the initiative sought to elaborate new and more effective means to manage territoriality that could balance security and freedom, allowing desirable people and goods in and keeping the unwanted out. The list of proposed measures included the development of common standards for biometrics, an integrated approach for processing cargo away from the border, the sharing of customs data, a bilateral arrangement to streamline refugee applications, consultation on visa policy, and sharing of Advance Passenger Information and Passenger Name Records concerning high-risk travelers.

Policymakers and the business community in the US and, at least initially, in Canada, enthusiastically endorsed the project. Senior Canadian officials, however, were nervous about any policy that would leave them open to charges of compromising Canadian sovereignty. The Canadian government therefore quietly distanced itself from the notion of "perimeter" in its public statements, going out of its way to dispel the notion that the perimeter followed the European model. Telling is the response by the then Immigration Minister Elinor Caplan to a question about the project: "When you say 'perimeter,' people think the European model where you erase the internal borders. That is not what we are talking about."[21] The new term of reference thus became the more politically neutral "Zone of Confidence."

Despite the change in name and the attempts to distinguish it from the European model, the initiative's main rationale and content were still those of a regional security perimeter. As an official involved in the negotiations stated, the change in terminology notwithstanding, the security perimeter was "really what these Manley-Ridge discussions amount[ed] to."[22] Indeed, if we look more closely at its content and organization, we can clearly see that the Smart Border initiative contained *in nuce* some of the key features characterizing Europe's regional security perimeter as it has been envisioned in the Schengen border regime. This is the case, for example, of policy initiatives such as the Safe Third Country Agreement, the 2002 bilateral US-Canada arrangement tackling the issue of asylum seekers crossing their common border,[23] advanced visa policy coordination, joint law enforcement teams targeting cross-border criminal activity,[24] Immigration Officers Overseas,[25] and an electronic system for sharing of information on criminal records.[26]

The perimeter dimension of US-Canadian efforts to address their common security concerns became even more explicit with the Beyond the Border (BTB) initiative, the most recent attempt to revamp and expand the work initiated with the Smart Border declaration. With BTB, the "p" word is no longer taboo. As its full name suggests, the initiative entails "a shared vision for *perimeter* security and economic competiveness" (emphasis added).[27] As for the Smart Border Plan, BTB contains initiatives aimed at coordinating and, when possible, harmonizing territorial security practices whose content and form are reminiscent of the Schengen regime, such as enhancing travel identity and biometrics requirements, developing joint privacy protection principles, expanding the scope of integrated cross-border law enforcement operations, sharing information between law enforcement agencies, and organizing joint patrols of common waterways.[28]

Unlike the multilateral approach adopted by European governments, the discussion about the North American security perimeter has been restricted mostly to the US and Canada. Over the last decade, however, there have been attempts to "trilateralize" the approach to territorial security in North America with the participation of the Mexican government. After the signing of the US-Canada Smart Border Declaration, calls for the expansion of the North American perimeter became louder. The idea of a trilateral approach to homeland security was at the core of the "Security and Prosperity Partnership of North America" (SPP). The SPP—which was launched in March 2005—was meant to provide a forum for ongoing dialogue and cooperation on a variety of economic and security issues, including border facilitation, the environment, food and product safety, and economic competitiveness. The decision to bring together the security and economic dimensions into a single multilateral regional framework, and thus the acceptance of the principle that security and prosperity are mutually dependent and complementary, clearly echoes the European experience with the Schengen border regime. As in the European case, the SPP approach to achieve greater integration was incremental. The initiative was, in fact, built on existing bilateral and trilateral arrangements in the region—including the Smart Border Declaration.

Despite a promising beginning, progress on the SPP agenda was uneven, and political will to support it ebbed. Canadian officials were the most skeptical about expanding the geographical and functional scope of the security perimeter.[29] In the last part of the second Bush administration, there were attempts to revive the initiative, but with few results. For the Obama administration, deeper American cooperation has not been a foreign policy priority. The consequence of this shift in focus was that the SPP was shelved in 2009. The SPP's demise leveled a serious blow to the quest to create a European-style formal regional institutional framework to manage territorial security in North America. One of the initiative's most innovative aspects was, in fact, the establishment of a trilateral mode of governance based on a series of multilateral forums where Canadian, American, and Mexican government officials could meet face to face on a regular basis to discuss and ensure the successful implementation of the items on the agenda.[30] The US-Canada Beyond the Border initiative signals a return to the bilateralism that characterized the pre-SPP period. The BTB's governance mirrors the Smart Border initiative, with an assistant deputy minister/assistant secretary–level US-Canadian Executive Steering Committee responsible for overseeing the implementation of the plan of action, as well as a series of operational groups led by individual departments within each government (e.g., working group on biometrics, asylum, Joint Port Operations committees at airports and land borders). The lack of a formal multilateral framework does not mean, however, that a regional dimension is missing from the ongoing project to create a North American perimeter. The governance of territorial security in North America, if not trilateral is, in fact, "triangular" in so far as the content of the ongoing bilateral discussions between the three governments significantly overlaps, and joint initiatives have taken into consideration existing relations with all countries in the region. This form of "interlocking bilateralism"[31] was a feature of the Smart Border initiative, as it was characterized by two parallel agreements that Canada and Mexico signed with the US. The overlap between the two initiatives is apparent in the agreements' list of proposed activities, such the favored travelers programs (Nexus between the US and Canada and SENTRI between the US and Mexico). Parallel negotiations for these programs were conducted, and despite the dissimilar nature of the two borders, and their separate challenges, efforts were made to share best practices stemming from both experiences. This triangular governance mode was also what characterized an ostensibly trilateral arrangement such as the SPP. The practical implementation of some of the items on the agenda was, in fact, delegated to bilateral working groups, whose activities were carried out in coordination with existing trilateral forums. The SPP was therefore not a purely trilateral, but a "bi-trilateral" initiative.

The lack of face-to-face interaction and common initiatives between the three partners means that the ties that bind the US, Canadian, and Mexican governments and that render territorial security a *regional* policy field are more indirect and thus less apparent than in the case of a bilateral or multilateral configuration. In the North American context, even more than in Europe, this regional dimension stems from national government officials' ongoing performance of similar territorial security practices (e.g., the activities that require "pushing borders out"), rather than from a conscious and coordinated effort. These practical performances show how government officials, despite having different national affiliations and, in some cases, a lack of direct personal contact, share with their colleagues a similar pragmatic understanding and increasingly regional perspective on the challenges that dealing with territorial security in North America entail, and how to address them. The elements, taken together, indicate that a North American community of territorial security practitioners is in the making. Although it is not formally organized, such a community is more coherent and tightly knit than the lack of an overarching institutional framework might suggest.

A true North American security perimeter is still far away from being realized. The experience with the Smart Border initiative and SPP suggests that policy convergence in territorial security matters is a slow and patchy process, especially in regard to harmonization.[32] Yet it should be noted that even in Europe convergence on territorial security practice is still a work in progress, despite the presence of a thick regional institutional framework that should guarantee a swifter and more coherent pace to this process (add reference). Thus, the lesson of the European experience for North America is that a pragmatic approach to policy-making can be instrumental in overcoming apparently insurmountable political and technical obstacles on the path to a regional security perimeter, although this project's trajectory will not necessarily be consistent and linear.

CONCLUSIONS: TOWARD A PRACTICAL TRANS-ATLANTICISM?

Europe and North America's political worldviews are often at odds with each other, and these differences are reflected in the different policy options that governments in the two regions have pursued in a variety of policy areas. As this chapter has shown, when it comes to territorial security, these differences at times tend to be overblown. On one hand, territorial security in Europe, despite the important steps taken towards its "supra-nationalization" in the context of the European Union, remains a mainly intergovernmental affair. On the other, territorial security in North America has become more regionalized, despite the lack of formalized trilateral institutional architecture. In turn, both regions are characterized by a pragmatic and flexible approach/method to policy-making, and by a network of like-minded and mainly national policy officials who apply this method in their everyday practices and who reproduce and strengthen it in their regular interactions.

This reformulation of the comparison between North American and European approaches to territorial security sheds new light on the dynamics characterizing the relations between the United States, Canada and Mexico. There is, in fact, a tendency to argue that the transformations in territorial security matters in North America are not as far reaching as those occurring across the Atlantic. Although not in the same manner as their European counterparts, North American governments have nonetheless moved away from traditional territorial models and embraced a "post-national" approach to territoriality, an approach that is based on a new conceptualization of territory, security, sovereignty, and international relations. The premise of a "post-national" argument is the recognition that modern states face new and unprecedented challenges to their ability to operate autonomously within their borders and on the world stage (e.g. economic globalization and international terrorism).[33] These challenges have not, however, leveled a fatal blow to the state and made it irrelevant in contemporary world politics. The case of territorial security in Europe shows that states (or, more precisely, national governments) still matter, although not in the same way they did in the past, and that regional system/integration can occur even without or despite the use of formal institutions.

The North American parallels with Europe, however, also show some of the limits and contradictions of this practical method of policymaking and its potential implications for the continent. On one hand, nonelected officials represent a vital component of this policy field, as they provide crucial continuity and momentum in the face of ebbing political support. On the other hand, their central role has turned policymaking into a technocratic exercise. Indeed, the spread of security practices is occurring behind closed doors and involves unelected career bureaucrats shielded from public scrutiny. The dynamics taking place within this field are not necessarily apolitical, however. Arguably, the very attempt to depoliticize territorial security by shielding it from public scrutiny (a move that might not necessarily be the stated objective of those involved, but that these very policymakers are helping to reproduce through their actions) can, in fact, be read as a political maneuver to prevent potential domestic and international criticism.[34] (To address these concerns, the Canadian government has allowed the population to participate in its formulation, although criticism remains.)

This chapter has focused on Europe as a reference point from which to assess the recent evolution of North America's territorial security practices. This does not mean, however, that the relationship between the two regions in this policy field goes in one direction; on the contrary, during the last decade, North America has also become a model for its transatlantic partners. The European Commission, for example, has for a long time been vocally critical of some US-led initiatives affecting Europe and its citizens (e.g., exchange of passenger data), and is currently working on similar arrangements for Europe (e.g., a "European PNR"). It has also advanced policy proposals first introduced by its North American counterparts (e.g., an Entry-Exit system applicable to European external borders). Indeed, what we are witnessing is the convergence of two approaches to territorial security, which in turn are leading to the emergence of a distinctive *transatlantic* policy field. The key components of this field are practices regarding the protection of the "homeland" by air (e.g., preclearing, sharing data, implementing an integrated approach to border control), land (preferential travelers programs, controlling passengers), and sea (preclearing cargoes, joint patrolling). These practices target goods and persons, using a combination of human, physical, and electronic techniques such as screening, data collection and exchange, interdiction, regulation, and interrogation. They take place inside a country's territory, at its borders, and abroad, and their goal is the prevention and management of terrorism and other serious threats to the "homeland." Finally, the policy actors populating this new transatlantic field are policymakers and practitioners affiliated with national institutions (e.g., ministries of interior) supported by private agents (e.g., airline carriers).

Considering homeland security as an ever-expanding field of practices also has implications for the future of this domain at global level. Some of the initiatives spearheaded by North American and European governments have, in fact, recently spread beyond the transatlantic arena. One case in point is the adoption by a growing number of countries of passenger screening systems similar to the US and EU PNR, and the resulting call for the establishment of an international standard in this area. A number of the homeland security initiatives formulated by North American and European governments have also been inserted in other global and regional fora agendas. For example, the G8, the annual meeting of the leaders of the world's most industrialized countries, has developed a set of guidelines and best practices to improve the security of travel documents, including the use of biometrics, which, in turn, the International Civil Aviation Organization (ICAO) has agreed to adopt as its international standard.[35] What these episodes show is that not only are North America and Europe becoming more integrated in this policy field, but also that they are actively shaping the rest of the world to their image. For the countries outside North America and Europe affected by these trends, the future of territorial security, as has been the case for North America after 9/11, could indeed turn out to be radically different than today's.

NOTES

1. Capling and Nossal 2009; Clarkson 2008; Hussain, Pattnayak, and Hira 2008.
2. See, e.g., Rudolph 2005; Brimmer 2006; Dalgaard-Nielsen 2004. One exception is Pastor 2001. His view of the "lessons" that the Old Continent can teach the New, however, predates 9/11 and it is centered on economic rather than security issues.
3. Wallace (2000) has defined the approach to the governance of European security as "intensive transgovernmentalism." Arguably, arguments contrasting North America with Europe in territorial security matters tend to conflate the latter with the European Union and its economic realm. As we will see shortly, this characterization does not reflect this policy field's actual features and dynamics.
4. On the concept of "practice" and its application to the study of international relations, see Adler and Pouliot 2011.
5. NCTA 2004, 339.
6. Since 2001, "homeland" and "homeland security" have become common terms in the US official and public discourse to define the new policy field. Canada and Mexico have shied away from using this terminology. Canadian officials prefer talking about "public safety," while Mexico has stuck with the more traditional "internal security." Despite their reservations about some of the implications of the new approach to territorial security that the new term *homeland* implied, the two governments have in practice accepted its key premises, especially that a more aggressive stance regarding border security is necessary in the post–9/11 world.
7. White House 2002b, 2 (emphasis added).
8. Flynn 2000.
9. US Customs and Border Protection 2011. Zolberg (1999) has defined this type of policy as "remote control."
10. White House 2002b, 22.
11. Canada Privy Council Office 2004, 46.
12. As the 9/11 Commission put it, "The US government cannot meet its own obligations to the American people to prevent the entry of terrorists without a major effort to collaborate with other governments." NCTA 2004, 390.
13. White House 2002b; Canada Privy Council Office 2004, 37–40.
14. NCTA 2004, 428. Mexico, unlike its northern neighbors, has historically relied on a European-style ministry of interior (Secretaría de Gobernación) as the lead agency responsible for the management of territorial security.
15. The nexus between foreign policy and the protection of the EU external frontiers was first explicitly made in the action plan on illegal migration that the European Council adopted in February 2002. See EU 2002.

16. Since the 1990s, one of the options put on the table in some scholarly and policy circles has been that of a "North American Community," which would involve a deeper degree of integration of various sectoral fields, including homeland security, and an advanced regional institutional framework (Pastor 2001). This vision, however, was put on the backburner in the aftermath of 9/11, in favor of more securitarian measures to protect the North American Homeland. Although there has been renewed interest in recent times (see, for example, Council on Foreign Relations 2005), North American governments have not officially endorsed the initiative.
17. The recent spat between Italy and France (two of the most influential EU members) over the handling of migrants who crossed the Mediterranean as a result of the turbulence that followed the so-called Jasmine revolutions in North Africa is a good example of the continuing centrality of national governments in the European Union. Carrera et al 2011. In April 2011 the French government in fact unilaterally reinstated border controls with its southern neighbor without consulting with EU institutions, thus violating the spirit of the Schengen agreement.
18. Stubb 2002.
19. One of them is the so-called *Prüm group*. This intergovernmental group, which initially included representatives of interior ministries from five EU member states (Belgium, Netherlands, Luxembourg, Germany, and Austria), and was later joined by their French, Spanish, and Italian counterparts, was formed outside the EU institutional framework with the aim of elaborating and expanding the scope of the Schengen regime. Discussions within this group have led to the drafting of the Treaty of Prüm, also known as "Schengen III," which was signed in May 2005 and whose objective is to advance police cooperation in the field of security. Other willing and capable countries can sign the Treaty, but they have to do so by accepting its entire content without modifications.
20. Noble 2005.
21. Quoted in Alberts 2001.
22. Ibid.
23. The concept of "safe country of asylum" is the key component of the Dublin Convention, which European countries signed in 1990 and which became effective in 1997. According to this agreement, if an alien applies for asylum after traveling through a country that is party to the protocol relating to the status of refugees and thus considered to be "safe," he or she will be sent back to that country to file his/her application.
24. The Integrated Border Enforcement Teams (IBET) were originally established in 1996 along the border in the western region of Washington state to combat drug smuggling and illegal immigration. The Smart Border Plan expanded this project to the entire US-Canada border. Since the 1990s, EU member states have organized several joint operations to manage Europe's external borders, such as Operations Triton and Orca (sea borders), Operation Visa (air border), and Operation Eastern External Borders (land borders).
25. These officers are government-appointed civil servants posted in selected third countries whose job is to obtain and exchange information on illegal immigration and related issues; to assist, advise, and train consular and diplomatic staff as well as airline companies; and to cooperate with the authorities of the host country. European countries had deployed Immigration Liaison Officers (ILOs) since the 1990s as part of their "remote control" policy.
26. The idea of a common database system for the purpose of maintaining and distributing information related to border security and law enforcement is behind the Schengen regime's Schengen Information System (SIS).

27. In the joint statement that officially presented the Beyond the Border initiative, US President Obama and his Canadian counterpart, Prime Minister Harper, referred to their common objective to be that of "pursu[ing] a perimeter approach to security, working together within, at, and away from the borders of our two countries to enhance our security and accelerate the legitimate flow of people, goods and services between our two countries." US Department of Homeland Security 2011.
28. US DHS 2011, 1–27.
29. A major concern is that Mexico has not taken part in regional security arrangements in the past, and thus its integration with the other two partners might be difficult. Another issue raised by Canadian officials is the difference between the problems at the US-Canadian border and those at the US-Mexican border (illegal immigration, drug and arms trafficking). From a practical perspective, the addition of a new partner could have therefore rendered existing informal cooperation more cumbersome.
30. In the security realm, the main trilateral forum was the Working Group on Security, whose mandate was to coordinate the activities of various specialized working groups (Traveler Security, Cargo Security, Border Facilitation, Aviation Security, Maritime Security, Law Enforcement, Intelligence Cooperation).
31. Acharya 2000, 18.
32. Rudolph 2005.
33. On post-nationalism as a term to portray recent social, political, and spatial developments affecting Europe and the rest of the world in areas such as citizenship, law and governance, democracy, and territory, see Soysal 1994; Zurn and Joerges 2005; Curtin 1997; Appadurai 1996.
34. For a critical view on the politics of homeland security, see Bigo 2008 and Bigo and Tsopukala 2008.
35. US Department of State 2004.

REFERENCES

Acharya, Amitav. 2000. "Regional Institutions and Security Order in Asia," paper prepared for the second workshop on *Security Order in the Asia-Pacific*, Bali, Indonesia, May 29–June 2.

Adler, Emanuel, and Vincent Pouliot. 2011. *International Practices*. Cambridge, UK: Cambridge University Press.

Alberts, Sheldon. 2001. "Border Deal Would Screen Travellers Before They Arrive," *National Post*, November 9, A4.

Appadurai, Arjun. 1996. "Sovereignty without Territoriality: Notes for a Postnational Geography" (pp. xx), in Patricia Yaeger, ed., *The Geography of Identity*. Ann Arbor: The University of Michigan Press.

Bigo, Didier. 2008. "The Emergence of a Consensus: Global Terrorism, Global Insecurity, and Global Security" (pp. 67–94), in Ariane Chebel d'Appollonia and Simon Reich, eds., *Immigration, Integration, and Security: America and Europe in Comparative Perspective*. Pittsburgh: University of Pittsburgh Press.

Bigo, Didier, and Anastassia Tsoukala, eds. 2008. *Terror, Insecurity and Liberty: Illiberal Practices of Liberal Regimes after 9/11*. New York: Routledge.

Brimmer, Esther. 2006. *Transforming Homeland Security: US and European Approaches*. Washington DC: Center for Transatlantic Relations.

Canada Privy Council Office. 2004. "Securing an Open Society: Canada's National Security Policy," April. http://publications.gc.ca/collections/Collection/CP22-77-2004E.pdf

Capling, Ann, and Kim Richard Nossal. 2009. "The Contradictions of Regionalism in North America," *Review of International Studies* 35 (1): 147–167.

Carrera, Sergio, Elspeth Guild, Massimo Merlino, and Joanne Parkin. 2011. A Race Against Solidarity: The Schengen Regime and the Franco-Italian Affair," *CEPS Working Paper*, April.

Clarkson, Stephen. 2008. *Does North America Exist?* Toronto: University of Toronto Press.

Council on Foreign Relations. 2005. "Building a North American Community: Task Force Report," May. www.cfr.org/canada/building-north-american-community/p8102

Curtin, Deirdre M. 1997. *Postnational Democracy: The European Union in Search of a Political Philosophy*. The Hague; London: Kluwer Law International.

Dalgaard-Nielsen, Anja. 2004. "Homeland Security: American and European Responses to September 11th" (pp. xx), in Jess Pilegaard, ed., *The Politics of European Security*. Copenhagen: Danish Institute for International Studies.

European Union. 2002. "Proposal for a Comprehensive Plan to Combat Illegal Immigration and Trafficking of Human Beings in the European Union," *Official Journal* C 142 of 14.06.2002.

Flynn, Steven E. 2000. "Beyond Border Control," *Foreign Affairs* 79 (6): 57–68.

Imtiaz Hussain, S.R. Pattanayak, and Anil Hira. 2008. *North American Homeland Security: Back to Bilateralism?* Westport: Praeger.

National Commission on Terrorist Attacks upon the United States (NCTA). 2004. "Final Report of the National Commission on Terrorist Attacks upon the United States" [9–11 Commission Report], Official Government Edition, July 21. http://govinfo.library.unt.edu/911/report/index.htm

Noble, John. 2005. "Fortress America or Fortress North America?" *Law and Business Review of the Americas* 15 (3/4): 461–526.

Pastor, Robert A. 2001. *Toward a North American Community: Lessons from the Old World for the New*. Washington: Peterson Institute.

Rudolph, Christopher. 2005. "International Migration and Homeland Security: Coordination and Collaboration in North America," *Law and Business Review of the Americas* 11 (3/4): 433–460.

Soysal, Yasmin N. 1994. *Limits of Citizenship: Migrants and Postnational Membership in Europe*. London; Chicago: University of Chicago Press.

Stubb, Alexander. 2002. *Negotiating Flexibility in the European Union*. Houndsmill: Palgrave.

US Customs and Border Protection. 2011. "CSI in Brief," October 7. www.cbp.gov/xp/cgov/border_security/ international_activities/csi/csi_in_brief.xml

US Department of Homeland Security. 2011. "Declaration by President Obama and Prime Minister Harper of Canada: Beyond the Border: A Shared Vision for Perimeter Security and Economic Competiveness," February 4 2011. www.dhs.gov/xlibrary/assets/wh/us-canada-btb-action-plan.pdf

US Department of State. 2004. "International Travel Security High on G8 Agenda: Leaders' Action Plan to Focus Particularly on Air Travel," *State Department Press Releases and Documents*, June 8. http://usinfo.state.gov/xarchives/display.html?p=washfile-english&y=2004&m=June&x=20040608201500bzemog2.355593e-02&t=livefeeds/wf-latest.html

Wallace, Helen. 2000. "The Institutional Setting: Five Variations on a Theme," in Helen Wallace and William Wallace, eds., *Policy-Making in the European Union*. 4th ed.; Oxford: Oxford University Press.

White House. 2002a. "The National Security Strategy of the United States of America," September 17. http://georgewbush-whitehouse.archives.gov/nsc/nss/2002/

White House. 2002b. "The National Strategy for Homeland Security," July 16. http://georgewbush-whitehouse.archives.gov/homeland/book/index.html

Zolberg, Aristide. 1999, "Matters of State: Theorizing Immigration Policy" (pp. 77–93), in Charles Hirschman, Philip Kasinitz, and Joshua DeWind, eds., *The Handbook of International Migration: The American Experience*. New York: Russell Sage.

Zürn, Michael, and Christian Joerges, eds. 2005. *Law and Governance in Postnational Europe: Compliance beyond the Nation-State*. Cambridge: Cambridge University Press.

5 The Government-Designed Architecture of North America's Disaggregated Trade and Investment Arbitration Regimes

Stephen Clarkson

When humans construct buildings, they generally have a plan that seeks to achieve a specific functional or aesthetic goal. Mostly, the erection of social structures and the ways that peoples relate within and between them are the product of more spontaneous, less intellectually driven impulses. In considering the changing architecture of North America, which is made up of three huge federal states, each of which shelters a diverse mix of populations and encompasses vast land masses stretching from the Atlantic to the Pacific Oceans, this chapter will focus on those contours of this trinational space that were the product of deliberate plans executed by the three governments' trade-regime architects. To get a sense of the dramatic shifts that have transformed North America's governance in recent times, the text will place its discussion in the context of the US, Canada, and Mexico's economic relations with each other and with the rest of the world.

In addressing the editors' principal analytical concern—the relationship between Type I and Type II policymaking modes in North America's regional governance—this chapter will argue that, because of the secretive, intergovernmental treaty-negotiating processes that characterize international trade and investment policymaking, the continent's governance remains the preserve of top-down, hard-law-making, Type I government with whatever bottom-up, soft-law-centered, Type II networking that does take place continuing to play the generally secondary role that it has displayed for over a century.

The argument will proceed chronologically by assessing the past significance of the Type I/Type II interactions that produced North America's profound restructuring through both the Canada-US Free Trade Agreement, that was historically momentous for Canada (CUSFTA, 1989), and the North American Free Trade Agreement, which was paradigm changing for Mexico (NAFTA, 1994), both agreements being of globally strategic and continentally tactical importance to the US. It will proceed to the present by discussing the institutional and sectoral developments that CUSFTA and NAFTA set in motion both before and after 9/11 transformed the US's governing policy paradigm from the extroverted, border reducing, economic expansionism that had characterized the 1990s to the introverted, anti-terrorist security, border building that has prevailed since September 2001. It will end by considering the future prospects for North American integration by peering through the lens of the three member-states' recent economic negotiations with other countries and other regions. The concluding section will return the chapter's analysis to the editors' conceptual and analytical agenda.

The notion of "Type I" government covers a multitude of individual, sometimes competing state entities but will be used in this chapter as shorthand for constitutionally legitimate governments and international economic institutions that have been established with juridical personality. As for "Type II" governance, whose interactions with Type I are this book's chief concern, we must distinguish between that part of a country's business sector that is internationally competitive and seeks legal weapons with which to promote and defend its interests abroad and the rest of a country's corporate community, which demands protection against foreign competition. Each country's civil society may be largely missing from this story, but its presence—or absence—needs to be separately acknowledged.

Trade negotiation processes play out on the national and international levels, but subfederal jurisdictions are increasingly affected by ever-more intrusive norms being established by continuing international negotiations into the various international economic rulebooks. North America's subfederal jurisdictions—the US's fifty and Mexico's thirty-three states plus Canada's ten provinces, along with the three countries' thousands of municipalities—make hard law within their constitutionally defined areas of competence, but, being without status in international law, they can for our purposes be considered Type II actors who lobby in the federal-level negotiating process to defend their interests.

THE PAST: CUSFTA AND NAFTA'S NEW CONTEXT

The interplay between Type I government and Type II governance in North America did not begin with NAFTA. Throughout the previous century, the varied and varying interactions between constitutionally defined federal governments and the various business and civil-society communities battling for advantage both within and among the US, Mexico, and Canada set the stage for the climactic trilateral negotiations of NAFTA's more formalized continental regime.

Background

Each of North America's nation-states gestated as colonies within the womb of an overseas relationship that was framed by a European kingdom's hard law control but driven by settlers and entrepreneurs seeking freedom and fortune in the New World, where aboriginal resistance was overcome by superior military firepower. By the end of the nineteenth century, when the three states had fought out their boundaries with each other and established their federalized control from the Atlantic to the Pacific, each had developed its own domestic, government-governance characteristics.

The US's ebullient capitalism was establishing an intimate, "revolving door" in which government regulators and regulated industries constantly switched places, thus ensuring that the American state served the interests of the US market's most politically powerful interests, whichever party held the reins of power. Backed up by the British military, the young Canadian dominion had a relatively more powerful government, but the business community could on occasion decisively flex its muscles, working to defeat, for instance, Liberal Prime Minister Sir Wilfrid Laurier's trade liberalization initiative with the US in the 1911 federal election. Meanwhile in Mexico, long periods of dictatorship simply suppressed interests not favored by the government. Prolonged civil strife between chronically hostile factions often soaked the relations between antagonistic social forces in blood, most notably in the seven-year-long revolution that ultimately gave birth to the republic's still-revered 1917 constitution.

While each of the three states was autonomous in international law, the overwhelming power of the US's social and economic subsystems extended north and south across its formal borders.[1] In 1902, the American Federation of Labor took over the Canadian Labour Congress lock, stock, and barrel.[2] North America's transborder civil-society integration was extensive, with the major enterprises in such emerging American economic sectors as automobile manufacturing taking over their Canadian counterparts. By 1907 an American political economist could already write that, while Canadians might think of themselves as denizens of a separate country, they were actually integrated through gradually tightening financial, industrial, transportation, labor, and cultural ties with their dominant but more progressive neighbor.[3] Depending on the desires and the determination of the US's two neighboring states, this integration was only partly reversible. A prime objective of Mexico's prolonged revolutionary struggle at the turn of the twentieth century was to regain national sovereignty over the country's national resources from the foreign transnational companies (TNCs) that were developing the country's nascent petroleum industry. A similar will—to build a national culture in the face of US radio transmitters' control of Canada's airwaves—motivated the Conservative government of Sir Robert Borden to establish a Canadian Broadcasting Corporation in the early 1930s.

As the US and Canadian state systems became increasingly sophisticated through mobilizing their economies to fight in the Second World War II, they were largely influenced by Keynesian notions of government policies counter-cyclically stabilizing the marketplace's socio-economic functioning. At the same time, Mexico's one-party regime incorporated all business, agricultural, and labor associations under tight state control aimed at building an autonomous national economy through a protectionist strategy known as import-substitution industrialization (ISI).

Successful though these arrangements had proven to be by generating high rates of growth throughout the 1950s, 1960s, and 1970s, each country entered into what were hyped as such profound crises that previously dismissed, game-changing solutions were abruptly adopted. Mexico's autarchic ISI faltered, causing its bureaucratic elites in the 1980s to launch far-reaching privatizations of the state's monopolies and such other liberalization measures as joining the OECD that were designed to open the economy to international competition. At the same time, the Canadian business community's rage at Prime Minister Pierre Trudeau's alleged nationalism drove a royal commission to recommend abandoning his efforts to diversify Canada's economy (by strengthening its overseas linkages) in favor of maximizing its continental integration (through an economic integration agreement with Washington).[4]

Meanwhile, President Ronald Reagan's business-friendly administration was thinking more globally than continentally. It was determined to reverse the US's putative economic decline by pushing its fellow members in the General Agreement on Tariffs and Trade (GATT) to negotiate, in a new set of global palavers dubbed the Uruguay Round, powerful new global rules protecting foreign investment, bringing services under trade disciplines, and strengthening intellectual property rights—innovations that would favor the global expansion and increased profitability of America's internationally competitive TNCs. Given the resistance of both the European Community and Japan to the GATT's adopting such government-restricting norms, the Reagan administration responded positively to the 1985 proposal by Progressive Conservative Prime Minister Brian Mulroney that the two countries negotiate their own trade and investment deal. Because American TNCs already had very open access to the Canadian market, it would hardly have been worth devoting the US Trade Representative's (USTR) bureaucratic resources to such a secondary negotiation. But in the context of the Uruguay Round's log jam, negotiating with a relatively needy and compliant Ottawa gave Washington the chance to establish bold precedents that introduced its business communities' desired norms for trade in services into international economic law.

After failing to interest the European Union (EU) in negotiating a new economic relationship, Mexican President Salinas de Gortari asked Washington for a similar market-access arrangement in 1991. President George W. Bush's administration had a double reason to oblige. Not only did highly competitive American business interests want to open up the Mexican economy to absorb, for instance, US surplus corn, which had just lost its Soviet market, but also the threat that NAFTA would create a protectionist Fortress North America region could bring pressure to bear on Brussels and Tokyo to accept transforming GATT into a radically revamped World Trade Organization (WTO) rather than face a protectionist Fortress America.

This review reminds us that North America's three states have been globally engaged from their very foundation. Over the course of their subsequent historical phases, the continent's two peripheral states have been constantly involved in dealing with their overwhelming neighbor in whose economy and society most of their own sectors were inextricably integrated. As for the continental giant, it only gave priority to relations with its two neighbors—once it had settled its boundary lines with them—when dealing with them had some globally strategic value for it.

Foreground

When the Mulroney government initiated formal negotiations with the US government, it set up a special Trade Negotiators' Office (TNO) that was recruited from, but largely independent of, the federal government. The TNO's consultation processes were modeled on the direct institutional connections between the USTR and US organized business, an arrangement that empowered the latter to instruct the former about what rule changes it wanted. By establishing an ad hoc consultative process, the Canadian government was able to control the outcomes by offering places in its Sectoral Advisory Groups on International Trade to big, often US-controlled corporations, which favored further continental integration. Government thereby shut out small- and medium-sized business sectors, which were likely to suffer under freer trade. As for the civil society's community groups, native peoples' representatives, trade unions, environmental NGOs, women's organizations, and pensioners whose interests were threatened by the prospect of "free trade" shrinking the Canadian state on which they depended, they were simply excluded, on the grounds that the negotiations were strictly about economic matters.

Although it ran an authoritarian state, the PRI government needed business support and technical advice about the meaning and consequences of the various provisions Washington was demanding. During the actual negotiations, Mexican officials would constantly repair to the *cuarto al lado*, the room next door, where the business *camaras*' representatives proffered their reactions and their advice. It is not so much that Canada and Mexico were compelled to rely on transgovernmental networks to work out mutually acceptable commitments as that they selectively co-opted representatives from the business world who would support their project for the duration of the treaty's negotiations and its subsequent ratification.

In their form, the resulting economic integration agreements did represent exceptions to the previous patterns of the primarily informal Canadian-American relations and the primarily formal Mexican-American relationship. Because they were so comprehensive, detailed, and mandatory, CUSFTA and NAFTA could be understood as significantly deepening and constitutionalizing the periphery's two political economies' dependent and asymmetrical integration in the continent's US-dominated power system. Extending

National Treatment (NT) to US corporations imported an international norm as hard law, which had the same effect as the previous informal understanding that neither the federal, nor municipal, nor provincial governments should take actions that negatively affected the balance sheets of US branch plants. But NT went further by eliminating the possibility of any industrial policy aimed at developing a more autonomous economy based on fostering domestically owned national champions.

For Mexico, NAFTA represented much more of a sea change in its relationship with Washington, which had tended to resolve specific irritants by imposing terms that met the short-term demands of its most vociferous interest groups. Whereas NAFTA mandated relatively inconsequential changes for the US, whose Congress would accept no diminution of its constitutionally enshrined trade-policy competence, it required Mexico to make major modifications to regulations in various economic sectors such as pharmaceuticals and banking. It even required the government to insert what amounted to a new trade-law process in its legal system to empower US or Canadian corporations to challenge the Mexican government's anti-dumping and countervailing duty determinations. Only for the energy sector was Mexico City able to draw the line. With its 1938 nationalization of foreign oil companies still being annually celebrated as the country's de facto declaration of independence, it refused to open up its energy sector to American and Canadian participation.

Beyond connecting the national to the continental levels, NAFTA also connected the three economies to the global level in both government and governance terms. In its Chapter 11 the signatory governments shut down one part of their legal systems, grafting on instead an arbitration process adapted, under the World Bank's auspices, from the domain of private international corporate law. To this extent NAFTA provided a partial opt-in to a global judicial regime, which boosted foreign TNCs' capacity to short circuit a signatory government's legal systems by taking their complaints against national measures to private arbitration whose rulings had direct effect in the host country. In this respect, NAFTA disaggregated its signatory states by amputating a part of their legal system and relocating it in an external legal system.

Chapter 11's creation of a means whereby foreign TNCs could win large financial awards against a host economy's regulatory measures that impinged on their profits had a linked side effect. The policy chill resulting from bureaucrats' fear that policy aimed at improving environmental sustainability or public health might provoke a "Chapter 11" case helped cut back the signatory states' regulatory powers. This regulatory chill in turn weakened those civil-society forces that lobby for government intervention to protect the environment, culture, or labor market.

By cutting civil society out of their negotiation process, CUSFTA and NAFTA significantly changed the balance of power within Canada's and Mexico's polities. These binding treaties were used by their neoconservative negotiators to permanently cut back their own state's capacities in the domain of economic development as well as forestall the reintroduction of state-centered policies by future activist governments. For the US, the two agreements resolved some "irritants" with its neighbors, but they were more significant in creating powerful new international norms, opening national service sectors to more foreign investment, and increasing intellectual property rights for Big Pharma. Rephrasing this reality in the thematic of this book, the historically unique moment of each North American country experiencing a separate crisis caused the two periphery governments to carry out a paradigm shift by closing down old, national pathways in favor of opening new continental and global ones for the US. Whether "free trade" affected Type I/Type II realities in North America can now be explored.

THE PRESENT: POST-NAFTA INSTITUTIONAL AND SECTORAL DEVELOPMENTS

When NAFTA entered into force on January 1, 1994, North America was seen by many as no longer just a geographical expression[5] but a bona fide member of the club of world regions with an integrated economic space.[6] This section makes four probes into the government/governance linkages across the borders of North America:

- North America's regionalism displays a low regional government capacity;
- North America's economic regionalization is being diluted by globalization pressures;
- A growing global regulatory capacity is displacing continental regionalism;
- Continental border security is a function of hegemon-driven intergovernmental relations.

North America's Regionalism Displays a Low Regional Government Capacity

By world-region standards, North America's institutionalization is remarkably hollow. Unlike the EU, NAFTA created no international legal personality for North America, which, therefore, cannot negotiate international agreements. Although NAFTA sports a North American Free Trade Commission, this executive body has no staff, no address, and no budget. Despite the substantial responsibilities for managing NAFTA's implementation conferred on it by the Agreement, the Commission consists solely of sporadic meetings by the three countries' trade minister, secretary, or representative, who, in practice, have turned out to be loath to make major decisions.

As for a legislative capacity to add to or amend NAFTA's norms, rules, or rights—a necessary feature of any multilateral body that hopes to retain its relevance as conditions evolve—this world region has none. Changes in NAFTA's normative structure require trilateral intergovernmental negotiations followed by the three governments' ratification, an event that has occurred only once, when a clause in Chapter 11 was clarified.

Nor does NAFTA have much in the way of an administrative arm. Buried in each of the three governments' trade departments, there is a small office responsible for documenting NAFTA-related business. Its sole intergovernmental bureaucratic sinew consists of some thirty committees and working groups mandated by the Agreement's various chapters. These trinational groupings, which are, in theory, staffed by middle-level civil servants from each federal government, barely exist in practice.[7]

The environmental and labor commissions that were added to NAFTA as side agreements as a result of pressure from the newly elected Clinton administration in 1993 shed interesting light on North American regionalism. The North American Commission on Labor Cooperation (NACLC) was designed to make it virtually impossible for unions to win cases against illegal labor practices. The three labor movements ultimately boycotted the organization. In the end the NACLC closed its doors: weak Type I government capacity inhibited the development of a continental Type II labor-union engagement. The North American Commission on Environmental Cooperation (CEC) has survived, but has done so by shirking its official mandate, the mitigation of the environmental externalities generated by increased cross-border trade and investment. The CEC has been particularly successful in fostering Mexican civil-society engagement in public environmental issues, but the three governments have kept it from dealing with NAFTA-generated issues: limited Type I government capacity generated limited Type II civil-society engagement at the continental level.

Of its half-dozen dispute settlement mechanisms, two (relating to energy and financial institutions) have remained dormant, and two (housed in the Environmental and Labor Cooperation Commissions) have proven ineffectual.[8] Disputes between the national governments over the interpretation and implementation of NAFTA's provisions were to be resolved by panels established under Chapter 20, but their rulings merely take the form of recommendations submitted to the NAFTA trade commission—that is, the three trade ministers—who, in turn, can only offer suggestions to their governments about how they might proceed. When, for instance, after yearlong delays caused by Washington's obstruction, a NAFTA Chapter 20 panel ruled that the US government had failed to honor its obligation to allow Mexican truckers access to its market, Washington did not change its ways and still persists in its noncompliance.

Putatively binding rulings established under Chapter 19 on cross-border disputes over anti-dumping (AD) or countervailing duties (CVD) are made by binational panels, which replace domestic legal appeals against the AD or

CVD determinations that were previously made by individual states' trade-administrative tribunals. While useful in resolving low-profile issues, the US government's refusal to comply with these rulings in such high-profile cases as its long-drawn-out softwood lumber dispute with Canada underlines the point that, as a continental governance regime, NAFTA's Type I institutions have strikingly little muscle when it comes to containing the capacities of the region's hegemon.[9]

The single arbitral function with patent hard law muscle is the investor-state dispute process established in Chapter 11 that allows NAFTA's TNCs to initiate an arbitration process governed by World Bank rules in order to seek compensation for any host state's domestic measure, which they claim has expropriated their assets. Because the arbitrators' rulings have direct effect in the defendant's jurisdiction, they have been the cause of both great delight and much dismay among jurists. While the delighted could celebrate continental corporations' new rights to challenge government measures at all levels, the dismayed bemoaned the new arbitration system's marginalization of domestic judicial sovereignty, lamented the process's disrespect for long-established norms of due process, and concluded that an ultimate regulatory chill would inhibit the effective regulation of corporate polluters. Both sides have been proven correct. TNCs have successfully launched investor-state arbitration cases against government measures with the result that policy chill in host states has inhibited their environmental, social, and human-rights legislative measures.

With the major exception of this foreign investment protection, the transborder governance established by NAFTA's ineffectual institutions was considerably less than what observers had had cause to expect when listening either to proponents or opponents of what President Ronald Reagan had called North America's "economic constitution." In one specific sense, Reagan had been right. NAFTA's Type I norms, rules, and rights were "constitutional," at least for Mexico and Canada, because they were mandatory in domestic law and extremely difficult to change. These components of each signatory state's external constitution[10] significantly disaggregated some of the governments' processes and affected the resulting outcomes in the two peripheral states' practices, though not those of the US. Applying national treatment to investment nailed shut the coffin of Mexico's ISI development model.

North America's Regionalization Is Being Diluted by Globalization Pressures

Even if North America's regionalism is less institutionally imposing than the original fanfare over NAFTA had led many to hope (or fear), the continent's regionalization may have political-economic substance in other, more commercial respects. Some economic sectors demonstrate significant continental governance, particularly where geographical proximity is economically important. In agriculture powerful US transnational corporations have generated elements of a continental political economy. In the wheat and corn markets in particular, US food processing transnationals have largely overcome domestic farm producers' resistance to imports—whether of Canadian wheat to the US or of American corn to Mexico. This section will consider three instructive cases: steel, automobiles, and textiles.[11]

Steel. In spite of the fact that steel provides the backbone of the three manufacturing economies, it did not do well under NAFTA. Because the agreement failed to eliminate or even reduce the protectionist anti-dumping and countervailing-duty actions with which the US steel industry had long been protecting itself against imports of their more efficiently produced steel, Canadian steel companies found themselves having to locate their new facilities inside the US market. Their American subsidiaries then became active members of such US industry associations as the American Iron and Steel Institute (AISI). They proceeded to lobby—along with the US steelworkers' union—to exempt Canada (and also Mexico) from the George H.W. Bush administration's safeguard duties that were imposed on US steel imports in 2003. This collaborative action suggested that, in the steel sector, an informal continental governance space was developing in which Canadian, and later Mexican, firms partially Americanized themselves within the US's borders, rather than create a continent-wide industry containing nationally competitive elements.

Symptomatic of this US-centered asymmetrical trilateralism was the AISI setting up the North American Steel Trade Committee (NASTC) as an instrument of trinational governance. In a continent-wide consultative process the NASTC brought together the three governments with their respective industry associations in order to develop common North American policy positions at the OECD, the WTO, and the Free Trade Area of the Americas (FTAA) negotiations. The acquisition in 2006 of the six largest domestically owned Canadian steel corporations by Brazilian, Indian, and American competitors suggested that NASTC's apparently continental regulatory consolidation was being trumped by the steel industry's corporate globalization. Even under global ownership, however, the sector remained a predominantly regional production system.

Automobiles. If NAFTA produced any winners, these were the US auto and textile sectors, which had managed to obtain rules-of-origin protection—at least for a time—from their Asian and European competitors. As the culmination of many years of lobbying by US automotive TNCs, NAFTA was thought to have set up a fully integrated system of production for those automobile manufacturers—principally the Detroit Three—which could meet its protectionist rules-of-origin requirements. However, the trilateral government-led working groups created to negotiate continental safety and emissions standards proved incapable of producing the recommendations for regulatory coordination that would have been necessary for a fully integrated continental production system to emerge.

Meanwhile, global competition undermined the American auto assemblers' oligopolistic dominance in the continent. Trans-oceanic corporate consolidation through mergers and equity linkages was developing a regime of accumulation that was truly universal, thus generating pressures to create a globally rather than continentally coordinated system of regulation. At the same time, continuing foreign auto and auto-parts investment in both Ontario (whose excellent transportation infrastructure and public medical system lowered costs for employers) and Mexico (which offered well-trained labor power at one-fourteenth the level of US wages) equalized production volumes in the three economies. When the 2008 global economic crisis occurred, the dominant role played by Washington and the major funding contributed by Ottawa to the bailout of Chrysler and General Motors showed how vulnerable was market governance to regulatory recapture.

Textiles. NAFTA's rules of origin also appeared to succeed in fusing the three countries' disparate textile and apparel industries into a common North American production system, in which the interests of US corporations combined more intimately with burgeoning Mexican firms than they did with shrinking Canadian companies. The asymmetries in this trilateral matrimony grew as continental market governance collapsed in the face of two global-level adversities—the expiry of the WTO's Multi-Fibre Agreement (which had allowed industrialized countries to impose draconian limitations on apparel imports from the Third World) and China's emergence as the dominant supplier to the North American market. Continental government in this sector amounts to little more than NAFTA's ageing rules of origin, which were made increasingly irrelevant by Washington's independent pursuit of its industry's interest through negotiating agreements with trading partners in other regions. Continental production in a severely shaken textile and apparel industry still revolves around an American hub, with the US industry pushing its government to respond unilaterally to its challenges, a battered Mexican industry retreating to the informal economy, and a hollowed-out Canadian sector sitting on the sidelines.

A Growing Global Regulatory Capacity Is Displacing Continental Regionalism

Regionalism becomes irrelevant when it is trumped by global government. Indeed, in economic sectors where geography plays no significant role, trinational regulatory harmonization results less from continental than from hard law government at the global level. For instance, changes to intellectual property rights (IPRs) for pharmaceuticals in North America were driven not by the IPRs specified in NAFTA's Chapter 17 but by the almost identical Trade-Related Intellectual Property Rights (TRIPs) agreement, which represented the lobbying triumph of US Big Pharma, together with its European and Japanese pharmaceutical counterparts, in achieving a new global legal regime for their sector. In effect, global hard law government has displaced continental government in the pharmaceutical industry.

Continental Border Security Is a Function of Hegemon-Driven Intergovernmental Relations

The economic integration fostered by NAFTA reduced the hard law generated barriers to trade along the US's two territorial borders and so allowed the continental marketplace freer rein to accelerate human and economic flows across the continent. As a result, North America's share of global domestic product increased from 29 percent in 1994 to 35 percent in 2000. Throughout the 1990s, business coalitions lobbied their governments to make increased investments in transportation and security technology and pressed for more intergovernmental policy coordination in order to create a near-borderless continent.

The US's sudden move to a security paradigm was dramatized for North Americans on September 11, 2001, by its immediately, if temporarily, blockading its land boundaries. Following the shock of this attack, Washington moved to terror-proof its borders, whatever the economic cost. This demonstrated that, when it deemed its national security to be at stake, the US government could unilaterally reassert its Type I control over the policy space it had previously vacated in the name of Type II–led trade liberalization. Washington's subsequent demands that Canada and Mexico do what it felt was necessary for them to securitize their cross-border flows of goods and people showed how much Washington still directed North America's border-security governance, however much the latter might still involve a complex mix of federal, state, and provincial agencies acting cooperatively with leading business associations.

Since 9/11, bilateral intergovernmental relations have reasserted themselves, Washington dealing separately with Ottawa and Mexico City. While the first years following September 2001 showed North America to be a more unilaterally, US-government-defined policy space, the proclamation of a Security and Prosperity Partnership for North America (SPP) by the three governments' leaders in 2005 and the creation of a short-lived North American Competitiveness Council in 2007 appeared to herald a shift toward a more trilateral continent with closely knit, Type II transborder government-business networks.

The bulk of the SPP's several hundred proposed measures dealt bilaterally with either US-Canada or US-Mexico issues, yet the informal, three-way telephone and e-mail communications among the bureaucrats who had put them together suggested that some useful trilateral networks were being created. At the same time, the SPP's security measures extended Washington's control across its borders beyond anything it had previously achieved. As for whether the SPP would lead ineluctably to the implementation of a common market, vehement opposition from civil society in each state and stubborn resistance within the US government to creating more continental institutions made this scenario unlikely even before its collapse under the weight of President Barrack Obama's indifference.

This review of how the tensions in North America between regulatory institutionalization and economic integration at the national, regional, and global levels are countervailed by the sovereignty-driven imperatives of national security suggests that there is no fixed end point to power relationships that are continually changing. But we can nevertheless propose a double inference linking hard government and soft governance: Where a continental government capacity has not developed, it will not attract governance relations (NACLC). Where a government capacity has developed, it will attract governance relations (NAFTA Chapter 11's investor-state dispute settlement).

Although the three countries' executives had engaged the upper ranks of their bureaucracies in trying to breathe life into the SPP, they paid virtually no attention to each other's interests when negotiating new trade agreements with other countries, the subject this chapter now addresses as it turns its attention to the future.

THE FUTURE: TRADE AND INVESTMENT-PROTECTION AGREEMENTS

Neither the three countries' government officials nor the business press who has supported their integration paradigm will utter other than relentlessly positive statements about the great successes achieved by "free trade." But the three North American governments' actions speak a different language. To shift our analysis toward assessing the future prospects for policy coordination in North America, we need to take stock of how the three capitals are adjusting their policies in an attempt to find alternatives to their failed strategy to grow through continental integration.

The United States of America

However huge the US government may appear in comparison with smaller states, its capacities are limited to negotiate complex economic agreements that both please its competitive, and reassure its defensive business, interests while satisfying the anxieties of its principal civil-society communities. Because Washington had had to accommodate Brussels's and Tokyo's concerns in Geneva, the WTO's new global economic constitution did not completely satisfy those American sectors that had specific concerns about other countries' regulations. Accordingly, USTR proceeded to negotiate further agreements, first plurilaterally, then bilaterally. At the 1994 Miami Summit of the Americas, President Bill Clinton proposed a "Free Trade Area of the Americas" for the Western hemisphere. In the interests of continental solidarity, Ottawa and Mexico City supported the US position—albeit reluctantly because they feared they would lose what special access to the

US market they thought NAFTA had gained them in exchange for having to make painful concessions that shrank their governments' internal autonomy. These concerns were laid to rest thanks to Brazil's stubborn resistance to the American agenda that laid out Washington's offensive demands while refusing the elimination of its subsidies to US agriculture that Brazil was demanding as quid pro quo.

North America's FTAA-induced solidarity was short lived. Washington was soon negotiating separately, as Mexico City and Ottawa discovered to their dismay. The twenty-one US bilateral investment treaties signed after NAFTA made a mockery of North America's pretensions to continental policy coherence. The US-Dominican Republic/Central America Free Trade Agreement (DR/CAFTA) gave Mexico's southern neighbors superior access in the American market for their textiles than what Mexico City had gained with NAFTA[12] and illustrated how NAFTA had failed to create any trilateral actorness for North America in the international arena.

In 2010, negotiations began for a Trans-Pacific Partnership with members drawn from North America (the US), Latin America (Peru and Chile), East Asia (Brunei, Malaysia, Singapore, and Vietnam), and Oceania (New Zealand and Australia). The processes and perceived outcome of the TPP's dynamics spoke volumes about North American policy coordination in the trade domain. Although Canada sought to join the group, its application was rebuffed by New Zealand and Washington, which wanted Ottawa to concede greater access to Canadian dairy and poultry markets as a precondition for its admission. When Mexico also applied to join the TPP, Washington imposed conditions that gave its two neighbors a second-class role: they had to accept without conditions the twenty-nine chapters that had already been negotiated, and they had to pledge silence for the first meetings they attended.

Despite their participating in the same negotiations, there is no evidence that the three countries have what could be considered a regional agenda. Indeed, the USTR's documentation on the TPP makes no mention of NAFTA, Mexico, or Canada. The US-imposed conditions relegating them to secondary status in the negotiations confirmed that Washington's trade negotiating processes have marginalized Mexico and Canada rather than enhanced their agency in a multilateral, transregional, intergovernmental process.

Given that the rules and principles of trade and investment agreements are locked in by formal treaties, a future activist government committed to recapturing its lost sovereignty in either of the peripheral countries would have enormous difficulty extricating itself from the constitution-like strictures adopted by its predecessors.

Mexico

After 9/11, intraregional trade stagnated in the shadow of stringent American anti-terrorist border controls. With 80 percent of its commerce integrated with the slow-growth and crisis-prone US, Mexico City, like

Ottawa, looked outside North America for partners with whom it could diversify its economic links. Using NAFTA as its template, Mexican government proceeded to negotiate new free trade and investment-protection agreements globally. Twenty of its next twenty-three bilateral investment treaties were negotiated with countries outside Central and South America.

That North American regionalism was not fulfilling its aspirations was made clear in 2012 when Mexico joined with Chile, Peru, and Colombia to form the Pacific Alliance, whose objective was to create a fully integrated economy of like-minded neoliberal states. Not only was Mexico trying to defend its interests in Asia through the TPP; it was also taking steps to reestablish itself in its former sphere of influence to the south.

Canada

Having declined from being the world's seventh largest economy in 1984[13] to being fifteenth in 2012[14] and facing the likelihood of no longer qualifying for the G-20 leaders' summits, Prime Minister Stephen Harper resurrected former Prime Minister Pierre Trudeau's once-scorned strategy of diversifying the economy's international connections. That Harper had given up on the three-state North America as the prime locus for Canada's economic prospects became clear when Ottawa imposed stringent visa requirements on Mexicans wishing to visit Canada. Although he tried to resurrect the imagined golden age of the Canadian-American relationship, Harper found himself having to fight against congressional protectionism (Buy-American legislation) and executive indifference (President Barrack Obama's unwillingness to support the Keystone pipeline).

Consequently Ottawa has negotiated trade and investment agreements with willing partners everywhere in the world. The Canadian mining industry's interest in legal weaponry to use against host-government measures affecting its investments has pushed the Department of Foreign Affairs and International Trade to negotiate twenty-four investment protection agreements, twenty of which were negotiated after NAFTA.

Initially, the European Commission was reluctant to accept the Canadian proposal that NAFTA's Chapter 11 be used as a model for the investment provisions to be contained in a comprehensive, state-to-region economic treaty. But since the Treaty of Lisbon shifted competence for investment from the EU member-states to the European level, Brussels has become a determined proponent of strong investment protection, insisting on provisions aimed at preventing Canadian provinces and cities from impinging on European investors' profits. In this region-to-government exchange, Ottawa was prepared to empower European TNCs vis-à-vis Canadian jurisdictions if it could reinforce the protections for Canadian mining companies it had already negotiated bilaterally with the dubiously democratic republics of eastern Europe.

THE IMPLICATIONS

By exploring the complex relationship between domestic networking and the intergovernmental negotiations of trade and investment agreements, this analysis can shed considerable light on the external linkages now built into North America's architecture.

The Relationship between Type I and Type II Modes of Governance

Rather than fostering the growth of fragmented, network-driven, specialized, functional, soft law governance, the intergovernmental trade- and investment-negotiating process supported by domestic, globally competitive corporate networks has proliferated muscular but private international arbitration systems. These have disaggregated the signatory states by replacing part of each state's previously autonomous judicial capacity with an international, hard law judicial arbitration system that empowers TNCs from every country that has ratified a bilateral investment treaty. It is not so much that governments were compelled to rely on transgovernmental networks to work out mutually acceptable commitments and practices as that they agreed to amputate part of their own government's corporate justice function and outsource it to an international arbitration institution under the aegis of the World Bank.

Nor does this analysis reveal a marked tendency to prefer coordinated, soft law executive commitments over formal, hard law legislation, market-driven over state-driven policy solutions, or problem-driven working groups of bureaucratic specialists over permanent councils. Instead, the international economic policy sphere displays executive unilateralism and hard law norms negotiated by government specialists, constitutionalized by treaties, and enforced through the World Bank's powerful International Convention for the Settlement of International Disputes.

The Enabling or Limiting Role of Domestic Institutions

Domestic constraints vary widely from state to state. If those directing their government's trade-negotiating process eschew political controversy, they do this by operating behind closed doors, not by avoiding institutional obstacles or choosing more informal, network-driven governance as a way to manage policy frictions. The pervasive consensus in the three countries' media that trade liberalization brings measurable, long-lasting economic growth and that protectionism is retrograde, selfish, and futile helps suppress the political backlash that might result from the restriction of each state's regulatory autonomy that is inherent in economic liberalization.

Like security, trade is a domain in which the three governments can affirm their traditional, superior role vis-à-vis civil society. Once empowered by

Congress with negotiating authority, USTR operates with considerable autonomy, constrained more by the politics of gridlock than by the separation of powers. Federal-provincial tensions have been co-opted in the process that Ottawa still leads, most recently and most notably for the Comprehensive Economic and Trade Agreement with the European Union at whose negotiating table the provinces' representatives were physically present. Although they were committed to being silent there, they were fully consulted by both the Canadian and the European Union's chief trade negotiators so that they would buy into the ultimate document.[15] Mexico's international economic agreement negotiators display no lack of administrative capacity: like their North American counterparts, they are highly trained and work with some autonomy from legislative-executive gridlock. Their chief constraint comes from business *camaras*, whose members lobbied against more trade liberalization because they have had trouble coping with the increased foreign competition generated by previous trade agreements.

The Nature of North America's Regional Governance

In the domain of North America's international economic negotiations, there is no evidence of an already-established but still-evolving complex of regional governance. Following NAFTA's negotiation, the three national ratification processes had a temporarily cohesive effect, as the three business communities supported the cause, but the three governments' subsequent separate treaty making underlined the continent's politically disintegrated reality. The ideational commonality of trade and investment negotiators' views suggests a high level of consensus within this transgovernmental epistemic community concerning the merits of their neoconservative trade-liberalization paradigm. But this uniformity does not in itself confirm the existence of active, specifically North American trade negotiators' networks. The trade negotiators in each country may well network with their continental colleagues, but there is no indication that they do so more than they do with fellow negotiators overseas.

As a decisive moment in an essentially permanent multilateral process, NAFTA was both important strategically for the US's global negotiating objectives in the GATT and important tactically for strengthening its economic preeminence in the continental periphery. For Canada and Mexico, the prime concerns were bilateral: weighing the trade-offs between their hoped-for greater access to and greater security in the US market against the autonomy-reducing concessions that Washington demanded in return. Their bilateral relationship with each other remained secondary.

NAFTA's negotiations were centralized and intergovernmental but short lived, making no progress in developing more permanent structures for intergovernmental decision making at the regional level. The three governments' subsequent negotiations of separate state-to-region or state-to-state trade and investment agreements with other partners confirmed the absence of any spirit of regionalism. Transcontinental networks in the form of significant working groups of bureaucrats are notable by their absence from this policy domain.

Unlike other issues discussed in this book, North American "region-ness" has not so much been constructed as diminished by the three countries' pursuing trade negotiations in separate silos. Nor does the evidence support the notion that the three governments look to regional policy coordination as a vehicle for building distinctive and effective policy models, which can leverage competition with rival regional models. However, it does confirm that North America's region-ness remains highly contested and that the political elites in all three countries—and particularly in Canada—have actively challenged the idea of a trilateral North America.

Far from the US-Mexico relationship being stifled on the Mexican side by political centralization and entrenched anti-Americanism, the Mexican government's trade-liberalization wing is run by technocrats who have long ingested the logics, assumptions, and hypotheses of neoconservative economics in US graduate schools.[16]

Trade and investment agreements are quintessentially structured, multi-issue initiatives, but the forms of policy coordination that they engender lie more on the side of policy outputs resulting from the negotiations than policy inputs that are generated in partial response to business' inputs and civil society's resistance. Any policy harmonization that does occur derives more from Washington's success in pressing its neighbors to incorporate such US standards as powerful intellectual property rights in their own legislative orders. Such one-way flows of norm diffusion resulting from the system's extreme power asymmetry can well be considered one of the distinctive structural and institutional features of North America as a region.

Whereas the European Union now behaves as a single actor in both trade and investment treaty negotiations, North America features three players, each pursuing its own international economic agenda with virtually no effort to achieve continental coordination. North America's absent institutionalization contributes to the disjunction between each country's international economic agenda and reinforces the continent's lack of actorness as a world region.

The continent's particular form of governance follows logically from North America remaining a giant's region. When it wanted a new rulebook, Washington agreed to negotiate and then dominated the negotiating process to secure its desired outcomes. When it was no longer interested in new rules in the trade-policy field, nothing much transpired. Indeed, the hegemon withdrew from playing a leadership role in updating the continental rulebook that it had caused to be written from the late 1980s the mid-1990s. Abroad, the continent's three member-states are separate policy entrepreneurs, negotiating independently at the level of government-to-government negotiations, which are separately driven by their own corporate constituencies and illustrate the unexpected disintegration that characterizes the North

American region. Tellingly, Mexico negotiated a trade agreement with the European Union in 2002. After long negotiations, Ottawa was on the verge of signing a Comprehensive Economic and Trade Agreement with Brussels in 2014, by which time Washington's negotiations of a Trans-Atlantic Trade and Investment Partnership were just getting off the ground. This spectacle of three separate negotiations with their European counterparts over more than a decade made a mockery of the admonition "for the countries of North America to negotiate trade agreements as a bloc."[17]

OUR CONCLUDING PARADOXES

What characterizes North America's mode of regional governance in international economic negotiations after NAFTA is its constitutional incoherence: the three governments have negotiated and ratified dozens of trade and investment agreements independently of each other. Paradoxically, the resulting "spaghetti bowl" of agreements is characterized by their normative coherence: the resulting rules appear increasingly similar, but this harmonization has not been generated by a specifically continental governance system.

The ultimate paradox is that, while foreign-investor protection agreements have been negotiated and ratified intergovernmentally, the resulting investor-state dispute arbitration system has hived off a significant judicial function from each signatory state's legal system and thereby created an autonomous international judicial institution that has vastly increased the power of transnational corporations vis-à-vis the host states in which they operate. Interstate, Type I diplomacy has, in effect, generated a new facet of international Type II judicial government driven by transnational corporations.

NOTES

1. Redekop 1976.
2. Babcock 1969.
3. Moffett 1907.
4. Government of Canada 1985.
5. Pastor 2004.
6. Castro-Rea 2006.
7. Clarkson, Davidson Ladly, Merwart, and Thorne 2005.
8. Vega and Winham 2002.
9. In contrast with having the concept signify the coercive control exercised by an imperial power, "hegemon" is used in this chapter to denote the leader of a regime whose weaker members participate in formulating and implementing the norms and rules by which their power system is governed.
10. For an extended elaboration of the argument that continental free trade agreements combined with the World Trade Organization comprise an external constitution for their member-states, see Schneiderman 2008; for a shorter exposition, see Clarkson 2004.

11. This section is based on material published in Clarkson 2008.
12. Jaramillo 2006.
13. World Bank 2014.
14. CIA 2012.
15. Author's confidential interviews in Brussels, July 2012 and July 2013.
16. The author's extensive confidential interviewing in the Mexican government's Secretaría de la Economía, 2006–2009.
17. Wilson and Biette 2014.

REFERENCES

Babcock, Robert Harper. 1969. *The A.F. of L. in Canada, 1896–1908: A Study in American Labor Imperialism*. Durham, NC: Duke University Press.

Castro-Rea, Julián. 2006. "Are US Business Priorities Driving Continental Integration?" *Edmonton Journal*, March 27, A14.

CIA. 2012. "Country Comparison: GDP," World Factbook. www.cia.gov/library/publications/the-world-factbook/rankorder/2001rank.html

Clarkson, Stephen. 2004. "Canada's External Constitution under Global Trade Governance" (pp. 1–31), in Ysolde Gendreau, ed., *Dessiner la société par le droit/Mapping Society through Law*. Montréal : Les Éditions Thémis, CRDP, Université de Montréal.

———. 2008. *Does North America Exist? Governing the Continent after NAFTA and 9/11*. Toronto: University of Toronto Press and Washington: Woodrow Wilson Center Press.

Clarkson, Stephen, Sarah Davidson Ladly, Megan Merwart, and Carlton Thorne. 2005. "The Primitive Realities of Continental Governance in North America" (pp. 168–194), in Edgar Grande and Louis W. Pauly, eds., *Complex Sovereignty: Reconstituting Political Authority in the Twenty-First Century*. Toronto: University of Toronto Press.

Government of Canada. 1985. *Royal Commission on the Economic Union and Development Prospects for Canada, vol. 1*. Ottawa: Queen's Printer.

Jaramillo, Carlos. 2006. *Challenges of CAFTA: Maximizing the Benefits for Central America*. Washington DC: The World Bank.

Moffett, Samuel. 1907 [1972]. *The Americanization of Canada*. 2nd ed., Toronto: University of Toronto Press.

Pastor, Robert A. 2004. "North America's Second Decade," *Foreign Affairs* 83 (1): 124–135.

Redekop, John H. 1976. "A Reinterpretation of Canadian-American Relations," *Canadian Journal of Political Science* 9 (2): 227–243.

Schneiderman, David. 2008. *Constitutionalizing Economic Globalization: Investment Rules and Democracy's Promise*. Cambridge UK: Cambridge University Press.

Vega, Gustavo and Gilbert Winham. 2002. "The Role of NAFTA Dispute Settlement in the Management of Canadian, Mexican and U.S. Trade and Investment Relations." *Ohio Northern University Law Review* 28 (3): 651–706.

Wilson, Christopher, and David Biette. 2014. *Is Geography Destiny? A Primer on North American Relations*. Washington DC: Woodrow Wilson Center Press.

World Bank. 2014. "Data." http://data.worldbank.org/indicator/NY.GDP.MKTP.CD/countries?order=wbapi_data_value_1984 wbapi_data_value&sort=desc&page=5

6 Lacking Linkages

Labor, Civil Society, and Subfederal Trade Policy in North America

Christopher J. Kukucha

One of the shortcomings of Type I and Type II regional models is the failure to adequately incorporate the relevance of nonstate actors. In an effort to address this, the following chapter focuses on the actions of civil society at the provincial and state levels in North America on matters of foreign trade policy. Specifically, has the absence of formalized institutions at the federal and trinational level in North America altered patterns of civil society activism on trade issues? Have coalitions of subfederal governments, the private sector, and civil society emerged, resulting in significant influence on North American trade policy? Do transnational linkages between subfederal actors exist and, if so, are they serving as a new mode of governance in North America?

Not surprisingly, the activity and relevance of subfederal societal actors is shaped primarily by the form and practice of federalism in all three countries. In Canada, intergovernmental mechanisms have evolved due to the constitutional legitimacy of provinces in this issue area, albeit with limited access for societal interests. In the US, subfederal societal interests focus on state legislatures in an attempt to influence the national agenda, where openings are limited for nongovernmental actors. In Mexico there is virtually no state interest in foreign trade policy due to corporatist traditions of engagement at the federal level within Mexican federalism. As a result, civil society has limited impact on trade policy in all three states, at least from an institutional perspective. Societal initiatives in Canadian provinces also focus mainly on services, forestry, agriculture, and the environment, although limited institutional access has shifted attention to municipalities and transnational movements. US societal interests, on the other hand, do pursue legislative initiatives within states regarding the review of international agreements, Presidential Fast-Track Authority, and the creation of Citizen Commissions, albeit with mixed success. Somewhat surprisingly, Mexican labor groups have sought transnational ties with other groups in Canada, the US, and Latin America, but this activity is driven by national organizations, and reinforces Mexico's overall lack of engagement and influence by societal interests at the subfederal level. Ultimately, there are no transnational ties between provincial and state societal interests indicating a shift toward a new model of North American governance.

CANADA

Canadian provinces have a degree of international legitimacy not granted to subfederal governments in other federations due to Canada's constitution and previous decisions by the Judicial Committee of the Privy Council (JCPC) and the Supreme Court of Canada. For the most part, the institutions of Canadian federalism have successfully responded to international pressures in this policy area. Starting with the Tokyo Round of the General Agreement on Tariffs and Trade (GATT), principles of executive federalism were adopted to increase consultation between both levels of government. This process continued to evolve in subsequent GATT rounds and during negotiations for the North American Free Trade Agreement (NAFTA) and the Canada-US Free Trade Agreement (CUSFTA). Today, Ottawa and the provinces discuss international trade in regular meetings of CTrade. There are also additional ad hoc sectoral discussions related to ongoing negotiations, such as the Canada-EU Comprehensive and Economic Trade Agreement (CETA), and assorted Mutual Reciprocal Agreements (MRAs).[1]

At the provincial level, the policy process is also driven by institutional actors. Surprisingly, the role of the political executive is somewhat marginalized, typically limited to crisis situations, the late stages of international negotiations, trade missions, or high-profile trade disputes, such as softwood lumber. In addition, provincial legislatures also play a minor role, outside of ratifying some international agreements, due to party discipline, a lack of legislative activity in this policy area, and the failure of most voters to identify with international trade at the constituency level. In contrast, provincial bureaucrats make significant contributions to policy outcomes, despite suffering from a lack of bureaucratic resources, especially in terms of budget and staffing. It is also important to note that Canadian provinces have an institutional capacity in this policy area that is lacking in US and Mexican states. This provides an access point for subfederal societal actors often missing in a North American context.

Historically, the impact of civil society at the subfederal level has shifted from region to region in Canada. In Ontario, most societal engagement focused on contentious issue areas, such as services or trade and the environment. Pressure, however, was not usually directed at the Ministry of Economic Development and Trade (MEDT), which had minimal contact with societal groups.[2] On water issues, for example, nongovernmental interests focused on the Ministry of Environment. For services, attention was usually directed at the Ministry of Education. Ontario also engaged First Nations groups in terms of the forestry sector.[3] In other cases, contact points with government are less clear. Due to the environmental implications of agricultural practices, these issues were often handled by the Ontario Ministry of Agriculture and Food.[4] In recent years, however, societal engagement with MEDT has increased. Ministry officials have consulted and shared working papers with the Canadian Centre for Policy Alternatives (CCPA), which has developed some expertise on services. According to one senior policy advisor, however, the input from the CCPA was productive, but it did "not define the province's final negotiating position on these issues."[5]

Quebec, on the other hand, has a corporatist tradition that does not exist in other provinces, with a high degree of labor involvement and nongovernmental engagement. The province's largest trade unions provide an organizational base for labor interests. Unlike other provinces, Quebec civil society also benefits from "peak associations." Such as the Fédération des Femmes du Québec, which draws together groups with similar interests.[6] In matters of foreign trade policy, however, contact is made directly with line departments and information is then passed to other relevant officials within the provincial bureaucracy. In response to pressure from civil society before and after the Organization of American States (OAS) Summit of the Americas in Quebec City, the Parti Québécois (PQ) also created a formal panel, the Quebec Observatory on Globalization, in the fall of 2001, although it failed to produce any meaningful engagement.[7] The subsequent election of Jean Charest's Liberal government ended efforts to further institutionalize these linkages. Instead, the Liberals relied on specialized think tanks and university groups for its nongovernmental input.[8]

Manitoba has a history of activist interest groups representing labor, gender, First Nations, and agriculture. Access to government, however, depended on which party was in power. Conservatives tended to favor agriculture, business, and Métis groups, while the NDP focused on organized labor and aboriginal interests.[9] In matters of foreign trade policy, consultation tends to be organized across a wide range of ministries. Engagement with societal actors is also often connected with efforts at the federal level, always with the goal of including a range of divergent interests, albeit with a limited impact on actual policy.[10] Saskatchewan also has a historical tradition of agrarian grassroots politics, but the increasingly pluralist nature of Saskatchewan's urban cities did create a number of new gender- and ethnic-based societal groups. Engagement with societal actors in the area of foreign trade policy, however, is usually with industry associations and tied to specific line departments. Much like Manitoba, Saskatchewan often partners with the federal government during its consultations. Regardless, limited bureaucratic resources restricted societal engagement in both Manitoba and Saskatchewan.[11]

In contrast to Saskatchewan and Manitoba, Alberta does not have a history of active civic engagement, although this shifted in the 1980s and 1990s with growing opposition to projects such as the Oldman River dam and proposed pulp mills in the northern part of the province.[12] For the most part, however, these trends were not reflected in consultation related to foreign trade policy. As in other provinces there is some contact with line departments and the Ministry of International and Intergovernmental Relations (MIIR), but this tends to be dominated by industry. In the past, however, MIIR has organized information sessions on services with a wide range of interests, including representatives from labor, teachers, and health care professionals.[13]

As with other provinces, most societal consultation related to trade policy in Atlantic Canada occurs in line departments. New Brunswick and Nova Scotia typically engage nongovernmental interests as part of larger federal consultations. The impact of these actors, however, tends to be minimal in this policy area, due to concerns related to the partisan nature of their input.[14] In Prince Edward Island, on the other hand, there is minimal engagement with provincial trade representatives beyond a narrow range of business interests.[15] Not surprisingly, societal groups in Newfoundland and Labrador are tied to the province's resource-based economy, especially the Grand Bank fisheries, offshore oil, and hydro electricity. Historically, there were close ties between merchants and political elites, but as these linkages declined, numerous sectoral and labor associations emerged. In most cases, however, efforts to access government occur at the ministry level.[16] Ultimately, the number of groups seeking access for international trade policy is limited in Atlantic Canada.

As in Quebec, British Columbia has a long legacy of societal engagement with labor, environmental groups, and First Nations interests. Environmental issues first gained prominence in BC during NDP governments in the 1990s but are less dominant today.[17] First Nations communities also increased access to the policy process in the 1990s due to judicial land claims and the Nisga'a Treaty.[18] As with environmental groups, however, First Nations do not have significant interest in provincial foreign trade policy. Labor, on the other hand, does have an interest in this policy area. In fact, it was pressure from a number of labor organizations that motivated BC to adopt its observer-only status position during NAFTA negotiations. The significance of labor was also evident in BC's position on WTO negotiations related to labor standards and services.[19] Having said that, it would be incorrect to overemphasize the impact of labor during this period. As one senior representative suggested, these groups "did not drive government policy, especially on matters of international trade."[20] Not surprisingly the relevance of societal groups further declined during the Liberal governments of Gordon Campbell and Christy Clark.[21] The exception appears to be the current controversy over the proposed Northern Gateway pipeline running from Alberta through Northern BC. For the most part, however, foreign trade policy issues are historically not priorities for societal interests in BC.

Despite these regional differences, societal groups did target the provinces during recent CETA negotiations. As early as 2008, societal groups such as the Council of Canadians (COC) became aware of provincial efforts, notably in Quebec, Ontario, and Manitoba, to promote trade talks with EU officials. Interest in the provinces was heightened as EU representatives repeatedly expressed concerns related to implementing a new agreement in areas of provincial jurisdiction. The COC responded by approaching provinces potentially receptive to input from the group. Manitoba and Nova

Scotia were targeted due to NDP governments with strong ties to labor and other social movements, as were Ontario and Quebec, due to predictable provincial concerns related to procurement, supply management, and liquor distribution boards. Over a span of three years the COC met with officials from Nova Scotia and Manitoba on several occasions. In Quebec, another group, the Rèseau Quèbecois sur l'Intègration Contintale (RQIC), also met with provincial officials, as did the Canadian Centre for Policy Alternatives and the Trade and Investment Research Project (TIRP) in Ontario. The Canadian Union of Public Employees (CUPE) also commissioned a legal opinion on potential provincial vulnerabilities related to CETA and services.

Typically meetings between government officials and civil society consisted of a briefing from a senior trade representative, followed by a question-and-answer session. Ultimately, however, civil society groups had mixed opinions of the effectiveness of CETA consultations. Although some provinces were very open to meeting and receiving unsolicited reports, others were less receptive. Quebec groups were initially optimistic about the potential openness of the newly elected PQ government that followed the Charest's Liberals, but were ultimately disappointed. Frustrated by a lack of progress with provincial officials, these groups soon refocused efforts on consultations at the municipal level, the mobilization of the pan-Canadian Trade Justice Network (TJN), as well as attempts to engage EU officials and European nongovernmental groups. The goal also shifted from influencing federal and provincial negotiating positions to a formal public review of CETA prior to it being signed by the Canadian government.[22] This did not occur prior to the chapter's publication.

THE US

There is less constitutional ambiguity in the US regarding the international activity of American states. For the most part, international relations are the sole domain of the federal government. During the past three decades, however, US states have gained increasing international relevance. A number of states, for example, have opened foreign offices seeking trade and investment. International dispute panels have also started examining issues of subfederal jurisdiction, including the GATT's *Beer I*, the WTO *Antigua-Barbuda Internet Gambling* case, and *Methanex* and *Loewen* cases under NAFTA Chapter 11. For all of these reasons, new forums of intergovernmental relations have evolved in the US related to subfederal foreign activity.

The primary conduit for American states in matters of trade policy is the Intergovernmental Policy Advisory Committee (IGPAC), established in 1975. In 2011, IGPAC's membership consisted of twenty-nine members selected from executive and legislative bodies of state, county, and municipal levels of government. The Office of the US Trade Representative (USTR) determines IGPAC's membership.[23] Initially, IGPAC provided selective recommendations during various rounds of the GATT. During the Uruguay Round, however, IGPAC produced its first comprehensive report covering the full range of the agreement.[24] Following NAFTA and the creation of the World Trade Organization, IGPAC's activity was suspended. It was renewed during the presidency of George W. Bush, when the 2002 Trade Act required IGPAC to report to the President, the USTR, and Congress no later than thirty days after the legislative branch was advised of a pending international trade agreement.

These developments prompted the USTR to alter the IGPAC process. Originally, elected officials dominated IGPAC membership, with staff from state governments serving on various working groups. With new tight timelines, however, officials with some expertise in trade policy were appointed to IGPAC to ensure that comprehensive reports would be produced within thirty days. Although IGPAC was expanded and nonelected officials became members of the advisory group, the forum still encountered problems. One specific issue was the need to receive security clearance to review confidential trade documents for pending international agreements. Several members of IGPAC were slow to apply and were not able to review relevant documentation. This resulted in a small number of IGPAC members writing the majority of the reports. A lack of staffing and support from the USTR also placed additional burdens on IGPAC members with clearance.[25]

In response to these concerns, IGPAC produced a memorandum calling for improved federal-state coordination on trade policy in 2004. The first recommendation called for the creation of a "Federal-State International Trade/Investment Policy Commission" to provide regular consultation between Washington and state governments.[26] The memorandum also suggested the Commission have bipartisan leadership with equal federal and state co-chairs, supported by a staff with appropriate knowledge of trade policy issues. Following the Canadian CTrade model, the new Commission would meet at least four times annually. Linkages would be established with national associations such as the Council of State Governments, National Governors Association, and the National League of Cities. The report also called for ties with business-oriented nongovernmental groups, such as the National Forum on Trade Policy and various Centers for International Business Education and Research (CIBERs). To date, however, the federal government has not moved to adopt any of these recommendations.

States not currently included in IGPAC, therefore, must seek other forms of federal representation. One mechanism, created by the USTR for NAFTA and WTO implementation purposes, was the State Single Point of Contact (SPOC) system. In each state the governor selects a representative who interacts with the USTR on matters of international trade. In most cases, SPOCs receive information in the form of USTR press releases and Federal Register notices.[27] Unfortunately, not all states are enthusiastic about the SPOC process. In a report released by the Forum on Democracy and Trade the USTR's use of the SPOC system was cited as "inconsistent," with the primary problem being inadequate information.[28] In addition to SPOC, states also have the option of pursuing matters of trade policy through Congressional delegations, although this is limited by a lack of interest and resources in Washington. Historically, Maine is one state active at the federal level due to Senator Olympia Snowe, a long-serving member of the Committee on Finance and its Sub-Committee on International Trade and Global Competitiveness.

Other states have engaged trade policy issues in "nontraditional" forums. One mechanism is State International Development Organizations (SIDO), which is associated with the Council of State Governments. Its mandate is trade promotion and skill development for state officials. In recent years, however, SIDO has increasingly focused on trade policy. The organization, for example, continues to push Washington for improved state-level data on services, exports, and imports. SIDO also hosts an annual "Washington Forum," in conjunction with the White House Office of Intergovernmental Affairs, where state representatives meet directly with senior staff from the Department of Commerce and USTR.[29] Another trade promotion platform is the US District Export Council, which consists of regional District Export Councils (DECs). Members of DECs are typically from the business community but also include representatives from the public sector. As with SIDO, the National DEC Steering Committee recently expanded its mandate and initiated a series of subcommittees on electronic communications, education/outreach, and legislative affairs. The National DEC also created a subcommittee specifically for trade policy.

A lack of access is also evident for nongovernmental interests on matters of trade policy. Historically, US trade policy was dominated by the economic priorities of producers who wielded considerable influence in Congress. Civil society was, for the most part, silent on international trade. Business leaders, academics, and unions engaged in debates on the issue, but most groups supported liberalized trade. In fact, during the postwar period, up until the 1960s, the American Federation of Labor-Congress of Industrial Organizations (AFL-CIO) supported the pursuit of free trade agreements under the assumption that American competitiveness would ensure employment and high wages for US workers.[30]

By the 1980s, however, trade negotiations began focusing on issues with a broader societal context. Attempts to reduce subsidies had the potential to impact domestic agricultural production, viewed as part of an "American" way of life, and intellectual property issues had implications for the pharmaceutical industry and the health and welfare of American citizens. Ultimately, it was NAFTA that highlighted divisions between labor, trade, and environmental groups. The NAFTA Side Deals were enough to defuse criticism from environmental interests but not organized labor. In fact, the AFL-CIO continued to oppose NAFTA as President Clinton fought to get the agreement through Congress.[31]

At the subfederal level, however, state and local interests have only become active on international trade issues during the past decade. For the most part, this activity focused primarily on legislative initiatives, which in some states were packaged together in one bill, consistently titled the *Jobs, Trade and Democracy Act*. Legislation in other states, however, had a more limited focus, usually introducing a broader legislative role for international trade policy and the creation of citizen commissions.

A state summary of legislative initiatives indicates a wide range of activity.[32] In Oregon Representative Brad Witt introduced House Bill 3340, calling for the creation of an Office of Trade Enforcement, and the creation of a Citizens' Commission on globalization, at the request of the Oregon Fair Trade Coalition in March 2007. Iowa also failed to pass bills in two consecutive sittings of the legislature. In 2007 SF 171, the *Jobs, Trade and Democracy Act*, and SF 168, calling for an advisory council on international trade and globalization, were defeated. The following year (February 2008) SF 2239 again called for an international trade and globalization advisory council. In Hawaii, Senate Bill SB1030, and its companion legislation House Bill HB30, calling for state legislative approval on procurement rules, was passed by the House and Senate in May 2007, subsequently vetoed by the Governor in July, and the veto rescinded by the legislature later that month. In the same year House Resolution 63, requesting a replacement of presidential Trade Promotion Authority (TPA), was also adopted. Similar house resolutions for Fast Track Authority were passed in Alabama (HR 121) and Pennsylvania (HR 276) in 2007. Other states pursuing similar legislative agendas, with varying degrees of success, include Minnesota, Wisconsin, Montana, California, New York, Maine, Vermont, New Hampshire, Utah, and Washington State.

In addition to state oversight, commissions and committees are a wide range of civil society groups with a focus on international trade. At the national level, Public Citizen, founded by Ralph Nader in 1971, relies primarily on private donations and funding. The organization has focused on a wide range of issues, including pharmaceuticals, the automobile industry, and nuclear power. Today it divides its interests into five main policy groups, the Congress Watch division, the Energy Program, Global Trade Watch, the Health Research Group, and its Litigation Group. The trade section of Public Citizen has an eclectic focus that includes "alternatives to corporate globalization, democracy, sovereignty, and federalism, deregulations and access to services, import safety, environment and health, jobs, wages and economic outcomes, and NAFTA, WTO and international trade agreements." All of these issues have some relevance to US states. In fact, Public Citizen was closely linked to state legislative programs in this policy area, often supporting legislation dealing with TPA and other pertinent international trade issues.[33]

As noted, the AFL-CIO is a labor-based organization with the support of fifty-six US unions representing over 12 million American workers. It also engages a wide range of issues, including health care, retirement, education, immigration, and workers rights. Unlike Public Citizen, however, the AFL-CIO concentrates primarily on current international trade negotiations with only minimal engagement on matters of subfederal trade policy. Comparatively, The Forum on Democracy and Trade covers a wide range of foreign trade issues with direct implications for US states, including services, procurement, and investment. In contrast to the AFL-CIO, Forum membership consists of US public officials from state and local governments usually with IGPAC affiliation. In recent years, however, the Forum has not engaged new international trade issues, such as the Trans-Pacific Partnership (TPP), or other US driven trade negotiations.[34]

A unique dynamic in the US, however, is the existence of civil society groups with an emphasis on international trade at the state level. Many of these groups are coalitions consisting of members from organized labor, churches, environmental groups, and other social justice and democratic rights organizations. In most cases, these groups emerged concurrently as state legislatures were considering legislative agendas focusing on international trade. The majority of these groups are also closely affiliated with, or are members of, Citizens Trade Campaign (CTC), a nationally based coalition founded in 1992 during the NAFTA process. Lori Wallach of Global Trade Watch, one of the founding members of the CTC, also has close ties with Public Citizen. In fact, much of the information on both the Public Citizen and CTC websites is overlapping.[35]

One of the oldest state-level groups, established in 2004, was the Maine Fair Trade Campaign, which was created at the same time the state government was passing its *Jobs, Trade, and Democracy Act*.[36] The Oregon Fair Trade Campaign was also founded in 2004 by Oregon branch of the AFL-CIO and the Sierra Club.[37] In Washington State, the Washington Fair Trade Coalition serves a similar function.[38] Other CTC-affiliated state coalitions also exist in Wisconsin, Florida, California, New York, Minnesota, Ohio, Pennsylvania, and Texas. In many cases these state organizations are nothing more than a name and contact information. Those subfederal groups with an online presence, however, post similar information and agendas, often with direct links to the main Public Citizen website.

This subfederal societal focus on international trade policy is undeniably unique in North America. CTC coalitions in Washington State and Oregon, for example, continue to have active agendas and frequently update their websites. At the same time, however, this activity needs to be considered in context. In fact, on closer examination, many of these initiatives appear to have stalled, or no longer exist. The New Hampshire Citizens Trade Policy Commission, for example, was eliminated in 2011, and Vermont's commission last took action in 2010 with a series of letters related to Korea-US trade negotiations and domestic regulation.[39] The reality is that a total of thirty-three US state legislatures did not pass or consider similar legislation related to international trade.

MEXICO

The form and practice of Mexican federalism does not facilitate intergovernmental relations on matters of foreign policy, especially in terms of international trade. Historically, Mexico has a centralized system of government, with extensive executive control. The President is both the Head of State and Government and from 1929 to 2000 was selected from one party, the *Partido Revolucionario Institucional* (PRI). During that period, the President, as leader of the PRI, held extensive powers of appointment within government and also had the authority to remove state Governors, usually by negotiated resignations. Historically, subfederal governments in Mexico are also fiscally constrained, with the federal government controlling over 80 percent of public revenue. Mexican states were also limited by rules against consecutive reelection, preventing elected officials from advocating state rights on an ongoing basis.[40]

Considerable decentralization has occurred in Mexico, however, since the 1980s. One initiative was electoral reform at the municipal level, which resulted in the election of *Partido Acción Nacional* (PAN) candidates in thirty-one cities. A new primary process for electing PRI candidates in state governor elections was also introduced. In addition, attempts were made to increase the revenue-generating capacity of municipal governments. Most significantly, the spending of Mexican subfederal governments increased by more than 40 percent during the last decade.[41]

One result of decentralization is the establishment of subfederal forums of consultation. The first attempt to institutionalize dialogue between state governments was the *Asociación Nacional de Gobernadores* (ANAGO). Formed in 1999, ANAGO was primarily a forum for *Partido de la Revolución* (PRD) party governors of Nayarit, Mexico City, Tlaxcala, and Zacatecas, to promote decentralization within Mexican federalism, including the delivery of services. In a notable federal-state dispute the Governor of Tlaxcala threatened to transfer the devolving educational system back to the federal government if more financial resources were not provided to the state. PRI governors from Oaxaca and Puebla soon followed with similar demands. Subsequent disputes, focused on health care and prisoners in state jails convicted of federal crimes, also began to include a wider range of PRD and PRI governors. As such, calls were made to move ANAGO beyond a PRD-based forum, which led to the creation of the *Conferencia Nacional de Gobernadores* (CONAGO) in 2002. CONAGO's primary purpose is to continue decentralization in Mexico. ANAGO still exists but functions as an organization for PRD state-based activities.

Not surprisingly, CONAGO has focused most of its attention on fiscal reform. One of its earliest lobbying efforts was for changes to the *Programa de Apoyos para el Fortalecimento de las Entidades Federativas* (PAFEF), created in 2000 to improve state finances from surplus oil revenues. Under the terms of PAFEF, state governors had to spend 50 percent of these funds on infrastructure projects. Not only did CONAGO successfully pressure for increased funding to PAFEF, but it also encouraged governors to not follow the 50 percent guidelines. Another financial success pushed by CONAGO was increased support for the *Acuerdo Nacional Hacendaria* (ANC), or Agricultural Pact, which supports state agricultural projects for peasants and other small producers. CONAGO also established the *Convención Nacional Hacendria* in 2004. Although three previous conventions had been held, the last in 1947, they focused primarily on the centralization of Mexico's fiscal relations. The 2004 convention, however, prioritized the opposite agenda. The conference unanimously approved 350 proposals, most on fiscal issues.[42]

Despite decentralization it is important to note that foreign policy remains the exclusive domain of the federal government. To date, only two Mexican states have bureaucratic departments exclusively committed to international affairs (Jalisco and Chiapas). The Mexican constitution also has no provisions allowing for intergovernmental consultation on matters of foreign policy. Any discussions that do occur with state or municipal officials are ad hoc and limited to specific issue-areas.

Issues of access are even more pronounced for subfederal Mexican societal interests. One obvious constraint is the absence of any significant nongovernmental activity for much of the twentieth century. Much of this was due to the dominance of the ruling PRI, which practiced formal corporatism and less institutionalized clientelism in its efforts to manage and co-opt potential dissent. Starting in the 1930s, for example, PRI efforts focused on the military but also peasants, labor, and other agrarian groups that served as the foundation for Mexico's revolutionary past. As Mexican society evolved, however, PRI methods became more sophisticated, with the need to incorporate traditional groups but also new urban middle-class professionals.

The PRI's focus on working- and middle-class Mexicans continued in the postwar period, with the government's protectionist trade policies and state investment in specific sectors of the economy. These economic priorities rewarded citizens responsible for manufactured goods but also those who could afford to purchase these products. State subsidies for food, gas, transportation, and housing also benefited these segments of Mexican society. The result was a labor- and middle-class that enjoyed comparatively high wages, a favorable standard of living, better education, and increased life expectancy. A shift occurred in the 1970s and 1980s, however, as the Mexican economy entered a period of steep decline. Citizen unrest also increased, as government resources were diverted to debt servicing, the dismantling of previous protectionist policies, and privatization. Ultimately, the PRI was no longer able to provide state-based patronage and support to its traditional political base. Wages also dropped, resulting in greater inequality in Mexican incomes.

The PRI's inability to continue its corporatist approach provided an opportunity for opposition parties and other citizen groups in Mexico, including independent unions, community organizations, and indigenous movements. Among these actors were also farming and middle-class interests that previously supported the PRI.[43] Initially these groups called for a return of services, increased wages, and social programs. Quickly, however, the agenda expanded to include fair elections and human rights. Linkages between civil society groups also began to increase, as did protests against state and municipal offices. A number of nongovernmental interests ran candidates in elections and offered support to unions, indigenous groups, debtors, and peasants, including the Zapatista rebels. The result was a mix of organizations linking middle-class interests with lower-class working and peasant groups.

Despite this coalescence, it was clear that different strategies were adopted by varying factions. Middle-class efforts were focused primarily within NGOs focusing on electoral reform and human rights. These actors did not focus on mass mobilization but instead adopted strategies designed to create legislative and electoral pressure. Lower-class interests tended to adopt different strategies, such as demonstrations, hunger strikes, barricades, and other forms of public protest. The linkages between middle- and lower-class groups, however, created larger and more representative coalitions, which represented a significant shift in Mexico's democratization process.

The institutionalization of this dissent occurred with the formation of the *Partido de la Revolución Democrática* (PRD). The democratization movement now had an official political presence and enjoyed success in state and local elections. Special efforts were made to select important and high-profile social movement members to run for office. Middle-class NGOs also continued to work with Mexico's most poor and vulnerable citizens, especially on issues related to fair elections and electoral reform. Despite this success, the PRD was limited in its impact. The rise of other legitimate opposition parties undercut its electoral support, numerous militants in the party hierarchy were jailed at various times, and the divergent interests of members often resulted in significant internal party divisions. Ultimately, it would be the *Partido Acción Nacional* (PAN), under Vincente Fox, that would sweep to power in federal elections in 2000.[44]

Although civil society groups in Mexico have concentrated attention on elections and human rights, it is important to note that some organizations have links to international trade. These groups, however, were relatively silent on trade issues prior to the negotiation of NAFTA. It was during this period that labor began to mobilize but not with a unified perspective. The Mexican Confederation of Labor (CTM), for example, supported NAFTA in contrast to most US and Canadian labor groups. Initially, the Mexican government actively engaged the CTM and other labor groups by allowing access to various consultative forums. As in Canada and the US, however, it was soon clear that these efforts did not result in any tangible impact on Mexico's final NAFTA negotiating position.[45]

In the aftermath of NAFTA, US and Mexican labor groups began to pursue cross-border cooperative initiatives in an attempt to strengthen their role in future trade negotiations. In 1998 John Sweeney, the president of the AFL-CIO, became the first prominent labor leader to visit Mexico in seventy-four years. The lack of American transnational coalition building during the Cold War reflected the strong protectionist attitudes of American labor during this period. Put simply, foreign workers were viewed as a threat to US jobs, which provided limited incentive for cooperation. This attitude began to change following NAFTA, however, and provided the catalyst for Sweeney's visit to Mexico. During his visit Sweeney met with a wide range of groups including the CTM but also new organizations such as the National Union of Workers (UNT). This broadening of engagement also subsequently strengthened the Inter-American Regional Workers Organization (ORIT), a regional organization coordinating labor groups throughout the Americas.

This initial cooperation, and a revitalized ORIT, began to raise the expectations of labor leaders throughout Latin and North America. The relatively negative NAFTA experience for many labor groups resulted in a call for greater cooperation between civil society in order to avoid labor's perceived marginalization in future negotiations. These efforts were not limited to the US and Mexico but also included the involvement of the Canadian Labour Congress and large organizations in Brazil and Chile, such as the Unified Workers' Central (CUT). This cooperation also resulted in the creation of the Hemispheric Social Alliance (HSA), a broad coalition of labor, NGOs, and other civil society groups, that actively opposed the Free Trade Area of the Americas (FTAA) negotiations between 2000 and 2004. Almost immediately, however, tensions began to emerge between groups advocating an end to capitalism and international trade, and "moderate" organizations such as ORIT and the AFL-CIO. Some groups, such as the CMT, refused to participate in the HSA. The broadening of the coalition also resulted in an agenda that transcended trade and included a wide range of environmental and social issues.[46]

It is important to note that the role of Canadian civil society in this emerging transnational cooperation extended beyond the Canadian Labour Congress. In fact, during the negotiation of NAFTA opposition groups emerged in Mexico to challenge the pro-trade position of the CTM. The Mexican Action Network on Free Trade (*Red Mexicana de Acción Frente al Libre Comercio* [RMALC]), for example, was an umbrella organization for over one hundred grassroots environmental, indigenous, labor, women's rights, and neighborhood groups. Many of the labor groups within the RMALC had ties with Quebec-based unions dating back to the 1970s. Some observers have suggested it was these initial Canadian ties that sparked interest amongst Mexican groups to strengthen linkages with US labor in the post-NAFTA era.[47]

Following the implementation of NAFTA, a number of public sector unions in Canada also began forging alliances with US and Mexican labor groups. These included the Canadian Union of Postal Workers, the Public Service Alliance of Canada, and the Canadian Union of Public Employees.

For the most part, these ties were limited to information sharing and research, especially related to the impact of liberalized trade on public services. One example was the Coalition to Defend Public Education, a group of over 500,000 teachers in the US, Canada, and Mexico, concerned about the potential commercialization of public education. Telecommunications was another sector of cooperation with evolving ties between the Communications, Energy, and Paperworkers of Canada; the Communication Workers of America; and the *Sindicato de Telefonistas de la República Mexicana* or Telephone Workers' Union of the Mexican Republic (STRM). These efforts resulted in joint cooperation in this sector on issues related to pay equity. Mexican unions also directly engaged US disputes due to the high level of Mexican migrants working in the telecommunications industry. In one case, Mexican representatives traveled to California to participate in a protest at a Sprint call center in San Francisco. In another example the United Steelworkers of America and the Canadian Autoworkers jointly participated in NAALC proceedings.[48]

LACKING LINKAGES: CHALLENGES FACING SUBFEDERAL CIVIL SOCIETY IN NORTH AMERICA

This chapter set out to answer three questions regarding the nature of subfederal societal activity related to trade policy in North America. The first focused on institutional realities at the subfederal, federal, and trinational levels. Ultimately, the role of subfederal societal actors is primarily defined by the form and practice of federalism in all three countries. As noted, subfederal governments in North America have varying levels of legitimacy in the negotiation and implementation of international trade agreements. Canadian provinces, for example, have the longest history of involvement due to a level of constitutional ambiguity on matters of foreign trade policy. In the US and Mexico, however, international trade is clearly a federal responsibility, outside of a small number of sectors such as procurement. Arguably, this could change as international agreements become more intrusive into domestic policy space and WTO dispute resolutions have binding implications for subfederal governments in North America. At the current time, with the possible exception of Canada, there is limited access for subfederal institutional actors in the foreign trade policy of all three North American states.

Not surprisingly, these institutional realities had a direct impact on the activity of subfederal societal actors, which tended to focus efforts at the state and provincial levels. In Canada, for example, there are distinct sectoral and regional differences influencing the activity of nongovernmental actors. In Ontario, linkages tend to be driven by business, although First Nations groups have established a role in the forestry sector. Quebec has attempted to initiate formal consultative frameworks in the past, but the

Liberals and PQ have returned to a more elite driven process of interaction. Alberta, on the other hand, faces negligible demands from societal considerations and continues to focus on concerns raised by industry. Although the NDP in British Columbia improved access during the 1990s, the role of labor and environment has diminished considerably during the past decade. The recent CETA negotiations also suggest a limited impact for societal actors at the provincial level.

The US also has a pattern of subfederal activity by nongovernmental actors related to foreign trade policy. Well-funded national groups such as Public Citizen, with some involvement from organized labor, led by the AFL-CIO, have targeted numerous state legislatures in an attempt to introduce legislation focusing on state involvement in the negotiation and implementation of international trade agreements and presidential TPA. These legislative initiatives also helped create a number of state citizen commissions that include elected and bureaucratic members of government, as well as representatives from civil society. Another unique feature of US states is the existence of societal groups with an emphasis on international trade. In most cases, these organizations consist of members from organized labor, churches, environmental groups, and other social justice and democratic rights organizations. The majority of these groups are also closely affiliated with, or are members of, the Citizens Trade Campaign or Public Citizen.

Despite this proliferation of activity, it is clear that US subfederal initiatives have only a minor impact on either state or federal foreign trade policy. First, interest in sub-federal international trade peaked during a small window of activity between 2004 and 2009. During the first wave of activity, these groups targeted the expiration of TPA in 2007, which was ultimately not extended. Building support for the Democratic challenge to the Republicans in the 2008 presidential election was also part of the strategy, thereby illustrating Tip O'Neil's famous observation that "all politics is local." Today, however, Public Citizen and labor have shifted attention and resources away from subfederal international trade to other campaigns, such as governor recall efforts and the 2016 US presidential election.[49]

This raises a question as to why national groups, such as Public Citizen, would adopt a strategy of targeting US states in an attempt to influence Congress. Again, one possible explanation is the nature of American federalism. Specifically, the US has a tradition of weak party linkages between federal and state governments. There is also an absence of robust party discipline, which, combined with an executive branch that is typically less powerful than the legislature, creates an environment conducive for lobbying by individuals, firms, and state governments. Although Canadian parties also have difficulty transcending federal and provincial politics, durable traditions of party discipline and strong executive government tend to promote a less confrontational form of federalism. Donald Smiley described this interaction as "executive federalism," which he argued was due to the lack of effective brokerage mechanisms for provincial representation within federal institutions.[50] Although Canada has similar nationally based groups with a focus on international trade, such as the Council of Canadians and the Canadian Centre for Policy Alternatives, these organizations have typically engaged provinces by providing studies critical of specific trade issues or informal conversations and lobbying. Regardless, executive federalism is often cited as a key difference between "cooperative" and "coercive" systems of intergovernmental relations. This study supports these conclusions.

Finally, Mexico also has a different pattern of subfederal involvement, once again driven by the realities of Mexican federalism. Historically, societal activity was tied to corporatist relations between the ruling PRI party and select labor and nongovernmental groups until the economic crisis of the 1970s and 1980s. The emergence of new groups representing the interests of Mexico's middle and lower classes, however, challenged the status quo but focused on human rights and fair elections as opposed to international trade. Many of these groups also adopted very different strategies to influence government, with some coalitions highlighting legislative electoral pressure and others pursuing other forms of mass mobilization, such as demonstrations, hunger strikes, and other protests. These new groups, however, did capture the attention of new political parties, such as the PRD and PAN, which both attempted to tap into their potential electoral support.

Ultimately, this chapter makes it clear that subfederal civil society has only a limited impact on foreign trade policy in North America. Where activity does occur, it is limited to "process" issues and cannot be tied to policy outcomes at the federal or international level. It is important to note, however, that challenges for societal groups are not solely tied to federalism. Organized labor, for example, has suffered from a decline in manufacturing jobs where most well-paid, secure, unionized jobs existed. The rise of the service sector, with minimal union representation, as well as a new generation of workers with a general antipathy for unions, all further contribute to a decline in influence. Even public sector unions remain particularly vulnerable in the aftermath of the 2008 global economic crisis, as opinion turns against the perception of high wages, overly generous benefit packages, and rich pensions. Traditional political influence within the NDP in Canada and the Democrats in the US is also in decline, as these parties begin to distance themselves from electorally unpopulated allegiances.[51]

On another level, broader societal engagement is limited by a series of other problems. One example is consultation fatigue. Just as governments face limited resources, so do nongovernmental interests, and most groups do not have the capacity to engage in dialogue with different ministries at both levels of government. There is also the reality that "civil society" is not a monolith and different groups have varying interests. In Canada, for example, organized labor, the environment, and aboriginal groups have all actively engaged government on softwood lumber and have enjoyed some success at various times, despite very different agendas.[52] A third point is that foreign trade is an extremely complicated and technical issue that often goes beyond the basic understanding of observers not directly involved in the actual policy process. It is also clear that the events of September 11, 2001, shifted the North American policy agenda from completing the FTAA and Doha Round negotiations to broader security concerns.[53]

Finally, the third purpose of this chapter was to examine existing transnational linkages and determine if they represented a new form of governance in North America. It is clear that transnational linkages tied to international trade exist in North America, but they do not include significant participation from labor groups organized at the subfederal level in Canada, the US, and Mexico. For the most part these ties also focus primarily on domestic bargaining and other local issues. Unfortunately, much of the initial success and optimism surrounding transnational civil society in North America has faded. Part of this is due to the collapse of the NAFTA NAALC process. Initially the NAFTA Labor Side Deal and the NAALC hearing and dispute process provided a focus for labor cooperation. This eventually ended, however, as few meaningful cases moved forward and culminated with the closing of the Commission for Labor Cooperation (CLC). At a more basic level, transnational solidarity in North America was doomed to fail, due to the primary concerns of all labor groups, namely to "lobby against the negative impacts of free trade on the domestic labor market."[54]

NOTES

1. Kukucha 2008.
2. Personal interview, May 30, 2002.
3. Lindquist and Wellstead 2001, 422–23; Levasseur and Paterson 2006, 221.
4. Montpetit 2003, 99.
5. Personal interview, August 31, 2005.
6. Montpetit 2004, 169–70.
7. Michaud 2003, 32.
8. Personal interview, June 4, 2003.
9. Brock 1996, 110–11.
10. Personal interview, June 2, 2004.
11. Personal interview, May 31, 2004.
12. Laycock 1990.
13. Personal interview, July 19, 2004.
14. Personal interview, May 29, 2003.
15. Personal interview, May 28, 2003.
16. Personal interview, September 2, 2005.
17. Hoberg 2002, 24–27.
18. Poelzer 2002.
19. BC Ministry of Labour 1999, 1.
20. Personal interview, July 14, 2004.
21. Personal interview, August 28, 2002.
22. Trew 2013.
23. Intergovernmental Policy Advisory Committee 2006, 5.
24. Intergovernmental Policy Advisory Committee 1994.
25. Ibid.

26. Wilkie 2004, 2–3.
27. Office of the US Trade Representative, *How USTR Consults with State and Local Governments*. www.ustr.gov/Benefits_of_Trade/States/How_USTR_consults_with_State_Local_Governments.html
28. Forum on Democracy and Trade 2006, 6.
29. State International Development Organizations, Programs and Resources. www.sidoamerica.org/programs.htm
30. von Bülow 2009, 6.
31. Destler 2005, 253–55.
32. Public Citizen, *Spotlight on your State*. www.citizen.org/Page.aspx?pid=1195
33. Public Citizen, *Globalization and Trade*. www.citizen.org/Page.aspx?pid=1328
34. Forum on Democracy and Trade, *Trade and Federalism*. www.forumdemocracy.net/section.php?id=121
35. Citizens Trade Campaign, *What Is Citizen Trade Campaign?* www.citizenstrade.org/ctc/about-ctc/what-is-citizens-trade-campaign/
36. Maine Fair Trade Campaign, *Home*. www.mainefairtrade.org/
37. Oregon Fair Trade Campaign, *Home*. www.citizenstrade.org/ctc/oregon/
38. Washington Fair Trade Coalition, Home. http://washingtonfairtrade.org/
39. The Vermont Legislature, Commission on International Trade & Sovereignty, *2011–2012 Legislative Session*. https://leg2.vermont.gov/sites/legislature/Committees/CTFWG/VTCITSS/default.aspx
40. Ward et al 1999, 66–67; Weldon 1997.
41. De Remes 2006, 185.
42. Ibid, 188–96.
43. Foweraker 1993; La Botz 1988; Williams 2001.
44. Shefner 2007, 188–93.
45. von Bülow 2009, 7.
46. Ibid, 8–15.
47. Nolan Garcia 2001, 95.
48. Clarkson 2008, 107–8.
49. Yakabuski 2012, A17.
50. Smiley 1987, 85.
51. Allemang 2012, F1.
52. Wilson 1998.
53. Wolfe 2007, 31–32.
54. Clarkson 2008, 110.

REFERENCES

Allemang, John. 2012. "Organized Labour is Fighting to Survive," *Globe and Mail*, March 24, F1.

BC Ministry of Labour. 1999. "BC Seeks Federal Support for Labour Standards in WTO," *News Release*, November 26.

Brock, Kathy. 1996. "Lifting Impressions: Interest Groups, the Provinces, and the Constitution" (pp. 95–122), in Christopher Dunn, ed., *Provinces: Canadian Provincial Politics*. Peterborough: Broadview Press.

Clarkson, Stephen. 2008. *Does North America Exist? Governing the Continent after NAFTA and 9/11*. Toronto: University of Toronto Press.

De Remes, Alain. 2006. "Democratization and Dispersion of Power: New Scenarios in Mexican Federalism," *Mexican Studies/Estudios Mexicanos* 22 (1): 175–204.

Destler, I.M. 2005. *American Trade Politics*. 4th ed., Washington DC: Institute for International Economics.

Forum on Democracy and Trade. 2006. *The Maine Citizen Trade Policy Commission: A Model for State Oversight and Communication on International Trade and Investment Issues*, November 29: 1–16.

Foweraker, Joe. 1993. *Popular Mobilization in Mexico: The Teachers Movement, 1977–87.* Cambridge: Cambridge University Press.

Intergovernmental Policy Advisory Committee. 1994. *The Uruguay Round of Multilateral Trade Negotiations: Report of the Intergovernmental Policy Advisory Committee*, January 11: 1–33.

———. 2006. *The US-Colombia Trade Promotion Agreement (TPA): Report of the Intergovernmental Policy Advisory Committee*, September 15: 1–25.

Nolan Garcia, Kimberley A. 2011. "The Evolution of United States-Mexico Labor Cooperation (1994–2009): Achievements and Challenges," *Politics and Policy* 39 (1): 91–117.

Hoberg, George. 2001."Policy Cycles and Policy Regimes: A Framework for Studying Policy Change" (pp. 3–30), in Benjamin Cashore, et al., eds., *Search of Sustainability: British Columbia Forest Policy in the 1990s.* Vancouver: UBC Press.

Kukucha, Christopher J. 2008. *The Provinces and Canadian Foreign Trade Policy.* Vancouver: UBC Press.

La Botz, Dan. 1988. *The Crisis of Mexican Labor.* New York: Praeger.

Laycock, David. 1990. *Populism and Democratic Thought in the Canadian Prairies, 1910–1945.* Toronto: University of Toronto Press.

Lindquist, Evert, and Adam Wellstead. 2001. "Making Sense of Complexity: Advances and Gaps in Comprehending the Canadian Forest Policy Process" (pp. 419–446), in Michael Howlett, ed., *Canadian Forest Policy: Adapting to Change.* Toronto: University of Toronto Press.

Levasseur, Karine, and Stephanie Paterson. 2006. "Forest Sector Regulation and Communities" (pp. 209–233), in G. Bruce Doern and Robert Johnson, eds., *Rules, Rules, Rules, Rules: Multi-Level Regulatory Governance.* Toronto: University of Toronto Press.

Montpetit, Éric. 2003. *Misplaced Distrust: Policy Networks and the Environment in France, the United States, and Canada.* Vancouver: UBC Press.

Montpetit, Éric. 2004. "Can Québec Neo-Corporatist Networks Withstand Canadian Federalism and Internationalization?" (pp. 165–181), in Alain G. Gagnon, ed., *Québec: State and Society.* 3rd ed., Peterborough: Broadview Press.

Michaud, Nelson. 2003. "Quebec and Continental Integration: The Characteristic Strategies of a Federated Actor," paper presented at the annual meeting of the Canadian Political Science Association, Halifax, Nova Scotia, May.

Poelzer, Greg. 2002. "Aboriginal Peoples and Environmental Policy in Canada: No Longer at the Margins" (pp. 87–106), in Debora L. VanNijnatten and Robert Boardman, eds., *Canadian Environmental Policy: Context and Cases.* 2nd ed., Toronto: Oxford University Press.

Shefner, Jon. 2007. "Rethinking Civil Society in the Age of NAFTA: The Case of Mexico," *Annals of the American Academy of Political and Social Science* 610: 182–200.

Smiley, Donald V. 1987. *The Federal Condition in Canada.* Toronto: McGraw-Hill Ryerson.

Trew, Stuart. 2013. "Correcting the Democratic Deficit in the CETA Negotiations: Civil Society Engagement in the Provinces, Municipalities, and Europe," *International Journal* 68 (4): 568–575.

von Bülow, Marisa. 2009. "Networks of Trade Protest in the Americas: Toward a New Labor Internationalism?" *Latin American Politics and Society* 51 (2): 1–28.

Ward, Peter M., Victoria Rodríguez, and Enrique Cabrero. 1999. *New Federalism and State Government in Mexico: Bringing the States Back In.* Austin: The University of Texas at Austin.

Weldon, Jeffrey A. 1997. "The Political Sources of Presidentialism in Mexico" (pp. 225–258), in Scott Mainwaring and Mathew S. Shugart, eds., *Presidentialism and Democracy in Latin America.* Cambridge: Cambridge University Press.

Wilkie, Kay. 2004. "Intergovernmental Policy Advisory Committee Memorandum: Recommendations for Improving Federal-State Trade Policy Coordination," August 5: 1–12.

Williams, Heather. 2001. *Social Movements and Economic Transition: Markets and Distributive Conflict in Mexico.* Cambridge: Cambridge University Press.

Wilson, Jeremy. 1998. *Talk and Log: Wilderness Politics in British Columbia, 1965–1996.* Vancouver: UBC Press.

Wolfe, Robert. 2007. "Transparency and Public Participation in the Canadian Trade Policy Process" (pp. 21–73), in Mark Halle and Robert Wolfe, eds., *Process Matters: Sustainable Development and Domestic Trade Policy.* Winnipeg: International Institute for Sustainable Development.

Yakabuski, Konrad. 2012. "Democrats in a Fretful State over Wisconsin," *Globe and Mail*, May 26, A17.

7 Security, Technology, and Market Restructuring in North America's Energy Industries and the Demise of Mexico's State-Oil-Monopoly Regime

Isidro Morales

Extensive integration of energy supplies in North America began with the negotiation of the 1989 Canada-US Free Trade Agreement (CUSFTA) and intensified through the 1994 North American Free Trade Agreement (NAFTA). As part of the CUSFTA, Canada guaranteed energy supplies to the US, and through NAFTA, Mexico began liberalization of cross-border energy trade in gas and electricity, but it maintained the state monopoly on both upstream and downstream activities. After NAFTA came into effect, security concerns—mainly in the US—spurred further cooperation and coordination through ad hoc mechanisms, such as the North American Energy Working Group (NAEWG), launched in 2001, and the Security and Prosperity Partnership (SPP), which ran from 2005 to 2009. However, the driving force behind continental integration of energy markets in North America has not been intergovernmental cooperation, but rather policy choices and market restructuring taking place *within* each of the three countries, as each government sought to respond to its own energy opportunities and challenges. These policy choices and market developments triggered the so-called energy revolution that began in Canada and was followed with impressive success in the US.

This energy revolution is impacting both energy supply, by making available a huge amount of nonconventional hydrocarbon resources (i.e., tar sands, shale/tight oil, and gas), and energy demand, by increasing focus on energy conservation and substitution—through, for example, the promotion of renewables (mainly in electricity generation) and the marketing of hybrid and plug-in vehicles. The leading country of this revolution is the US, which since the turn of the century has launched myriad policies targeting technology innovation for exploiting and marketing nonconventional fuels and renewables, conservation, and a new generation of automotive engines able to substitute liquid fuels with electricity or fuel-cells. The results are becoming apparent since the turn of the present decade: Canada has become a tar sands powerhouse, while the US has rapidly increased the domestic supply of nonconventional oil and gas, and there is an expanding market for nonconventional automobiles. These impressive changes are transforming the role to be played by North America in global energy markets in the years to come. Furthermore, the energy revolution taking place within the US is setting up that country as a "nonconventional" energy power. The first and second parts of this chapter will explain, in a summarized way, the major features of these changes taking place in Canada and the US.

In contrast to the rapid changes in Canada and the US, Mexico has struggled to undertake market reforms in the energy sector, traditionally monopolized by two state firms. Most involved have agreed that the status quo in the way the industry is managed has become unsustainable, but there is no consensus on how to transform it. The third part of this chapter will review post-NAFTA energy reforms attempted to introduce market competition in this sector, and it will explain their limited or dysfunctional results. The fourth and final part of the chapter will summarize the purpose and implications of the reform bill submitted to Congress by President Peña in August 2013 and passed December 18. This bill enacted a major constitutional amendment, which marks the end of the state-oil-monopoly regime in almost all aspects of the hydrocarbon and electric industries, a dramatic departure from the model that prevailed in Mexico through most of the twentieth century. I argue that the political obstacles to energy sector reform in Mexico—and the specific policy mechanisms that the Peña administration introduced to get past those obstacles—are reflections of the country's own distinct historical experiences and political institutions. Yet the pressures for policy change and the design of the specific reforms passed by the Mexican Congress are also intimately connected with the industry and policy changes taking place in Canada and the US, and are thus an integral part of the broader transformation of the regional energy agenda in North America.

Although NAFTA and the SPP failed to put in operation a "cooperative regime" on energy matters among the three nations, I conclude that energy policy in North America has been characterized by a form of multi-level governance. Policy coordination in this area has not been led by federal government agencies, or embedded in formal agreements or institutions, but rather played out at the subregional or subnational levels, in ways similar to parallel developments in other related issue-areas, such as climate change policy and electricity trade.

THE LOOMING OF NONCONVENTIONAL FOSSIL FUELS IN NORTH AMERICA

Although North American countries have traditionally been major world hydrocarbon producers and consumers, their positioning in world markets has changed rapidly over the past ten to fifteen years. The region is emerging as a major reservoir and producer of nonconventional fossil fuels (i.e., oil sands and oil and gas from shale and tight geological formations). While in 1998 overall proved oil reserves of the region amounted to 100 billion barrels (Bbls), by 2011 they had more than doubled to 217.5 Bbls, accounting for 13 percent of world reserves. Figure 7.1 traces this major transformation on North American resources, mainly due to the rapid increase, at the end of the 1990s, of Canadian oil sands resources, located in Alberta and along the Western Canada Sedimentary Basin (WCSB).[1] At that time, Mexico also thoroughly reassessed its own proved reserves following international standards, stemming a rapid decline in its assets, which has had a major impact in Mexican production and exports, as discussed in more detail in the third part of this chapter.

Canadian production has steadily increased from the late 1990s to the present, from 2.7 to 3.8 million barrels per day (Mbl/d) in 2012. The country is anticipated to become a major global liquid fuel supplier in the years to come, with a production forecast of 6.6 Mbl/d in 2035.[2] Virtually all of Canada's oil and gas surpluses are traded to American outlets because its energy industry is heavily integrated, by pipelines, to the lower forty-eight states. Three companies operate most of the export pipelines to continental America: Enbridge, Kinder Morgan, and TransCanada, the latter having a major stake in export gas lines as well. Most of these pipelines are dedicated to serving the US system, particularly the Illinois and Oklahoma terminals. While the most heavily populated Canadian provinces (Ontario and Quebec) are primarily served by imported oil, Canada's net exports have steadily increased south of the border, consolidating its position as the major foreign oil and gas supplier to the US market.[3] If the oil sands boom continues, however, and oil and gas shale production in the US continues to expand rapidly, Canadian producers are bound to diversify their export markets,

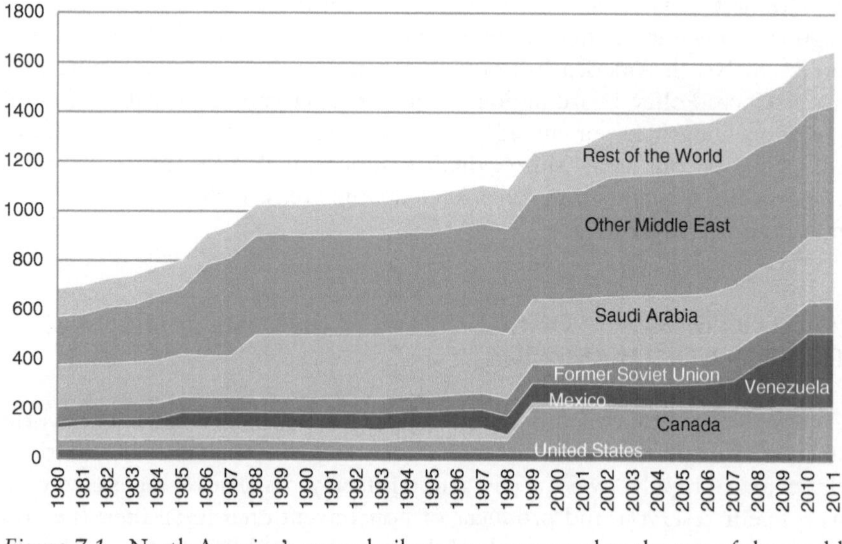

Figure 7.1 North America's proved oil reserves compared to the rest of the world (billion barrels), 1980–2011

Source: British Petroleum, Historical Workbook 2013

probably to Asia. One major constraint for expanding foreign markets is infrastructure and transmission pipelines, which are subject to regulatory mandates and environmental concerns, as reflected in the controversy surrounding TransCanada's Keystone XL pipeline.[4]

Before the US shale gas boom, it was anticipated that Canadian gas exports will not be enough to meet growing American requirements, thus prompting the siting and construction of liquefied natural gas (LNG) plants in the US. However, the rapid increase in American production over the last decade is dramatically changing the gas scenario throughout North America.

By contrast with Canada, Mexico's energy scene looks quite gloomy. Proved reserves of oil and gas have severely declined, and the country is struggling to confront infrastructure, institutional, economic, and political constraints in order to further develop its vast nonconventional fossil fuels potential. While still a major oil and gas producer, Mexico has become a net importer of gasoline and natural gas, and risks becoming a net importer of crude oil due to growing oil consumption outpacing the expansion of domestic supply. Because, as discussed in greater detail later in the chapter, Mexico's state-oil-monopoly regime is centered around self-sufficiency, this has spurred political pressure for a sweeping "energy reform," to boost reserves and production. Today, about 80 percent of crude oil exports go to the US, and most of Mexico's imports of gas and petroleum products come from the US. Although pipeline interconnection is not as extensive and sophisticated as that between Canada and the US, Mexico's oil and gas industries are de facto integrated with US markets for geographical and logistical reasons.

The US remains the major oil and gas producer and net importer in North America and globally. US oil and gas addiction deepened through the last decade, while domestic supply of crude oil continued its secular decline, until 2007, when production from tight formations joined the shale gas boom initiated some years before. These trends explain why US net oil dependence reached a historical high of 60 percent of its domestic consumption in 2005, then declined to 40 percent in 2012. A similar trend dominates gas markets. Throughout these major market transformations, Canada and Mexico have remained key partners, with increasingly continentalized energy industries.

Sixty percent of US crude oil imports comes from just four countries: Canada, Saudi Arabia, Venezuela, and Mexico. Canada rapidly increased its share since the turn of the century, from 16 percent of overall imports in 2000 to 28 percent in 2012. (Figures 7.2 and 7.3 clearly show Canada's strategic position as a liquid and gas fuel supplier to the US.) During this same period, Saudi Arabia, Venezuela, and Mexico reduced their shares (Mexico from 12 to 10 percent of all imports during the same years) but remain major suppliers to the American market. Overall Mexico's crude oil exports declined from a peak of 1.8 Mbl/d in 2004 to just 744,825 bl/d in 2012. In spite of political tensions between Washington and Caracas during the Chavez administration, Venezuela has also remained a key supplier to the American market, in as much as US refineries have the capacity to process Venezuelan heavy oils.

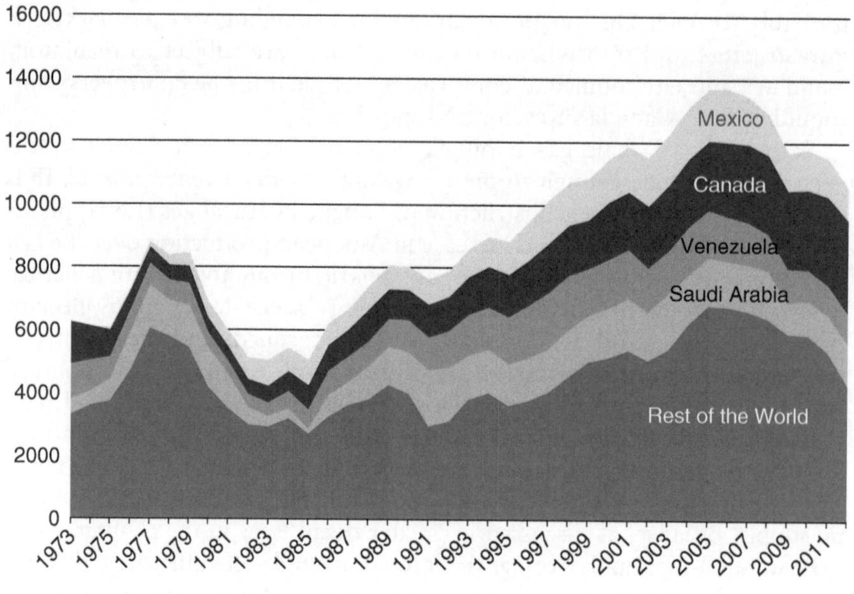

Figure 7.2 US crude and petroleum products imports from main suppliers (thousand barrels per day), 1973–2012

Source: US Department of Energy.

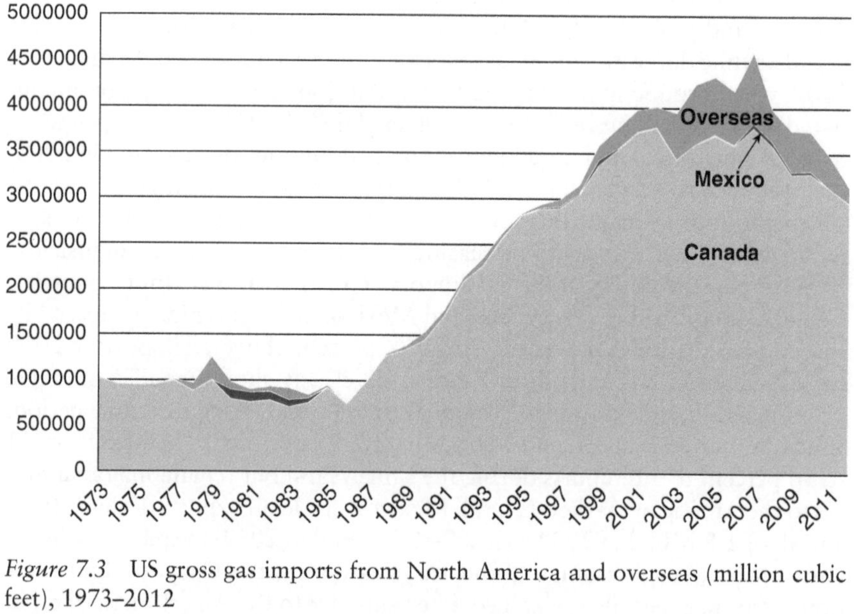

Figure 7.3 US gross gas imports from North America and overseas (million cubic feet), 1973–2012

Source: US Department of Energy

Although North America accounts for 5.2 percent of world proved reserves of natural gas, only Canada is a net provider to the US. Mexico used to export some marginal production north of its border, as shown in Figure 7.3, but has become a net importer from Texas. Currently, gas imports account for 19 percent of Mexico's domestic consumption. The gas scene in the region is changing very rapidly since the irruption of shale and tight gas production in the US.

Table 7.1 summarizes the most updated assessment of technically recoverable (TR)[5] shale oil and gas resources in the region. It compares nonconventional resources of each country and region with their respective proved reserves. In the case of the US, shale gas reserves (including tight gas resources) more than double their current proved reserves, and account for 9 percent of currently assessed worldwide shale gas resources. Canada's and Mexico's numbers are even more impressive, as nonconventional gas reserves multiply manifold their current proved gas reserves.[6] As a region, North America accounts for 24 percent of current TR world shale gas potential. China is the only individual country that rivals each of the three North American countries in terms of TR resources. As for nonconventional oil resources (tight and shale oil), North America accounts for 24 percent of overall assessed assets, the US alone representing 17 percent. Although shale resources come from different geological deposits than tight resources, they

Table 7.1 Technically recoverable shale oil and gas resources compared with proved and overall prospective nonshale reserves

	Shale oil		Oil, proved reserves		Shale gas		Gas, proved reserves	
Country	billion barrels	%	billion barrels	%	trillion cubic feet	%	trillion cubic feet	%
Canada	9	3	175	11	573	8	70	1
Mexico	13	4	11.7	1	545	7	12.5	0.2
US	58	17	30.9	2	665	9	299.7	4
Total North America	80	24	217.6	14	1783	24	382.2	5.2
Russia	75	22	88.2	5	285	4	1574.3	21
China	32	9	14.7	1	1115	15	107.7	1
World total	**345**	100	**1,652.6**	100	**7,299**	100	**7,357.8**	100
Total technically recoverable reserves of nonshale oil, gas	**11%**		**3,012**		**32%**		**22,882**	

Source: EIA, *Technically Recoverable Shale Oil and Shale Gas Resources: An Assessment of 127 Shale Formation in 41 Countries Outside the United States*, Washington, DC, June 2013, p. 10, and BP Statistical workbook, 2013.

have in common the technology used for their recovery: hydraulic fracking and horizontal drilling. In the following section I will briefly summarize how this major revolution in resource recovery and enhancement was possible in the US and has impacted energy markets, and will continue to do so during the following years.

SECURITY AND TECHNOLOGICAL CHANGE AS THE BACKBONE OF THE AMERICAN "ENERGY REVOLUTION"

Energy security returned to the forefront of US energy and foreign policies in 2001, when incoming Vice President Dick Cheney released the National Energy Policy (NEP), which mapped out most of the energy bills and initiatives that were discussed or passed since that time, under both the Bush and Obama administrations. The September 11 terrorist attacks took place not long after the NEP was released, and longstanding energy challenges were subsequently redefined as a security issue, with warnings that America's prosperity and standard of living would be threatened if the growing imbalance between its energy production and consumption were not addressed. The Cheney report advocated conservation (through technological innovation), infrastructure development, the increase of domestic energy supplies (both nonconventional fossil fuels and renewable sources), and stronger links with both Canada and Mexico as major policy steps to enhance the country's energy security.[7]

In that same year, and consistent with the recommendations of the Cheney Report, US President George W. Bush, Mexican President Vicente Fox, and Canadian Prime Minister Jean Chrétien launched the North American Energy Working Group (NAEWG), an interministerial task force with the goal of sharing information and data for improving and enhancing energy trade and interconnections within North America. The meetings and publications of this trilateral group became more relevant after the Gulf of Mexico was buffeted by a series of hurricanes in the fall of 2005. In that same year, trilateral dialogue through the NAEWG was reframed as co-management of a "continental" energy system, as part of the launch of the Security and Prosperity Partnership (SPP).

Although the primary concern of the SPP—at least in the eyes of the Bush administration—was a strengthening of border security,[8] the SPP's June 2005 report called for the creation of a "policy environment" in which a sustainable supply and efficient use of energy could be promoted.[9] It also recognized that energy had become "critical to the prosperity and security" of the three nations. Both NAEWG and SPP released data, studies, and declarations highlighting the importance of considering energy policies of party members under a continental view, but they did virtually nothing to create the necessary "policy environment" for enhanced continental cooperation on energy matters. With the arrival of the Obama administration in 2008, the SPP process was terminated, and no new regional initiative took its place; the governance of security and energy issues in the region shifted decisively back to national policymaking. International policy coordination, as noted in the introduction to this chapter, had little impact on the regional energy picture; much more important to the evolution of the regional market were the rapid technological changes and increased output of shale gas and oil plays, particularly in the US.

Under the Bush and Obama administrations, the energy scene in the US has been shaped by a set of legislative and administrative measures, including a variety of tax incentives, neither consistent nor continuous, and not always coming from the federal agencies. The most significant of these legislative and regulatory measures were the Energy Policy Act (EPA) of 2005 and the Energy Independence and Security Act (EISA) of 2007, both undertaken by the Bush administration. Under the Obama administration, by contrast, Congress has not passed any comparable bill, in spite of the president's efforts to promote a wider mix of clean and renewable energy. Both EPA and EISA created a series of tax incentives and research programs designed to stimulate the domestic supply of unconventional fossil fuels and to encourage the development of renewables and energy conservation measures.

These measures taken at the federal level, together with the introduction of the portfolio renewable standards enforced at the state level (including mandatory quotas for consumption of renewable resources in electricity generation), have unchained a real revolution in the US featuring the spectacular growth of unconventional fossil fuels output, especially shale gas. A first consequence of this rapid increase has been the drop in gas prices vis-à-vis crude oil and the possibility that the US could become a net gas exporter in just seven years. Figure 7.4 includes the Department of Energy's (DOE) most recent forecast estimating a continuous growth in shale gas production during the next twenty-five years, which could eventually yield export surpluses. Although gas prices might increase due to an anticipated growth in domestic demand, they will remain below crude oil prices.

According to DOE's most recent estimates, the TR reserves of nonconventional gas in the US (shale and tight) amount to 665 trillion cubic feet (TCF), more than double US proven reserves of conventional gas. In any case, the amount is equal to 27 percent of the total recoverable reserves of gas (conventional or not). Although those impressive figures might be downsized—for geological and economic reasons—they could also be revised upward, depending on geological and technological variables. Over the past two decades, technological innovation in terms of exploration, exploitation, recovery, and consumption of energy resources has proved to be crucial to the new supply boom of nonconventional energy resources and renewables.

Regarding export surpluses, Figure 7.5 shows a possible scenario in which the US could eventually cease to import gas from Canada, which—as noted above—would prompt that country to find new markets, probably in Asia. Under this scenario, American net exports are shipped via pipeline to

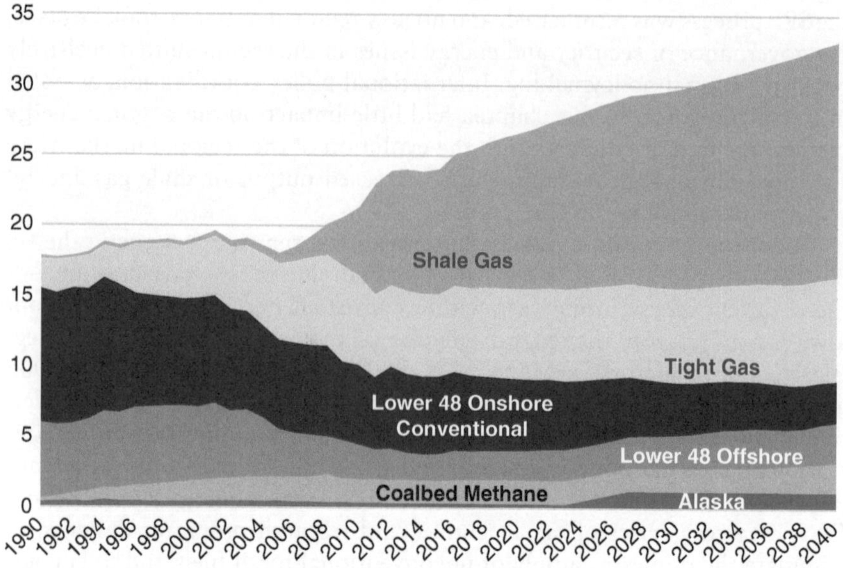

Figure 7.4 Natural gas production by source (trillion cubic feet), 1990–2040
Source: EIA 2013.

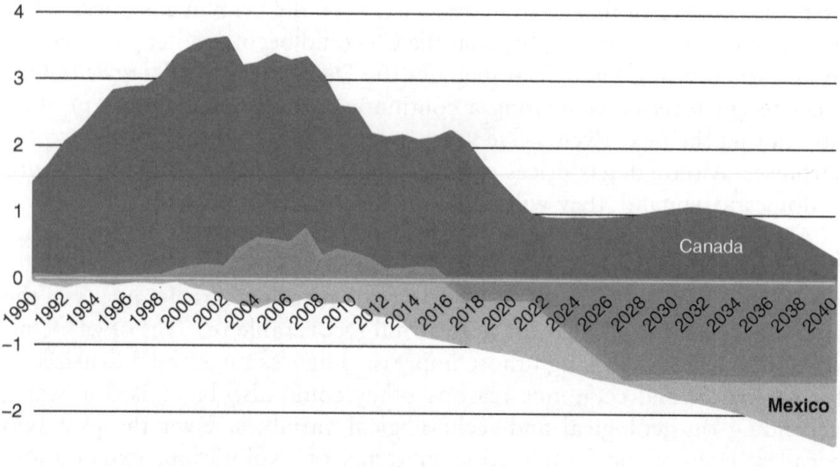

Figure 7.5 US net imports/exports of natural gas by source (trillion cubic feet), history and projections 1990–2040
Source: EIA 2013a, 73.

Mexico and to other markets as liquefied natural gas (LNG). It is unclear however, whether Mexico will be able to absorb, or would be interested in absorbing, much of the US surplus. While import prices would be attractive, Mexico does not have the transport infrastructure needed to harness a greater volume of gas inflows. On the other hand, Mexico has considerable potential of its own in both conventional and nonconventional oil and gas resources, but the technological and institutional capabilities for developing those resources is yet to be built.

Energy policies implemented in the US since the beginning of this century have also impacted the production of domestic crude oil production. The secular downward trend in the production of conventional oil that began in 1986 came to a halt in 2009 due to the increasing supply of tight oil. In 2012 annual production reached 6.34 Mbd and could peak at 7.5 Mbd in the middle of the next decade, according to the most recent estimates (see Figure 7.6). Alaska's declining production will be offset by the growth of nonconventional plays. However, tight oil production could peak at the end of the incoming decade, with an average production of 2.7 Mbd.

Despite the recent success in the extraction of nonconventional fossil fuels, there are many uncertainties pending in their future development. The recovery rate by well is different than that of conventional fossil fuels;

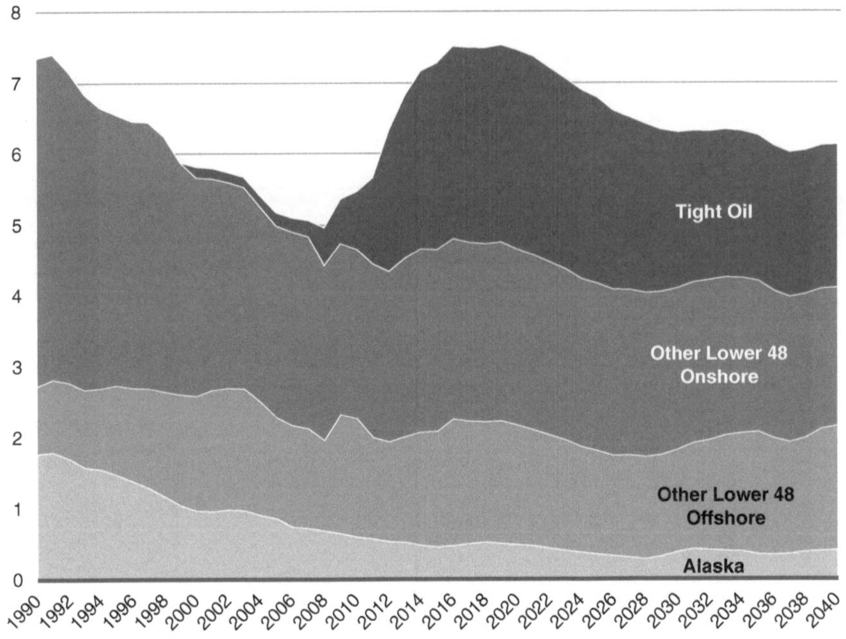

Figure 7.6 US domestic crude oil production by source (million barrels per day), history and projections 1990–2040

Source: EIA 2012.

it might increase or decrease depending on the geological characteristics of the fields, as well as of the technological improvements reached in drilling and extraction. In other words, the projections presented in the reference scenario should be treated with some caution. There is a possibility that prospective resources could be as much as 50 percent lower than estimated, or on the contrary, more than 100 percent higher.[10] The productivity of the wells is independent of the economic conditions of exploitation and the policies implemented to encourage the development of the industry. In the most "optimistic" alternative scenario, where productivity is 100 percent higher than the reference scenario, the US could actually become self-sufficient, with enormous consequences for Mexico, Canada, and world's energy markets.

If, on the other hand, the productivity of the wells is significantly less than originally estimated, the American economy will continue its dependence on net imports of oil. Figure 7.7 attempts to incorporate some of these variables. It presents five scenarios, all of them estimating the share of net imports of liquid fuels vis-à-vis consumption trends for the next twenty-five years. As shown, under the reference scenarios, "energy dependence" (net imports as a percentage of overall consumption) will reach almost 40 percent at the end of the study period, which is not much higher than the currently prevailing 37 percent (see Figure 7.7). If we assume that the US could become a net

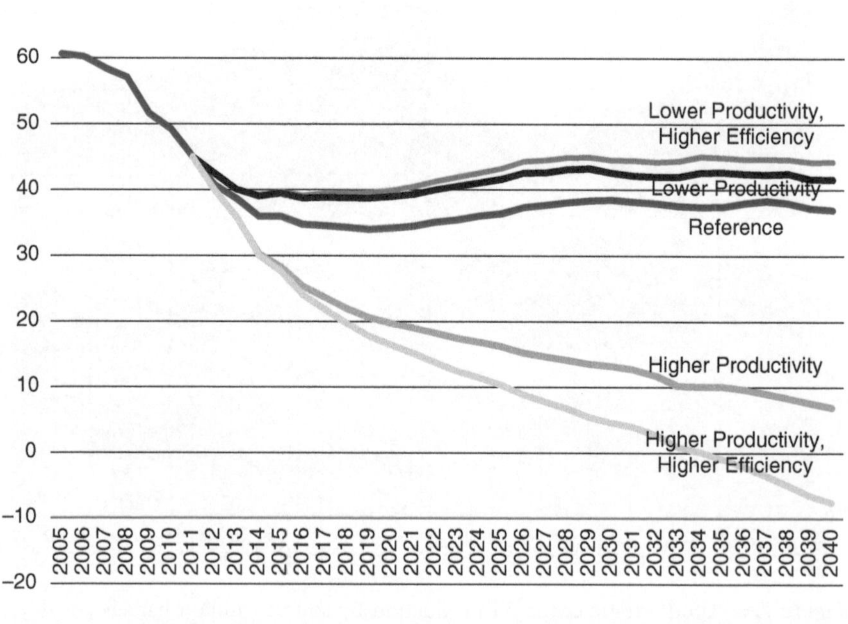

Figure 7.7 Net import share of liquid fuels in five cases (percent), 2005–2040
Source: EIA 2013, 37.

exporter of gas in a span of seven years, net imports of energy could drop from 17 to 8 percent from 2012 to 2040.

None of these scenarios take into account another variable that could also overturn—or at least modify—current trends: climate change policies. The Obama administration has focused on penalizing greenhouse gas emissions (GHG), an approach that helps renewable sources to better compete with coal, and to a lesser extent with natural gas, especially in the generation of electricity. The exploitation of nonconventional gas has also generated concern and opposition by groups interested in the protection of the environment. Until now, however, and as evidenced by the case of the state of Pennsylvania,[11] regulations to abate negative externalities caused by the new methods of exploitation have been confined to the individual states. The future of environmental legislation in the US depends more on political variables, played out in both federal and state legislatures. That legislation, moreover, entails a differentiated impact in the production and consumption of fuels. To cap and penalize emissions of CO_2 could dampen the consumption of fossil fuels, but all would benefit from exports in the case that surpluses are higher than anticipated. By contrast, if the exploitation of nonconventional fossil fuels is subject to stricter environmental regulations, this would undoubtedly have a greater impact on the production of such fuels than on their consumption.

THE SCOPE AND LIMITS OF MEXICO'S POST-NAFTA ENERGY REFORMS

Of the three North American countries, Mexico is the most dependent on oil and gas as the primary source of energy for domestic consumption. At present, oil represents 57 percent of total primary energy supply (subtracting exports and adding imports) for the country, while gas amounts to 27.4 percent. This contrasts sharply with its North American partners, where oil represents 39 percent of total primary energy supply for the US and 35 percent for Canada, and gas represents 23 percent and 29 percent respectively.[12] Mexico's energy mix will remain heavily dependent on hydrocarbons in the years to come, and this is why any attempt to open the hydrocarbons industry to private participation had traditionally been anathema in Mexico's energy policy debates.

State-run oil monopoly and resource nationalism became and have remained two major paradigms in the governance of the energy mix in Mexico from the turn of the twentieth century to the present. State monopoly over hydrocarbon resources aims at managing them as a strategic stock with the ultimate goal of strengthening state capabilities and serving state interests—economic, political, or ideological. In the case of Mexico, hydrocarbons and any other natural resource existing in the subsoil and continental shelves belong by constitutional mandate to the nation.[13] This is at the basis of what some authors have called "resource nationalism," meaning that energy resources should be exploited in such a way that all nationals of a country should benefit.[14]

In contrast to other countries in which oil wealth also belongs to the nation, such as Canada, Brazil, or Venezuela, oil nationalism in Mexico has specifically made the state and its government agencies the only entities legally entitled to exploit both upstream and downstream activities. In practice, this has meant that two government-managed firms—Petróleos Mexicanos (PEMEX) and the Comisión Federal de Electricidad (CFE)—have exercised an effective monopoly over the exploitation, production, and distribution of hydrocarbon fuels and electricity, respectively. This is what I refer to in this chapter as the state-oil-monopoly regime, a model of governance that differs from other forms of resource nationalism in which the subsoil wealth is not necessarily monopolized by the state, and the participation of private capital (either local or international) is managed through contracts or concessions.

From the expropriation of foreign oil companies in 1938 by President Lázaro Cárdenas (1934–1940) until the signature and enforcement of the NAFTA in 1994, the strategic management of energy resources by government monopolies became the equivalent of a *raison d'État* through which the state ensured its own political strength and survival. PEMEX's monopoly profits effectively made Mexico a rentier state, and the appropriation and distribution of those rents through taxation has been the basis for perpetual bargaining among all relevant stakeholders.[15] Although PEMEX gross income has traditionally been much higher than the company's operational costs, the state oil monopoly suffers from an endemic deficit once a myriad of taxes are deducted. For instance, in 2012 overall sales income amounted to US $126.6 billion, out of which almost 50 percent came from exports. Although gross income before taxes amounted to US $69.6 billion, PEMEX transferred to the federal government $69.4 billion on federal contributions levied to oil production, creating a general deficit of $28.7 billion once other deductions are taken into consideration.[16]

PEMEX deficits are balanced either by loans or direct transfers operated by the Ministry of the Treasury. However, those transfers are conditioned to annual negotiations by which the Mexican Congress and the Treasury craft the budgeted expenses for the fiscal year. The Ministry of the Treasury set an anticipated price for the Mexican oil export mix, and congressmen set in general terms how government resources—of which 35 to 40 percent come from oil—will be expended. Even in the case of windfall profits—that is, when oil revenues are significantly above the budgeted price—the expenditure of surpluses is determined and directed by the executive agencies, usually with very low transparency. While this "extractive" rentier regime has enhanced the capabilities of the Mexican state—in terms of nationalist support, political patronage, and economic dirigisme—it also put constant pressure on the state oil firm and prevented any sound fiscal reform.[17]

While in 1980 oil transfers represented 3.7 percent of Mexico's GDP, from 1982 to the present that figure has ranged between 6 to 8 percent.[18] These figures, which normally amount to 35 to 40 percent of overall government income, highlight the severe dependency of the Mexican state on the production and export of oil wealth, as well as the entrenched interests shared among policy and political stakeholders that had become the major defenders of the status quo.

While PEMEX official information states that oil income transferred to the government is being channeled to the improvement of education and health services, roads and dwelling construction, rural support, electricity generation and distribution, national security purposes, law enforcement, and transfer to state and municipal authorities, among other things, in practice it is difficult to track how these resources are effectively disbursed. Fragmented information coming from some studies suggests that public expenditure is being expanded or contracted according to the fluctuation of oil revenues, highlighting the vulnerability of public finances to the volatility of the international oil market. Furthermore, these resources are neither efficiently assigned nor intended to reduce inequalities between poor and rich regions in the country.

Take, for example, transfers to state governments. According to a study tracking these transfers during the Fox administration (2000–2006), about 50 percent were channeled to rich governments such as that of Mexico City, the states of Mexico, Jalisco, Nuevo León, Veracruz, and Tabasco. Poor states such as Chiapas, Guerrero, and Oaxaca only received 9 percent of overall transfers.[19] Furthermore, states are not accountable for the effective expenditure of these transfers.

In the year 2000, the state launched the Petroleum Revenue Stabilization Fund (PRSF), the goal of which was to create a saving fund fed by windfall profits. The idea was to use this fund as a counter-cyclical policy tool in order to cushion shocks coming from a downturn in international oil markets. The creation of this fund is a major departure from the "oil boom" years, during which windfall profits were exhausted on a short-term basis, and falling oil prices often led to the onset of major financial crises.[20] The PRSF therefore represents the advent of an energy security approach, which is essentially unprecedented in Mexico.[21]

However, the record shows that the PRSF funds have been used for all kinds of purposes, including the support of normal government expenditure, in spite of the fact that since 2000 international oil prices have been above the anticipated price budgeted by the Ministry of the Treasury. The lower house of Congress sets the parameters, on a yearly basis, for the expenditure of these windfall revenues from a nonrenewable resource. In 2000, for example, 60 percent of the resources allocated to the fund were geared to debt payments, and 40 percent to state transfers. The following year, however, only 33 percent of the revenues were destined to state transfers, while 33 percent was channeled to balance the public budget. The legislation was revised at the end of the Fox administration, to make the use of PRSF funds more transparent, and giving priority to the support of PEMEX investments. However, the executive branch and local state authorities still benefit from large extraordinary discretionary faculties for making use of those revenues coming from the PRSF. The record shows that during the Fox administration part of those resources was used for paying increased wages to public school teachers, for funding pensions, and for covering other expenses that do not necessarily imply productive investments. The record also shows that local governments have used part of these oil-revenue transfers for purposes that do not encompass infrastructure enhancement, but rather normal expenses of all sorts.[22]

During the Calderón administration, moreover, it seems that PRSF resources were also used to subsidize fuel consumption. The Mexican government has traditionally subsidized domestic prices of gasoline, diesel, LP gas, and electricity. Subsidies vary and do not imply a direct transfer to consumers, but function as different types of price discounts depending on the location and type of the final user. For instance, gasoline is normally commercialized at prices below the international equivalent. The subsidy increases if international prices increase suddenly, as was the case in 2008 and again in 2011. Diesel has a special discount price for rural workers, while electricity is heavily subsidized for residential consumers below a certain threshold and industries benefit from different rates. In other words, the maintenance and governance of subsidies remain anchored at the core of the state-oil-monopoly regime in Mexico, and their supporters claim the social benefits of the distributive effects. From 2008 to 2010, the Mexican government channeled US $5.106 billion on average from the PRSF for supporting subsidies to hydrocarbon fuels. Just in 2008, the amount reached US $14.481 billion,[23] suggesting that, just as with government expenditures, energy subsidies follow the rhythm of international markets. As long as prices remain high, subsidies do as well.[24]

However, energy subsidies do not necessarily benefit the least favored people in the country. Traditionally championed as a means to promote "social justice" or "equality," most of these energy subsidies seem to be regressive, artificially fueling demand for gasoline and electricity far above their opportunity cost, with toxic effects on the environment and increasing pressure on the domestic supply of fuels. According to some studies, 75 percent of gasoline subsidies, whose imports reached 54 percent of consumption in 2011, benefit 40 percent of the better off of the Mexican population. Only 12.5 percent of those subsidies benefit 40 percent of the worse off.[25] Sixty percent of subsidies geared to electricity consumption in rural areas benefit the richest 10 percent of farm growers.[26]

While the PRSF was launched with a stock of US $766 million in 2000, by the beginning of 2006 the reserve had been increased to US $1.061 billion. According to some estimates, however, that amount represented just 3 percent of windfall revenues for that time period.[27] At the end of May 2012, the stock of the fund reached US $1.3 billion, while windfall revenues from 2007 to that date were estimated at US $54.6 billion.[28] It is clear that most of the windfall profits are not being collected for energy security purposes; on the contrary, they are being appropriated, allocated, and expended with no accountability by the Ministry of the Treasury. This suggests that the exploitation of Mexico's oil wealth, under the hands of state monopolies, subordinates the financial health of PEMEX, the energy security of the country, and the general interest of the nation—if by this we mean the entire community of Mexican citizens—to the particular interests of policy and political stakeholders who control oil and energy policies in the country. This is what was at stake in the state-oil-monopoly regime in Mexico.

Post-NAFTA reforms have attempted to introduce competition in the energy sector, and some administrative changes in the corporate governance of PEMEX. While they have raised some interest among private investors in participation in the industry, these reforms have failed to tackle the problem at its very core—i.e., the subordination of the oil and gas industry to the short-term interests of a political class that is determined to avoid real accountability, and that sustains fiscal dependency on oil income and a growing consumption of carbon fuels, even through direct subsidies, in an era in which other countries are taxing the use of carbon fuels for environmental and security reasons.

Mexico's Post-NAFTA Energy Reforms

NAFTA launched its own revolution in Mexico's economic organization and earmarked the end of the state dirigisme of the successive PRI governments whose legitimacy had been anchored in the principles, rulings, and practices of the Mexican Revolution. The implementation of the agreement accelerated major constitutional reforms to facilitate the liberalization of historically highly protected areas such as agriculture, foreign direct investment, foreign trade, intellectual property rights, government procurement, and services.[29] The fact that these reforms were anchored in a hard law, a trilateral agreement signed with the US and Canada, had the effect of locking in a state economic reform that transcended the Salinas administration. In many ways we could say that Mexico's economy and politics are still adapting to those long-term reforms.

It is well known that Mexico's hydrocarbon sector remained aloof from this major state reform, as a negotiation tactic vis-à-vis both the US and nationalistic groups at home.[30] Mexico's constitution regarding the hydrocarbon sector was not modified, and the industry remained a "strategic sector" only to be exploited by the state. However, Chapter 6 of NAFTA set out the principles and conditions for a gradual liberalization of Mexico's overall energy sector. Through NAFTA Mexico liberalized the power industry by making a distinction between the supply of electricity as a public service, reserved solely for the state, and the production of electricity by private firms—including foreign firms—under the following categories: 1) production for own use, 2) co-generation, and 3) independent power producers

(IPP). However, Mexico's power utilities—Comisión Federal de Electricidad (CFE) and Luz y Fuerza del Centro (LFC)—retained a monopoly on transmission, so private producers, independently of the categories to which they were assigned, were compelled to sell their production or surpluses to CFE.[31] NAFTA electricity liberalization was preceded by changes in regulatory bills, which allowed IPP to generate and sell electricity to CFE in order to supply it under the category of "public service."

NAFTA also privatized most of the petrochemical industry,[32] liberalized cross-border trade in electricity, and set the grounds for doing the same for natural gas. This was furthered under the administration of Ernesto Zedillo (1994–2000), who introduced changes through regulatory bills—without making any constitutional changes—to allow private firms to participate in cross-border trade in natural gas, and in the construction of transmission lines, distribution, and storage facilities.

Even though Mexico attached many explicit exceptions to Chapter 6 of NAFTA, it became the major framework from which "gradual liberalization" of the sector would evolve. And this would and could be done without necessarily making constitutional reforms, by introducing "tactical modifications" in regulatory bills, as was done in the case of electricity and gas. President Zedillo failed, for instance, in making a constitutional reform for allowing a further privatization of the power sector, which undermined the possibility of a regulatory reform being submitted by president Vicente Fox (2000–2006) to Congress. President Calderón submitted an energy reform that attempted to allow the participation of private firms in the refinery of crude oil and in the transportation, distribution, and storage of petroleum products without making constitutional reforms. This was also rejected by Congress, and the final regulatory changes remained constrained to the modification of the corporate governance of PEMEX and to a further clarification of the role of private firms as service contractors and suppliers of the state monopoly.[33]

In other words, over the last twenty years, NAFTA's regulatory body (Chapter 6, but also principles regarding services, government procurement, dispute settlement, and investments in the case of private electric utilities) had remained the major energy reform implemented in the country affecting the monopolies of the state over the sector and the scope of participation of private firms. The "energy reform" passed by Congress in 2008, made major changes in the corporate governance of PEMEX, but it did not modify as substantially as NAFTA did the role of state and firms in the sector overall. The agreement raised and put momentum behind the principle that a minimum of market competition was needed in order to improve the competitiveness of Mexico's energy industry, but to this day it remains highly inefficient and ineffective in serving the interests of the whole Mexican society.[34]

NAFTA also framed Mexico's energy sector in a continental perspective. Although during the "oil boom" years, Mexico attempted to diversity its exports from the US, geography virtually compelled some kind of continental integration. Because a cluster of refineries are located along the US

Gulf of Mexico coast, mainly in Texas and Louisiana, Mexico's crude oil production coming from the south is "gravitationally" attracted by those refinery outlets. PEMEX has co-invested in a refinery with Royal Dutch Shell, in Deer Park, Texas, from which gasoline processed with Mexican crude is exported to Mexico. Most of PEMEX's export mix is heavy crude oil (Maya), furthermore, and American refineries are the best suited technically and economically for processing this type of product. By liberalizing foreign trade in fuels, NAFTA made feasible the possibilities of exploiting economies of scale in the energy sectors of the two countries—as is the case between Canada and the US—and the emergence of cross-border regional markets for some products, in order to improve efficiency and security in their exploitation and distribution. In 1990, 56.4 percent of Mexican exports went to the US; that number has since risen to 80 percent.

As for natural gas imports, they come either by pipeline from the US or by ship tanks as liquefied natural gas (LNG). So far, most imports come from the US by pipeline via several border interconnection points, concentrated in major border cities, such as the urban areas of Tijuana, Mexicali, Ciudad Juárez, and Reynosa. Imports are mainly handled by PEMEX and CFE, and only minor amounts are carried by private utilities. LNG imports currently pass through three regasification plants, one located in Altamira, Tamaulipas, in the Gulf of Mexico; the second plant, which came on-stream in 2008, located in Ensenada, Baja California; and a third one, located in Manzanillo, Colima, on Mexico's west coast, which came on-stream in March 2012. Imports of LNG amount to 27 percent of overall imports, and they are anticipated to grow in the foreseeable future because the development of shale gas is still uncertain. However, anticipated LNG imports could be replaced by imports coming from US shale plays, as forecasted by the US DOE, and shown in Figure 7.8 here. However, there are infrastructure constraints—particularly lack of needed cross-border transmission lines—which could create pressure for higher LNG imports, in case Mexico is unsuccessful or decides not to develop its own shale plays.

Indeed, Mexico has failed to develop an export market for its huge natural gas potential, mainly due to the lack of infrastructure for efficiently recovering its associated gas and pumping it to commercial outlets. Mexico's gas industry still lacks an interconnected and efficient gas-line grid, similar to those already existing within and between Canada and the US, in order to benefit from and exploit economies of scale for this industry. This explains some of the bizarre anomalies in this sector, such as the fact that Mexico is importing almost 19 percent of its national gas consumption while still venting part of its production.

The de facto integration of Mexico's energy trade in the North American market has put additional pressures to Mexico's energy system. As noted above, Canada has become the leading oil supplier to the US, and its huge potential in both nonconventional oil (tar sands) and gas (shale) has made this country a real powerhouse within the North American region. Additionally, Venezuela's

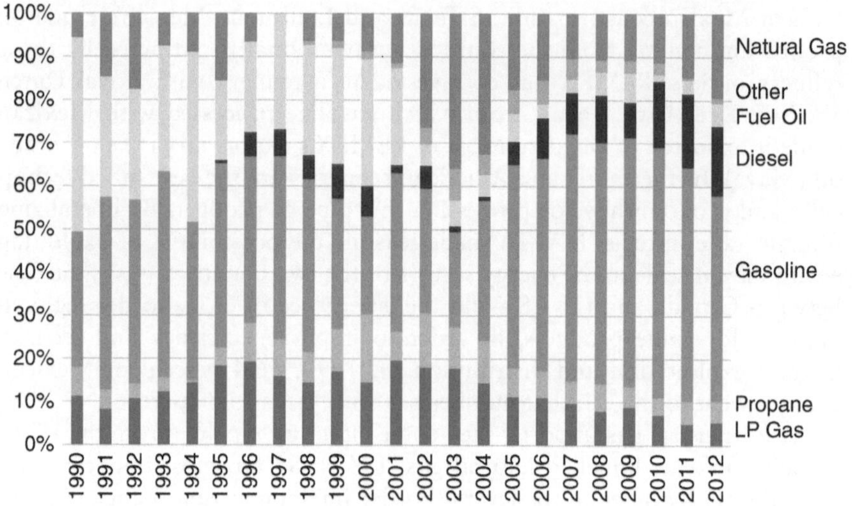

Figure 7.8 PEMEX imports of fuels estimated by volume (percent), 1990–2011

heavy oil is directly competing with Mexico's when supplying American refineries located in the Gulf of Mexico. The rapid development of shale gas and the revolution that is taking place in the US market with the entrance of bio-fuels and renewable energy is prompting Mexican industries, especially automotive and energy-intensive ones, to shift their demand for alternative fuels.

But the major impact of the North American energy revolution on Mexico's energy situation has been the contrast between the Mexican outlook and those of its regional neighbors. Unlike Canada and the US, the hydrocarbon situation in Mexico is critical, to say the least. After a downward reclassification of proven reserves by PEMEX in 2002, the three types of reserves that the company traditionally typifies (proven, probable, and possible) have persistently declined, barely stabilizing in recent years at about 44.530 million barrels of oil equivalent (MBOE). From this stock, proven reserves (13.868 MBOE) equal thirteen years of current production (including natural gas liquids). Crude oil production peaked in 2005, reaching 3.3 Mbd, and progressively declined in subsequent years. In 2012, production was 2.547 Mbd, a fall of almost 24 percent compared to 2005. The same thing has happened with exports, which peaked in 2006 at 1.79 Mbd then declined to 1.25 Mbd in 2012, a fall of 31 percent.[35] At the same time, imports of petroleum products, especially gasoline, have increased because the processing capacity of Mexican refineries has been overwhelmed and the construction of new sites has not yet begun. The production of natural gas, after having known a significant growth over the past decade, with 7,031 BCF of annualized production in 2009, began its fall to reach 6,385 BCF in 2012. With a domestic consumption whose growth has exceeded the increase in production, driven by electricity generation, which has gradually shifted from fuel oil to gas, imports of natural gas have also hiked in the past few years, going from 592.5 MCFD in 2002 to 1,089.3 MCFD in 2012.[36] Figure 7.8 depicts these trends; in recent years, imports of gasoline have represented 50 percent of overall PEMEX's imports.

The decline in reserves and in the production of both crude oil and natural gas is largely due to the exhaustion of the last super giant well, Cantarell, discovered during the oil boom of the late 1970s and early 1980s. This reservoir, which supplied until quite recently more than 60 percent of the total crude oil production, now contributes with only 17 percent.[37] Other wells located in the marine region, such as the complex Ku-Maloob-Zaap, have increased their production in recent years, but without being able to compensate for the steep decline in Cantarell. Notwithstanding, in addition to the probable and possible reserves located mainly in the region of Chicontepec, Mexico has a significant amount of prospective reserves of both conventional and nonconventional resources. In early 2013, the Secretary of Energy (SENER) estimated in 54.500 MBOE the amount of prospective reserves, almost half of them located in Gulf of Mexico deep waters. Likewise, the SENER recognized, for the first time, an estimate of prospective reserves of nonconventional hydrocarbons of 60.200 MBOE.[38]

In other words, in addition to the three types of reserves that Pemex currently recognizes, at 44.530 MBOE, SENER additionally estimates that the country has 114,700 MBOE of prospective resources, conventional and unconventional. These calculations could be conservative, however, because SENER estimates the prospective reserves of shale gas at 141.5 TCF, while the US DOE estimates it at a much higher 545 TCF.[39] Once the Mexican government finally recognized the huge potential of nonconventional fuels in the country, the question that immediately arose among public officials and experts was whether PEMEX had the technological and institutional capacities to develop and exploit them.

Peñas's Energy Reform: Are Mexicans Ready to Overcome the State-Oil-Monopoly Model?

As noted above, from the oil expropriation in 1938 until the 1960s, the Mexican energy sector, from crude oil exploration up to the generation of electricity, was vertically integrated and monopolized by two public companies, PEMEX and the CFE. Articles 25, 27, and 28 of the Mexican Constitution, and a myriad of bills and regulations concerning the operation of the energy sector and of public enterprises, have considered all the value chains of the hydrocarbon industry to be strategic, thus confining their exploitation to state monopolies. Consequently, in parallel to resource nationalism earmarked by the Constitution of 1917, which reached its highest momentum in 1938 with the expropriation of foreign companies in Mexico, the state-oil-monopoly regime became progressively reinforced in such a way that virtually all chains of the hydrocarbon, electrical, and nuclear industries, including the so-called basic petrochemicals, were virtually monopolized under the two state-owned companies.

In the field of energy, as explained above, nationalism and state monopolism are not the same. While the first refers to the subsoil resources and offshore shelves as the property of the nation, the latter refers to the strategic nature of an industry, or of the value chain of a sector, which, according to Article 25 of the Constitution, is the basis for sole management by the state. Article 27, however, accepts the prospect of concessions and contracts with third parties for the development of subsoil resources, although a reform in 1960 explicitly forbade this legal possibility in the realm of hydrocarbons, unlike, for example, mining or even coalbed methane.

It was not until NAFTA came into force that a bundle of constitutional reforms and administrative bills were enacted in order to introduce openness and competition within the energy sector. From that time to the present, including the regulatory modification made during the administration of President Calderón, the succeeding "reforms"—or attempted reforms—aimed at opening to market competition some value chains within the industry, such as electricity generation or the refining of oil products, always took the form of amendments to administrative bills, without challenging constitutional mandates. The results were fruitless. The 2008 reform, for example, only introduced changes to the internal organization of PEMEX, by enlarging its Governing Board to include four "professional" advisors, and by creating a supervisory agency, the Comisión Nacional de Hidrocarburos (CNH), whose mission has been to revise the criteria under which PEMEX has operated upstream activities, such as those located in Chicontepec. At any rate, the 2008 reform made no significant changes to address the more serious constraints facing the industry, particularly in the area of upgrading technology and expertise for ensuring a more efficient exploitation of energy resources.

In August 2013, then-recently elected President Enrique Peña, elected from the Partido Revolucionario Institucional (PRI), submitted to Congress a new reform bill that immediately provoked a response from the two main opposition parties, the Partido Acción Nacional (PAN) and the Partido de la Revolución Democrática (PRD). The essence of the PRI reform was to modify Articles 27 and 28 of the Constitution, to end the state-oil-monopoly regime currently prevailing, without compromising the constitutional guarantee that all hydrocarbon and subsoil resources would be the collective property of the nation. This was a departure from previous reforms because a constitutional amendment was requested and finally enacted, aimed at liberalizing all value chains within the hydrocarbon industries (and the majority of the electricity sector, except for the national transmission system) by removing their designation as "strategic" resources, and thereby overturning the legal rationale upon which the state-oil-monopoly regime was built. PRI's proposal also suggested that the participation of private firms—both national and international—ought to be done under the contracts, explicitly banning the possibility of granting concessions.

A reform of this kind will certainly reduce the ambiguity under which private contractors have operated with PEMEX since 1960, the year the constitution was amended to explicitly prohibit the signature of contracts with the state-run company (although in practice PEMEX has persistently engaged with private contractors). Under the new bill, private contractors are enabled not only to undertake work for PEMEX, but also to participate directly in the operation and development of upstream and downstream activities. The modality regulating the participation of private contractors, either under the formula of production sharing, profit sharing, or risk-sharing agreements, will be defined in subsequent regulatory and administrative bills.

A reform of this sort will no doubt ease the pressures on PEMEX to develop deep-water deposits or to initiate the development of unconventional resources of gas, where PEMEX's production costs are more than double those in similar basins in Texas.[40] An opening of this type will probably boost downstream operations, not only in the refining area, but in transmission and distribution networks as well. It could give momentum to the petrochemical industry because the reform liberalized once and for all the so-called basic petrochemicals—i.e., the supply of methane and ethane—and opened to greater competition the generation of electric power, especially from renewables.

The PRI proposal thus dissociated resource nationalism from the state-oil-monopoly regime, which was built in parallel with it since the original post-revolutionary expropriations. It challenged the very basis of the latter model without compromising the national property rights of the mineral resources, at least under the constitutional mandate. However, by challenging the state-oil-monopoly regime, and regardless of the virtues and vices that this model entailed for the country, the PRI proposal opened the central question—without this necessarily being its original intention—of how the "nation" (rather than a state monopoly) will administer and allocate the benefits deriving from Mexico's oil wealth.

The PRI proposal maintained a disconcerting silence in this regard, while the PAN and PRD positions did address the matter. In effect, the PRD and the PAN proposed the creation of an oil fund, which finally was accepted, to be fed by revenues coming from the oil rent and to be managed independently from the Ministry of the Treasury, through which—as explained earlier—most of PEMEX's transfers are currently administered. The way the Ministry of the Treasury has used and distributed these rents, and the way the government itself manages the PRSF, amounts to a de facto political appropriation of oil revenues, raising questions and concerns about the extent to which these resources really benefit Mexican society overall, and not just a handful of privileged groups. This is why PRD and PAN proposals to create an oil fund, administered by autonomous institutions, became important. According to the bill finally enacted, this fund will be administered by Mexico's Central Bank, an institution that has proved to be autonomous from government officials since the turn of the century.

Traditionally, post-NAFTA energy reform debates in Mexico have been primarily concerned with the advantages and/or disadvantages of allowing private firms to participate in different value chains within the industry, without challenging the state-oil-monopoly regime. This has led to a confusing polarization of debate between those calling for "privatization" of national resources and those calling for the "defense" of state sovereignty over them. This sort of debate has been influenced more by ideological/political positions than by an attempt to differentiate and delink the question of the ownership of the resources—which belong to the nation and will continue to do so according to the enacted bill—from the question of how those resources will be exploited and managed (state monopoly, public-private partnership, contracts or concessions to private investors, etc.).

This sort of debate, which came back once again after the PRI submitted its proposal to Congress, puts aside discussion about the appropriation, expenditure, distribution, and conservation of the oil rent; this wealth ultimately belongs to the nation—that is to say, to all Mexicans. Until now, and due in good part to the prevalent model of monopolistic exploitation, such income has been appropriated by a political class, made up of public officials, partisan congressional blocs, and trade union leaders, whose managerial objectives lack the transparence and accountability needed if part of those resources are to be preserved for future generations. A sort of "re-nationalization" of the oil rent is crucial, if those revenues are to be reinvested and used for achieving more far-reaching goals. This is what is now at stake in the creation of the oil fund in the last bill enacted at the end of 2013.

The re-nationalization of the oil rent would mean a delinking of PEMEX and the entire energy sector from the budget of the Ministry of Finance, and the creation of new independent budgetary and administrative regulatory bodies responsible for monitoring and disclosing accumulated income, once PEMEX's or private contractors' profits have been discounted. Pending secondary legislation is expected to spell out the scope and attributes of these productive public firms. This would also require a more rigorous and transparent process of tendering for contracts, managed by autonomous institutions (PAN's proposal was to empower the CNH with independent budget and decision-making process in order to fulfill this task, a proposal that was finally accepted), and a major revision of subsidies and different types of transfers—such as those to the oil trade union—most of which favor already-privileged sectors. Needless to say, a strong and autonomous regulatory body overseeing the accountancy and disbursement of the oil rent ought to be a watchdog agency to combat and denounce the widespread corruption currently prevailing in Mexico's energy sector. Last but not least, a re-nationalization of the oil rent calls for a needed debate about the most efficient way to optimize that rent—that is, an assessment of the opportunity costs for exploiting some basins, say deep waters, against others (shale oil and gas, for instance), the amount of production and proved reserves that the country needs or desires to sustain, and, consequently, the volume of net exports. These decisions cannot be made in a superficial way, without considering the evolution and impact of the North American energy revolution in oil and gas markets, or left solely in the hands of the presidential branch and its entourage, as during the López Portillo (1976–1982) "oil boom" years. At that time, those important decisions were confined to the executive branch's inner circle, which, at the end of the day, proved to be more costly for all Mexicans.

CONCLUSIONS

While Chapter 6 of NAFTA did not challenge Mexico's state-oil-monopoly regime, it certainly created the basis for a gradual liberalization of its energy industry. NAFTA also initiated an intergovernmental trade regime through which a continental approach on energy markets was envisioned, with the potential for creating a suitable "policy environment" at the regional level. This was the rationale for the founding of the NAEWG at the turn of the century, and it explains why energy became a security issue under the creation and activities of the Washington-led SPP process. Indeed, during the two terms of the George W. Bush administration, American security concerns became the driving force for consolidating a trilateral understanding on energy issues.

Twenty years after NAFTA came into force, and almost a decade after the launching of the SPP, North American energy markets have become more integrated and are witnessing a rapid transformation that is impacting world energy markets. Canada is currently ranked third in terms of proven oil reserves and has become a major oil net exporter, thanks to the coming on-stream of its massive tar sands resources. Canadian production could be more than 6 Mbd within twenty years. The US is witnessing a gas revolution, which has already impacted world gas prices and is making it possible for the US to become a net gas exporter within seven years. This will impact North American gas markets, prompting Canada to find new overseas outlets (mainly in Asia) and forcing Mexico to decide whether to rely on cheap gas imports from its northern neighbor or to set the right policy incentives for developing its own huge shale gas potential in the years to come. Furthermore, US domestic oil production is rapidly increasing thanks to newly developed tight/shale oil resources, and liquid fuel consumption is about to witness a major transformation if markets for hybrid and electric vehicles are consolidated. If technology and geology play out the right way, the US could become an energy self-sufficient country in the span of twenty years. Finally, Mexico has put an end to the state-oil-monopoly regime that was built up in parallel to resource nationalism, both grounded in the narrative of the Mexican Revolution, whose values, political institutions, practices, and imageries hegemonized most of the country's political and social life in the twentieth century. With the new bill passed by Congress, major constitutional amendments were made, allowing private firms, either national or international, to invest and/or participate in all chains of Mexico's oil, gas, and power industries, aimed at transforming the country's energy industry in a way that was unthinkable at the time when NAFTA and the SPP were launched.

All those major transformations, however, have not been the result of intergovernmental cooperation, or policy coordination among the three North American partners, as called for in NAFTA, the Cheney report, and the SPP. On the contrary, the sudden changes that North America is witnessing at the policy and resource endowment level have been the product of energy constraints and of policy and technological responses taken at the national and subnational levels. Although the energy revolution started with Canadian oil sands, the US policy environment that loomed since the first term of the George W. Bush administration was decisive in explaining the nonconventional hydrocarbons revolution that is taking place in this country. This revolution has made of the US a "nonconventional" energy powerhouse.

Until recently, the major players in the international market of hydrocarbons were divided among major producers/exporters of crude oil or gas (Saudi Arabia, the key countries of the OPEC, Russia, Norway, Mexico, Qatar, and Bolivia) and large consumers/importers (the US, Japan, continental Europe). Under those circumstances, it became crucial to estimate, taking into account the asymmetric allocation of energy resources, the demand for exports from major producers to major consumers. At present, the American energy revolution is impacting both production and consumption patterns. This seems to be a structural trend that will continue during the next two decades, which will make of the US a net gas exporter in just seven years and eventually a self-sufficient country in energy matters. Never before has any hydrocarbon producer achieved this double impact on world markets.

Traditionally a great producer/exporter, such as Saudi Arabia in the case of oil, or Russia in the case of gas, could influence world prices and articulate a resource diplomacy based upon its wealth. Large consumers/importers could coalesce and coordinate contingency measures—such as the use of strategic reserves—or common policies geared to the containment of demand. This was in fact the rationale for the establishment of the International Energy Agency (IEA), shortly after the first oil shock (1973–1974). Today, the US can have an impact on both fronts, and it has the wherewithal to articulate a resource diplomacy that would simultaneously promote a shift to nonconventional fossil fuels and the marketing of alternative and renewable resources. US leverage is based, among other factors, on its endowment of nonconventional energy resources, policy measures implemented to develop and transport those resources, and most importantly, the technological innovation transforming their exploitation, marketing, consumption, substitution, and replacement.

Needless to say, this major revolution, driven by policy incentives and market and technological changes, has had a decisive impact on Mexico's energy policy options. Post-NAFTA energy reforms had traditionally attempted to widen the scope of private participation in Mexico's energy sector in order to increase competition without modifying constitutional mandates. By modifying regulatory legislation, the Mexican state widened the scope for private firms' participation in areas that, in principle, could be better exploited by them, such as electricity generation not considered as "public service," and gas transmission, storage, distribution, and foreign trade. However, post-NAFTA energy policy change has also traditionally polarized Mexico's political class and society, between those advocating reforms and denounced as "privatizers" by their detractors, and those defending the status quo and self-labeled as "nationalist" or "sovereignty keepers." This polarization has been poisonous for launching a real debate about the policy options for coping with the energy quandaries pending in the country. By disqualifying any reform initiative as a challenge to Mexico's sovereignty, Congress and political actors were just preserving a risky status quo and postponing the real changes needed to develop Mexico's full energy potential.

In this sense, the energy reform passed by Congress in December 2013 came as a major breakthrough. President Peña's proposal directly challenged the monopoly regime upon which energy resources had been exploited and managed in Mexico. The reform aimed at decoupling resource nationalism—which must doubtless remain as a constitutional principle in the governance of subsoil resources—from state monopolism in the realm of hydrocarbons and electricity. That is, it has opened to competition all the value chains of these industries without alienating the sovereign ownership of resources. However, and argued here, the opening of these value chains to competition is not a magic key to guarantee the revival of Mexico's hydrocarbon and power industries. It is equally urgent to make PEMEX an independent and competitive firm, and to build strong public regulatory institutions, independent from the interests of the Ministry of the Treasury and other government officials, which are capable of monitoring and protecting the extraction of the oil rent that state and private companies will continue to generate. If the present reform lays the groundwork to "re-nationalize" the oil rent for the nation, currently in the hands of partisan interests and political cliques, it will mark a historic milestone in the Mexican energy industry.

At any rate, the continentalization of energy markets in North America will continue and become deeper in the years to come. The cooperative regime that failed to be implemented throughout NAFTA and SPP will probably be reactivated as a need to better exploit and regulate economies of scale, cross-border pipelines and exchanges, environmental externalities, price fluctuations, and resource allocation in a petroleum and electricity industry whose cross-border regionalization is more and more driven by rapid technological changes and shifting market preferences. The new cooperative regime will not necessarily follow the classic intergovernmental pattern of collaboration, as in NAFTA or the SPP. Most likely it will emerge from cross-border initiatives that already exist, grounded at the subnational, or subregional, level, such as the North American Electric Reliability Corporation (NERC), the Western Climate Initiative (WCI), or others created for addressing specific needs and challenges provoked by a growing intertwining of the energy industries located in the three North American partners. Under this emerging multi-level governance architecture, the future of those interdependent industries will be commanded not just by addressing the policy choices coming from government agencies or firms, but by taking into consideration the needs and policy preferences of private firms, consumers, technology innovators, environmental organizations, and other actors capable of impacting a multidimensional energy agenda.

NOTES

1. Canada is currently ranked third, after Venezuela and Saudi Arabia, in proved oil reserves.
2. EIA 2012, 4.
3. Canadian net exports grew from 739 thousand barrels in the year 2000 to 1.6 Mbl/d in 2012. Canada now represents nearly 90 percent of all imported gas in the US market.
4. EIA 2012, 10.
5. Technically recoverable resources means that it is physically and technologically possible to exploit them, but the term does not consider economic and environmental costs. Economically recoverable reserves consider the cost/benefit rationale for their exploitation.
6. Mexico's most updated official estimates for shale oil and gas prospective reserves amount to 31.9 billion barrels and 141.5 trillion cubic feet (TCF), respectively. The latter figure is significantly lower than that used by the US Department of Energy. For PEMEX's estimations, see SENER 2013, 44.
7. NEPDG 2001.
8. See Bélanger 2011.
9. Council on Foreign Relations 2005.
10. EIA 2013a, 34.
11. See Rabe and Borick 2013.
12. IEA 2010.
13. Article 27 of the Mexican Constitution allows for concessions to private firms in order to exploit most subsoil natural resources, but specifically bans them, as well as private contracts, in the case of hydrocarbons. In practice, however, contracts between state firms and private companies have nonetheless been accepted and regulated under administrative bills.
14. Mares 2011.
15. According to SENER, the oil rent is the amount of income left from deducting the overall value of hydrocarbons production, priced at international prices, minus all costs incurred in the production and marketing of products. Consequently, all sorts of subsidies, discounts and transfers from PEMEX to unions of state agencies, should be discounted from the oil rent. See SENER 2008.
16. PEMEX 2013, 6.
17. See also Farfán-Mares 2010, 4.
18. In 1983 and 1984 oil income represented 11.3 percent and 11.6 percent of the country's GDP respectively. However, the figures of those years could be biased because the Mexican economy sunk into a severe crisis, provoking a sharp

decline in the national accounts. All figures concerning oil income comes from official estimations, published by the Mexican Congress at www3.diputados.gob.mx/camara/001_diputados/006_centros_de_estudio/02_centro_de_estudios_de_finanzas_publicas__1/005_indicadores_y_estadisticas/01_historicas/02_ingresos_publicos_1980_2012/01_ingresos_presupuestarios_totales_1980_2012/(offset)/12.
19. Moreno 2006, 20.
20. Morales at al 1988.
21. In principle, a strategy of energy security should target the reduction of vulnerabilities—social, economic, or political—vis-à-vis unexpected or critical changes impacting the energy system of the country.
22. Moreno 2006, 22–23.
23. OECD 2011, 214.
24. According to OECD figures, while subsidies in Mexico amounted to 1.7 percent of GDP in 2007, the figure reached 2.1 percent in 2008, dropped to 0.39 percent in 2009, and increased again to 0.92 percent in 2010 (OECD/IEA 2012). Ratios were calculated by the author according to GDP figures (in current US dollars) from the World Bank.
25. CIDAC 2012, 25.
26. Ibid, 22.
27. Moreno 2006, 19.
28. De la Fuente 2012.
29. For the details of the NAFTA agenda, see Vega 2010.
30. Mayer 1998, 140–41.
31. LFC was merged into CFE in 2009.
32. Morales 1997.
33. Elizondo 2011.
34. According to a study done by Hartley and Medlock (2011), comparing technical efficiency of oil firms around the world, either public owned, private owned or mixed capital, during nine years of the past decade, PEMEX ranked thirty-seventh out of sixty-two firms. Technical efficiency is understood by the capacity of a firm to generate revenue from a bundle of inputs—such as reserves of oil and gas, distillation capacity, employees—and output prices, mainly for oil and gas. According to this ranking, PEMEX is far below most big private firms (e.g., BP, Exxon/Mobil, Shell, or Chevron), which is not particularly surprising because national oil companies (NOCs) normally pursue political and social goals other than private profits. However, the Mexican firm is also far below some major NOCs, such as Norway's Statoil/Hydro (62 percent government participation), ranked sixth; China's SINOPEC (China, with 68 percent government participation), ranked tenth; and Saudi Aramco (100 percent government owned), ranked twentieth (Ibid, 21). According to the same study, PEMEX is overstaffed, ranking fifty-second in the overall sample by measuring revenue per employee. While NOCs such as Statoil, Saudi Aramco, Petrobras, and Petróleos de Venezuela have revenue/employee ratios of 1.8, 3.3, 1.0, and 1.5 million dollars, respectively, PEMEX's ratio is 0.58 million (Ibid, 14–15). Last but not least, the study concludes that PEMEX "would have been able to earn more than 48 percent additional revenue, on average, in each year by more efficiently employing the resources at its disposal" (Ibid, 12).
35. PEMEX 2013.
36. PEMEX 2013.
37. Cantarell peaked with 2.035 Mbd production in 2005, while in 2012 only produced 454.1 thousand barrels daily (Tbd). Part of this abrupt decline has been compensated for by increasing production of other major fields, such as Ku-Maloob-Zaap, located in the Northeast Marine Region as well. These

fields produced 288.7 Tbd in 1999, while thirteen years later were producing 855.1 Tbd. PEMEX 2013, 17.

38. SENER 2013, 43.
39. Ibid.
40. While at Eagle Ford costs per well reach US $4–6.5 million, the Emergente well, a shale well already developed by PEMEX in a similar geological formation to that of Eagle Ford, reached US $11.9 million. Apart from that huge cost differential, PEMEX must internalize in its operations the cost of using 4 million gallons of water per well (the equivalent to 15,000 cubic meters, approximately) plus other industry safety requirements developed by Mexican agencies for exploiting nonconventional resources (SENER 2012, 42; EIA 2013b).

REFERENCES

Bélanger, Louis. 2011. "Governing the North American Free Trade Area: International Rulemaking and Delegation in NAFTA, the SPP, and Beyond" (pp. 27–64), in Isidro Morales, ed., *National Solutions to Trans-Border Problems? The Governance of Security and Risk in a Post-NAFTA North America*. Farnham UK: Palgrave Macmillan.

CIDAC. 2012. *No más subsidios injustos*. June 6. www.cidac.org

Council on Foreign Relations. 2005. "Security and Prosperity Partnership of North America: Report to Leaders," trilingual version, June. www.spp.gov/spp/report_to_leaders/Trilingual_Report_to_Leaders.pdf

De la Fuente, Aroa. 2012. "Ingresos petroleros excedentes, ¿el gran despilfarro del sexenio?," *Animal Político*, May 31. www.animalpolitico.com

Elizondo, Carlos. 2011. "Stuck in the Mud: The Politics of Constitutional Reform in the Oil Sector in Mexico" (pp. xx), in *The Future of Oil in Mexico*. Houston: James A. Baker III Institute for Public Policy.

Energy Information Administration (EIA). 2012. *Canada*. December. Washington.

———. 2013a. *Annual Energy Outlook 2013*. June. Washington.

———. 2013b. *Technically Recoverable Shale Oil and Shale Gas Resources: An Assessment of 137 Shale Formations in 41 Countries outside the US*. June. Washington.

Farfán-Mares, Gabriel. 2010. "Mexico's Curse," *Perspectives on the Americas*, Center for Hemispheric Policy, University of Miami.

Hartley, Peter and Medlock, Kenneth B., 2011. "The Revenue Efficiency of PEMEX: A Comparative Approach" (pp. xx), in *The Future of Oil in Mexico*. Houston: James A. Baker III Institute for Public Policy.

International Energy Agency (IEA). 2010. *2007 Energy Balances*. Paris: OCDE. www.iea.org/

Mares, David. 2011. "Oil Policy Reform in Resource Nationalist States: Lessons for Mexico"(pp. xx), in *The Future of Oil in Mexico*. Houston: James A. Baker III Institute for Public Policy.

Mayer, Frederick. 1998. *Interpreting NAFTA: The Science and Art of Political Analysis*. New York: Columbia University Press.

Morales, Isidro. 1997. "Mexico's Post-NAFTA Deregulation Policies: The Case of the Petro-Chemical Sector," *New Political Economy* 2 (3): 427–450.

Morales, Isidro, Cecilia Escalante, and Rosío Vargas. 1988. *La Formación de la Política Petrolera en México. 1970–1986*. Mexico City: El Colegio de México.

Moreno, Rocío. 2006. *Ingresos petroleros y gasto público. La dependencia continúa*, FUNDAR, Centro de Análisis y de Investigación, A.C., Mexico City.

National Energy Policy Development Group (NEPDG). 2001. *National Energy Policy*. May. Washington.
OECD. 2011. *Inventory of Estimated Budgetary Support and Tax Expenditures for Fossil Fuels*. Paris. www.oecd.org/site/tadffss/oecd-ieafossilfuelsubsidiesandothersupport.htm
OECD/IEA. 2012. *IEA Estimates of Fossil Fuel Consumption Subsidies*. OECD/IEA, Paris. www.oecd.org/general/searchresults/?q=IEA%20Estimates%20of%20Fossil%20Fuel%20Consumption%20Subsidies
PEMEX. 2013. *Anuario Estadístico 2013*. Mexico City.
Rabe, Barry G., and Christopher Borick, 2013. "Conventional Politics for Unconventional Drilling? Lessons from Pennsylvania's Early Move into Fracking Policy Development," *Review of Policy Research* 30 (3): 321–340.
Secretaría de Energía (SENER). 2008. *Iniciativas de Reforma Energética: La renta petrolera*. Mexico City. www.energia.gob.mx/
———. 2012. *Estrategia Nacional de Energía*, February. www.energia.gob.mx/
———. 2013. *Estrategia Nacional de Energía, 2013–2027*. www.energia.gob.mx/
Vega, Gustavo. 2010. *El Tratado de Libre Comercio en América del Norte: Visión retrospectiva y retos a futuro*. Mexico City: El Colegio de México.

ELECTRONIC DATABASES

British Petroleum (BP). 2013. Statistical Workbook. www.bp.com/sectionbodycopy.do?categoryId=7500&contentId=7068481
Energy Information Administration. 2013. www.eia.gov
Secretaría de Energía (SENER). 2014. *Sistema de Información Energética* (SIE). http://sie.energia.gob.mx/

8 "Exceptional," Immovable, Adaptable

Congress and the Limitations of North American Governance

Geoffrey Hale

The development and evolution of North American governance—the interaction of national, international, subnational, market-based, and other forms of governance processes within North America—has always been heavily contingent on the priorities, internal trade-offs, and institutional constraints of the US as its largest and most powerful country. Isabel Studer has noted that the creation of a minimalist institutional framework for North American integration during the late 1980s and 1990s reflected two overarching US domestic constraints echoed by corresponding responses in Mexico and Canada.[1]

First, American political culture reinforces a strong normative and pragmatic orientation toward what Studer and others describe as "exceptionalism": the assertion of institutional and cultural distinctions between the US and other countries, including strict limits on binding international commitments capable of undermining national sovereignty, policy autonomy, and political responsiveness to domestic constituencies.[2] Moreover, the US government is far from being a unitary actor. American foreign policy reflects a *variety* of national traditions and agendas of different ideological and electoral segments, noted by Mead[3] and others, which must be reconciled to achieve reasonable coherence and consistency over time.

Secondly, US policies in North America are heavily influenced by domestic partisan, factional, sectoral, and special interest politics.[4] Domestic politics, mediated through Congress, structure the context and limits for exercising presidential discretion and that of executive departments and agencies—making it the "pivot" for US policies toward its North American neighbors. Members of Congress often approach bilateral and North American policies, whether at systemic, sectoral, or micro levels, through the prism of their impact on constituents.[5] Although this approach can impede transnational economic and societal interaction, it injects practical human and societal concerns into the workings of government bureaucracies—if often in idiosyncratic ways. However, it also reinforces the unpredictability and contingency of American domestic politics, particularly in the context of persistent internal party cleavages and growing partisan polarization.

Such debates have had five practical effects. First, they have increasingly limited the capacity of the US Executive Branch and other NAFTA governments to pursue "Type I" forms of regional integration discussed by Bow and Anderson to periodic issue sets around which a critical mass of support can be mobilized across party lines. Secondly, they have made Congressional support for further integration contingent on the accommodation of varied sectional, factional, or ideological interests and coalitions. Thirdly, these pressures have also contributed to the emergence of crosscutting coalitions of transnational (and sometimes, transgovernmental) interests to pursue, obstruct, or broker compromises among these agendas. Fourthly, they have also limited North American integration by encouraging both Canadian and Mexican governments to limit their vulnerability to the vicissitudes of American domestic politics by maintaining policy discretion to secure their own national interests and diversifying their trade relations and export markets while working with counterparts in Washington on narrower issues of mutual interest.

This chapter suggests that, for the foreseeable future, these realities have largely eliminated the basis for the kinds of bipartisan, large-scale agreements contributing to the substantial extension or "deepening" of North American integration. It considers the constitutional and institutional positions that make any movement toward deeper North American integration subject to Congressional authorization and oversight—often as subsets of US domestic policies and politics. It suggests that the likelihood of constructive Congressional engagement with bilateral or North American policy processes depends on the interaction of broader presidential agendas with those of relevant Congressional party and committee leaders, which, in turn, are driven largely by internal and domestic political considerations.

INSTITUTIONAL AND CULTURAL BARRIERS: CONGRESS AS "GUARANTOR" OF AMERICAN INTERESTS

Formidable political obstacles stand in the way of the three countries of North America deepening their integration along European lines. However, the most important political impediments exist in the US, where deeply engrained biases against the creation of supranational institutions prevail, especially in Congress.[6]

The US Constitution was and is designed to limit and structure the exercise of governmental power through its separation of powers and systems of checks and balances. Pastor and Fernandez de Castro have emphasized the centrality of Congressional autonomy and "insularity" in enabling this "pivot" of the American political system to "shape the banks within which the river of North American integration runs its course."[7] This insistence reflects both deeply rooted elements of American political culture and calculated responses to what Rodrik has described as the "globalization trilemma": the fundamental trade-offs among "democracy, national determination, and economic globalization"[8] by leaders and elected representatives of both major parties.

There have always been debates within American society over the nature and extent of these trade-offs, but American political institutions have generally resisted the transfer of governmental authority to supranational institutions. Presidents may exercise extensive discretion on national security issues and aspects of foreign policy. However, the binding of domestic laws through international treaties is subject to the "advice and consent" of the Senate, requiring an affirmative two-thirds vote. Moreover, the Senate may attach interpretative conditions, which then have force of law in American courts upon treaty implementation.[9]

The Senate's robust exercise of these powers has led presidents to resort to executive agreements, which only require passage by a majority of both houses of Congress for trade and other international agreements.[10] Even so, the Senate retains an effective veto over legislation through its members' right to extended debate (the "filibuster") which has become a de facto requirement for a super-majority of sixty votes for any measure[11] to secure a vote of the full Senate. As neither party has enjoyed a working sixty-seat majority since 1979, this reality forces the majority to maintain effective cohesion while winning support from some members of the minority party. Doing so often requires both the accommodation of sectional interests and the idiosyncrasies of individual Senators from both parties.[12] However, the extent and nature of such cooperation is heavily contingent on the broader legislative and electoral strategies of party leaders (including the president) and, on some issues, of individual senators.

The mediating and constraining roles of Congress are predominant on issues of "low politics," which shape the interaction between traditionally domestic aspects of policy or legislation and international commitments designed to regulate or facilitate the interactions of businesses, states, and citizens. Congressional leaders have long insisted on establishing conditions and limits on the delegation of power through international agreements—or to international institutions—to secure their own constitutionally mandated powers.[13]

Moreover, the management of domestic and foreign policy trade-offs has long involved the projection of national (or factional) policy priorities into the international arena through the use of domestic legislation. In trade (and other) policies, these conditions frequently include principles of reciprocity in dealing with foreign countries, and prior legislated constraints on presidential negotiating authority. American politicians across the political spectrum (including presidential candidates) speak regularly of "enforcing" American trade laws to protect or enable the competitive positions of various interests—whether in attempting to "protect American jobs," create a "level playing field" against foreign imports or foreign government subsidies, correct human rights abuses, or apply domestic environmental policy goals to imported products.[14]

However, Congress itself is not a unitary actor. The nature of Congressional policy processes (and leadership) varies significantly between the Senate and House of Representatives, reflecting different (and evolving) institutional and party cultures in each chamber.[15] These processes remain largely opaque, with the public roles of senior party and committee leaders often concealing an "inside" game, which, by its very nature, tends to be contingent and subject to the personal, institutional, and partisan priorities and judgments of individual leaders and members.

On trade issues, the effective presidential capacity to negotiate trade agreements is heavily contingent on Congressional extension of Trade Promotion Authority (TPA)—the so-called fast-track approval process that requires that treaties negotiated under Congressional authority be subject to an "up-or-down" vote of both houses without right of amendment.[16] Congressional refusal to extend TPA to the Clinton Administration after 1997 and to the Bush (and Obama) administrations since 2007 has severely limited presidential flexibility in conducting international trade negotiations, and made periodic approval of trade treaties heavily contingent on bipartisan support within Congress.[17] However, skepticism toward trade liberalization among Senate Democratic leaders has effectively precluded TPA renewal during the 113th Congress.[18]

Regulatory measures favored by the president, whether mainly domestic or involving "intermestic" elements combining domestic and international policies, are often advanced through "omnibus" bills. This legislative practice bundles numerous related measures (and often unrelated measures included to secure the support of particular members of Congress) into a single piece of legislation. Congressional scholars often point to such processes as examples of "shared" legislative authority in which Congressional authority is balanced by the threat or exercise of presidential veto. However, the far-from-transparent deal making usually needed to secure intraparty, cross-party and House-Senate agreement often require presidents to defer to Congressional leaders and even individual members on many issues in order to secure their core policy priorities.[19]

Moreover, the greater the range of issues addressed in such legislation, the greater becomes the number of competing domestic interest groups to be accommodated, and the less the likelihood that the interests of foreign governments will be accommodated unless they overlap significantly with those of influential US domestic interests.[20] Secondary policy and regulatory issues are also subject to Congressional oversight and influence through annual appropriations processes, which may be used to fine-tune or obstruct the implementation of previous legislation.[21] These realities help to explain why, without a national crisis that requires the subordination of partisan or particular interests to a timely legislative response, presidents often find it difficult to impose their agendas on Congress, even when both Houses are controlled by a majority of the president's party.

More frequently, members of Congress are successful in promoting measures with extra-territorial application which advance the interests of particular economic or social interest groups. These measures may be embodied in discrete legislation such as the 1996 Helms-Burton Act, which allowed US citizens injured by the Castro government's expropriation of private property to seek legal damages against foreign firms, which subsequently acquire such property,[22] or be embedded in broader legislation, such as regulations stemming from the 2010 Dodd-Frank Act, which threatened to disrupt sovereign bond markets in Canada and elsewhere until changes made in response to extensive lobbying.[23]

Constraints on executive leadership in North American governance have taken two major forms: one longstanding, the other an intensification of previous domestic political trends. First, the persistent decentralization of power within Congress, described by Gotlieb as the "sub-separation of powers," has enabled the chairs of committees and subcommittees to exploit the fragmentation of *operational* responsibilities within Congress to assert control over or negotiate the basis of consent over sizeable portions of the Congressional agenda—often in the service of particular domestic interest groups.[24]

The second is a progressive polarization of American politics and ideological discourse since the mid-1990s, which has largely undercut the capacity of Congressional party leaders to broker interparty compromises capable of projecting a consistent sense of *national* interest. Beginning in 1994 (and subsequently in 2006 and 2010), a series of "backlash" elections has intensified partisan majoritarianism in the House of Representatives, limiting presidential power without necessarily resulting in greater policy cohesion or coherence. It has become increasingly difficult for administrations to negotiate the terms of major domestic policy changes with Congress, particularly those with significant implications for the distribution of economic costs and benefits in across American society. These trends take different forms in each house, as well as in the House-Senate and congressional-executive interactions associated with legislative agenda setting and implementation.

Polarization may have contributed to greater centralization of power, especially in the House. However, competition among party factions and the different styles (e.g., "authoritative," "brokerage," "accommodative," or "erratic") of senior party leaders reinforces the contingency of policy outcomes, reflecting partisan, policy, and electoral contexts for debates on particular issues. DiSalvo notes that relative (de)centralization in each house may be more formal (rule driven) or informal (culture driven), with centralization reflecting "leader-driven" or "caucus-driven" decision making depending on the interests, agendas, and relative strength of major factions at different times.[25] These realities reinforce the complexity and crosscutting cleavages of Congressional processes, and hence, the Congressional autonomy often decried by advocates of closer North American integration.

Conversely, growing polarization in the Senate, while not as intense as in the House, has reinforced its historically *anti*-majoritarian character, thus privileging incremental brokerage politics over broader initiatives for structural policy change. As a result, the governments of Canada and Mexico have generally been reluctant to negotiate major changes in bilateral or regional governance relationships with the equivalent of "two executive branches: the Executive Branch and Congress"[26] in the absence of clear procedural measures to facilitate Congressional approval.

PUSHING NORTH AMERICA TO THE MARGINS: PARTY POLITICS AND THE EXTERNALIZATION OF NATIONAL CHALLENGES

Major "progress" in cross-border and North American relations—however this concept is defined in practice given the presence of diverse governmental and societal agendas—may depend on presidential leadership. However, securing necessary Congressional approval typically requires the presence of policy champions within Congress, whether in providing rhetorical leadership or the hard work of assembling bipartisan support for presidential initiatives. The more consuming partisan and ideological agendas—whether of the right or left—become in legislative processes on "North American" issues, as opposed to the brokerage politics of Congressional and interest group trade-offs, the more likely that costs of adjustment to policy changes will be externalized to America's neighbors and other countries. This reality has been visible in deep divisions over energy, environmental, and immigration policies, among others, during the past decade. It also reflects intense opposition on both right and left to policies fostering aspects of North American integration that might diminish their influence in domestic politics—or perpetuate the relative stagnation of domestic living standards since the 1990s.[27] Under such circumstances, any movement toward "North American" approaches to governance is likely to be subordinated toward domestic political, electoral, and policy agendas—as has consistently been the case since the mid-1990s.

The nature of Congressional leadership is highly contextual. John Owens describes this process as an "interactive approach towards leadership," based on two core principles: 1) "that leaders cannot be separated from their historical and other types of contexts in which they operate or the culture of their working environment; and 2) that leaders are accountable for the performance of their organisation or the success of their party or movement that they lead regardless of the context in which it occurs."[28] Institutional differences in each house have reinforced three broad trends since the late 1980s. Hargrove and Owens have noted that "in the contemporary congressional environment, the ability of leaders to juggle leadership strategies that juggle party, electoral and policy contexts has become an important requirement for effective leadership."[29]

These contexts can often be crosscutting in character. Volden and Bergman have noted that the most significant factors contributing to increased party cohesion are the growth in differences between parties' median ideological preferences in each house, and moving from minority to majority status. Increased ideological partisanship in the majority party generally triggers a parallel response by the minority party. Although DiSalvo suggests that this process began as early as the 1960s with the efforts of liberal Democrats, followed by conservative Republicans, to secure control of their parties' respective agendas, it intensified sharply during the late 1980s.[30] Conversely, the broader the ideological and interest distributions of either party, the greater the possibility that detailed policy trade-offs may shift toward the preferences of median or "centrist" voters. Volden and Bergman have noted that the most significant factors contributing to a decline in party cohesion are growth in a caucus' internal ideological preference spreads, followed by growth in party size.[31]

However, the accentuation of party and ideological polarization since NAFTA's passage has undermined and redefined the basis for cross-party cooperation on major legislative issues, without necessarily contributing to greater deference to party leaders.[32] This trend reflects a serious weakening of centrist elements in both parties historically most receptive to North American integration—as noted in Tables 8.1 and 8.2—although the extent and nature of polarization has differed between House and Senate. Table 8.1 notes the progressive intensification of ideological polarization in the House since the late 1980s, particularly as more moderate and conservative Democrats in Republican-leaning states (most recently described as "New Democrats"),[33] and more moderate and liberal Republicans in

Table 8.1 The shifting centers in Congressional politics, 1987–2013

Congress	100th	104th	110th	112th	% Change
House	1987–89	1995–97	2007–09	2011–13	100–112
Democratic Median*	**–0.336**	–0.417	**–0.404**	–0.441	31.3%
Republican Median*	0.347	**0.379**	0.433	**0.474**	36.6%
Δ Party Medians	0.683	0.796	0.837	0.915	34.0%
% "Centrists"	22.6%	12.1%	8.5%	3.7%	
Senate					
Democratic Median*	**–0.328**	–0.323	**–0.341**	**–0.335**	2.1%
Republican Median*	0.338	**0.338**	0.407	0.407	20.4%
Δ Party Medians	0.666	0.661	0.748	0.742	11.4%
% "Centrists"	19%	13%	12%	9%	

Bold print indicates majority in each house.

*Median refers to median for each party of first dimension DW-NOMINATE scaling of lifetime ideological voting patterns for each member of Congress.

"Centrists" are members whose lifetime DW-NOMINATE scales are between –20 and +20.

Source: Keith T. Poole and Howard Rosenthal, DW nominate database, www.voteview.com; author's calculations.

Table 8.2 US Senate: Regional segmentation, 1987–2013

	Percent of Party	Total	Centrist < +/–20	Moderate +/–20–35	"Core" +/–36–50	Hard Core > +/–50
100 Congress (1987–89)						
NE/WC Republicans	28.3%	13	8	3	1	1
Southern Democrats	27.8%	15	8	6	1	0
103 Congress (1993–95)						
NE/WC Republicans	28.9%	13	7	2	2	2
Southern Democrats	29.8%	17	7	8	2	0
104 Congress (1995–97)						
NE/WC Republicans	25.5%	14	8	3	2	1
Southern Democrats	25.5%	12	5	6	1	0
106 Congress (1999–00)						
NE/WC Republicans	22.8%	13	7	3	2	1
Southern Democrats	23.4%	11	4	7	0	0
108 Congress (2001–03)						
NE/WC Republicans	19.6%	10	5	3	2	0
Southern Democrats	20.4%	10	5	5	0	0
110 Congress (2007–09)						
NE/WC Republicans	16.0%	8	4	2	2	0
Southern Democrats	12.0%	6	2	4	0	0
112 Congress (2011–13)						
NE/WC Republicans	10.6%	5	3	1	1	0
Southern Democrats	17.0%	9	4	5	0	0

NE—Northeastern (New England + NY, NJ, PA); WC—West Coast (AK, CA, HI, OR, WA). Ideological scaling: 100 = "pure" conservative/libertarian; –100 = "pure" liberal.

Sources: Keith T. Poole and Howard Rosenthal, DW Nominate database, www.voteview.com; author's calculations.

Democratic-leaning states retired or were defeated—particularly in the "backlash" elections of 1994, 2006, and 2010 when "out"-party leaders succeeded in nationalizing Congressional elections.

Polarization in the Senate, while more asymmetrical and less intense than in the House, has also reflected regional realignments in broader political support (see Table 8.2), resulting in declining numbers and influence for southern Democrats and northeastern and west coast Republicans who have usually been more open to trade liberalization, subject to the accommodation of constituents' concerns. These trends have shifted the leadership "pivots" of both parties toward their respective liberal and conservative cores—although these patterns have taken different forms in each house.

Secondly, greater cohesiveness of party voting in each house has changed the nature of partisan agendas and related leadership styles—narrowing the windows for substantive legislative changes within each electoral cycle and the range of issues that can be addressed in such legislation without triggering institutional and partisan deadlock. Agenda setting by party leaders tends to focus on issues that increase internal party cohesion, while often seeking opportunities to exploit internal differences within the opposing party and among its supporters. As American policies toward Canada, Mexico and, more broadly, toward North America have generally been subsets of broader US domestic or foreign policies, these realities have reinforced the marginalization of North American policies—elements of which divide both parties—and the tendency of US domestic interests to narrow and segment policy initiatives to address specific policy problems in a piecemeal fashion: the topic of the next section.

These factors have increased the temptation to externalize the costs of adjustment to structural policy changes—whether in strengthening border and homeland security measures after 9/11,[34] addressing the social disruptions resulting from large-scale illegal immigration and American employers' demand for undocumented labor,[35] the fifteen-year campaign to limit access to the US by Mexican truckers, unsuccessful proposals to shift the costs of adjustment to climate-change to importers of foreign goods,[36] the extension of "Buy American" rules to construction materials in federally funded construction projects in 2009,[37] or more recent efforts to limit Canadian oil imports in order to increase oil prices and with them, the economic viability of alternative fuels and transportation technologies.[38]

Some of these initiatives, reflecting the broader trends noted above, were calculated measures of party policy. Others were driven by the agendas of particular committee chairs and other policy entrepreneurs who succeeded in mobilizing a congressional (and often public) following for their proposals by appealing to insecurities among core constituencies of each party and often broader publics. However, taken together, they have made it difficult for leaders of either major party to contemplate, let alone develop a coherent North American agenda.

Although both Presidents Bush and Obama have attempted to pursue more consensual approaches on numerous issues relevant to cross-border or North American cooperation, neither has typically been willing to risk much political capital by challenging a majority of his own party in Congress on broader North American issues. The two-fold result has been to resort to administrative and regulatory measures primarily within the jurisdiction of the executive branch, and a tendency to defer to Congress on most aspects of the development of major economic, energy, security, and environmental legislation of relevance to North American governance. (President Obama's more assertive use of executive orders on domestic policy issues since his reelection in 2012, while challenging Republicans in Congress, has not affected these realities substantially.) These tactics have contributed to the decentralization of policy development on major issues relevant to ongoing economic integration—the "Type II" approaches to integration discussed by Bow and Anderson—reinforcing Congress' default orientation towards policy incrementalism, brokerage and special interest politics on complex policy issues.

POLICY DECENTRALIZATION IN CONGRESS: IMPLICATIONS FOR NORTH AMERICAN GOVERNANCE

> Strong leadership occurs only when copartisans want or expect it; which occurs only when copartisans are in agreement on what leaders should do.[39]

Most aspects of US North American policies, as noted earlier, are either subsets of broader hemispheric policies or of domestic policies applied deliberately or inadvertently to Canada and/or Mexico.[40] Apart from clear, consistent White House leadership on a North American agenda that is capable of mobilizing either a sustained Congressional majority or some degree of bipartisan support—conditions that have not applied since NAFTA's ratification in 1994—the default position of Congress is to deal with policies toward Canada and Mexico through a decentralized sectoral or issue-specific prism. Thus, Congress retains its pivotal role as the arbiter and broker for substantial changes in North American governance.

Relative Congressional autonomy on North American policies is reinforced by the growing tendency of cross-border policy relations to address primarily domestic issues subject to the largely decentralized legislative mandates, ongoing appropriations, and oversight processes of both houses of Congress. In recent years, these issues have included energy and related environmental policies, homeland security, immigration and border management, transportation and infrastructure, and other industry- and sector-specific policies and regulatory measures.

These trends also reflect a second major set of factors influencing North American integration: broad shifts in economic activity from Western industrial nations to Asia-Pacific countries and other developing economies[41]—despite modest signs of the "reshoring" of some manufacturing activities. These realities reinforce the likelihood that US (and Canadian and Mexican) policies toward North America are likely to be contingent upon broader trends in international trade policies, private sector business and investment trends, and incremental steps toward regulatory cooperation. These trends have contributed to new developments in transgovernmental and transnational cooperation that may serve as complements or substitutes for multilateral treaty negotiations—while respecting domestic constitutional and political arrangements in participating countries. Such initiatives are responses to the proliferation of major actors with diverging interests in multilateral negotiations, and the interdependence between regional and plurilateral policy initiatives. They also reflect the growing complexity of policy issues, and the greater ease of developing shared epistemic communities and related policy initiatives among policymakers and related economic and societal interests in narrower policy sectors and subsectors.[42]

The extension of international negotiations to include matters ranging from intellectual property rights to technical product standards traditionally subject to domestic regulatory primacy expands the range of Congressional committees and related special interests likely to be drawn into policy discussions and political debates. Such negotiations are likely to have implications that go well beyond North America—with or without deliberate Executive Branch decisions to negotiate common positions with Mexico and/or Canada as part of a multi-track strategy to project American interests and objectives in a broader international context. The Obama administration's evolving regulatory cooperation agenda, which has involved parallel "hub-and-spoke" discussions by Executive Branch officials with the European Union, Canada, and Mexico on numerous technical regulatory issues and processes, utilizes one variation of this approach—albeit with limited outcomes to date. Broader negotiations for the expansion of the Trans-Pacific Partnership reflect another.[43] Although such activities may be pursued independently of Congress, the Executive Branch's capacity to implement anything more than purely incremental measures remains dependent on legislative action by Congress, along with Congressional authorization of related appropriations.

In practice, therefore, the development of such initiatives requires prior engagement with relevant Congressional committee leaders to determine the limits and conditions likely to apply to the use of executive discretion in international negotiations. They also require formal and informal processes to identify complementary domestic and cross-border interest group coalitions whose members can either facilitate or impede each measure. Initiatives that cultivate support across traditional partisan and ideological divides and that engage existing policy communities have a better chance of steering clear of partisan conflicts in Congress, and thus of securing the accommodation and support of Congressional leaders.[44]

The practical effects of *domestic* policy decentralization in Congress reinforce committee-, sector- (or issue-) specific and constituency-specific incentives for legislators, even if mediated to different extents by broader party-political considerations. Moreover, the greater the range of competing intraparty (and related constituent) interests engaged on particular sets of issues, the greater the likelihood that relevant committee leaders will compete to control or influence relevant legislative processes—or to extract desired concessions through appropriations processes.

Such contexts may facilitate the activities of sector-specific cross-border or North America–wide coalitions supportive of sector-specific policy initiatives—as long as these measures accommodate key interest groups central to each party's ongoing coalition-building and maintenance efforts. However, they are inimical to the kinds of "grand bargains" that trade policy and integration theorists frequently argue are necessary to transcend the joint-decision traps that are built into large-scale Congressional legislation on primarily domestic issues.[45]

These realities leave American presidents with several different options in engaging Congress—ranging from the development or extension of transgovernmental networks intended to avoid direct Congressional involvement at one end of the spectrum to the investment of substantial political capital in an effort to mobilize Congressional support for major policy changes at the other. However, the greater the range of American domestic interests affected by actual or prospective legislation, the greater becomes the likelihood either of protracted negotiations between the White House and party leaders in Congress—or of presidential deference to Congressional processes in the working out of domestic legislation. These realities make the governments of Canada and Mexico reluctant to risk much political capital on protracted cross-border or trilateral negotiations whose outcomes are largely subject to domestic political trade-offs in Congress.[46]

These realities help to explain the failure of both Presidents George W. Bush and Barack Obama to engage Congress on administrative and regulatory issues arising from the Security and Prosperity Partnership process of 2005–2009, or subsequent negotiations with Mexico and Canada as extension of the latter's regulatory reform agenda. Instead, the latter has attempted to cultivate existing cross-border networks of sectoral interests in pursuit of targeted improvements in border management and regulatory cooperation in separate processes with Mexico and Canada. This approach has certainly suited Ottawa's North American agenda (and that of major Canadian business interests) in recent years—wary as they are of seeing Canadian interests entangled in bitter US domestic disputes over Mexico-related security and immigration policy disputes.

However, these processes remain vulnerable to unilateral Congressional action—as demonstrated by protracted disputes over market access by Mexican truckers and by "Buy American" provisions, which mandated domestic sourcing for all construction materials financed through the 2009 federal "stimulus" bill.[47] Since its proposed cap-and-trade legislation failed to win Senate approval in 2010, the Obama administration has sought to sidestep both partisan and internal Democratic party divisions on energy policy by pursuing an "all of the above" policy strategy reminiscent of the 2005 energy bill passed under the Bush administration. Such policy processes may create opportunities for the selective accommodation of selected cross-border interests in the Congressional logrolling process. But unless relevant executive agencies give a high priority to specific measures for transgovernmental cooperation—a comparative rarity when their domestic agendas are internally contested—the pressures of domestic and interest group politics are likely to shift broader North American concerns to the margins of the policy process.

CONCLUSION

Congress continues to play a central, and indeed, "immovable" role in the evolution of American policies toward its North American neighbors. Its defense of American "exceptionalism" and related policymaking autonomy remains inseparable from its defense of its own prerogatives, and of the ability of its leaders to frame and serve their own partisan, ideological, and constituency-based interests within the domestic political context in which they function. The legislative, budgetary/appropriations, and oversight functions of Congress establish both the conditions and limits of North American governance. Although these functions may be exercised in ways that serve the interests of constructive relations with Canada and/or Mexico, and so prove to be "adaptable," they do so primarily in the context of American domestic and interest group politics.

Because presidential and transgovernmental policies within North America function as multi-level games balancing executive-Congressional, interagency, societal, partisan, and ideological objectives and interests with those related to broader US foreign and sectoral policy goals and the complementary goals of other governments, it is only reasonable to expect that the strategic and tactical approaches of Canadian and Mexican governments will attempt to maintain their own evolving balance as well.

Following Rhode and Shepsle, changes in the broader Congressional culture necessary to enable deeper North American integration will require shifts in the underlying societal and political conditions that have contributed to partisan and ideological polarization—and with it, somewhat greater party cohesion.[48] Thus, greater cross-party cooperation in Congress, and the potential for political legitimization that goes with it, is largely contingent on the emergence of a new "middle ground" in American politics not defined by zero-sum politics, which affects the geographic and ideological composition of both Congressional parties.[49] Historical instances of such cross-party cooperation may be seen in a US-Canadian context following the 1910 reforms of Congressional governance in which Democratic agrarians and Republican progressives cooperated to reduce tariffs in conjunction with broader domestic reforms supported by elements in both parties. More recently, in a North American context, they are visible in collaboration between business-oriented Republicans and centrist Democrats during the late 1980s and early 1990s to secure passage of the Canada-US Free Trade Agreement, NAFTA, and the broader Uruguay Round agreements that created the World Trade

Organization, as well as complementary shifts in US domestic fiscal, agricultural, and social policies.

The pursuit of sectoral policy cooperation in various areas may facilitate reciprocal initiatives (whether bilateral or trilateral) that accommodate the domestic and broader international policy agendas of each North American government with domestic political and interest group sensitivities. However, just as such approaches have typically lent themselves to incremental policy adaptation rather than grand policy visions during the almost two decades since NAFTA's ratification, these realities are likely to persist in the absence of fundamental changes to the political, cultural, and institutional contexts for policymaking in the US.

NOTES

1. Studer 2007, 53–75.
2. Ibid, 58; see also Slaughter 2004.
3. Mead 2002.
4. Doran and Sokolsky 1985; Gotlieb 1991; Clarkson 2008; Hale 2012.
5. Pastor and Fernandez de Castro 1998b, 46; see also Gotlieb 1991.
6. Studer 2007, 71.
7. Pastor and Fernandez de Castro 1998a, v.
8. Rodrik 2011, xviii.
9. *Constitution of the United States of America*, Article 2, Section 2; Congressional Research Service 2001.
10. Congressional Research Service 2001, 4–5; Grimmett 2004.
11. Amended in November 2013 to preclude filibusters on Senate authorization of presidential nominees to the executive branch and the judiciary, other than the Supreme Court.
12. For example, the *Washington Post* lamented delays in extending the General System of Preferences (GSP) unilaterally reducing American tariffs on imports from developing countries because one Senator's use of procedural rules to block a vote on the measure to preserve protection for a sleeping bag manufacturer in his state. *Washington Post* 2011.
13. Destler 2005.
14. Ibid.
15. Patterson 1989; Volden and Bergman 2006; Strahan 2007.
16. Destler 2005, 346–47.
17. Trade agreements with Colombia and Panama negotiated by the Bush administration in 2006 did not receive Congressional approval until February 2011, along with the Korean trade deal negotiated by the Obama administration in December 2010. A majority of House Democrats rejected all three treaties, despite the extension of Trade Adjustment Assistance programs demanded as a condition for Democratic support. Goldfarb and Montgomery 2011, A1.
18. Scheiber 2014.
19. Krutz 2001, 124–34.
20. Hale and Gattinger 2010, 271.
21. For example, see Hale 2012, 167–68, 268–69, 284.
22. Pastor and Fernandez de Castro 1998, 29–30.

23. Robertson and Kiladze 2012; Goldfarb and Schneider 2012; Shecter 2013.
24. Gotlieb 1991, 28, 35, 43ff.
25. DiSalvo 2009, 30–47. This distinction (reinforced by Newt Gingrich's erratic leadership) may help to explain both Republican conservatives' tactical shift from a Speaker-dominated process to Dennis Hastert's "majority-of-the-majority" strategy after 1998, subsequently adapted by John Boehner. It may also explain liberal Democrats' shift from pursuing a decentralization of power in the 1970s and 1980s to the progressive centralization between the Speakerships of Jim Wright and Nancy Pelosi. See also Sinclair 1999; Owens 2002.
26. Novak 2006.
27. Hale 2012, 88–89; Angus Reid Associates 2012. This outlook is reflected more broadly in American public opinion on liberalizing international trade, particularly as it affects domestic employment levels. See www.pollingreport.com/trade.htm.
28. Owens 2005.
29. Hargrove and Owens 2003, 8.
30. Volden and Bergman 2006, 83–84; DiSalvo 2009, 40–41, 44–45; see also Barry 1989.
31. Volden and Bergman, 2006, 84.
32. Ornstein 1998, 103; Stanton 2012.
33. DiSalvo 2009, 46–47.
34. Andreas and Biersteker 2003; Alden 2008.
35. Alden 2008.
36. Mufson 2007.
37. Hale 2012, 294–99.
38. Ibid, 158, 316, 319; Nocera 2012.
39. Owens 2002, 4.
40. This observation is an extension of the author's analysis in *So Near Yet So Far*, 13–21. Its substance is consistent with analyses by Davidow 2007 and Weintraub 2007, among others.
41. For example, output in developing economies increased by 41 percent, compared with 5 percent in advanced industrial economies between 2005 and 2010. Card and Daschle 2011.
42. Slaughter 2004; Buthe and Mattli 2011; Herman 2012.
43. White House 2012; Hunt 2012.
44. For discussion of international negotiation as two-level and multi-level games, see Putnam and Bayne 1987; Milner 1997; and Hale 2012.
45. Manley, Aspe, and Weld 2005; Burney 2010; Hale 2012, 332–34.
46. For example, see Hale 2010 and Gattinger, 24–43; Lizza 2010.
47. Hale 2012, 294–99; Waddell 2010, 150–67; Seelke 2012, 35.
48. At time of writing, there is considerable uncertainty over the capacity of Republican Congressional leaders to manage internal and primary challenges from the GOP's "Tea Party" wing.
49. Rohde and Shepsle 1987.

REFERENCES

Alden, Edward. 2008. *The Closing of the American Border: Terrorism, Immigration and Security since 9/11*. New York: Harper.

Andreas, Peter and Thomas J. Biersteker, eds. 2003. *The Rebordering of North America*. New York: Routledge.

Angus Reid Associates. 2012. "Americans, Canadians Feel that They Have Lost Out with NAFTA," Vancouver, May 17. www.angus-reid.com/wp-content/uploads/2012/05/2012.05.17_NAFTA.pdf

Barry, John M. 1989. *The Ambition and the Power*. New York: Viking.

Burney, Derek. 2010."Canada-US Relations at 150." Paper presented at "Canada @ 150: Rising to the Challenge" Conference, March 28. Calgary: Canadian Defence and Foreign Affairs Institute.

Buthe, Tim and Walter Mattli. 2011. *The New Global Rulers: The Privatization of Regulation in the World Economy*. Princeton, NJ: Princeton University Press.

Card, Andrew and Tom Daschle. 2011. "US Trade and Investment Policy," *Independent Task Force Report* 67, September. New York: Council on Foreign Relations.

Clarkson, Stephen. 2008. *Does North America Exist?* Toronto: University of Toronto Press.

Congressional Research Service. 2001. "Treaties and Other International Agreements: The Role of the United States Senate," report prepared for Committee on Foreign Relations, US Senate, 106th Congress, 2nd Session, January. Washington: US Government Printing Office. www.au.af.mil/au/awc/awcgate/congress/treaties_senate_role.pdf

Davidow, Jeffrey. 2007. *The Bear and the Porcupine: The US and Mexico*. Princeton, NJ: Marcus Weiner Publishers.

Destler, I.M. 2005. *American Trade Politics*. 4th ed., Washington: Institute for International Economics.

DiSalvo, Daniel. 2009. "Party Factions in Congress," *Congress & the Presidency* 36 (1): 27–57.

Doran, Charles F. and Joel J. Sokolsky. 1985. *Canada and Congress: Lobbying in Washington*. Halifax: Centre for Foreign Policy Studies, Dalhousie University.

Goldfarb, Zachary A., and Lori Montgomery. 2011. "Congress Approves 3 Trade Accords," *The Washington Post*, October 13, A1.

Goldfarb, Zachary A., and Howard Schneider. 2012. "Local, Foreign Governments Slam Volcker Rule," *The Washington Post*, February 29, A12.

Gotlieb, Allan. 1991. *I'll Be with You in a Minute, Mr. Ambassador*. Toronto: University of Toronto Press.

Grimmett, Jeanne J. 2004. "Why Certain Trade Agreements Are Approved as Congressional-Executive Agreements Rather than as Treaties," CRS Report 97–896, July 28. Washington DC: Congressional Research Service, Library of Congress.

Hale, Geoffrey. 2012. *So Near Yet So Far: The Public and Hidden Worlds of Canada-US Relations*. Vancouver: UBC Press.

Hale, Geoffrey and Monica Gattinger. 2010."Variable Geometry and Traffic Circles: Navigating Canada's Policy Relations in North America" (pp. 262–282), in Monica Gattinger and Geoffrey Hale, eds., *Borders and Bridges: Canada's Policy Relations in North America*. Toronto: Oxford University Press.

Hargrove, Edwin, and John E. Owens. 2003. "Introduction: Political Leadership in Context" (pp. 1–16), in Edwin Hargrove and John E. Owens, eds. *Leadership in Context*. Lanham MD: Rowman and Littlefield.

Herman, Lawrence L. 2012. "The New Multilateralism: The Shift to Private Global Regulation," CD Howe *Commentary 360*. Toronto, CD Howe Institute, August.

Hunt, Alex. 2012. Comments to symposium on "US-Canada Regulatory Cooperation Council Action Plan at Six Months," Woodrow Wilson Center, Washington DC, July 26.

Krutz, Glen S. 2001. *Hitching a Ride: Omnibus Legislating in the US Congress*. Columbus OH: The Ohio State University Press.

Lizza, Ryan. 2010. "As the World Burns," *The New Yorker*, October 11.

Manley, John P., Pedro Aspe, and William Weld. 2005. *Building a North American Community: Report of an Independent Task Force*. New York: Council on Foreign Relations, May.

Mead, Walter Russell. 2002. *Special Providence: American Foreign Policy and How It Shaped the World*. New York: Routledge.

Milner, Helen V. 1997. *Interests, Institutions, and Information: Domestic Politics and International Relations*. Princeton, NJ: Princeton University Press.

Mufson, Steven. 2007. "House Democrats at Odds Over Energy Bill Provisions," *The Washington Post*, June 28, D03.

Nocera, Joe. 2012. "The Politics of Keystone, Take 2," *The New York Times*, February 11, A21.

Novak, Robert. 2006. "The Politics of Ports," *The Washington Post*, February 27, A15.

Ornstein, Norman. 1998. "The New Congress" (pp. 97–120), in Robert A. Pastor and Rafael Fernandez de Castro, eds., *Controversial Pivot: The US Congress and North America*. Washington DC: The Brookings Institution.

Owens, John E. 2002. "Late Twentieth Century Congressional Leaders as Shapers of and Hostages to Political Context: Gingrich, Hastert and Lott," *Politics and Policy* 30 (2): 236–281.

Owens, John E. 2005. "Style, Skills, and Context: An Interactionist Exploration of Dennis Hastert's Speakership," paper presented to annual meeting of the Southern Political Science Association, New Orleans, January 5–9.

Pastor, Robert A. and Rafael Fernandez de Castro, eds. 1998a. *The Controversial Pivot: The US Congress and North America*. Washington DC: The Brookings Institution.

Pastor, Robert A. and Rafael Fernandez de Castro. 1998b. "Congress and Mexico" (pp. 29–47), in Robert A. Pastor and Rafael Fernandez de Castro, eds., *Controversial Pivot: The US Congress and North America*. Washington DC: The Brookings Institution.

Patterson, Samuel C. 1989. "Party Leadership in the US Senate," *Legislative Studies Quarterly* 14 (3): 393–413.

Poole, Keith T., and Howard Rosenthal. n.d. *DW NOMINATE* database. www.voteview.com

Putnam, Robert and Nicholas Bayne. 1987. *Hanging Together: Co-operation and Conflict in the Seven-Power Summits*. Cambridge, MA: Harvard University Press.

Rohde, David W. and Kenneth A. Shepsle. 1987. "Leaders and Followers in the House of Representatives: Reflections on Woodrow Wilson's *Congressional Government*," *Congress and the Presidency* 14 (2): 113–133.

Robertson, Grant, and Tim Kiladze. 2012. "Banks Warn Volcker Rule Could Violate NAFTA," *The Globe and Mail*, January 20, B4.

Rodrik, Dani. 2011. *The Globalization Paradox: Democracy and the Future of the World Economy*. New York: WW Norton.

Scheiber, Noam. 2014. "Obama Is Foundering on Trade because He's Too Much Like Bill Clinton, Not Too Little," *The New Republic Online*, February 23.

Seelke, Clare Ribando. 2012 "Mexico: Issues for Congress", CRS Report RL-32724. Washington, DC: Congressional Research Service, 15 February.

Shecter, Barbara. 2013. "Canada Dodges Volcker's Full Impact," *Financial Post*, December 11, FP1.

Sinclair, Barbara. 1999. "Transformational Agent or Faithful Agent: Principal-Agent Theory and House Majority Party Leadership," *Legislative Studies Quarterly* 24 (3): 421–449.

Slaughter, Anne Marie. 2004. *A New World Order*. Princeton: Princeton University Press.

Stanton, John. 2012. "Who's Afraid of John Boehner?" *Roll Call*, February 29.

Strahan, Russell. 2007. *Leading Representatives: The Agency of Leaders in the Politics of the US House.* Baltimore: Johns Hopkins University Press.
Studer, Isabel. 2007. "Obstacles to Integration: NAFTA's Institutional Weakness" (pp. 53–75), in Isabel Studer and Carol Wise, eds., *Requiem or Revival: The Promise of North American Integration.* Washington DC: The Brookings Institution.
White House. 2012. "Promoting International Regulatory Cooperation," Executive Order 13609, *Federal Register* 77 (67), May 4, 26413–15.
Volden, Craig, and Elizabeth Bergman. 2006. "How Strong Should Our Party Be? Party Member Preferences over Party Cohesion," *Legislative Studies Quarterly* 33 (1): 71–104.
Waddell, Christopher. 2010. "The Auto Industry Bailout: Industrial Policy or Job-Saving Social Policy?" (pp. 150–167), in G. Bruce Doern and Christopher Stoney, eds., *How Ottawa Spends: 2010–2011.* Montreal: McGill-Queen's University Press.
Washington Post, The. 2011. "Mr. Sessions and the Need to Trade," *The Washington Post,* editorial, February 12.
Weintraub, Sidney. 2007. *Energy Cooperation in the Western Hemisphere.* Washington DC: Center for Strategic and International Studies.

9 Polls, Parties, Politicization, and the Evolution of North American Regional Governance

Brian Bow and Arturo Santa Cruz[1]

Most of the preceding chapters in this volume are concerned with the roles played by various political and economic elites in shaping the pace and direction of regional integration in North America. Especially prominent have been closed networks of bureaucrats and lawyers working collaboratively outside of the conventional channels for political accountability (i.e., transgovernmental networks). In addition to questions about efficacy and distribution, this raises important questions about democracy and legitimacy. What does the general public—in each of the three countries—think about the process and outcomes of regional policy coordination? When and how do public attitudes and expectations have an impact on the regional agenda?

These have become increasingly important questions in Europe, which is often seen as a model or template for the theory and practice of regional integration more generally. The early decades of European integration were characterized by a "permissive consensus," in which publics were seen to be passively supportive of regional cooperation, and willing to defer to policymakers in designing and implementing joint European policies.[2] Beginning with the negotiation of the Maastricht Treaty, however, regional integration became increasingly politicized in Europe, with a larger proportion of survey respondents holding strong views on regional issues, greater polarization of opinion, and some political candidates and parties developing clear and explicit positions on regional integration per se.[3] Based on extensive opinion surveys over the last twenty years, students of European integration are developing a clearer picture of public attitudes on regional issues, and a more nuanced understanding of the nature and sources of "Euroskepticism," in all its various forms. Even before the eruption of the ongoing monetary crisis, there were clear indications of widespread opposition to regional integration in Europe, and signs of broad-based national and transnational coalitions seeking to contain or even roll back the region-building project. However, even in this more politically charged context, the process of regional institution building continued in Europe, with policymakers pressing ahead aggressively (though not always successfully) with the building of a single regional market and shared currency in the 1990s, and with the drafting of a European constitutional structure in the 2000s.

The North American experience has been strikingly different. In fact, as we will explain later in this chapter, the pattern in North America is almost exactly the opposite of what we have seen in Europe. Whereas European integration was not politicized at the outset and then became politicized over time, North American integration was intensely politicized at the outset (i.e., at the time of the free trade ratification debates), but then depoliticized almost immediately afterward, and it has remained depoliticized since. Whereas regionalism and regional integration in themselves seem to have become more salient as focal points for political mobilization in Europe over the last twenty years, in North America regional integration per se seems to have become less salient, except for small (but vocal) minorities, mostly operating outside of the political mainstream. Whereas anti-regionalism in Europe has become embedded in party platforms and coalition making, and therefore plays itself out through traditional party-led political competition, in North America—or at least in the US and Canada—none of the major parties have staked out clear and consistent positions on regional integration per se, and there has been no sustained interparty debate on these issues since NAFTA came into force. And, finally, whereas the rise of a fairly robust anti-regionalist coalition did not deter European political leaders from pursuing more ambitious forms of regional institution building, in North America the anticipation of latent opposition has played a part in dissuading American and Canadian political leaders from overt region building.

The rest of this chapter is organized into three main parts. First, we consider the argument, raised in the introduction to this volume, that popular anti-regionalism deflected or constrained the potential for a "deepening" of regional integration in North America after NAFTA. We note that political elites in all three countries—but particularly in the US—did perceive a latent opposition to further regional integration immediately after NAFTA, and this did dissuade some of them from exploring options for more ambitious forms of regionalism. However, we argue that policymakers *did* pursue a form of "deepening" after NAFTA, based on informal policy coordination, rather than formal treaty making and institution building. Policymakers were more inclined to pursue this more informal approach anyway, for longstanding structural and strategic reasons, so the perception of latent public opposition to formal region building after NAFTA merely reinforced an inclination that was already well established.

Second, we briefly review some recent literature on public opinion in North America, with particular attention to the question of whether or not there is a substantial reservoir of latent opposition to regionalism (i.e., anti-regionalism), which could deflect or constrain further regional integration. We find that there is little in the extant survey literature to support either the conventional wisdom that there is widespread popular opposition to regional integration, or Robert Pastor's revisionist reading of the polls, which suggests that the public actually wants much closer cooperation between the three countries, and the absence of further regional integration after NAFTA is attributable to a lack of political will and creativity among political elites.[4]

Finally, we consider the specific form that politicization of regional integration took during the NAFTA debates, and the depoliticization of these issues afterward. More specifically, we argue that the different form, scope, and timing of politicization in the North American context may be at least partly attributable to different electoral systems, which generate different mechanisms for politicization and mobilization, and different incentives for politicians with an interest in these issues.[5] Most western European countries have proportional representation (PR) electoral systems, which create incentives for small parties to explicitly adopt strong positions on regional integration, and choose electoral coalition partners accordingly. The US and Canada, on the other hand, have single-member plurality (SMP) systems, and Mexico has a SMP system for its presidential elections, with a mixed system for its national legislature. Within SMP systems, mainstream parties have few incentives to adopt clear-cut positions on issues about which very small minorities are passionate, but most potential supporters are either ambivalent or indifferent; thus regional integration after NAFTA has remained a marginal issue in the US and Canada, and there is a deep sense of disenfranchisement and frustration among opponents of regional integration. As we will discuss in the concluding section of this chapter, this generally underappreciated institutional dimension has important implications for the future of regional integration in North America.

POPULAR ANTI-REGIONALISM AND POST-NAFTA REGIONAL GOVERNANCE: ONE CAUSE AMONG MANY

As noted in the introduction to this volume, theory and research on European integration has found that when political leaders attempting to coordinate policies with regional neighbors find themselves "blocked" by inflexible supranational or national institutions, or by widespread and intense popular opposition, they will often eschew formal institution building, and rely instead on informal coordination, particularly through transgovernmental networks. Thus the intense controversies surrounding the Single European Act in the early 1990s and the constitutional treaties in the mid-2000s were each followed by a slowdown of intergovernmental diplomacy and a marked increase in the intensity and importance of transgovernmental network activity as an engine for policy coordination.[6] One could argue that something similar took place in North America as well, as the controversy surrounding the negotiation and ratification of NAFTA was followed by a marked shift toward informal coordination, particularly the kinds of "bundled" transgovernmental networks described in VanNijnatten and Craik's contribution to this volume.[7] However, we should be careful not to overstate the importance of popular anti-regionalism as an explanation for the particular form that regional governance has taken in post-NAFTA North America. There are, as we will explain below, a number of other factors in play, and public opposition—actual or potential—seems to play only a supporting role in the story.

Historically, trade policy has only very rarely stirred much controversy in North America, and has not often been prominent in national election campaigns. However the Canada-US Free Trade Agreement (CUSFTA) and the North American Free Trade Agreement (NAFTA) triggered intense political debates in Canada and the US, respectively, and had significant impacts on subsequent national elections. CUSFTA was the focal point for intense debate in Canada, before and during the 1988 election, with polls finding the electorate evenly—and often intensely—divided on the issue. NAFTA enjoyed broad support in the US at the outset of negotiations in 1991, but once lobbying against it began in earnest, public opposition grew rapidly, reaching 57 percent in September 1992 and 63 percent in March 1993.[8] Given the extent and the intensity of the controversy surrounding the free trade agreements, it is not surprising that policymakers in all three countries—and particularly in the US—were convinced that there was a substantial reservoir of latent opposition to regional integration in North America, and that any move to further "deepen" regional ties would risk provoking a dangerous political backlash.[9]

The "lessons" of NAFTA were played out in several different ways, and reinforced through multiple iterations, for both of the two major parties in the US.[10] It began when outsider candidates within both the Democratic and Republican primaries seized on NAFTA as a wedge issue to challenge mainstream frontrunners. On the right, Pat Buchanan attacked George H. W. Bush's decision to negotiate free trade with Mexico, arguing that it would undermine national sovereignty and democratic accountability, and accelerate the "Hispanicization" of American society. On the left, Jerry Brown, Ralph Nader, and Jesse Jackson condemned Bill Clinton's support for NAFTA as a betrayal of core party supporters in the unions and environmental NGOs, arguing that the deal would create pollution and destroy jobs on both sides of the US-Mexico border. Then, once the presidential election got under way, Ross Perot made NAFTA the centerpiece of his ill-fated third-party challenge, mixing right- and left-wing critiques of the agreement, and thereby stripping votes from both of the major parties.

The most important moment, though, at least in terms of making a lasting impact on political elites in Washington, came in the fall of 1993, when it became clear that, even with broad Republican support, the Clinton administration did not have the necessary votes in Congress to secure ratification of the agreement.[11] The new administration's credibility was on the line, and the White House was ultimately forced to engage in a desperate campaign of last-minute vote trading and pork peddling to win over a handful of recalcitrant legislators.[12] Although Clinton was ultimately able to deflect pressure from within his party base by tacking on the labor and environmental "side agreements," Washington insiders were impressed by the political clout wielded by the new tacit alliance between unions and environmentalists, before and after the 1992 presidential election. Even more striking was the way these groups rallied the support of a broader bloc of civil society NGOs and ordinary voters, part of which eventually emerged as the leading edge of the popular anti-globalization movement of the 1990s and 2000s.[13]

Before the dust had settled on NAFTA ratification, moreover, Mexico was hit in quick succession by a "Zapatista" insurgency in the south, a series of high-profile corruption scandals, and a financial crisis that required a multibillion-dollar US bail-out. Thus NAFTA continued to be a lightning rod for criticism in the US, from the left and right, even after it was passed into law.[14] Twenty years later, we can see that "NAFTA" has become a powerful symbolic marker in American society, evoking popular anxieties about the political and social implications of economic globalization, demographic and cultural transformation, and questions about popular sovereignty in an increasingly "internationalized" political space.[15]

Canada had of course negotiated its own free trade agreement with the US back in 1987, and Brian Mulroney's Progressive Conservative government had narrowly won the national election the following year. But the next time out, in the October 1993 election, the party was smashed at the polls, at least partly because of popular misgivings about free trade, and it spent the next decade in the political wilderness.[16] The leader of the resurgent Liberal party, Jean Chrétien, had campaigned on promises to renegotiate the NAFTA deal he had inherited from Mulroney, but then backtracked right after he was elected, drawing intense but short-lived criticism from Canadian labor and environmental groups.[17]

Overall there was not a great deal of public opposition to NAFTA in Mexico, and, as we will discuss later in the chapter, there seems today to be broad popular support for—or at least receptiveness to—closer integration in general. But there were some in Mexico who were alarmed about the sovereignty and social implications of NAFTA, and the agreement became a focal point for resentment among groups that felt threatened and disenfranchised by rapid change. Even solid supporters of free trade argued that Carlos Salinas has promised too much to secure popular support for NAFTA, and worried that the resulting dislocations and disappointments could trigger a broad backlash against the agreement, particularly from less-educated and less-skilled workers, rural areas, and southern states, all of which were integral to the PRI's political base.[18]

In all three countries, there was clearly still a robust elite consensus around liberalization of domestic economies and closer integration with regional neighbors, but this had clearly been tempered by the political turbulence stirred up when regional agreements had passed through formal treaty-ratification processes. Given the lessons drawn from the NAFTA debates, it is not surprising that politicians in the US and Canada would be wary of further regional cooperation, particularly where it might aggravate the same groups that had most aggressively opposed NAFTA: geographically concentrated economic interests, organized labor, environmental NGOs, and "civil society" organizations from the further left and right of the political spectrum.[19] Thus, a number of observers have argued that politicians were generally reluctant to focus on regional issues in the late 1990s, and, when forced to grapple with these issues after the 9/11 terrorist attacks, they made a deliberate choice to approach policy coordination through informal channels, which would insulate them from public oversight and circumvent formal decision-making processes, which might serve as focal points for interest group and popular opposition.[20]

In Mexico, political elites connected with the PAN and, to a lesser extent, the PRI, were inclined to try to build on NAFTA through further rounds of formal institution building, in order to win the attention of US policymakers, tie up political and legal loopholes in NAFTA, and create tighter constraints on the US. This was most clearly reflected in Vicente Fox's diplomatic push for a "NAFTA-Plus" accord, which ultimately withered and died in the face of US indifference.[21] Ultimately, Mexican officials accepted the SPP model as a "best-available" option, and tried to get what they could from it. The SPP, one Mexican official reflected,

> attempts to achieve what is possible, not what is ideal. . . . We are going to do everything that is administratively possible to do, because the three countries consider that going through Congress is quite [a bit] more complex. . . . There are very adverse conditions in the three countries for achieving a more integrationist scheme, because we are in a period of certain skepticism towards more integrative positions in the three countries.[22]

There were some in Canada who also favored some kind of formal institution building, perhaps in the context of a "grand bargain" that would address America's post–9/11 security concerns.[23] But proponents of a "big deal" were few and far between in Canada, outnumbered and out-positioned by those who wanted to move away from trilateral relations, and back to informal policy coordination with the US, perhaps based on a revival of the Cold War–era "special relationship."[24]

Most important, of course, were the preferences of the US, and there was a clear consensus in Washington that formal institution building in the regional context was not politically viable.[25] Thus, reflecting on the origins of the 2005 Security and Prosperity Partnership (SPP), former Deputy Assistant Secretary Roberta Jacobson—for example—described it as a conscious choice by policymakers not to try to pursue a more ambitious "NAFTA-like step," but rather to "aim smaller" because of "the electoral and political realities in all three countries."[26] This interpretation was echoed by former Assistant Secretary Thomas Shannon:

> . . . [A]s we developed this we really thought we were operating kind of at the far edge of the envelope of what was possible politically in all three countries. . . . I think all three countries had to work very carefully internally in order to shape an approach to the SPP that allowed us to do as much as possible without provoking a political backlash that would actually set back North American integration.[27]

The formula that was ultimately chosen was based on the technical working groups developed to manage policy frictions associated with the negotiation and implementation of NAFTA. These involved networks of policymakers, both political appointees and technical experts, with some intermittent direction from the political leaderships, and some selective engagement with relevant private sector stakeholders. These networks were tasked with identifying, negotiating, and implementing relatively "easy" forms of policy coordination, in areas like regulation, infrastructure, and information sharing.[28] This same basic model was applied in the Security and Prosperity Partnership, and then broken up and reformed on bilateral basis through the 2007 Mérida Initiative, the subsequent Beyond the Border initiative, US-Canada Regulatory Cooperation Council, US-Mexico High-Level Regulatory Cooperation Council, and various other named and unnamed network processes.

This approach was not particularly successful in terms of reconciling difficult policy frictions between the three countries, but it was very successful in terms of avoiding or minimizing interference and criticism from within the three countries. In that sense, it seems to have been tailor-made as a response to the lessons political leaders learned from NAFTA. However, while the timing and the motivations "fit," it is important not to overstate the importance of popular anti-regionalism in shaping the evolution of regional governance structures in North America.

As briefly outlined in the introduction to this volume, all three governments had their own structural, institutional, and strategic reasons to prefer informal coordination as the predominant mode of regional governance, before and after NAFTA. The US, as the dominant state in the region, would naturally prefer to avoid creating regional institutions that could set limits on its freedom of action, or shift bargaining leverage to regional neighbors.[29] Canada and Mexico, as weaker states living in America's shadow, hoped that regional agreements might set some limits on the exercise of US power, but were anxious about participating in regional institutions that might undermine their sovereignty, or force them to accept US policy preferences.[30]

These structural features were reflected in the institutional design of NAFTA itself, and this has had important implications for subsequent policy coordination efforts. Following theory and research in institutional economics, Alexander Cooley and Hendrik Spruyt have characterized NAFTA as an example of relatively shallow but "complete" contracting, in which the parties elected not to pool a significant share of sovereignty in supranational institutions, but instead worked out very clearly the rules governing regional trade and investment and the terms by which those rules might be applied and adjusted.[31] This is in contrast to the European experience, where early treaties were relatively "incomplete," but involved a much more extensive pooling of rule-making authority within regional institutions. Thus whereas in Europe the creation of supranational institutions had a self-reinforcing and self-extending effect, in North America, the clear rejection of supranationalism in NAFTA reinforced the three states' national sovereignty, but created an inflexible institutional structure that could not adapt to new policy challenges.

Louis Bélanger has picked up on this line of thinking, but argues that the important question is not how much rule-making authority has been handed over to supranational authorities (i.e., international delegation), but rather how much the regional institution and existing national institutions provide for concentration of rule-making authority in national executives (i.e., domestic delegation).[32] NAFTA set some limits on national legislatures and subfederal governments, and thereby created new space for more autonomous policymaking by national executives, through executive orders and discretion over resource allocation, implementation, and regulation. Because NAFTA and subsequent initiatives like the SPP do not provide for any meaningful supranational rule-making authority, progress in regional policy coordination has mostly depended on the degree of policymaking autonomy that national executives happen to have within any given issue area. Thus, while there has been virtually no movement over the last twenty years on rules-of-origin, the three governments were able to coordinate relatively quickly and easily on post–9/11 border controls and law enforcement cooperation. Moreover, political leaders have been inclined to take advantage of opportunities to reinforce and deepen their rule-making authority wherever possible, and have therefore tried to use post-NAFTA regional initiatives like the SPP not only to iron out policy frictions among them, but also to assert and strengthen their claims to policy autonomy against various political challengers (e.g., legislatures, states/provinces, courts).

In Europe, regional identity and support for supranationalism have been reinforced by pressures from outside the region, based on the expectation that a regional institution might more effectively respond to complex, transnational problems, and protect shared values against the homogenizing, sovereignty-diminishing effects of globalization.[33] In the US, however, there are signs that the pressures of globalization have reinforced traditional conceptions of national identity and sovereignty, as well as culturally rooted anxieties about supranationalism, particularly where it evokes the supposedly inefficient and hyper-bureaucratized European Union.[34] This aversion to supranationalism played an important part in discouraging post-NAFTA coordination in the late 1990s, and encouraging the reliance on low-profile "working groups" after 9/11. However, the underlying suspicion of "big government" probably undercut the post-NAFTA working group model as well, because the lack of transparency surrounding the SPP process sparked alarm, on the further right and left of the ideological spectrum, that—beneath its boring, technocratic façade—lurked a more ambitious, supranationalist agenda (i.e., "North American Union").[35]

Thus policymakers in all three countries had a number of compelling reasons to prefer informal coordination over formal institution building, before and after NAFTA. The perception after the NAFTA debates that there was deeply rooted opposition to regional integration does seem to have reinforced these incentives. But, contrary to some accounts, which have tended to see public opposition as the key obstacle to Europe-style region building in North America, it is probably more useful to think of this is as a relatively minor part of the much more complex explanation for the scope and form of regional governance in North America today.

THE SCALE AND STRUCTURE OF ANTI-REGIONALISM IN NORTH AMERICA

Ann Capling and Kim Nossal have argued that North America is strikingly different from Europe, and possibly unique among world regions, as an example of extensive regionalization without regionalism.[36] That is, it represents a case where neighboring countries have recognized extensive policy interdependence, and have effectively coordinated policies with one another across an array of issues, in spite of the fact that virtually no one identifies with the region nor strongly favors the creation of formal regional institutions. This fits with the conventional wisdom about North America, which holds that most voters in the three countries are opposed to further regional integration, or at least deeply skeptical about it. One of the very few public advocates of closer regional ties, Robert Pastor, challenged this conventional wisdom, arguing that opinion polls actually indicate that citizens of all three countries want their governments to cooperate more effectively with their regional neighbors, are open to the prospect of more integrated policies, and may even be developing a nascent sense of regional identification.

Based on our review of recent survey-based research, we argue that reality is somewhere in between the conventional wisdom and Pastor's revisionist reading. We agree with the conventional wisdom that there is widespread skepticism about regional integration in North America, but we argue that the scale of "latent" opposition is less important than the potential for that opposition to be mobilized and translated into political pressure. And, while agreeing with Pastor's general point that there is nothing inevitable about popular opposition to regional integration in North America, we challenge his reading of recent opinion poll numbers.

Given the obvious importance for each country of its relations with its North American neighbors, it is striking how little we know about public attitudes toward regional cooperation. This is in sharp contrast with the European experience, where wide-ranging and long-running opinion surveys like the Eurobarometer and European Values Survey have provided researchers with abundant raw material for sophisticated studies of public attitudes and their connections to specific policy debates.[37] In North America, relatively few opinion surveys have asked specifically about regional integration per se, the few questions that have been asked are very broad, and few of these questions have been asked the same way repeatedly, in order to make it possible to properly track changes over time. The survey-driven research we do have so far has naturally attempted the get as much mileage as possible out of this meager pool of resources, but the results raise as many questions as they answer.

One commonly asked and analyzed question is about identification with nation and/or region, as a way of assessing the degree to which people identify with the broader regional community. This is an important question in the European context because proponents of regional integration have actively tried to foster a sense of European identity that complements or even supersedes national identity, and their success in doing so could also be read as an indication of political momentum for regional integration more generally.[38] But, as noted earlier, regionalization has proceeded in North America without any real effort to cultivate regional identification, and the presence or absence of such a self-image wouldn't necessarily tell us much about the latent potential for regional integration.

Not surprisingly, opinion polls have found that very few people, in any of the three countries, identify themselves primarily as North American. Pastor and his co-authors cite surveys that have found the number of people who identify primarily with North America, rather than their respective nation-state or some other collectivity, varying between 2 and 8 percent at various times over the last thirty years, with the most recent number (October 2013) at 4 percent.[39] Pastor argues that it is an interesting, counterintuitive finding that anyone at all would identify with North America, given the absence of any effort to build a regional identity. But we ought to be cautious about drawing any such conclusions from this figure, given that it isn't much higher than the poll's margin of error (2.5 percent).[40]

More interestingly, Pastor also cites polls that show that, when given the choice to identify as national *and* "North American" (as opposed to either nation-state only or region only), significant minorities picked this option: 41 percent in the US, 31 percent in Canada, and 27 percent in Mexico. These are surprisingly high numbers, with that for the US only slightly lower than the number of Europeans who chose "nation and then Europe" in answer to similar poll questions (i.e., generally varying between 40 and 50 percent since the early 1990s).[41] Pastor explains this surprisingly high figure for dual identification in terms of increased numbers of "binational" people in North

America, mostly living near the US-Canada and US-Mexico borders. This is a plausible interpretation, but again we should not read too much into these numbers because they are based on a very small number of polls, and because the even larger number of respondents choosing a national identity only could be read—as it often is in the European context—as evidence of a conscious, deliberate rejection of the dual-identification option.[42]

There is a well-established literature showing that self-identification with Europe is consistently associated with support for European integration.[43] Parallel studies have found a similar relationship in North America. In a 2004 study, David Rankin looked more closely at the connection between national identity and attitudes toward NAFTA.[44] He found that indicators for education, income, and ideology were not good predictors of Canadians' and Americans' attitudes toward the agreement, but respondents putting a greater emphasis on national identity and values were consistently more likely to have unfavorable views of the free trade agreements. More specifically, the respondents with the most negative views of NAFTA were also those with a more patriotic self-image in Canada, those with a more "restrictive" concept of national identity and culture in the US, and those with more traditional views on national sovereignty in both countries.

Similar results have been found in subsequent studies over the last ten years, including a recent study by Constantine Boussalis and her co-authors, which found that those indicating a stronger sense of identification with North America were more likely to have positive views of NAFTA (particularly in Canada and Mexico), and to express greater openness to regional integration more generally, even if it might compromise national sovereignty.[45] This then brings up the more important questions, raised by Boussalis et al, of whether or when those connections are stable across question frames and political contexts, and when and how those attitudes translate into political mobilization.

Closely related is the question of survey respondents' attitudes toward their regional neighbors. Particularly in the North American context, where there are only three states in play, one would expect that those who have negative views of regional neighbors will be less likely to support regional integration. Pastor reviews relevant poll data, and—based mainly on Chicago Council polls—finds that the number of respondents in all three countries with favorable views of the other two countries are consistently higher than those with unfavorable views.[46] However, a wider survey of poll results finds very different numbers, with clear majorities of Americans often expressing unfavorable views of Mexico—particularly after 2008—and pluralities of Canadians sometimes having negative views of the US, particularly in the mid-2000s. The most recent Pew Global Attitudes surveys found that majorities in Canada and Mexico have favorable views of the US (64 percent and 66 percent, respectively); the vast majority of Americans have positive views of Canada (81 percent), but far fewer have positive views of Mexico (39 percent favorable, 52 percent unfavorable).[47] These results probably bear out Pastor's argument that North Americans don't "hate each other," but it doesn't necessarily indicate any sense of common purpose or openness to regional integration. In fact, as Pastor points out, all of these figures fluctuate with perceived changes in each bilateral diplomatic relationship, and can be shifted—sometimes quite significantly—by media reports of specific policy frictions.[48] These context effects may also carry over into attitudes toward NAFTA or specific post-NAFTA regional initiatives, but so far we do not have well-developed empirical analysis to confirm this.

A variation on this theme is the question of trust between North American partners. Paul Brewer and his co-authors have shown that a sense of trust in other nations is associated with support for closer diplomatic and political cooperation with those countries, and similar results have been found in survey-based research on European integration.[49] Alejandro Moreno has explored this question in the North American context and found that the number of Canadians expressing trust in the US had increased between 1990 and 2005, from 55 percent to 65 percent, and that the number for Mexicans had gone up during that same period from 20 percent to 36 percent.[50] Pastor reads these figures as a positive sign, as the overall level of trust seems to be increasing as the number of demographic and economic connections between the societies increases in the wake of NAFTA.[51] We should not lose sight, however, of how low some of these numbers are in absolute terms. Moreno gives a detailed breakdown of figures for Mexicans in 2003, showing that only 23 percent of respondents trusted the US "a great deal" or "quite a lot," while 77 percent trusted them "not very much" or "not at all." Mexicans expressed even less trust in Canadians, with the corresponding figures at 20 percent and 80 percent.[52]

One way to get more direct traction on the question of regional integration per se is to look at publics' attitudes toward NAFTA. This is one dimension that can be tracked over time with some confidence because the question has been asked repeatedly, in essentially the same form, since 1994. Unfortunately, NAFTA has picked up so much political baggage over the last twenty years that it may represent different things to different people, from trade policy to cultural and ethnic diversity.[53] Some observers have focused on the way that public's views of NAFTA worsened after it came into effect in 1994, but, as Pastor shows, attitudes toward NAFTA have pretty consistently gone up or down in line with perceptions of national economies' overall performance, just as have attitudes toward free trade in general.[54] A few details are worth mentioning. Canadians and Mexicans believe that Americans have gotten more out of NAFTA than they did, and Americans think it's the other way around. Americans generally think that Canada is a fair trader; the number for Mexico is lower, but it has increased significantly since NAFTA came into effect. Again, these attitudes are sensitive to national economic performance, with clear dips after 2008.

Other kinds of poll questions have looked more directly at attitudes toward regional integration, but it is sometimes difficult to know how to interpret the results. Basanez, Inglehart, and Nevitte looked at WVS data on respondents' attitudes toward "forming a single country" with a regional neighbor, under certain conditions.[55] The results found surprisingly high numbers supporting a hypothetical political merger in 1990, particularly where it was linked to improved economic fortunes and quality of life. "Would you favor or oppose having Canada/Mexico and the US form one country, if it meant that you would enjoy a higher standard of living?," for example, was answered positively by 81 percent of Americans, 64 percent of Mexicans, and 50 percent of Canadians. Those numbers went down markedly when the question was asked again in 2005—after diplomatic tensions had erupted over the war in Iraq—but still remained remarkably high (77 percent, 51 percent, and 43 percent, respectively). Even this ostensibly regionalism-friendly result should be kept in perspective, however. Viewed from another angle, the same results also show that nearly half of Canadians and Mexicans in 2005 would categorically reject political merger with the US, even if that merger were somehow guaranteed to improve their standard of living.[56] Priming is clearly crucial here, moreover, because the numbers are very different when the consequence of political integration is an anticipated loss of cultural identity, with only 10 percent of Americans supportive in 2005, 12 percent of Mexicans, and 5 percent of Canadians.

In 2005, Ekos Research asked survey respondents whether they thought the three North American countries "should have an economic union like the European Union," and found higher-than-expected support for the idea: 45 percent agreeing in the US, 57 percent in Canada, and 59 percent in Mexico.[57] However, as Pastor concedes, it is not at all clear whether respondents understand what would be involved in such a union, nor what sort of terms or time frame they would accept.

The Ekos 2005 poll also asked respondents whether they would prefer to see more "independent" or more "integrated" policies on a list of eleven issues.[58] Pastor reviews the results and argues that "the public is clear in their preference for North American approaches to a wide group of issues." A closer look at the results, however, raises questions about this inference. "Fully integrated" and "somewhat integrated" have been lumped together in the reported results, so that even those respondents who preferred a very small degree of policy coordination—perhaps even less than the level actually found at that time—are counted as supporters of further integration. "Independent" might therefore be read as indicating a preference for deliberate pursuit of differentiated policies, or even a reduction of existing policy coordination. In any event, majorities from all countries can agree on greater integration with respect to fewer than half of the issues on Ekos's list: environment, border security, defense policy, transportation, and (especially vaguely) "economic policies." If there is a clear pattern in this data, then it is that Canadians are either skeptical of or divided/ambivalent about closer integration on most issues, often with very small differences between the number preferring "somewhat or fully integrated" policies and those preferring "independent" policies. Mexicans are clearly more open to integrated policies across the spectrum, with some reservations about energy, banking, and currency.

Graves, Pastor, and Basanez ask a very similar set of questions again in 2013, but with responses on a seven-point scale.[59] American respondents tilted toward integrated policies on environment and border security; were ambivalent on economic policy and energy; and inclined toward independent policies on currency, banking, and defense. Canadians also preferred integrated policies on environment and border control, were divided over energy, and inclined to independent policies on everything else. Most Mexicans were inclined toward integrated policies across the board (with the important exception of energy), but Mexicans were also much more likely to tilt strongly toward the ends of the seven-point scale, meaning that there were also substantial minorities in favor of independent policies, particularly with respect to defense, economic policies, and currency.

This brief review of poll findings suggests that while we do have some interesting questions to ask, we do not yet have enough of the right kinds of survey results to draw confident conclusions about the nature and bases for public support or opposition to regional integration in North America. Most of what we do have so far is either so broad as to be inherently ambiguous, or so skewed that it is probably better seen as "spin" than science. Following the much more substantial research on public opinion and regional integration in Europe, survey research on North America needs to move away from vacuous "thermometer" questions, try to get more directly at attitudes toward (and knowledge about) specific policy initiatives, and try to parse out context and framing effects.

ELECTIONS, PARTIES, AND POLITICIZATION IN NORTH AMERICA

In the introduction to this chapter, we noted the striking difference in the sequencing of politicization between Europe and North America: Europe was characterized for decades by a "permissive consensus," but over the last twenty years it has become increasingly politicized. In North America, regional integration was politicized very rapidly during the free trade debates, but then depoliticized just as rapidly, and has remained so ever since.

One possible explanation for this pattern is the occurrence of formal treaty-making "moments," which naturally become focal points for political contestation. The early European treaties, such as the 1957 Treaty of Rome, did not impinge much on national sovereignty and had minimal impacts on voters' day-to-day lives and livelihoods. Later treaties, beginning with the 1987 Single European Act, removed national vetoes on important policy questions, and could be readily seen to have big potential effects on countries and individuals. Politicization in Europe has consistently been most widespread and intense during periods leading up to and immediately after major treaty showdowns—i.e., the late 1980s and early 1990s, and the mid-2000s.[60] North America's treaty-making moments were the two free trade agreements—CUSFTA in the late 1980s and NAFTA in the early 1990s—and the politicization we have seen in North America is very neatly confined to those two periods.

Because the treaty that was eventually negotiated in North America clearly specified the parties' obligations and further rule-making procedures for trade and investment, there was little "demand" after NAFTA for further formal institution building. Because the ratification debate was so contentious, moreover, policymakers were anxious to avoid further political risks, and therefore inclined to pursue further integration through informal policy coordination that would minimize public criticism and reinforce national executive control. This interpretation is plausible up to a point, but it implies that there is only one political elite, when of course there are different groups of rival elites in play, in all three countries, competing to outmaneuver one another within the electoral process. How is it then, given the political and symbolic importance of some of the issues pursued since NAFTA through informal coordination (e.g., border control, law enforcement information sharing, regulatory coordination) that no mainstream party has sought to politicize these issues, or to challenge regional cooperation more broadly?

One part of the explanation must be that while opposition to regional integration may be widespread, it tends to be an "outsider" issue, with relatively few voters and organizations actually mobilized against it. That opposition, moreover, tends to come from the further left and right of the political spectrum. This pattern was frequently remarked on during the NAFTA debates in the US, with observers commenting on the "bizarre" left-right alliance working to derail the agreement.[61] This in itself is not unique to North America, however, as opposition to regional integration in Europe also tends to come from both the further left and right, with the right most concerned about national identity and sovereignty and the left most concerned about job security and living standards.[62] The important difference here seems to be not in the sources and structure of anti-regionalism itself, but rather the way that the different electoral systems affect the potential for politicization.[63]

Europe has a variety of different electoral systems, but many western European countries have some version of proportional representation (PR) for their national parliaments. Proportional representation systems make it easier for smaller parties to have an impact on national policy, by having elected representatives whose support may be needed in the formation of coalition governments.[64] The US and Canada, on the other hand, have single-member plurality (SMP, or "first-past-the-post") electoral systems, which—following Duverger's Law—tend to generate two-party competition, and encourage both parties to become broad, "catch-all" coalitions, each seeking the support of the median voter.[65] Mexico has an SMP system for its presidential elections, and—like some European countries—a hybrid system that mixes SMP and PR voting for the national legislature.

Thus in Europe there are opportunities for relatively small groups to form parties based on their support for or opposition to regional integration, and for small parties to form tactical alliances with other like-minded parties on these issues, even where they disagree on many other issues.[66] In North America, on the other hand, small parties tend to be eliminated from electoral competition—or at least marginalized—and the political landscape is dominated by a small number of powerful "brokerage" parties.[67] Thus, given that there is not a broad, ready-made coalition opposing regional integration in any of the three North American countries, those who oppose regional integration can only have an impact on the political debate by working *within* the major parties. To be clear, coalition building is pivotal in both contexts, but in Europe, the coalition building happens between parties, and in North America it happens within parties.

This is a reasonably useful way to start thinking about the NAFTA debate in the US. The big question there was always whether the Democratic presidential candidate would endorse or oppose NAFTA. Opposing the deal would provide a lever to attack George H. W. Bush's Republicans going into the 1992 elections, but it would run contrary to the advice of mainstream economists, alienate the export-oriented business community, and carry potentially serious diplomatic costs. As a moderate "new Democrat," Bill Clinton was quick to endorse NAFTA, and his focus shifted to pacifying traditional Democratic Party supporters like organized labor and increasingly important civil society groups like the environmental lobby.[68] Once it became clear that both of the two front-runner candidates supported NAFTA, the struggle was played out within the presidential primaries, with Bush attacked by Buchanan from the right, and Clinton challenged by Brown, Nader, and Jackson from the left. These "outsider" candidates sought to use their opposition to NAFTA to fuel their attempts to control the party platform and, if elected, probably (but not certainly) would have sought to translate their anti-regionalist ideas into policy.

We can also use this view of electoral politics to think about the absence of politicization after NAFTA, particularly in the US. When the George W. Bush administration signed on for the trilateral Security and Prosperity Partnership in 2005, it did so primarily because of the advice of leading officials and well-connected party insiders. The initiative provoked strident opposition, mostly from the conservative fringe, which reinforced the idea that there might be political risks associated from a more formal process with Congressional involvement, but did not provide for any means for these conservative critics to directly challenge the policy from within the Republican party machinery.[69] Obama's decision to terminate the SPP in 2009, moreover, seems to have been primarily an opportunistic rejection of a Bush initiative; the White House might have hoped that it would deflect marginal criticism from the left wing of the Democratic base, but the decision was not driven by intense pressure from a mobilized domestic constituency. Nor did it prevent the Obama administration from pursuing similar forms of policy coordination bilaterally through the Beyond the Border, High Level Economic Council, and Regulatory Cooperation Council initiatives.

There are of course all kinds of potential pitfalls with counterfactual reasoning, but it seems likely that a different electoral system in the US might have brought about a different pattern of politicization on regional issues. A PR system in the US would encourage the fracturing of the two dominant parties, most likely leading to the formation of a breakaway conservative-nativist party and/or a "red-green" party, favoring a more restrictive approach to trade and investment. These ideologically rooted parties would have strong incentives to politicize regional cooperation, particularly with respect to labor mobility and regulatory coordination, and would almost certainly have opposed the SPP. The political outcome might ultimately have been the same, but the extent and nature of politicization, and probably of popular mobilization as well, would likely have been quite different.

This is not to say, of course, that the SMP electoral system makes politicization of regional cooperation impossible. There was, as noted above, nothing inevitable about Democratic Party support for NAFTA in the 1992 election or afterward. More importantly, there *was* of course some interparty contestation of NAFTA in the US, in the form of Ross Perot's ill-fated third-party campaign. However, this is probably better read as an exception that proves the rule, in the sense that, while Perot's campaign did succeed in stirring opposition to NAFTA, and did (temporarily) steal support from both of the two major parties, it collapsed at the polls, and ultimately failed to shift the public debate on NAFTA.[70]

This interpretation of the depoliticization of regional cooperation after NAFTA fits less well in the Canadian and Mexican cases, but does so in a way that plays up the importance of electoral systems and party organization. In both Canada and Mexico, opposition parties have challenged sitting governments on high-profile regional integration initiatives, and these debates were prominent in some election campaigns. This is not particularly surprising, however, because both countries deviate from the "two-party" model imagined in Duverger's Law, and maintain political "space" for a handful of more programmatic/ideological small parties.

Since 1911, the question of free trade with the US had been the epicenter for a number of massive electoral earthquakes in Canada, and a number of observers had characterized it as an untouchable "third rail" for Canadian political parties. After Mulroney's Conservatives made the "leap of faith" to free trade in 1986, the Liberals positioned themselves firmly against CUSFTA, and made that opposition the centerpiece of their campaign in the next federal election. The 1988 contest, in fact, is often recalled by historians as "the free trade election."[71] In that sense, opposition to economic integration was as intensely politicized in this case as the interparty struggles over the constitutionalization of Europe in the mid-2000s. Since the 1988 election, however, regional issues have faded into the background in Canada. The Liberal party (as the official opposition) talked about "renegotiating" NAFTA during the 1993 federal election, but then quickly and quietly backtracked after they won. The more ideological New Democratic Party (NDP) and the Green Party have been critical of post-NAFTA regional initiatives, including the SPP, but have done so as minor parties with little leverage on political outcomes. After the NDP's surprising successes in the 2011 federal election, and during its subsequent tenure as the official opposition in Canada, the party was more circumspect in its attention to and attitude toward regional cooperation.

There are also clear-cut partisan divisions on regional issues within Mexico, although these have often not been focal points for partisan debate, at least partly because of the breadth and diversity of popular support there for regional cooperation. The Partido Revolución Institucional (PRI) was essentially hegemonic until the late 1990s, so the formal electoral system had little to do with political cleavages and issue politicization at the time of the NAFTA decision.[72] There was some opposition to NAFTA from within the PRI, but it was marginal and remained virtually invisible to the general public. The opposition Partido de la Revolución Democrática (PRD) was critical of the market liberalization strategy undertaken by the PRI, and of Salinas's negotiation of the free trade deal with the US, but tacitly acceptant of the necessity to secure access to the US market through some kind of trade agreement. Since the collapse of the PRI "perfect dictatorship" in 2000, the center-right Partido Acción Nacional (PAN) has consistently been more supportive of regional integration, and the PRD more critical, with the PRI occupying a middle ground that is generally inclined toward close cooperation with the US, and openness to trilateral coordination, but still holding on to nationalist rhetoric designed to maintain support from traditional bases of support among public sector workers, in the south, and in rural areas. Both the PRI and the PRD seem to have recognized and adapted to the broad pattern in Mexican public opinion, where—as noted above—there seems to be a broad base of support for further regional integration, based on pragmatic expectations about jobs and living standards, but also a relatively small but robust segment of the public that is opposed, based on a mixture of traditional nationalist concerns about sovereignty and geographic or sectoral concerns about job security and social turbulence.

These examples of party contestation over regional issues do not necessarily undercut the general argument that electoral systems have important effects on politicization. The premise here is not that SMP (and similar) electoral systems make politicization of these issues impossible, but rather that they make it less likely, and perhaps also more totalizing. In post-Maastricht Europe, where PR electoral systems are common, there is always permanent, low-level party contestation of regional integration; it may become consequential at specific times and places, when an anti-Europe party happens to hold the balance in national coalition-making dynamics.[73] In North

America, with its various SMP and SMP-hybrid systems, the politicization of regional issues depends mostly on coalition building within the major parties. If anti-regionalist leaders or groups happen to have influence on party priorities, then these issues may become intensely politicized, as they were in the 1988 Canadian election and 1992 US presidential election campaign. If not, then they will tend to disappear, save for those rare moments when light is shined on internal leadership struggles within the parties, as in the criticism of NAFTA by candidates Clinton and Obama in the 2008 Democratic primaries.

This is not necessarily undemocratic or illegitimate because it helps to guard the regional agenda against opportunistic challenges from fringe candidates or "capture" by highly organized interest groups. But it does mean that those who oppose regional integration will tend to feel disenfranchised by the system, and this will tend to bring the "conspiracy theory" element to the forefront of the opposition.[74]

CONCLUSIONS: WHAT THE PAST MIGHT TELL US ABOUT THE FUTURE

This (somewhat eclectic) chapter sought to make some progress in working through three problems associated with regional integration in North America: How can we best characterize the nature, extent, and sources of popular opposition to regional integration in North America? What impact has popular opposition had on the pace, trajectory, and form of regional integration since NAFTA came into effect twenty years ago? And how can we explain the explosive politicization of these issues in the late 1980s and early 1990s, and depoliticization since then?

A number of observers have approached these questions from the premise that there has been (and perhaps still is) a region-building project in play in North America, which was effectively derailed or delayed by popular opposition in one form or another. This is a view common among both opponents and proponents of closer economic integration. Thus critics such as Jeffrey Ayres (1998) have highlighted the efforts of transnational labor unions and civil society networks in challenging the free trade agreements and post-NAFTA initiatives for "deepening" of regional ties.[75] And proponents such as Robert Pastor (2011) have argued that policymakers who might otherwise have been strong advocates of regional cooperation have been cowed by populist critics. We agree with Ann Capling and Kim Nossal, however, who have argued that there never really was much political momentum behind regional integration per se, and very few proponents of region building per se (i.e., regionalism). The supposed "failure" of the North American project is therefore better seen as a reflection of an underlying preference among political leaders for informal modes of policy coordination, which are believed not only to maximize national autonomy but also—and perhaps more importantly—to increase central executive branch control over the policy agenda, insulating it against obstruction and criticism from legislatures, subnational governments, national and transnational interest groups, the media, and the general public.

So public opposition has probably played a less decisive role in forestalling regional institution building than some analysts have supposed. Public opposition had important effects on the form, intensity, and possibly even the outcome of the original CUSFTA and NAFTA debates, but its salience has evidently declined since then, and its effects have become more indirect. The overall level of public opposition has apparently declined significantly since the original free trade debates, although it is difficult to be certain given the limited opinion survey data available. Our review of recent survey research suggests that there may be a significant number of voters in each of the three countries who are receptive to more extensive policy coordination—and perhaps even to more thoroughgoing forms of political integration—as long as it would lead to tangible policy benefits (e.g., security, jobs). There are, however, also clearly (still) quite a number who are clearly opposed to these kinds of initiatives, based on misgivings about their anticipated policy effects and/or their implications for national sovereignty. Again, it is difficult to know with any certainty, based on available data, but that skepticism seems to be much more widespread in Canada and the US than in Mexico, albeit for different kinds of reasons.

More concretely, there seem to be particular issue-areas and formulations that hit a nerve for respondents in particular countries. Significant numbers of Americans are generally skeptical about close cooperation with Mexico, mistrustful of their own government's commitment to protect national sovereignty, and anxious about the implications of formal supranationalism. Many Canadians are evidently skeptical about formal institution building and trilateralism in general, and about policy integration in economic policy, finance/currency, and defense in particular. Mexicans seem to be most pragmatic about regional coordination in general terms, but many are opposed—often adamantly opposed—to more integrated policies in specific policy areas, particularly energy, banking, and finance/currency.

However, for all of these respondents and on all of these issues, context clearly matters, both in terms of the timing of the poll and the framing of the questions. Thus when asked about whether or not they would consider closer integration in order to improve their standard of living, the number of respondents receptive to this idea fell dramatically in the mid-2000s—in all three countries—when diplomatic tensions erupted over US defense policy. Context matters so much, in fact, that it raises questions about the coherence and stability of voters' opinions on these issues, and about whether or not any level of popular opposition can be seen to be a "permanent" obstacle to regional cooperation. Even issues that might today seem to be untouchable lightning rods might become tractable areas for policy coordination in the future, just as free trade itself—previously seen as an unapproachable "policy frontier"—was successfully framed as a policy imperative during the CUSFTA and NAFTA debates, and then receded into the background as a "normal" feature of national economic policy in a globalized world economy.[76]

Given the structural pressures for informal coordination outlined in the first part of this chapter, and the configuration of popular attitudes outlined in the second part, there seems little reason to expect renewed politicization of regional integration in North America. This is further reinforced by the effects of the SMP electoral system, particularly in the US, in terms of the incentives for politicians to be responsive to minority opinions and opportunities for minority coalitions to have an impact on the policy agenda. Because the opposition to regional integration in North America is geographically fragmented, disjointed across issue-areas, and—most importantly—drawn from the traditional constituency bases of multiple parties (e.g., the right wing of the Republican Party and the left wing of the Democratic Party), it seems to be locked into its current position as an "outsider" movement, with limited traction on the mainstream party leaderships.[77]

Outsider candidates may have opportunities to publicly challenge regional initiatives within US presidential primaries, in American and Mexican Congressional races, and in the Canadian party caucus process. And they may be in a position, from time to time, to drive mainstream candidates to strike anti-regionalist poses, as Clinton and Obama did over NAFTA in some of the 2008 Democratic primaries.[78] But, given the nature of the electoral system, opponents of regional integration will generally not have opportunities on the broader public stage afforded to national political candidates unless and until they are successful in "capturing" the party platform. This seems unlikely, at least for the foreseeable future. The post-NAFTA "working group" model has not delivered big and important breakthroughs in terms of resolving difficult policy coordination challenges, but it has demonstrated some tangible progress in areas like border control and law enforcement coordination, while—more importantly, as noted earlier—avoiding broad popular backlash. The only reasons national policymakers would give up on this model would be if it clearly proved to be functionally inadequate to cope with new and urgent problems, or if there were powerful political reasons for one or more countries (especially the US) to insist on the consecration of a new agreement through formal treaty making.[79]

NOTES

1. Thanks to John Mitton and Ben O'Bright for excellent research assistance. Both authors gratefully acknowledge financial support for this research from the Programa Interinstitucional de Estudios sobre la Región de América del Norte (PIERAN). Bow also acknowledges support, in the form of a Standard Research Grant, from the Social Sciences and Humanities Research Council of Canada.

2. The phrase was coined in Lindberg and Scheingold 1970.
3. Hellstrom 2008; Hooghe and Marks 2009; De Wilde and Zürn 2012.
4. Pastor 2011, 73–79.
5. The general argument is developed (in the European context) in Carrubba 2001.
6. Franklin et al 1994; Jönsson 1998; Eberlein and Grande 2005.
7. For general overview and appraisal of post-NAFTA integration in North America, see Pastor 2001; Hufbauer and Schott 2005; Studer 2007; Pastor 2011.
8. Gallup polls, cited in Klamer and Meehan 1999, 76. See also Lawrence 2002.
9. See Hart 1990; Weintraub 1996; Anderson and Sands 2007; Pastor 2008.
10. For general overviews of NAFTA as an issue in the 1992 presidential primaries and election, see Mayer 1998; Cameron and Tomlin 2000; Hufbauer and Schott 2005.
11. Conybeare and Zinkula 1996; Kahane 1996.
12. Mayer 1988, 311–19; Conybeare and Zinkula 1996; Shoch 2011.
13. Destler and Balint 1999; Shoch 2011.
14. Cameron and Tomlin 2000, 208–44; Hufbauer and Schott 2005, 9–14; Hufbauer and Schott 2008.
15. Pastor 2011; Bennett 2004; Shoch 2011.
16. Cairns 1996; Ayres 1998.
17. Ayres 1998.
18. Golob 2003; Cameron and Wise 2004.
19. Weintraub 1996.
20. Ayres and Macdonald 2006; Anderson and Sands 2007; Pastor 2008.
21. Leiken 2001; Miller and Gabriel 2008.
22. Santa Cruz interview of Alejandro Estivill, Washington, July 3, 2008.
23. These arguments are reviewed and assessed in Barry 2003.
24. See Sands 2011.
25. Weintraub 1996. For more on the question of a "big deal" after NAFTA, see Blank's contribution to this volume.
26. The full quotation is: "[T]he real debate in some respects I think was how big did you want to aim? Were you going to aim for something very large, a NAFTA-like step on integration? Or were you, because of the electoral and political realities in all three countries and the growing controversy over free trade in the US, going to have to aim smaller? And I think the decision was taken by all three leaders at the time that we were going to have to move incrementally. And there is I think pros and cons on both sides of the argument as to whether that was a good thing, but as it was structured SPP was not, and I don't think ever really has been, a sort of big lead." Santa Cruz interview of Roberta Jacobson, Washington, July 15, 2008.
27. Santa Cruz interview of Thomas Shannon, Washington, July 25, 2008.
28. Anderson and Sands 2007; Studer 2007; see also contributions to this volume by VanNijnatten and Craik and by Ackleson and Lapid.
29. Pastor 2005; Hurrell 2006.
30. The administration of Mexican President Vicente Fox is—as noted earlier—a partial exception to this pattern, as it advocated formal institution building, at least until it ran into opposition in Washington.
31. Cooley and Spruyt 2009, 142–84.
32. Bélanger 2007.
33. Mittelman 1996; Rosamond 2005.
34. On the historical and institutional sources of Americans' apprehensions about "big government," see Bennett and Bennett 1996. Of course, Americans' aversion to supranationalism has not necessarily prevented the US from

participating in international institutions, including relatively "deep" ones like the World Trade Organization. But it has tended to reinforce American political leaders' general preference for reciprocal executive commitments and "soft law."

35. Capling and Nossal 2009, 161–62.
36. Capling and Nossal 2009. A clear example of this kind of interpretation, from the right wing of the political spectrum, is Corsi 2007.
37. On the availability of survey data in various regional contexts, see Norris 2009. There is, however, also a near-consensus in Europe that even these fairly extensive public opinion resources are inadequate to a proper understanding of popular attitudes toward regional integration, and that scholars will have to "dig deeper" to properly understand the effects of context and framing. Hooghe and Marks 2001; see also Risse 2004; Checkel and Katzenstein 2009.
38. Carey 2002; Hooghe and Marks 2005; Christin and Trechsel 2002; Luedtke 2005.
39. Graves et al 2013, 12–13. See also Graves 2007, 107–09; Pastor 2011, 67.
40. Indeed, we should be cautious about the interpretation of any survey results featuring very small minorities because past polls have consistently found small minorities (< 20 percent) holding a variety of unorthodox and/or ill-informed views, including the 18 percent of Americans who apparently believe that the Sun revolves around the Earth. Crabtree 1999.
41. Pastor 2011, 67. For recent updating of the European trends, see Polyakova and Fligstein 2013. Graves (2007) compared the breakdown for North America and for Europe in 2002 and found some clear differences: in Europe, 59 percent chose "nationality and continental," "continental and nationality," or "continental only," while 39 percent chose "nationality only"; in North America, the corresponding figures were almost exactly the reverse—38 percent and 61 percent, respectively.
42. Or, more mundanely, it is possible that many of the people who "identified with" both nation and region were saying something about their knowledge of geography, rather than their own (political) self-concept.
43. E.g., Carey 2002; Hooghe and Marks 2004, 2005; Christin and Trechsel 2002; Luedtke 2005.
44. Rankin 2004; see also Rankin 2001.
45. Boussalis et al 2013.
46. Pastor 2011, 61–62.
47. Pew 2013a; Pew 2013b. See also Chicago Council 2013.
48. Pastor 2011, 60–62.
49. Brewer et al 2004; Sánchez-Cuenca 2000.
50. Moreno 2007.
51. Pastor 2011, 61–62.
52. Moreno explains that Mexicans seem to have a culturally rooted lack of social trust in general, which is reflected in the fact that only 16 percent of Mexican respondents expressed trust in other Mexicans. Research in other contexts suggests that trust in other societies is often based on direct experience (e.g., travel), business and family connections, and ideological concurrence. In that sense, there may be some room for optimism about the cultivation of trust within North America as a support to closer regional cooperation, but there is clearly a long way to go along this road.
53. Rankin 2004.
54. Pastor 2011, 62–63.
55. Basanez et al 2007, 35. See also Inglehart et al 1997.
56. In their October 2013 poll, Graves, Pastor, and Basanez asked Americans and Canadians an even more leading version of this question ("Would you

consider forming a single North American country if it means that you would enjoy a higher standard of living, a higher quality of life, or an improved environment?"), and got similarly ambivalent results: 38 percent of Americans agreed, and 35 percent disagreed; 26 percent of Canadians agreed, and 69 percent disagreed. That means, presumably, that 69 percent of Canadians refused to consider a political merger, even if it somehow guaranteed them a higher standard of living, higher quality of life, *and* an improved environment.

57. Ekos 2005, as reported in Pastor 2011, 71.
58. Ekos 2005, as reported in Pastor 2011, 73–74.
59. Graves et al 2013.
60. De Wilde and Zürn 2012.
61. Some pundits derided this alliance of strange bedfellows as "the Halloween Coalition." See Mayer 1998.
62. De Vries and Edwards 2009; Halikiopoulou et al 2012.
63. Party organization and strategies have been recognized as pivotal to the politicization of regional integration in Europe. See, for example, Gabel 2000; Ray 2003; Tillman 2004; Steenbergen and Scott 2004; Steenbergen et al 2007; Hellstrom 2008; Almeida 2012.
64. Duverger 1954. Many of these countries have strict minimum-vote requirements to discourage fringe parties. The fact that some explicitly pro- and anti-Europe parties have surpassed these requirements in recent years is an indication that politicization of regional integration is no longer a "fringe" phenomenon.
65. Riker 1982. Of course, this basic distinction between PR and SMP systems only captures a few of the different dimensions across which we can compare electoral systems. See Gallagher and Mitchell 2005.
66. For examples and analysis, see Almeida 2012.
67. Canada has often "violated" Duverger's Law, by sustaining several more or less viable parties, some of which have not behaved like ideal-type "brokerage" parties (e.g., the secessionist Bloc Quebecois); this is attributable in part to the segmentation of Canadian politics along regional lines. Mexico was dominated throughout the post-revolutionary period by a single party, the PRI, but it was formally challenged by two major rival parties, the PRD and PAN. Since the collapse of the PRI monopoly in 2000, the electoral landscape has been dominated by these same three parties.
68. Shoch 2011.
69. Pastor 2011.
70. Holian et al 1997; Uslaner 1998; Mayer 1998. Some studies have argued, in fact, that voters' loss of confidence in Perot in the late stages of the campaign undermined opposition to NAFTA.
71. Brodie 1989.
72. Klesner 2005.
73. Steenbergen and Scott 2004; Steenbergen et al 2007.
74. Bow forthcoming.
75. See also Ayres and Macdonald 2009.
76. On the crossing of the "policy frontier," see Golob 2003 and Santa Cruz 2013; on the social construction of crises and their implications for regional integration, see Bow 2012.
77. This is, as noted above, less clear-cut in Canada and in Mexico, where left-leaning parties (i.e., the NDP in Canada and the PRD in Mexico) have been critical of successive regional integration initiatives. Note, however, that—apart from the NDP's unexpected surge in 2011—these parties have generally been outsiders at the national level, at least in part because of their refusal to play the "brokerage party" role demanded by SMP electoral competition.

78. Gross 2008.
79. Note, again, that Mexican political elites have always been more inclined to explore more ambitious forms of institution building (as seen most clearly during the Fox years), and might be expected to do so again if a window of opportunity were opened in the US.

REFERENCES

Almeida, Dmitri. 2012. *The Impact of European Integration on Political Parties: Beyond the Permissive Consensus.* New York: Routledge.

Anderson, Greg, and Christopher Sands. 2007. "Negotiating North America: The Security and Prosperity Partnership," *Hudson Institute White Paper* (Fall).

Ayres, Jeffrey M. 1998. *Defying Conventional Wisdom: Political Movements and Popular Contention against North American Free Trade.* Toronto: University of Toronto Press.

Ayres, Jeffrey M., and Laura Macdonald. 2006. "Deep Integration and Shallow Governance: The Limits of Civil Society Engagement across North America," *Politics and Society* 25 (3): 23–42.

Ayres, Jeffrey, and Laura Macdonald, eds. 2009. *Contentious Politics in North America: National Protest and Transnational Collaboration under Continental Integration.* New York: Palgrave Macmillan.

Barry, Donald. 2003. "Managing Canada-US Relations in the post-9/11 Era: Do We Need a Big Idea?" *CSIS Policy Paper on the Americas* 14. Washington DC: Center for Strategic and International Studies.

Basañez, Miguel, Ronald Inglehart, and Neil Nevitte. 2007. "North American Convergence, Revisited," *Nortéamerica* 2 (2): 21–60.

Bélanger, Louis. 2007. "An Unsustainable Institutional Design: Incompleteness and Delegation Deficit in NAFTA," in Gordon Mace, J.P. Thérien and Paul Haslam, eds. *Governing the Americas: Assessing Multilateral Institutions.* Boulder CO: Lynne Rienner.

Bennett, Linda L.M., and Stephen E. Bennett. 1996. *Living with Leviathan: Americans Coming to Terms with Big Government.* Laurence KS: University Press of Kansas.

Bennett, Scott E. 2004. "American and Canadian Assessments of NAFTA: Opinion on Continental Policy and Its Drivers," *American Behavioral Scientist* 47 (10): 1285–1318.

Boussalis, Constantine, Jennifer L. Merolla, and Carin A. Peiffer. 2013. "Identity and Public Support for North American Integration," paper presented at workshop on "The Legitimacy of Regional Integration in Europe and the Americas: Empirical and Comparative Perspectives," LMU Munich, July 19–20.

Bow, Brian. 2012. "Immovable Object or Unstoppable Force? Economic Crisis and the Social Construction of North America," in Jeffrey Ayres and Laura Macdonald, eds., *North America in Question: Regional Integration in an Era of Economic Turbulence.* Toronto: University of Toronto Press.

Bow, Brian. Forthcoming. "Legitimacy as the Key to Anti-Regionalism in North America," in Achim Hurrelmann and Steffen Schneider, eds., *The Legitimacy of Regional Integration in Europe and the Americas: Empirical and Comparative Perspectives.* Houndsmill: Palgrave Macmillan.

Brewer, Paul R., Kimberly Gross, Sean Aday, and Lars Willnat. 2004. "International Trust and Public Opinion about World Affairs," *American Journal of Political Science* 48 (1): 93–109.

Brodie, Janine. 1989. "The Free Trade Election," *Studies in Political Economy* 28: 175–182.

Cairns, Alan C. 1996. "An Election to be Remembered: Canada 1993," *Canadian Public Policy* 20 (3): 219–234.

Cameron, Maxwell A., and Brian W. Tomlin. 2000. *The Making of NAFTA: How the Deal Was Done*. Ithaca NY: Cornell University Press.

Cameron, Maxwell A., and Carol Wise. 2004. "The Political Impact of NAFTA on Mexico," *Canadian Journal of Political Science* 37 (2): 301–323.

Capling, Ann, and Kim Richard Nossal. 2009. "The Contradictions of Regionalism in North America," *Review of International Studies* 35 (1): 147–167.

Carey, S. 2002. "Undivided Loyalties: Is National Identity an Obstacle to European Integration?" *European Union Politics* 3 (4): 387–413.

Carrubba, C. J. 2001. "The Electoral Connection in European Union Politics," *Journal of Politics* 63 (1): 141–58.Checkel, Jeffrey T., and Peter J. Katzenstein, "The Politicization of European Identities," in Checkel and Katzenstein, eds., *European Identity*. New York: Cambridge University Press.

Chicago Council [on Global Affairs]. 2013. "As President Obama Heads to Mexico, Americans Have Mixed Views of Neighbor across the Border," April 29. www.thechicagocouncil.org/UserFiles/File/130429_Mexico_Brief.pdf

Christin, T., and A.H. Trechsel. 2002. "Joining the EU?" *European Union Politics* 3 (4): 415–443.

Conybeare, John A.C., and Mark Zinkula. 1996. "Who Voted Against NAFTA?" *The World Economy* 19 (1): 1–12.

Cooley, Alexander, and Hendrik Spruyt. 2009. *Contracting States: Sovereign Transfers in International Relations*. Princeton NJ: Princeton University Press.

Corsi, Jerome R. 2007. *The Late Great USA: The Coming Merger with Mexico and Canada*. Medford OR: WND Books.

Crabtree, S. 1999. "New Poll Gauges Americans' General Knowledge Levels," *Gallup Reports*, July 6. www.gallup.com/poll/3742/New-Poll-Gauges-Americans-General-Knowledge-Levels.aspx

Destler, I.M., and Peter J. Balint. 1999. *The New Politics of American Trade: Trade, Labour and the Environment*. Washington DC: Institute for International Economics.

De Vries, Catherine E., and Erica J. Edwards. 2009. "Taking Europe to Its Extremes: Extremist Parties and Public Euroscepticism," *Party Politics* 15 (1): 5–28.

De Wilde, Peter, and Michael Zürn. 2012. "Can the Politicization of European Integration Be Reversed?" *Journal of Common Market Studies* 50 (1): 137–153.

Duverger, Maurice. 1954. *Political Parties*. New York: Wiley.

Eberlein, Burkard, and Edgar Grande. 2005. "Beyond Delegation: Transnational Regulatory Regimes and the EU Regulatory State," *Journal of European Public Policy* 12 (1): 89–112.

Franklin, M., M. March, and L. McLauren. 1994. "Uncorking the Bottle: Popular Opposition to European Unification in the Wake of Maastricht," *Journal of Common Market Studies* 32 (4): 445–72.

Gabel, M. 2000. "European Integration, Voters and National Politics," *West European Politics* 23 (4): 52–72.

Gallagher, Michael, and Paul Mitchell. 2005. "Introduction to Electoral Systems," in Gallagher and Mitchell, eds., *The Politics of Electoral Systems*. New York: Oxford.

Golob, Stephanie. 2003. "Beyond the Policy Frontier: Canada, Mexico, and the Ideological Origins of NAFTA," *World Politics* 55 (3): 361–398.

Graves, Frank. 2007. "North America: Mosaic, Community, or Fortress?" *Nortéamerica* 2 (2): 105–129.

Graves, Frank, Robert A. Pastor, and Miguel Basanez. 2013. "The NAFTA Promise and the North American Reality: How to Narrow the Gap," October 31. www.american.edu/sis/cnas/upload/3_b_2013_CNAS_Survey_Full_Results.pdf

Gross, Daniel. 2008. "NAFTA Nonsense," *Slate*, March 4. www.slate.com/articles/business/moneybox/2008/03/nafta_nonsense.html
Hart, Michael. 1990. "The Future on the Table: The Continuing Negotiating Agenda under the Canada-United States Free-Trade Agreement," in Richard Dearden, Michael Hart, and Debra Steger, eds., *Living With Free Trade: Canada, the Free Trade Agreement and the GATT.* Ottawa: Centre for Trade Policy and Law and Institute for Research on Public Policy.
Halikiopoulou, D., K. Nanou, and S. Vasilipoulou. 2012. "The Paradox of Nationalism: The Common Denominator of Radical Right and Radical Left Euroscepticism," *European Journal of Political Research* 51 (4): 504–539.
Hellstrom, J. 2008. "Who Leads, Who Follows? Reexamining the Party-Electorate Linkages on European Integration," *Journal of European Public Policy* 15 (1): 1127–1144.
Holian, David B., Timothy B. Krebs, and Michael H. Walsh. 1997. "Constituency Opinion, Ross Perot, and Roll-Call Behavior in the US House: The Case of the NAFTA," *Legislative Studies Quarterly* 22 (3): 369–392.
Hooghe, L. and Marks, G. 2002. "Multiple Identities," in Hooghe and Marks, eds., *Multi-Level Governance and European Integration.* Oxford: Rowman and Littlefield.
Hooghe, Liesbit, and Gary Marks. 2005. "Calculation, Community and Cues: Public Opinion on European Integration," *European Union Politics* 6 (4): 419–443.
Hooghe, Liesbit, and Gary Marks. 2009. "A Postfunctionalist Theory of European Integration: From Permissive Consensus to Constraining Dissensus," *British Journal of Political Science* 39 (1): 1–23.
Hufbauer, Gary Clyde, and Jeffrey J. Schott. 2005. *NAFTA Revisited: Achievements and Challenges.* Washington DC: Peterson Institute.
Hufbauer, Gary Clyde, and Jeffrey J. Schott. 2008. "NAFTA's Bad Rap," *The International Economy* (Summer): 19–23.
Hurrell, Andrew. 2006. "Hegemony in a Region that Dares Not Speak Its Name," *International Journal* 61 (2): 545–566.
Inglehart, Ronald L., Neil Nevitte, and Miguel Basanez. 1996. *The North American Trajectory.* Hawthorne NY: Aldine de Gruyter.
Jönsson, Christer, et al. 1998. "Negotiations in Networks in the European Union," *International Negotiation* 3 (3): 319–344.
Kahane, Leo H. 1996. "Congressional Voting Patterns on NAFTA: An Empirical Analysis," *American Journal of Economics and Sociology* 55 (4): 395–409.
Klamer, Arjo, and Jennifer Meehan. 1999. "The Crowding Out of Academic Economics: The Case of NAFTA," in Robert F. Garnett, Jr., ed., *What Do Economists Know?* New York: Routledge.
Klesner, Joseph L. 2005. "Electoral Competition and the New Party System in Mexico," *Latin American Politics and Society* 47 (2): 103–142.
Lawrence, Robert Z. 2002. "International Trade Policy in the 1990s," in Jeffrey A. Frankel and Peter R. Orszag, eds., *American Economic Policy in the 1990s.* Boston: MIT Press.
Lindberg, Leon N. and Stuart A. Schiengold. 1970. *Europe's Would-Be Polity.* Englewood Cliffs NJ: Prentice Hall.
Leiken, Robert S. 2001. "With a Friend Like Fox," *Foreign Affairs* 80 (5): 91–104.
Luedtke, A. 2005. "European Integration, Public Opinion and Immigration Policy," *European Union Politics* 6 (1): 83–112.
Mayer, Frederick W. 1998. *Interpreting NAFTA: The Science and Art of Political Analysis.* New York: Columbia University Press.
Miller, Mark J., and Cristina Gabriel. 2008. "The US-Mexico Migration Honeymoon of 2001: A Retrospective," in Cristina Gabriel and Héllène Pellerin, eds., *Governing International Labor Migration.* New York: Routledge.

Mittelman, James H. 1996. "Rethinking the 'New Regionalism' in the Context of Globalization," *Global Governance* 2 (2): 189–213.

Moreno, Alejandro. 2007. "Trust in North America: Why Do Mexicans Distrust Their Continental Neighbors?" *Nortéamerica* 2 (2): 63–84.

Norris, Chuck. 2009. "The Globalization of Comparative Public Opinion Research," in Neil Robinson and Todd Landman, eds., *The Sage Handbook of Comparative Politics*. London: Sage.

Pastor, Robert A. 2001. *Toward a North American Community: Lessons for the New World from the Old*. Washington: Peterson Institute.

Pastor, Robert A. 2005. "North America and the Americas: Integration among Unequal Partners," in Mary Farrell, Bjorn Hettne, and Luk Van Langenhove, eds., *Global Politics of Regionalism: Theory and Practice*. Ann Arbor MI: Pluto Press.

Pastor, Robert A. 2008. "The Future of North America: Replacing a Bad Neighbor Policy," *Foreign Affairs* 87 (4): 84–98.

Pastor, Robert A. 2011. *The North American Idea: A Vision of a Continental Future*. Oxford UK: Oxford University Press.

Pew [Global Attitudes Project]. 2013a. "Attitudes toward the US," July 18. www.pewglobal.org/2013/07/18/chapter-1-attitudes-toward-the-united-states/

Pew [Global Attitudes Project]. 2013b. "Which Countries Americans Like . . . and Don't," December 30. www.pewresearch.org/fact-tank/2013/12/30/which-countries-americans-like-and-dont/

Polyakova, Alina, and Neil Fligstein. 2012. "Is European Integration Causing Europe to Become More Nationalist? Evidence from the Recent Financial Crisis," paper presented to the American Sociological Association annual conference, New York, August 9–12.

Rankin, David M. 2001. "Identities, Interests, and Imports," *Political Behavior* 23 (4): 351–375.

Rankin, David M. 2004. "Borderline Interest or Identity?: American and Canadian Opinion on the North American Free Trade Agreement," *Comparative Politics* 36 (April): 331–351.

Ray, L. 2003. "When Parties Matter: The Conditional Influence of Party Positions on Voter Opinions about European integration," *Journal of Politics* 65 (4): 978–94.

Riker, William H. 1982. "The Two-Party System and Duverger's Law: An Essay on the History of Political Science," *American Political Science Review* 76 (4): 753–766.

Risse, Thomas. 2005. "European Institutions and Identity Change: What Have We Learned?" in Richard Herrmann, et al, eds., *Transnational Identities. Becoming European in the European Union*. Lanham MD: Rowman & Littlefield.

Rosamond, Ben. 2005. *Globalization and the European Union*. Basingstoke: Palgrave.

Sánchez-Cuenca, Ignacio. 2000. "The Political Basis of Support for European Integration," *European Union Politics* 1 (2): 147–171.

Santa Cruz, Arturo. 2013. "La política exterior de Felipe Calderón hacia América del Norte: Crisis interna y redefinición de Fronteras," *Foro Intarnacional* 53 (3–4): 537–571.

Sands, Christopher. 2011. "The Canada Gambit: Will It Revive North America?" *Hudson Institute Briefing Paper*, March. www.hudson.org/research/7757-the-canada-gambit-will-it-revive-north-america

Shoch, James. 2011. "Grappling with Globalization: The Democratic Party's Struggles over International Market Integration," in James E. Cronin, George W. Ross, and James Shoch, eds., *What's Left of the Left? Democrats and Social Democrats in Challenging Times*. Raleigh NC: Duke University Press.

Steenbergen, Marco R., and David J. Scott. 2004. "Contesting Europe? The Salience of European Integration as a Party Issue," in Gary Marks and Marco Steenbergen, eds., *European Integration and Political Conflict*. Cambridge UK: Cambridge University Press.

Steenbergen, M.R., E.E. Edwards, and C.E. de Vries. 2007. "Who's Cueing Whom? Mass-Elite Linkages and the Future of European Integration," *European Union Politics* 8 (1): 13–35.

Studer, Isabel. 2007. "Obstacles to Integration: North America's Institutional Weakness," in Isabel Studer and Carol Wise, eds. 2007. *Requiem or Revival?: The Promise of North American Integration*. Washington: Brookings Institution Press.

Tillman, E.R. 2004. "The European Union at the Ballot Box? European Integration and Voting Behavior in the New Member States," *Comparative Political Studies* 37 (5): 590–610.

Uslaner, Eric M. 1998. "Trade Winds: NAFTA and the Rational Public," *Political Behavior* 20 (4): 341–360.

Weintraub, Sidney. 1996. "Next Steps: Policy Options after NAFTA," in Charles F. Doran and Alvin P. Drischler, eds., *A New North America: Cooperation and Enhanced Interdependence*. Westport CT: Praeger.

10 How Do We Get to North America?[1]

Stephen Blank

An out-of-towner asks a New Yorker, "How do I get to Carnegie Hall?"
The New Yorker answers, "Practice, practice, practice."
The same goes for North America.

Negotiations on NAFTA (North American Free Trade Agreement) began in 1992, and the agreement came into effect at the start of 1994. The twentieth anniversary of NAFTA is upon us at a moment of deep concern and uncertainty about the future of North American collaboration.

WHERE HAVE WE COME FROM?

Neither NAFTA nor its predecessor, the Canada-US FTA (CUSFTA), marks the beginning of deeper North American integration. NAFTA was a response to two profound changes in the North American environment that took place a decade before the agreement was negotiated.

The collapse of oil prices in 1982 opened the door for a North American trade deal, but the driving force for the agreement came from the profound transformation underway across North America's economies. Economic integration in North America intensified in the 1980s, largely as a result of changes in corporate structure and strategy. In key sectors, US companies rationalized their Canadian and Mexican branch plants and constructed integrated continental production, marketing, and sourcing networks, replicating developments since 1965 in the auto industry.[2] Other factors also contributed to deepening integration, including improved communications that facilitated longer-distance coordination, excess capacity on rails and highways, new transport technologies such as double stacking containers, and deregulation and privatization in the transportation industry, which led to consolidation and efficiency gains in the trucking and rail industries.

NAFTA is a classic trade pact, viewed by most trade specialists as innovative and important. It rests on the CUSFTA, which accomplished much of the heavy lifting, including agreements on services and the new dispute resolution mechanism.[3] NAFTA created the largest trading community in the world, provided the opportunity for a large developing nation to play in the developed league, and assured North American (and foreign) investors that the steps they had taken to build more deeply integrated continental production and distribution systems could be expanded without fear of government intervention.

NAFTA's public sector architects and private sector supporters never viewed it as the beginning of a scheme of economic and political integration. The counterpoint to NAFTA was Europe-1992, the creation of a single European market.[4] Experience (and liberal economic theory then ascendant) seemed to confirm that in the more entrepreneurial North America, government involvement was unnecessary and that markets and individual firms could be relied upon to create necessary arrangements.

Unlike the EU, NAFTA is institution-light. The agreement created only three new organizations. Two, the North American Agreement on Environmental Cooperation (NAAEC) and the North American Agreement on Labor Cooperation (NAALC), were the products of side agreements that won US Congressional support for ratification. The North American Development Bank is the third. The Commissions have been modestly funded and tightly controlled by the NAFTA partners, while the Development Bank is limited to funding environmental projects on the border. NAFTA did not establish a common customs territory, plan for a common currency or for the free movement of labor, or plan for citizens to travel across borders freely as in Europe's Schengen accord. NAFTA envisaged no "cohesion funds," used by Europe to bridge development gaps between member states.

Fundamentally, the agreements constituted commitments by the US, Canadian, and Mexican governments to do less rather than more, to permit more markets to function autonomously in a North American economic system that was already well advanced. Robert Pastor observes that the accord "did not envisage any unified approach to extract NAFTA's promise, nor did it contemplate any common response to new threats. NAFTA simply assumed that the peoples of North America would benefit from the magic of a free marketplace, and that the three governments would resolve old or new problems."[5]

Beyond the trade agreement was a North American "reality." Remarkable is not simply the dramatic increase in the exchange of raw materials and finished after 1994, but rather the striking increase in the movement of parts and components across the borders. This "trade in inputs" outlines the changing structure of the North American economy. And more, North Americans share highly integrated energy markets, provide the same customers with financial services, use the same roads and railroads to transport jointly made products, fly on the same integrated airline networks, and increasingly meet the same or similar standards of professional practice. By the 1990s, much of North America's economy could be visualized as a deeply integrated continental system of supply chains structured by networks linking production centers and distribution hubs across the continent.

This is what economists call "deep" or structural integration: we do not just sell goods to each other; we make them together. Viewing North America as a trade bloc is not an accurate way of understanding the substance of the North American economic system.

WHERE ARE WE NOW?

NAFTA did not transform North America into anything like the European Union. But while North America is not Europe, neither is it three autonomous countries simply engaged in a trade bloc. The North American nations are deeply interconnected and interdependent, with an unprecedented degree of collaboration among them. No one planned these developments. The most powerful drivers of change were corporate strategies and structures. The direction of change was largely "bottom-up" rather than "top-down" government decisions. Governments removed barriers but did not lay out plans.

The achievements of the previous decades were remarkable, but by the late 1990s, problems were brewing up. The process of integration slowed markedly.

Why? Post–9/11 security policies led to "thickened" borders, but security concerns were not the only, nor even the most important, reason for the slow down. Integration slowed for several reasons. Initial gains from tariff reduction were internalized, and further rationalization of production systems proceeded slowly. Integrated production systems were stressed by deteriorating transportation and energy infrastructure, growing transportation congestion at key choke points, and inadequate border facilities. The impact of dysfunctional regulations—the "tyranny of small differences"[6]—intensified as initial easy gains from bottom-up integration ran their course. Heightened international competition drew attention from North American ventures. The economic crisis of 2008 dramatically reduced cross-border activities, especially in the auto industry.

Moreover, the trilateral vision that formed around NAFTA eroded. US views of Mexico were increasingly shaped by a surge of illegal immigrants and worsening drug violence, while many Canadians sought to disengage from NAFTA enterprises and focus instead on a Canada-US "special" relationship. Despite irregular "leaders' meetings," the attrition of a trilateral vision has been most profound at the top level of our governments—the US and Mexican, as well as Canadian.

The era of bottom-up integration has ended. What has been done successfully in the past will no longer suffice to meet today's needs. We now confront looming issues demanding different approaches than those we have become accustomed to over the past decades. Many of these crosscut old political boundaries and revise established political landscapes. Some will require deeper continental collaboration. Increasingly rapid technological change and economic uncertainty has changed the game rules. Moreover, the bar has been raised. In the 1980s and 1990s, North American systems had to be efficient. After 9/11, they had to be secure, and now, with rising environmental concerns, sustainable.

****

The flaw at the heart of the NAFTA structure was the failure of the three national governments to acknowledge the obvious—that the free trade agreement was one element of a wider North American reality, and only a first step toward achieving a stable foundation for continental collaboration and growth. But Ottawa, Washington, and Mexico City continued to emphasize that the North American nations—the three "NAFTA partners"—were trading partners, nothing more.

Economic integration in Europe has been a means to achieve a wider political objective, initially to create a European political entity that could overcome the century of intra-European warfare and strengthen Europe in the face of the Soviet threat. And now, that goal has been to build a stronger, more efficient Europe in the global economy. Europeans have differed over the nature of that entity, but there has been no doubt—at least until the present moment—about the objective.

On our side of the Atlantic, this vision—a North American "project"—was never embraced. Political goals that frame European integration and the governmental apparatus constructed to achieve them are entirely absent here. The only people who talk about a North American Union are those who desperately oppose what has never been proposed.

Some of NAFTA's founders intended that the process would move beyond the trade agreement. But by the time the three national leaders signed the agreement, the storm over globalization had intensified, and NAFTA was its lightning rod. Facing this tempest, all were reluctant to push beyond the trade agreement. Any discussion of the future of "North America" was off the table. The system of Working Groups set up by NAFTA soon withered.[7]

The lack of a clear trilateral vision has critically impeded the development of institutions that could help connect the elements of the North American reality. Unlike the Europeans who quickly established "European" research and educational institutions after the Treaty of Rome in 1957, the notion of educating anyone about "North America" was viewed with horror.

Efforts to upgrade the NAFTA system have been painfully unsuccessful. Free trade proponents talked about NAFTA II and "Big Ideas," but nothing happened.[8] The failure of the Security and Prosperity Partnership (SPP) revealed that leaders in our governments were unprepared to confront wild and unfounded but politically potent charges that sovereignty would be undermined and a "North American Union" constructed.[9] The work of the Regulatory Cooperation Council has progressed more successfully than many people thought likely. But it is more modest—bilateral rather than trilateral and focused essentially on making the border more efficient and more secure. This is vital, but it is essentially old business, matters that have been on the table since 1994.

The slowdown of economic integration in North America must not be overestimated. Companies have navigated the border by participating in programs such as C-TPAT and PIP and by outsourcing border transport to specialized 3PL (third-party logistics) firms. Energy flows have continued to increase. Despite market setbacks, border slowdowns, and regulatory inefficiencies, trilateral trade and FDI have increased steadily to date: trilateral trade has recovered steadily since 2009 and overall has more than tripled since NAFTA's adoption.[10]

WHERE ARE WE GOING? NORTH AMERICAN SOLUTIONS

The incremental, bottom-up decision-making process that characterized North American integration in the last decades of the twentieth century no longer suffices at a moment when precedent-defining political decisions are required on issues dealing with energy, infrastructure, the environment, security, and more. What alternatives exist for North American governance, for making decisions on vital issues that affect us all?

First and most important, we must create a vision of North America in the mid-twenty-first century—in terms, for example, of energy, production, supply chains, infrastructure, demographics, and climate change. Second, we must begin to create institutions that provide a foundation for coping with these and other demanding issues.

We have not thought about a North American infrastructure for the twenty-first century—rails, highways, pipelines and wires, air- and sea ports, about how to improve our continental supply chains—and, indeed, what shape these might take in the next decades. Delighted with vast new energy reserves, we have not planned how to maximize efficient and sustainable use. We have given little thought to how we must collaborate in adapting to climate change. And we lack informed constituencies that would support new policies. Without these, the danger lies in attempting to find purely national answers to what are increasingly continental issues.

In his recent book, *The North American Idea: A Vision of a Continental Future*, Robert Pastor describes the "real choice" that must be made between "a bold vision of a North American Community" and "incremental approaches to the region's problems"—what he terms "gradual, minimal progress" on "*one issue, one country at a time.*" Pastor says that this is what we have being doing since 2000 and "it has accomplished very little, if anything."[11]

I disagree with Pastor's analysis. Trying to start new comprehensive negotiations to build a "North American Community" would be a mistake. Efforts to revitalize the movement toward economic integration in North America should not be directed toward the negotiation of a grand new bi- or tripartite trade deal. The goal cannot be a North American "Community." There is no way to delink this image from politically toxic squabbles about eroding sovereignties.

Instead, we should begin with a vision of three sovereign nations confronting common, shared, and increasingly urgent problems. The idea of "North America" should become a vehicle for collaboration rather than the goal of collaboration. I do not suggest that every problem that exists has a North American solution. But we have to stop being afraid to consider possible continental ideas and approaches to some of our most pressing problems. It should be natural—not unusual—to think of continental collaboration as a tool to deal with particular issues. We must work to de-demonize the idea of North America by adding North American solutions as an element in our policy arsenal.

This means that, instead trying to recreate an all-in NAFTA II negotiation, we should be prepared to deal with issues individually and probably differently—depending on the issue, the context, the interests involved, and the resources at hand. We must think of launching parallel initiatives dealing with issues such as energy, climate change, production and distribution systems, infrastructure, demographic change, and health care.

Energy

After bitter rows over energy in the 1970s, Canada-US energy relations after CUSFTA calmed, shaped by parallel policies of domestic liberalization and cross-border harmonization. Despite concern about Canadian energy vulnerability resulting from NAFTA (Mexican energy policy was largely exempted from the agreement), bilateral energy ties deepened as energy flows grew.[12] Today, however, we must view energy in continental terms rather than in national boxes. Canadians, Americans, and Mexicans alike benefit from North America's deeply integrated oil, gas, and electricity systems. What has changed is that North America is now energy rich. Increasingly, the main energy issue will be to determine an energy mix that optimizes availability, cost, and sustainability for the next generations. Joe Dukert, one of the few truly continental energy specialists, states that "the time has come for objective analysts within the private sector develop at least an initial North American Energy Outlook (NAEO) to illuminate the difficult path that lies ahead."[13] The Outlook must be continental in design, transcending the three-country parallelism of the North American Energy Working Group.

Climate Change

Leaders are beginning to understand the depth of the threat of climate change. We cannot see this as three separate national issues. Climate change does not stop at the Rio Grande or the forty-ninth parallel. Much of the environmental community and many business and political leaders are aware that policies for mitigation and adaptation must be considered, developed, and adopted in a common framework.[14] Canadian, US, and Mexican environmental groups and government agencies have cooperated on bilateral and regional projects, facilitated by the Commission for Environmental Cooperation. But much of the work is still highly fragmented and many resources are devoted to examining climate change in national perspectives.[15] The North American Commission on Environmental Cooperation has done well, given a very modest budget, but it has not connected sufficiently with many of the groups that share interests. Can the CEC build an ongoing, networked, coherent conversation on key environmental matters? It should improve its role in public education, particularly providing a clearer overview of issues, options, arguments, and data.

Production and Distribution Systems

The search for greater efficiencies in production and distribution has largely driven North American integration. In an increasingly competitive global economy, many Canadian, US, and Mexican firms depend on continentally integrated production and distribution systems that enable them to site units in the most efficient locations and link them with a highly efficient logistics-transportation system.[16] Our service industries depend on the same kind of continental networks and linkages. Yet it is remarkable how little is known about all of this.[17] The result is that we all depend deeply on something few know anything about. We need to focus serious attention on learning more about how North America works, more on factors that drive or inhibit our competitive advantage, and more about what a globally competitive North America might look like in the next half century. It is time to stop talking about trading partners and underline that we are production partners.

Infrastructure

Competitiveness requires efficient, safe, and sustainable transport (road, rail, air, and water), logistics systems, and border crossings. Energy from every source must move along wires and through pipelines or along roads and rails. But North Americans face a tremendous infrastructure crisis—collapsing roads and bridges and decaying pipelines, water systems, and electric wires. Our broadband carriers are reaching capacity, and sea- and airports are falling behind international competitors. Investment just to maintain let alone improve infrastructure in all three countries is insufficient.[18] North America needs new initiatives to address infrastructures that are both inadequate to serve huge volumes of traffic within the continent and uncompetitive relative to the rest of the world. We need to lay out alternative visions of an efficient, sustainable, and secure North American freight transportation system for the next decades—relating this to the impact of new technologies, changes in global production and trade flows, and demographic patterns. It is time to create a North American Commission on Freight Transportation. One goal would be to mobilize some significant part of the large transportation research community that now exists for this collaborative task.[19]

Demographic Change

All three North American nations are undergoing extensive demographic changes, which impose hard limits on policies for economic growth and fiscal balance and create political, economic, and social turmoil. Population movement—mainly Mexicans coming legally or illegally to the US—has been the most visible and politically potent dimension of this in recent years. Aging will be an increasingly powerful driver of change in North America.[20] All three countries are experiencing high levels of internal migration as people seek to follow jobs; all three face growing imbalances of the supply of medical and educational resources and changing levels of demand for these services. The costs and benefits of population movements in North America are both clear and frequently affect both sides of the border.

Health Care

Demographic change and population movements, together with growing ease of transportation and communication, are changing the nature of our health care systems. Increasingly large numbers of citizens cross borders to avoid lengthy waits for health care or to find lower prices. More Canadians and Americans have become permanent snowbirds—Canadians retiring in the US southeast and southwest and Canadians and Americans both moving to Mexico for their retirement years. The ability to bring health care plans across borders will become a necessity. Canadian health care faces its own challenges, but it would surely ease the system in, for example, Ontario, to establish OHIP-designated hospitals in an area such as Lake Chapala, which boasts over 700,000 Canadian retirees. The savings in health care provision in Ontario, combined with the jobs that would be supported in Mexico, makes this an idea worthy of serious consideration.

HOW DO WE GET THERE? PRACTICE, PRACTICE, PRACTICE

I have suggested a new vision of North America focused on building collaborative solutions to common problems faced by the three North American nations. But policy initiatives matter little without widespread understanding and support. With regard to building informed constituencies in North America, we start in a deep deficit. Little has been done to create the public understanding that is required to support the initiatives described above.

Assembling a much broader base of informed and active constituencies is critical to any effort to meet these problems. The NAFTA approach confined discussions about North America to a small number of players—bureaucrats in the national capitals, some industry advisers, a few trade specialists from the academic-research community and, willy-nilly, a swarm of anti-NAFTA publicists. But the issues we face today are large and difficult, and dealing with them is likely to force significant changes in our lives. Without widespread recognition and understanding, it will be extremely difficult to organize positive responses. Moreover, we are burdened with a history of misinformation (secret North American superhighways) and deeply imbedded fears (eroding sovereignties). When our leading newspapers ask why we cannot purchase a "made-in-America" car, we know we are in deep trouble.[21]

Instead of compressing the wide range of distinct issues into a single negotiation, discussions must involve many participants—in think tanks, universities, expert commissions, and groups of "wise people" and government agencies across the continent. Discussions should involve perspectives from different regions, different economic and social sectors, and from those who oppose as well as support further integration. We must stimulate dialogue, exchange, and controversy and mobilize communities of interest that network practitioners, policymakers, researchers, and teachers—so climbing beyond the repetitive ad hocism that has characterized our approach to most discussions of North America in the past.

The process must get outside of the beltways—it must give voice to community and economic leaders who are most deeply involved in this new system. If efforts to build a new North American system rest on the creation of a new Ottawa–Washington–Mexico City corridor, they will lack legitimacy in many parts of the continent.

Jean Monnet, one of Europe's "fathers," felt that people could only unite behind a vision they shared. He understood the importance of building informed and committed constituencies, groups that would press governments to realize a vision. Through the Action Committee, Monnet sought to mobilize constituencies that would support a European Community. He described the "constant outside pressure" that the Action Committee brought to bear, and "the moral influence the Committee exerted on the established authorities in each country."[22]

In North America, such constituencies do exist—people in companies that run continental production, supply, and marketing systems; in cities where jobs depend upon efficient North American transportation and logistics networks; and in border communities. There is no shortage of skilled, informed people, deeply involved in dealing with these issues. Networks linking mid-level managers in many federal and state/provincial government agencies talk about these issues across national borders.

But despite this wealth of assets, none has created a sense of the North American reality. Knowledge about North American issues is fragmented and specialized, with little communication among expert groups. For even the most informed, North America is typically the background to more pressing tasks of getting parts to loading docks, keeping oil and gas flowing in pipelines, matching electric demand and supply, considering how weather variations might affect water flows in the next months, and tracking threatening invasive species. Discussions—for example, on freight transportation or energy—have proceeded in a fragmented, ad hoc fashion. Decisions have been incremental and most efforts often directed at smoothing the edges of diverging national policies.

In general, there is a terrible ignorance about North America. In my own experience, teaching in universities across the continent, students were more likely to believe that there is a secret plan to build a sovereignty-eating North American super corridor than there is a desire to understand how automobiles are built in North America or how our energy systems work together. Media coverage is scarcely better. As in education, media views the North American nations as distant and—with regard to Mexican immigration in the US or US attitudes toward Albertan oil—threatening. One searches for a sense of common interests. Levels of knowledge about the North American experience among those who influence the policymaking process—our political, government, education, and media elites—are typically appallingly low. The result is that as we face demands for more concerted action, we have no sense of what has been accomplished, no case studies, and no reservoir of experience to guide our responses.

The task is to mobilize these constituencies, help them comprehend the wider North American map, and create appropriate ongoing vehicles to lay out policy ideas (backed by research and analysis) for each of the areas noted above—and others as well. Why haven't we been able to do this?

Looking at a couple of cases helps illustrate the situation. The second Detroit-Windsor Bridge provides a useful example of the problems we face in making decisions on critical matters of common concern and parallels issues of cross-border environmental governance. We know that leaders did not move either quickly or vigorously to make the case for the bridge, notwithstanding the US-Canada/Ontario-Michigan production relationship, particularly in the automotive sector. Government officials continued to speak about trade in automobiles, rather than just-in-time cross-border production systems. Given this lack of clarity, they were unable to frame the debate around the key reasons for building the bridge—our deep mutual interdependence. There was little sense of the Detroit-Windsor crossing as the chokepoint of a continent-wide system of converging supply chains. Leaders did not try to construct constituencies to support the project until the very end, when heroic action was required to keep the process moving forward.

A large number of grassroots local, sectoral, and single interest groups exist, all well versed on Michigan-Ontario relations. But their attention tracks many issues (water, the Great Lakes, invasive species, transport, trade corridors, and so on). The problem was not the absence of involved groups, but rather the lack of focus and the formation of separate micro-constituencies. Many groups did not want a seat at the table, but rather, their own table. And the widespread ignorance among political leaders, media, and the general public about how North American production actually work—the auto industry, for example—was a huge inhibition to successful policymaking. We saw again that ignorance opens the door to all sorts of misinformation and fear mongering.

These perspectives on the second Detroit-Windsor Bridge parallel those found in the Woodrow Wilson Center's excellent 2010 publication on "Environmental Governance on the 49th Parallel."[23] As Barry Rabe observes in the introduction, there is no shortage of players in this game, just as in Ontario-Michigan relations.

If sheer number of institutions and agreements is a proxy measure for volume of governance activity, Canada and the US clearly would have one of the most densely packed environmental governance systems of any two national neighbors on the globe. [The contributors to Rabe's volume] demonstrate an incredibly sizable and diverse set of governance arrangements, many of which overlap one another in both policy area and geographic territory.[24]

But did all of this apparatus make much difference? Not much. Substantial numbers of actors—individuals and organizations—were there. But collaboration among them remained modest and ad hoc. Institutions that encourage collaboration, that, over time, sponsor learning, training and experience were largely absent.

Rabe is careful here, staying focused on environmental issues. But his comments do apply equally to other cases of cross-border governance: "There is simply no governance entity currently in operation that has much if any role in promoting collaboration on greenhouse gas reductions, and all of the potential economies of scale and collaborative opportunities across policy arenas that this might entail. Instead, collective climate governance bringing together Canadian and American entities is largely nonexistent."[25]

The Ontario-Michigan region does not function as an integrated system with regard to most issues. No capacity exists to assess shared problems and needs, identify alternative solutions, formulate policy responses, mobilize coalitions among key stakeholders and constituencies, or manage continuing programs. Notwithstanding the existence of networks linking officials and community leaders, there is no formalized collaboration among senior government leaders. Research and educational assets are not involved in continuing, coordinated efforts to lay out programs of research, education, and training to improve regional capacities.[26]

This is where Europeans have a critical advantage. During the 1980s and 1990s, North Americans contrasted their bottom-up, entrepreneurial mode of integration with the ponderous, bureaucratic, top-down European style. But looking at developments over the past decade suggests that this image is no longer accurate. The author of a recent study of trade corridors in three continents comments on the case of one European corridor. Although sited in a very poor region, "in the space of five years through an initial phase of operation of the Corridor Secretariat, the countries have managed to jointly identify a list of priority infrastructure projects; recognize that even more important than infrastructure are harmonization of standards and coordination of border crossing procedures; and declare the intent to enter into a more binding organizational form to address the harmonization and coordination problems."[27]

She concludes that "grassroots organizing" is the strength of the US approach. The European strength (and the US weakness) lies in the formation of institutions at the transnational level to bring an overarching vision to corridor development and coordination to border management.

Europe has articulated a grand design for an integrated transport system. Under the aegis of its Steering Committee and Secretariat, the Corridor can be managed as a system, facilitating the identification of bottlenecks or other impairments to overall efficient functioning and providing a forum for joint redress of such problems. Official international cooperation of this sort does not exist to manage the corridors of North America. Development there moves rather in piecemeal fashion in response to interest groups contending through the political process.[28]

Over time and with a much clearer sense of building a European-wide political as well as physical infrastructure, Europeans have institutionalized conversations on these issues. A variety of organizations reach out to a spectrum of interests in each policy area and create inclusive fora for ongoing discussions. Bridges have been built to the research and teaching communities, providing continuing data collection and analysis as well extended informed constituencies. One result is a system of countervailing voices, so that, for example, even in periods of fiscal restraint, some groups still underline the need for investment in infrastructure. Compare this to North America, where almost every issue is viewed principally in the single context of security and border control and, increasingly, cuts in public spending. Over decades, the Europeans have recorded examples of success and failure and have tried to learn from experience. There has been movement up a learning curve, in which all participants gain greater understanding of the issue, options, and implications—in vivid contrast to our failure to advance discussions beyond an oft-reiterated starting point.

This is not, of course, to suggest that what Europeans have done in these areas is always correct, that policies embraced by Brussels have all been implemented at the national level, that vested interests never distort policy intentions, or that learning curves never spiral out in low-return directions. But across policy areas of growing importance to North Americans, a learning process has influenced participants, policymakers, and constituents alike and shaped over time the conversation on these issues. We will not imitate the European system or try to construct a North American Community. But we should try to learn from their experience.

"Looking ahead," Rabe concludes, "one great challenge will be developing institutions and policy professionals capable of cutting across traditional boundaries and achieving greater integration of effort."[29] How do we create these institutions?

In North America, not by starting at the top to negotiate a North American system of governance. In Europe, formats and routines for collaboration among governments and sectoral/regional organizations have evolved over decades. On this side, the public-private sector gap is much wider. A top-down structure, with government-owned or government-managed institutions, is not practical, workable, or desirable.

But governments must still play a vital role. Government leaders at the metro, state-provincial, and federal levels must set the context for individual issues. They must acknowledge the North American reality that our three nations are deeply interconnected and interdependent, and help encourage more information and education about North America. They must take a leadership role in helping to define agendas and structure conversations—what Roy Norton, the Canadian Consul General in Detroit during the storm over the second bridge, terms "signals from the top."[30]

Partly this is an issue of institutionalizing communications. A vital asset for creating new patterns for dealing with common problems is the dense network of contacts among agencies at every level of government in the three nations. At times, when facing an emergency, even senior government leaders work together. But in general, existing networks are not used to advantage. In particular, cross-border contacts at senior levels of government remain intermittent. Given the level of Michigan-Ontario interdependence, for example, it is remarkable that there was no forum where senior leaders met regularly to discuss emerging issues and lay out plans to engage in public discussion and build constituencies. Government leaders must champion collaborative institution building.[31] Lacking clear signals from the top, agendas blur amidst a cacophony of competing interests and demands.

For any of this to succeed, we must improve understanding about North America. The process of educating and mobilizing citizens is as important as the institutions themselves. This is "practice." Practice accustoms leaders and groups to think in terms of possible North American solutions to critical economic and social issues. Practice de-demonizes the notion of North America. Practice will help build leadership and management skills and networks that constitute the foundation for the kind of institution Rabe describes.

Improving this situation does not pose huge conceptual problems. With regard to education, creating North American study centers is not the answer. Canadian, Mexican, US, or North American studies programs are usually lumped on campuses with "language and area studies" programs as exotic regions of investigation. Embedding North American content in core courses across the university would be more economical and efficient, and not only in liberal arts programs: putting more North American content in transportation and logistics programs, schools of business, public health programs, and schools of journalism would spread knowledge about North American developments among critical emerging constituencies. Given the great importance of continental issues we are facing now, learning more about North America should not be exceptional, but normal, a central ingredient of our education.

Greater collaboration among think tanks is another area where modest changes in institutional behavior might produce significant results. Think tanks in North America produce piles of interesting and useful studies. But some of this work might be more valuable with a comparative dimension. Could a group of research directors at several US, Canadian, and Mexican research institutes agree to reach out to each other when developing certain projects, to discuss the possibility of including a comparative element?

Another example of tweaking institutions is case studies. There is very little information about how North America works. There are few studies of industrial sectors, corporate links, energy system, or cross-border demographics. We lack case studies of failures or successes, and should ask what we can learn from past initiatives such as the Auto Pact, the acid rain agreement, the SPP, and Enhanced Drivers Licenses; what resulted from the trade corridor bubble of the 1990s; and what resulted from organizations like PWNER on one border and the Arizona-Mexico Commission on the other. More important is creating institutional memory, so that we can build on past experience. Establishing a database for this type of material should not be too hard and itself would encourage more work.

A vital task is to educate representatives in state and national capitals about the impact of North American economic integration on jobs and economic development in their communities. Shouldn't universities in border regions (and elsewhere) have some responsibility for this?

Institution building has been inhibited by our governments' reluctance to acknowledge the levels of North American interdependence, preferring negotiations conducted "under the legislative and media radar." But without the support of informed constituencies engaged in the political process, the kind of decisions required to meet these issues cannot be made, institutions will not be constructed, and policies not be put in place. We have to be prepared to take on the most difficult questions such as how new North American decision-making arrangements will ensure transparency and participation, and the relationship between independence and interdependence. We must stop being afraid of public debate on the future of North America. For surely, if we act like conspirators, we will be accused of conspiracy—exactly what happened to the SPP when critics uncovered the dastardly plot to overturn US sovereignty and institute a North American Union.

How does the process of institution building start? Begin with a series of initiatives to inform and encourage active interest in North American developments.

What kind of initiatives? A group of university presidents and chancellors might announce that they will work together to encourage more teaching, training, and research on North American topics. Such a group might ask the Canada-US and Mexico-US Fulbright programs to reserve a number of awards for work on particular subject areas—for example, on climate change, energy, or infrastructure in North America—in cooperation with several universities that commit themselves to develop programs on these topics.

The same might work with directors of transportation institutes or schools of journalism. Directors of several North American think tanks might agree to add comparative elements on certain projects. Canadian, US, and Mexican university partnerships and student and faculty exchange should be investigated. Greater use of new technology should be made to develop joint courses. A website—like the late Portal on North America[32]—ought to explored, as a resource for information including a data bank, interviews, and cases. This was more expensive and unwieldy a few years ago than it would be today. Could a faculty member be given a course credit for editing such a site?

These projects should be launched at the same time, not linearly. The strategy must be to create a critical mass. Steps forward should be publicized and participants prepared to respond to anti-integration arguments.

At the center of this, a group is needed with a broad enough base and sufficient status to open discussions on such ideas with a wide range of business, government, and research groups. Neither the time nor the environment is right for an effort like Monnet's Action Group. But we should think about the "constant outside pressure" and "moral influence" Monnet described, to create voices that enunciate the goals of North America integration and press for new policies to achieve these objectives.

There is, I think, one pretty good example of such a group. From 1957 to the years leading up to the CUSFTA and NAFTA, the Canadian-American Committee (CAC) was a valuable source of research and discussion on key bilateral issues. The story of the CAC involves many actors. Its origins go back to the Washington-based National Planning Association (NPA).

The NPA was created as an independent, private, nonprofit, nonpolitical organization to conduct research and policy formulation in the public interest. It began in 1937, during the Great Depression, when conflicts among major groups (business, farmers, labor) threatened to paralyze national decision making on critical economic and social issues. It was dedicated, in the words of its statement of purpose, to the task of "getting [these] diverse groups to work together . . . to narrow areas of controversy and broaden areas of agreement . . . [and] to provide . . . programs for action . . . in the best interests of a functioning democracy."[33]

It "brought together influential and knowledgeable leaders from business, labor, agriculture, and the applied and academic professions to serve on policy committees . . . intended to identify and anticipate emerging problems confronting the US, both from internal and international sources, and to seek to develop and agree upon policies and programs for coping with them."[34]

In the mid-1950s, the NPA began to explore Canadian-American relations. It initiated discussions about forming a new Canadian-American Committee. The CAC emerged in 1957 with both Canadian and US members. This led to the foundation of the Private Planning Association of Canada (PPAC), which became the C.D. Howe Institute. For several decades, the NPA was supported by the CAC in the US and the PPAC/C.D. Howe Institute in Canada.

In an era of slower and more expensive travel and when publications had to be printed, mailed, and stored, the CAC (disclosure—I was a member of the CAC from the 1980s through to the end of the story) played a central role in mobilizing and educating leaders from different backgrounds. It also created a cadre of researchers who worked on many bilateral topics, some over many years. Soon after the formation of NAFTA, the CAC transformed itself into the North American Committee (NAC). The NAC struggled onward for several years, but finally collapsed.[35]

One reason for the collapse was the declining interest of major US firms. Senior executives from Canadian and Mexican firms were frequently disappointed that American firms did not send their top people. By the 1980s, the fact is that most American firms no longer viewed Canada (or Mexico a bit later) as a problem. Cross-border business was booming and attention was focused on problems further afield. Continental integration in many sectors had become normal, and North American divisions had fused older Canadian and Mexican branch plants. Leaders were reluctant to talk about continental production systems and supply chains—on one hand, because this was a source of competitive advantage and, on the other, because of the concern that they would be accused of exporting US jobs. Finally, no one was thinking about the longer-term implications of this emerging North American system or about problems that might arise in the future (such as congestion on highways or at borders). It wasn't broken and it didn't need fixing. Not yet. Who could have anticipated 9/11 and the emerging continental issues we now face?

But let's not miss the main issue: yes, interest lagged, but the demise of the NAC was caused largely by the failure of institutional support. The geriatric NPA wobbled in the Reagan era as money became tighter and the Howe said it would no longer be the Canadian NAC host. The Conference Board of Canada was importuned to take over the Howe's place but made it clear that it did not regard this as a long-term commitment. The Mexicans worked hard to keep the NAC going, but could not compensate for the lack of institutional support north of the borders. By the last years of the NAC, the NPA had pretty well ceased raising funds and recruiting members and the Canadian Conference Board was looking for a graceful exit.[36]

The sad ending of the story notwithstanding, my sense is that the CAC in its prime—particularly in the decade leading up to the CUSFTA and NAFTA—provides a useful model for a broadly based, network-oriented, deeply committed core institution. This is particularly the case when much of what drove budgets then—printing costs, inventory, mailings—are largely costless today.

The CAC was noteworthy because of the breadth of its membership, drawn from different sectors with some labor representation and close ties to key think tanks, and its longer-term perspective on bilateral (and later trilateral) issues.

Several efforts have been made to create a North American business voice. Two are particularly notable, the North American Competitiveness Council (NACC), the business group associated with the SPP, and the North American Forum.

The NACC was established to provide business input to the SPP by three top CEO-based organizations in North America—the US Business Roundtable, the Canadian Council of Chief Executives, and the Consejo Mexicano de Hombres de Negocios. When the SPP vanished, the NACC disappeared as well. Could the NACC have put enough light between it and the government-owned SPP to achieve a seriously independent status? We'll never know. We do know that when the SPP became the symbol of a North American Union, the NACC folded like a cheap suit.

For a moment, the North American Forum seemed that it might play a significant role. Composed of senior business leaders and former top government officials, its website states that the Forum "is a community of Canadian, Mexican and American thought leaders, whose purpose is to advance a shared vision of North America, and to contribute to improved relations among the three neighbors."[37] But the Forum's determination to be invisible has made it an obvious target for North American Union conspiracy mongers. An even more profound flaw, as far as can be known, the Forum has issued no policy papers, has not offered a vision of North America, and has developed no ties to universities or think tanks. It prides itself on its confidentiality.

Recreating the NAC or a similar organization might be a midterm objective, but the most likely place to start now is with the North American business community. Indeed, given that business was the main driver of continental economic integration and the importance of maintaining (or restoring) North American competitiveness in the global economy, it is odd that there is no broadly based North American business-focused organization.[38] It is time that such an organization—perhaps a North American Chamber of Commerce—should be created and then networked with business and workers associations, regional organizations, and research centers.[39]

Its mandate could be to present illustrations of how North America's economy actually works, looking at the benefits, costs, and difficulties of structural integration in various economic sectors; to describe how decisions are currently made (or not made) in a range of economic, social, and environmental arenas; and to indicate where North American solutions might be effective and efficient means to cope with some of the issues we now confront. It would seek to shift the conversation about North America from eroding sovereignties and secret plans for a North American Union to practical matters of how we might develop collaborative means to manage common problems.

It would call attention to areas where institutions with a broader, continental perspective are weak (freight transportation and infrastructure, for example). It would suggest new institutional arrangements. Some might build on existing bodies. It could identify organizations that have made useful contributions—perhaps the Pacific Northwest Economic Region (PNWER), the Border Trade Alliance (BTA), or the Border Policy Research Institute (BPRI), to mention a few—and publicize examples of successful cross-border collaboration (for example, the long-term work of the International Joint Commission; the more recent accomplishments of the Regulatory Cooperation Council; or the ongoing work of the North American Electricity Reliability Corporation[40]). It would seek to promote new initiatives—convening the ginger group of university leaders noted above. A key task would be to remind government agencies and think tanks that some of what they do might be more usefully undertaken in a continental perspective.

We are not talking about building North American constituencies from whole cloth. Unlike the Europeans in 1945, facing devastation and decades of enmity, we begin with systems in place and habits of collaboration on many matters. The goal is to pull these pieces together, into larger and more coherent networks to achieve a critical mass in which discussions of North America are commonplace. What this institution has to do is what Rabe and others found missing—to cut across traditional boundaries and promote collaboration and achieve greater integration of effort. It needs to be able to enunciate and legitimize a vision of the three North American nations developing collaborative solutions to common problems. It should encourage conversations about all of this at many levels and in many places, and be prepared to debate tough issues and mobilize support to respond to charges that this will undermine sovereignty, lead to waves of illegal immigrants, or establish continental US hegemony.

Given the reality of national sovereignties, the regional architecture of North America, and our decentralized systems of government, we must anticipate that institutional arrangements might well differ from issue to issue and, perhaps, from region to region. Part of the process—the practice—is going to be learning from a variety of experiments and experiences.

There is a North American reality—a complex North American system, many sectors of which are characterized by deep structural integration. This reality was not created by the CUSFTA or NAFTA but by changes in the North American economy that helped lay the foundation for these trade agreements. For more than twenty years, deepening integration in North America was driven from the bottom up, largely by the transformation of corporate structure and strategy, not by governmental plans.

Understandably, in these fat years, we did little to prepare for lean years. We dealt with problems incrementally. Fearful of confronting the anti-globalization, anti-NAFTA pack, governmental leaders refused to acknowledge that the North American relationship was anything more than a trade agreement. Only a few visionaries like Robert Pastor were even willing to think about the future shape of North America.

The result is that today, when we confront new concerns that demand continental responses, we are unprepared. We lack a vision of what North America might be in the next decades, we lack institutions that might translate this vision into reality, and we lack informed constituencies that will demand and support the actions that will be required to meet these new challenges.

One sure conclusion: there is much to do and little time in which to do it.

NOTES

1. An early version of this chapter was presented at the Canadian Political Science Association Annual Conference, Edmonton, June 2012. The argument builds on research presented in Blank and Jeffs 2012.
2. Blank and Haar 1998. See Hufbauer and Schott 2005 for detailed analyses of the North American agriculture, automotive, and energy sectors.
3. NAFTA has not lacked for critics, but most experts agree that its impact on the three national economies was positive, if less than had been promised. The best assessment of the agreement is found in Hufbauer and Schott 2005.
4. See "Background: NAFTA as the Anti-Europe," in Golob 2008.
5. Pastor 2001, 2.
6. Hart 2006.
7. Clarkson et al 2006. Clarkson 2008 discusses this in great detail.
8. Wendy Dobson's (2002) call for a "big idea" to restart the North American process after 9/11 was one of the most eloquent of these.
9. See the grand Sierra Club PowerPoint presentation titled "Threats to Our Water: NAFTA, SPP, Super-Corridors, Atlantica," which ties everything together in a neat conspiratorial package. Eaton 2007. Jerome Corsi (2007) tells the best story.
10. By October 2011, US-Canada trade in goods had almost equaled the high-water mark of 2008.
11. Pastor 2011, 28.
12. Gattinger 2010.
13. Dukert 2012, 170.
14. See the National Round Table on the Environment and the Economy's report on "Canada-US Climate Policy Choices" (2011), which notes that "Canada has embarked upon a path of climate policy harmonization with the United States . . . [which has] significant implications to our own [i.e., Canada's] climate policy ambitions and realizations" (Message from the Chair, no page).
15. Each year, the US Global Change Research Program produces a "National Climate Assessment" (see www.globalchange.gov/what-we-do/assessment). The

National Research Council, with members drawn from other august bodies, has issued an evaluation of this report, asking if any critical content areas are missing. It responds: "There is a clear need for more international context in the discussion of energy use and mitigation efforts, and in understanding US vulnerabilities that stem from impacts occurring elsewhere in the world." National Research Council 2013, 15. But the report provides no indication that climate change in the US should be viewed in the context of the impact of climate change on the North American continent nor a suggestion that this investigation ought to be carried out jointly by the three North American governments.

16. Stanley 2010.
17. Blank 2011.
18. See the semi-annual Report Card for America's Infrastructure issued by the American Society of Civil Engineers (www.infrastructurereportcard.org/).
19. In August 2012, the Secretary of Transportation announced the formation of a Freight Policy Council, which would develop a national plan for improving freight movement and meeting the President's goal of doubling US exports by 2015. In May 2013, he announced the members of the National Freight Advisory Committee, a diverse group of professionals that will advise on improving the national freight transportation system (US Department of Transportation 2013). There is no indication of the reality that key sectors of our economy are integrated continental systems, as is much of our freight transportation system, and that a vital need is to enable this transport system to meet twenty-first-century demands.
20. For a recent update, see Economist 2012. Canadians have been more aware of an impending demographic crisis; see Senate of Canada 2010.
21. See Jensen 2009.
22. Monnet 1976, 408.
23. Crist 2010.
24. Rabe 2010a, 12.
25. Rabe 2010b, 183.
26. Again, there is good work out there. See UCS/ESA 2003; Canada-US-Ontario-Michigan Border Transportation Partnership 2004; Anderson 2012; and many more one-off reports. The problem is that all of this work is fragmented, embedded in silos, and soon forgotten.
27. Wiemer 2009, 4.
28. Wiemer 2009, 4–5.
29. Rabe 2010a, 14.
30. Private conversation with the author, Detroit, August 2, 2012.
31. In his essay on "transborder environmental governance" in the Wilson Center publication, Don Alper writes (2010, 146) that "the importance of leadership, and of individuals who are willing to 'champion' the cause of promoting transboundary cooperation, cannot be overestimated. . . . [I]t is clear that the close personal and working relationships between different sets of BC premiers and Washington state governors have been crucial to elevating the profile of 'transboundary' work."
32. The old website still exists: www.cigionline.org/project/portal-north-america. But the content is no longer updated. (Disclosure: I was much involved with this project.)
33. Smith 1997, 113.
34. Smith 1997, 113.
35. It is tragic that the organization disappeared with barely a trace. I could not find a single Google hit on the CAC or NAC. Also, there was, I believe, a Canadian-American Chamber of Commerce about this time. But I can find no information on it either.

36. Disclosure: These are views drawn from my own experience in these organizations. As noted, there seems to be no literature on any of this.
37. See http://northamericanforum.org/.
38. At the regional and grassroots levels in North America, a garden of business-based organizations thrive—from trade corridor organizations to regional development bodies and cross-border chambers of commerce, not to mention many issue-focused groups that deal with transportation or environmental issues, for example, as well as a few better-known organizations such as PNWER and the BTA. But there are no coherent links among them, there is little learning from one another, and, as we have seen, the sheer number of these bodies can actually diminish rather than enhance their influence in the policymaking process.
39. One can think of several models. BIAC (the Business and Industry Advisory Committee to the OECD) has represented business interests in the OECD for more than fifty years (www.biac.org/index.htm). The network of business advisory groups in EU systems deserves to be closely examined. Recently created, the Business Coalition for Transatlantic Trade (BCTT) "seeks to promote growth, jobs, and competitiveness on both sides of the Atlantic through an ambitious, comprehensive and high-standard trade and investment agreement between the US and the European Union" (www.transatlantictrade.org). This comes very close to the model I have been suggesting; why is it so much more difficult to do this in North America?
40. On the North American Electricity Reliability Corporation, see Gattinger 2011.

REFERENCES

Alper, Donald K. 2010. "Transboundary Environmental Governance in the Pacific West," *Environmental Governance on the 49th Parallel: New Century, New Approaches*. Washington DC: Woodrow Wilson International Center for Scholars, Canada Institute, Occasional Papers.

Anderson, Bill. 2012. "The Border and the Ontario Economy," University of Windsor, Cross-Border Transportation Centre. www1.uwindsor.ca/crossborder/system/files/The_Border_Report2012.pdf

Blank, Stephen. 2011. "Building Autos: How North America Works and Why Canadian Studies Should Be Interested," *American Review of Canadian Studies* 41 (4): 330–344.

Blank, Stephen, and Jerry Haar. 1998. *Making NAFTA Work: US Firms and the New North American Business Environment.* Miami: Lynne Rienner/North-South Center, University of Miami.

Blank, Stephen, and Jennifer Jeffs. 2012. "The NAFTA Region: A Work in Progress," *Inside Policy: The Magazine of the MacDonald-Laurier Institute*, October: 39–44.

Canada-US-Ontario-Michigan Border Transportation Partnership. 2004. "Planning/Needs and Feasibility Study," January. www.partnershipborderstudy.com/pdf/a_PNFStudyReport_FINAL_updatedpgnumbers.pdf

Clarkson, Stephen. 2008. *Does North America Exist? Governing the Continent after NAFTA and 9/11*. Toronto: University of Toronto Press.

Clarkson, Stephen, Sarah Davidson Ladly, and Carlton Thorne. 2006. "A North American 'Community of Law' with Minimal Institutions: NAFTA's Committees and Working Groups" (pp. 105–122), in John Kirton and Peter Haynal, eds., *Sustainability, Civil Society, and International Governance: Local, North American, and Global Perspectives*. New York: Ashgate.

Corsi, Jerome. 2007. *The Late Great USA: NAFTA, the North American Union, and the Threat of a Coming Merger with Mexico and Canada*. Washington DC: WND Books.

Crist, Ken, ed. 2010. *Environmental Governance on the 49th Parallel: New Century, New Approaches*. Washington DC: Woodrow Wilson International Center for Scholars, Canada Institute, Occasional Papers.

Dobson, Wendy. 2002. "Shaping the Future of the North American Economic Space: A Framework for Action," *CD Howe Institute: The Border Papers* 162 (April).

Dukert, Joseph. 2012. "Energy: The Continental Bridge" (pp. xx), in Alex Bugailiskis and Andres Rozental, eds., *Canada Among Nations 2011–2012*. Montreal/ Kingston: McGill-Queen's University Press.

Eaton, Janet M. 2007. "Threats to Our Water: NAFTA, SPP, Super-Corridors, Atlantica," presentation to "Our Communities, Our Water" Forum, September 22–24, University of Massachusetts Amherst. www.sierraclub.ca/national/programs/health-environment/water/water-threats-nafta.pdf

Economist. 2012. "America's Demographic Squeeze: A Falling Birth Rate and Much Slower Immigration Presage Long-Term Trouble Ahead," *Economist*, December 15. www.economist.com/news/united-states/21568398-falling-birth-rate-and-much-slower-immigration-presage-long-term-trouble-ahead-double

Gattinger, Monica. 2010. "Canada's Energy Policy Relations in North America: Toward Harmonization and Supranational Approaches?" (pp. xx), in Geoffrey Hale and Monica Gattinger, eds., *Borders and Bridges: Canada's Policy Relations in North America*. Toronto: Oxford University Press.

Gattinger, Monica. 2011. "Canada-United States Electricity Relations: Test-Bed for North American Policy-Making?" *Canadian American Public Policy* 75.

Golob, Stephanie R. 2008. "Three Strikes and You're Out? The Security and Prosperity Partnership of North America (SPP) and the Future of North American Integration," Teaching Module for the Portal for North America, Center for International Governance Innovation, July. www.portalfornorthamerica.org/sites/files/PNA_Teaching_Module_Golob-SPP_0.pdf

Hart, Michael. 2006. "Steer or Drift? Taking Charge of Canada-US Regulatory Convergence," *CD Howe Institute: The Border Papers* 229, March.

Hufbauer, Gary Clyde, and Jeffrey J. Schott. 2005. *NAFTA Revisited: Achievements and Challenges*. Washington DC: Institute for International Economics.

Jensen, Cheryl. 2009. "For Baffled Buyers, a Guide to Cars Made in North America," *The New York Times*, June 19. www.nytimes.com/2009/06/21/automobiles/21intro.html?_r=0

Monnet, Jean. 1976. *Mémoires*. Paris: Arthème Fayard.

National Research Council. 2013. *A Review of the Draft 2013 National Climate Assessment*. Washington DC: The National Academies Press. www.nap.edu/catalog.php?record_id=18322

National Round Table on the Environment and the Economy (NRTEE). 2011. *Parallel Paths: Canada-US Climate Policy Choices*. Ottawa: NRTEE. http://neia.org/wp-content/uploads/2013/04/canada-us-report-eng.pdf

Pastor, Robert A. 2001. *Toward a North American Community: Lessons from the Old World for the New*. Washington DC: Institute for International Economics.

Pastor, Robert A. 2011. *The North American Idea: A Vision of a Continental Future*. New York: Oxford University Press.

Rabe, Barry. 2010a. "Trans-Border Environmental Governance in Canada and the United States: Introduction and Common Themes" (pp. xx), in *Environmental Governance on the 49th Parallel: New Century, New Approaches*. Washington DC: Woodrow Wilson International Center for Scholars, Canada Institute, Occasional Paper Series.

Rabe, Barry. 2010b. "The Absence of Governance: Climate Change in Canada and the United States" (pp. xx), in *Environmental Governance on the 49th Parallel: New Century, New Approaches*. Washington DC: Woodrow Wilson International Center for Scholars, Canada Institute, Occasional Paper Series.

Senate of Canada. 2010. *Fiscal Sustainability Report*, February 18. www.pbo-dpb.gc.ca/files/files/Publications/FSR_2010.pdf

Smith, Arthur J.R. 1997. "The Canadian-American Committee and the Private Planning Association of Canada," *Canadian Business Economics* (Winter/Spring): 113–116.

Stanley, Guy. 2010. "Borders and Bridges: Free Trade, Supply Chains, and the Creation of a Joint Trading Platform: Canada-US Industrial Development since 1980" (pp. xx), in Geoffrey Hale and Monica Gattinger, eds., *Borders and Bridges; Canada's Policy Relations in North America*. Toronto: Oxford University Press.

UCS/ESA. 2003. "Confronting Climate Change in the Great Lakes Region: Impacts on Our Communities and Ecosystems," report of the Union of Concerned Scientists and the Ecological Society of America, April. www.esa.org/science_resources/DocumentFiles/ucsgreatlakesFINAL4–7.pdf

US Department of Transportation. 2013. "US Transportation Secretary LaHood Announces National Freight Advisory Committee Members," US DOT Press Release 50–13, May 30. www.dot.gov/briefing-room/us-transportation-secretary-lahood-announces-national-freight-advisory-committee

Wiemer, Calla. 2009. "Three Cases of Cross-Border Economic Corridor Development with Lessons for the Greater Mekong Sub-Region," report prepared for the Asian Development Bank, July. http://callaweimer.com/Documents/Wiemer%20Corridor%20Study.pdf

11 Conclusion

Without Architecture, but Not without Structure

Greg Anderson and Brian Bow

The title of this volume was meant to evoke a process of formation, or expansion, without any sense of purpose or design to guide that process. In that sense, it was meant to draw out the comparison with European integration, which has always been guided by successive cohorts of regionalist policy entrepreneurs with a strong sense of both purpose and design. Even in the aftermath of recent financial crises, the debate about Europe's future is still about how best to restore momentum to a political project, and what design might best serve the next phase of the region's development. To the extent that North America can be seen as a meaningful regional complex, one could argue that it was formed as such almost entirely "by accident." It is, as Ann Capling and Kim Nossal noted long ago, a strange case of regionalization without regionalism. But even in the absence of design, there can be structure, and, because structures create path-dependency effects, they can be helpful to us not only in understanding past and present policy outcomes, but also in anticipating future outcomes as well.

As noted in the introductory chapter, the two core purposes of this volume have been to try to characterize the structure of regional governance in North America, and to try to account for that structure. Our first thoughts in this direction were based on a recognition that while North America and Europe are often seen as opposites (e.g., in terms of formal institution building), there was also a striking similarity between the two regions, in the growing prominence of network-driven policy coordination after the early 1990s. With North America turning away from formal intergovernmental negotiations after NAFTA, and Europe struggling to agree on next steps after Maastricht, both regions seemed to be "muddling through." To the extent that policies were being effectively coordinated, it was often through the negotiation of informal agreements to make unilateral adjustments, rather than through formal treaties, and this process was being driven by a much more complex array of political actors, including subfederal governments, bureaucratic networks, and transnational private and civil society actors. We found, however, that the literature on this kind of "multi-level governance" (MLG) was much less developed in the North American context, and so turned to recent theory and concepts from research on Europe, comparative regional integration, and international policy coordination.

Needing a relatively simple and user-friendly conceptual anchor, we chose as our starting place Liesbet Hooghe and Gary Marks's distinction between Type I and Type II modes of governance:[1] Type I, as described in the introduction to this volume, refers to the Westphalian ideal-type model of politics and diplomacy, with regional politics seen as negotiation between sovereign states, and states as unitary/hierarchical decision-making machines. Type II, on the other hand, refers to policy spaces where the state has been effectively "disaggregated,"[2] and representatives of some of its constituent parts are more or less free to collaborate with their counterparts across national borders, to design and implement policies that solve common problems—i.e., as imagined in most accounts of transgovernmental relations, and more generally what has been called multi-level governance.

This distinction resonates with past and present policy advocacy surrounding North American regional relations. Some advocates of closer regional cooperation have argued for a strengthening of Type I governance, through the creation of new regional institutions and/or negotiation of new treaties, or through new domestic mechanisms for strengthening executive control over regionally important issues.[3] Others have argued that there are too many political obstacles to effective Type I governance in North America, and—in the interest of making progress in working out coordinated policies to respond to pressing problems—have looked to Type II governance as the pragmatic alternative. This latter impulse is consistent with the findings of academic work on multi-level governance, within which there is a virtual consensus that "dispersion of governance across multiple jurisdictions is more flexible than concentration of governance in one jurisdiction."[4] While "flexibility" is undoubtedly a good thing, there are obviously trade-offs built into the shift from Type I to Type II governance, including questions about overall policy coherence and democratic accountability. In practice, moreover, central political leaders often seek to maintain control over the policy agenda, forcefully directing or setting limits on Type II engagements.

From the outset then, we were skeptical of some popular accounts of multi-level governance, which seemed to expect an inevitable, across-the-board shift from Type I to Type II models. First, we expected our contributors to find significant variation across issue-areas, with policy coordination in some domains more closely approximating the more centralized Type I model and others approximating some version of Type II. This first expectation was borne out in the empirical chapters, although not always exactly as we expected. The two chapters on border control and territorial security—by Ackleson and Lapid and by Zaiotti—both found significant transgovernmental network activity in day-to-day policy implementation. Some of the examples in these chapters, moreover, fit fairly neatly with the conventional account of transgovernmental networking as a form of Type II governance.

Other chapters, however, showed that old-fashioned Type I governance is still alive and well in North America, and raised questions about the relevance of Type II accounts, at least within certain issue-areas. Stephen Clarkson's chapter on trade and investment policy, for example, argues that central policymakers have effectively used traditional (Type I) mechanisms of top-down authority and diplomacy—and particularly international legal agreements—to selectively set limits on state autonomy, in order to further a neoliberal economic agenda.

Second, we expected that policy coordination in North America would never actually look exactly like either of Hooghe and Marks's ideal-type models, but rather tend to some kind of hybrid form. The chapter by VanNijnatten and Craik, on environmental policy, focuses on this kind of hybridization, and makes the case for "bundled" transgovernmental networks as a way to balance the strengths of Type I with the flexibility of Type II governance. On closer inspection, most of the other chapters also describe various kinds of hybrid regimes, although they are not always as clear about how the pieces fit together. Ackleson and Lapid's chapter on border security focuses on the day-to-day operation of transgovernmental networks, but it also reveals the importance of central political leaders in enabling and directing this activity. Kukucha's chapter on trade policy recognizes the way—in keeping with the basic expectations of the multi-level governance (MLG) approach—subnational governments have an impact on national goals and strategies; but, in pointing out the limited impact that civil society actors have on subnational governments, Kukucha also shows that there are limits to the decentralization of authority and perhaps of the applicability of the MLG approach more generally. And Morales's chapter on the evolution of Mexico's energy policy focuses squarely on national policymaking, with attention to fairly standard Type I dynamics (e.g., constitutional constraints, national party competition), but it also emphasizes the way that the political context in which the policy debate unfolds is powerfully shaped by "micro"-level trends (e.g., individual firms' responses to changing technology and market pressures).

Our aim in this volume was to get a sense of the predominant mode of regional governance in general, but with some attention focused on the variety of different forms across bilateral relationships and issue-areas. We did not begin with deductive propositions about how we might explain whatever patterns found across the chapters, and—looking back on what the various chapters have turned up—we are only just beginning to inductively work out possible explanations. Because we have been thinking about modes of governance as institutional structures, and reflecting on the pattern of centralized and decentralized decision making across different issue-areas, we are increasingly drawn to the New Institutional Economics (NIE), and its reflections on institutions as mechanisms for limiting transaction costs in the organization of private activity. We believe that the concepts and concerns of the NIE approach can help us explain some of the patterns unearthed within and between the chapters of this volume, and perhaps also serve as useful guideposts for future theorizing and research on regional governance in North America.

Like this volume, NIE as an academic project is chiefly concerned with understanding and explaining varying modes of governance. Whereas political scientists have been interested in the governance of public transactions in areas like border management, security, or the environment, economists working in the NIE tradition have focused on the governance of private transactions, particularly through their analysis of firms. Yet, the lessons to be learned from institutional design are relevant to both domains.

The NIE approach highlights two dimensions that might help us to understand the emergence of different institutional structures across issue-areas. First, it draws our attention to the type and scale of transaction costs associated with different kinds of activity, and the challenges involved in assessing and reducing those costs. Understanding the exchange relationships within particular policy areas might help us understand the types of institutions that emerge to manage the attendant transaction costs. Second, NIE emphasizes the way that institutions are durable, slow to change, and create path dependencies that shape subsequent activity and institution making. Thus the best explanation for a particular institutional form within a given issue-area might be the prior existence of other institutions, which encourage or discourage specific ways of regulating activity.

For scholars of the New Institutional Economics, the mitigation of transactions costs is all about the "varieties of governance." Moreover, one of the most enduring puzzles among this group of scholars is also one that animates this volume: how can we begin to explain both the varieties of governance we observe as well as changes to that governance over time? Whereas scholars of NIE have focused on the governance of private transactions, particularly through their analysis of firms, political scientists have been interested in the governance of public transactions in areas like border management, security, or the environment. Yet, the lessons to be learned from institutional design are relevant to both domains.

We add here a third dimension that can help to connect NIE concepts and concerns with those covered more explicitly in this volume: relative asymmetries of national power. Given the sheer scale of the power asymmetry between the US and its two neighbors, and the contrast with the European context, one might expect that this dimension would be at the forefront of theorizing about North America. In fact, it is often implicitly treated as "too obvious," and tends to fade into the background, as it does in this volume (Clarkson's chapter being a notable exception). Rather than thinking about power asymmetry as something that might explain policy coordination outcomes, however, here we are most concerned with it as a potential obstacle to coordination. As noted briefly in the introduction, the US, as the region's predominant power, has few incentives to compromise, and so might be inclined to hold back from regional dialogue, expecting its smaller neighbors to adapt themselves to American priorities and policies. And Canada and Mexico, as the weaker powers, would naturally be reluctant to engage with the US, for fear of being locked into an arrangement that constrains their already-fragile policy autonomy. Thus power asymmetry represents a "problem" that might be resolved through institutional design.

The remainder of this chapter will attempt to explore these questions in the course of working through a more traditional summary of the key findings of the preceding chapters. In the next section, the governance of private transactions and the language of "institutions" as governance structures is described alongside, and in conversation with, the literatures in governance highlighted by Hooghe and Marks. This section will also introduce the concept of investment-specificity as developed in scholarship on mergers and acquisitions of firms, where asymmetries are endemic. The third part of the chapter will then apply these insights to the North American setting and the findings of the contributors regarding the relative incidence of Type I or Type II governance. The final part will integrate the findings of our contributors into a broad discussion of recent events in North American governance and offer some conclusions about the interaction of Type II institutions and asymmetry, which, in turn, suggests avenues for future research and policy action.

INSTITUTIONS AND GOVERNANCE

An intrinsic element in the typology of governance developed by Hooghe and Marks is the role of institutions in optimizing the transactions costs associated with exchange at every level of granularity. The sections that follow are an effort to connect the "islands of theorizing" about governance of the state to similar "islands" regarding the governance of private firms, the basic rationales for which are remarkably similar. One of the foremost figures working in this stream is Douglass North, who argues that divergences in economic performance among countries are governed by the design and function of institutions shaping economic decision making. As he defines them: "Institutions are the humanly devised constraints that structure political, economic, and social interaction. They consist of both informal constraints (sanctions, taboos, customs, traditions, and codes of conduct), and formal rules (constitutions, laws, and property rights)."[5]

Put this way, the institutions of governance are more diverse and pervasive than those suggested in each of Hooghe and Marks's typologies. They govern our decision making in ways akin to the way the rules of the road govern traffic patterns but do not necessarily dictate where we drive. Political science tends to look at the roads and the road signs, and economics at the movement of the cars, but both are essentially concerned with the same things.

Classical economists like Adam Smith demonstrated how production and market exchange could be made much more efficient through the specialization and division of labor. This set of ideas was then extended and applied by David Ricardo to international trade via the specialization and division of labor inherent in comparative advantage-based trade. With limited specialization, production, or exchange, such as that restricted to a relatively autarkic subsistence family farm, the incidence of transactions costs is low. Transactions occur whenever there is specialization, a division of labor, and increasing degrees of interpersonal exchange that flows from them. As Williamson has observed, "a transaction occurs when a good or service is transferred across a technologically separable interface. One stage of activity terminates and another begins."[6] Where there are transactions, there are also transactions costs; with more transactions come more transactions costs.

One of the principal sources of transactions costs is uncertainty. Although the neoclassical model emphasizes choice under constraint, the constraints that economic actors work under are seldom finite or clearly defined. Although we are confronted on a daily basis with a range of economic choices, we also confront considerable uncertainty about those choices and choice sets. Most of that uncertainty involves the imperfect nature of the information at our disposal to help us make decisions. Moreover, cognitive scientists have for years been casting doubts upon the human rationality postulate central to the neoclassical model. They point out, for example, that humans routinely violate the most basic tenets of rational choice models, even when engaged in the simplest kinds of decision making.[7]

Economic decision makers much prefer risk to uncertainty. Institutions help mitigate the uncertainty within our choice sets by transforming uncertainty into risk. As Coase reminds us, productivity depends upon specialization and with it increased complexity in economic exchange, fraught with increasing uncertainty and numerous transactions costs. Were it not for the development of institutions to help guide economic activity, economic actors would be completely lost in a world where the cost and uncertainty of obtaining information upon which to base economic decisions would virtually prohibit economic exchange. Institutions, therefore, necessarily evolve along with economic specialization and serve to transform the uncertainty associated with imperfect information into risk, thereby reducing transactions costs, and facilitating the capture of the potential gains from trade.[8]

If we lived in the frictionless world of zero-transactions costs, the particular form of organization we employed to govern the process of exchange would be irrelevant; everything we produced and consumed could be procured through spot-market exchange.[9] Because we do not live in such a world, particular forms of organization or governance can have a tremendous impact on all manner of economic, political, and social decision making.

As the volume makes clear, there are multiple forms of governance institutions operational in the North American economic and security space, none of which materialized overnight. Hooghe and Marks note that different forms of governance are characterized by a high degree of embeddedness—Type II flowing from Type I, for example. But how can we begin to account for the varieties of governance we see on the continuum between Types I and II?

Hooghe and Marks observe that differing modes of regional governance may be reflections of differing strategies for reducing transaction costs among states. This is left somewhat vague, but it clearly resonates with the established economic literature on the organization of firms as mechanisms for reducing transaction costs in private economic activity. As Ronald Coase first explained in his seminal article on the theory of the firm, the firm's very existence is premised on the internalization of market transactions costs.[10] Yet, as the theory of the firm has evolved, questions about how firms organize for this purpose have proliferated. For example, if efficiency is the main function of internalizing market exchange transactions under one roof, why then are there so many different ways of organizing the firm itself? Why, in other words, are there so many varieties of economic governance?

As economies and polities become more sophisticated and move away from subsistence exchange and toward specialization, the division of labor, and economies of scale, significant gains from exchange can be had. However, with that exchange comes the uncertainty and transactions costs associated with more impersonal, intertemporal, and long-distance forms of exchange. Transactions costs involve three key elements: 1) uncertainty, or rather the resources required to mitigate uncertainty; 2) the frequency with which transactions occur (linked to uncertainty and extending the shadow of the future); and 3) the degree to which transactions-specific investment costs are incurred.[11] The first and second of these having been touched on above, we turn to the third.

Investment-Specific Transactions Costs

An important indicator of the incidence of transactions costs and, therefore, the structure of governance flowing from them, is the relative specificity of those costs. In order to carry out a market transaction, it is necessary to discover who it is one wishes to deal with, to inform people that one wishes to deal and on what terms, to conduct negotiations leading up to a bargain, to draw up the contract, and to undertake the inspection needed to enforce the terms of the contract. These operations are often extremely costly—sufficiently costly at any rate to prevent many transactions that would be carried out in a world in which the pricing system worked without cost.[12]

Transactions costs will fall most heavily on those exchanges that involve the most specific and specialized kinds of exchange (i.e., investment-specificity).[13] A key issue in any exchange between parties is whether the assets being exchanged are fungible; in other words, how rapidly can you redeploy assets committed to an exchange relationship should that relationship fall apart?[14] Defense procurement, for example, is a form of exchange with typically high asset-specificity, in which there are few alternative sources of supply (for the government) or demand (for the firm). Where the identity of the parties is important, as in the case of jet fighter procurement, both parties are likely to be more committed to a contract. Both parties have an interest in fulfilling the terms of the contract because, except where specialized training or investment capital are transferable to alternative buyers or suppliers, both are locked into the terms of the contract and may be more amenable to adapting or renewing contractual relationships; in other words, the parties become engaged in a kind of exclusive bilateral supply.[15] Parties to any contract are interested in appropriating as much of the rent from a contract as possible. However, the specificity of the investments within the contractual arrangement will dictate how those rents are distributed, how transactions costs are borne, and what kinds of institutions evolve to frame the rules of the contract.

In the case of many buyers and sellers, the standard spot-market contracting costs will be incurred and institutional structures arise. But in the case of high investment-specificity, a special set of institutions may arise to help structure the relationship and reduce the potential impact of transactions costs on the performance of the exchange relationship. The point to be made here is that the more highly specialized the assets within an exchange relationship are, the greater is the potential for transactions costs to be significant and hence, the greater the incentives for firms to bring such relationships under one roof through mergers and acquisitions—in other words, a significant change to patterns of corporate governance.

The incursion of either spot-market or investment-specific transactions costs also suggests the rationale for the rise of firms, states, or regions—that is, the internalization of some of those transactions costs. Rather than incur those costs through the creation of a web of contractual relationships, why not simply bring them under a single roof? According to the Coase Theorem, firm size is limited where its internal costs of organizing an extra transaction are equal to that of conducting it outside the firm.[16] From this premise, we can begin to reason through the rationale for mergers and acquisitions as well as the more recent practice of outsourcing.[17] Firms do not expand indefinitely, nor does a single firm produce everything. As the marginal costs (transactions costs) of exchange rise and fall in response to the standard determinants of supply and demand, the capacity of firms to change their governance structures can often determine the firm's survival. Hence, decisions about the vertical and horizontal integration of production are based upon whether that transaction can be done more efficiently inside or outside the firm's structure.

NORTH AMERICAN GOVERNANCE?

There are some important differences between firms and states as institutional structures. Firms respond to shareholders who expect dividends, and states respond to citizens who expect accountability. Both states and firms are under pressure to deliver both cost-efficiency and output-quality, although in practice states may be more concerned with outputs and firms with efficiency. Both, as part of their drive for efficiency, are concerned with optimizing transactions costs, and in both cases different states or firms will foster different governance structures. Thus, one airline might choose to internalize some transactions costs related to fueling its fleet by purchasing a refinery, while another carrier relies on more traditional market hedging strategies.[18] Similarly, the neoclassical theory of the state points to the utility of institutions like the US's Interstate Commerce Clause, as a means of internalizing transactions costs incurred in exchange among the fifty states.[19]

Notwithstanding the differences between states and firms, there are at least three ways in which the commonalities between them can shed light on North American governance. Firstly, consider the role of innovation in shaping the governance patterns of both firms and states. In the case of the firm, innovative technologies or processes may be adopted outside any particular firm, perhaps in a related industry, possibly in response to a specific need or problem. It may be attractive for the firm to internalize the transactions costs associated with that innovation, perhaps becoming more vertically integrated, or by expanding its business lines through horizontal integration. To put things concretely, when Facebook paid $19 billion for a little known start-up tech firm called WhatsApp, the social media giant was internalizing potential transactions costs by becoming a more vertically integrated firm.[20]

With respect to the three North American governments, the patchwork of governance modes has become an engine of problem solving and innovation. We see this in at least two contexts: within and between components of the federal executive, and within and between federal systems. With respect to the former, government departments and agencies often have quite a bit of latitude in the implementation of policies, and sometimes are empowered to make their own policies. Where the policy solutions they develop have broader applicability, those "best practices" may be copied or otherwise diffused to other departments or agencies within the national executive, or across borders in other capitals.

A similar pattern can be seen with respect to subfederal governments, operating within the different federal structures of the three North American countries. Former US Supreme Court Justice Louis Brandeis often referred to the US states as the "laboratories of democracy," wherein governance innovation often resulted in models or practices that could ultimately be adopted nationwide.[21] Local problems breed local solutions and processes to manage them. Depending on how widespread those problems are, the most innovative local solutions and processes are sometimes internalized on a larger state, regional, or national level in much the same way a firm internalizes transactions costs through mergers and acquisitions; in some instances, the state becomes more vertically integrated, in others, it "outsources" to more efficient and specialized expertise. This process of governance innovation on the part of subfederal actors underlies the evolving patchwork of interaction between civil society and subfederal governments described by Kukucha in Chapter 6 of this volume.

Second, the types of governance we see in firms and states are frequently embedded in one another, linked together by function and process. When, for example, an auto manufacturer decides to produce a new model, it may decide not to produce all of the components internally, and instead contract for some of them outside the firm. The governance relationship that evolves from that contract would not exist without the production of the new vehicle. The two firms are now tied to each other in a new contractual relationship different from either of those internal to each firm.[22] So it is with the state, wherein Type I governance initiatives spawn new Type II forms of governance. They are distinct, but tied to one another because the latter would not exist without the former. For example, cities are creatures of the state or province that chartered them in legislation (Type I). However, those same cities then experiment with multiple forms of stakeholder engagement, outreach, and organization in a variety of municipal-level processes that might at any given time be described as informal, diffuse, temporary, task specific, or advisory (Type II); all are embedded in Type I. The "embedded," path-dependent, and linked qualities of Type II and Type I governance have been revealed in several contexts throughout this volume, but perhaps most vividly in the pieces by Ackleson and Lapid (homeland security), Kukucha (subfederal civil society), and VanNijnatten and Craik (the environment), each of which traces the Type I sources of various forms of Type II activity.

Third, and possibly most important, is the asset-specificity of investments in exchange relationships because it can help us understand the dynamics of power asymmetry that is so pervasive in North America. As noted above, the greater the investment-specific nature of an exchange relationship (e.g., few other exchange partners), the stronger the incentives for both integration and robust institutional design to govern the relationship.[23] Yet, who bears the burden of those investment-specific transactions costs may depend on which party's asset-specificity is greater. In other words, if one party has fewer options for exchange than another, the asset-specificity of the relationship is higher for the former party relative to the latter. Examples of this kind of asymmetry are everywhere in mergers and acquisitions, where a weak firm may have few options other than to be merged with a healthier firm, or risk going out of business.[24] The result is that the asset-specific transactions costs of exchange will be more heavily borne by the weaker party. All of this is of importance for North American governance because it can help us understand the dynamics of asymmetrical power among the three countries, particularly the lack of Type I institutionalization and the expanding network of Type II.

Investment-Specificity of Governance Structures

The relative dependence of Canada and Mexico on US market access (as reflected in Table 11.1) entails a form of investment-specificity in their relations—costs that are unevenly distributed among the three parties depending on whether the governance process being pursued is Type I or Type II.

For the US, the investment-specificity of relations with Canada and Mexico is relatively low when in pursuit of Type I governance. Where economic relations are concerned, the US has a much more diversified set of potential exchange partners to which assets can be deployed than do Canada or Mexico. Indeed, as partly described by Geoffrey Hale in Chapter 8, the US has a large, global agenda, wherein Canada and Mexico seldom loom large. Because it has many more potential partnerships in which its assets could be deployed, the US has few incentives to invest in the construction of Type I institutions with Canada and Mexico—a kind of asymmetrical indifference. This suggests an entirely new way to interpret the US's disinterest in regional institution building. Most International Relations theory accounts explain the dearth of regional institutions in North America in terms of power, hegemony, and the preservation of hegemony.[25] Through the prism of the theory of the firm, however, the dynamics of asymmetrical interdependence can also be seen in terms of investment-specificity driving the relative institutionalization at many levels.[26]

Yet, where Type II processes are concerned, the dynamics of asset-specificity and asymmetry are different. A plethora of actors, processes, and relative symmetry of power, for example, within transgovernmental networks or among subfederal governments, often result in a higher degree of asset-specific investment by all parties; in short, it is more equitable with less structural indifference on the part of any of the parties.

The asymmetry of the asset-specific investments into the exchange relationship at the macro-level (e.g., high-level summitry) makes Type

Table 11.1 NAFTA asymmetries (in billions $US), 1975–2012

	1975	1987	1994	2000	2012
Canada GDP	$170	$420	$560	$770	$1,780
% of North American GDP	9%	7.9%	7.0%	6.5%	93%
Exports + Imports as %GDP	47%	53%	67%	85%	63%
Mexico GDP	$88	$140	$420	$581	$1,178
% of North American GDP	4.7%	2.6%	5.9%	5.2%	6.1%
Exports + Imports as %GDP	17%	33%	38%	64%	66%
US GDP	$1,600	$4,700	$7,017	$9,764	$16,240
% of North American GDP	86%	89.3%	87.7%	88.2%	84.5%
Exports + Imports as %GDP	16%	19%	22%	26%	29%

Source: World Bank

Table 11.2 NAFTA export partners, 2012 (rank order and percentage of total)

	Canada	Mexico	US
Exports to	US (74.5%) China (4.3%) UK (4.1%)	US (80.5%) Canada (3.6%) Germany (1.4%)	Canada (18.9%) Mexico (14%) China (7.2%) Japan (4.5%)
Imports from	US (50.6%) China (11%) Mexico (5.5%)	US (49.9%) China (15.4%) Japan (4.8%)	China (19%) Canada (14.1%) Mexico (12%) Japan (6.4%) Germany (4.7%)

Source: CIA World Factbook 2012.

I institutionalization in North America difficult. The stakes for the "weaker" parties, Canada and Mexico, are high due to the high level of asset-specificity placed on their relationship with the US. For Canada and Mexico, that high-stakes investment would yield a set of Type I institutions that formalized and deepened North America even further. By contrast, the US invests relatively little but gets a lot of what it wants out of North America through existing Type I institutions. It is a dynamic among the three countries that played itself out in both of the Type I negotiations of the late 1980s and early 1990s wherein Canada and Mexico each committed significant resources to negotiating the CUSFTA and then NAFTA.[27]

Yet, at many levels below this, there is far more symmetry in the investment-specificity of exchange relations, all of which facilitates the growth of the kind of Type II arrangements described in this volume that are structuring North American governance. In other words, the dynamics of asymmetry may lend themselves to more Type II forms of governance patterns: a plurality of stakeholders, task-specificity, informality, ad hoc, or advisory. One effect of establishing Type I governance is extending the "shadow of the future" of the exchange relationship between the two parties—in other words, institutional security. However, getting there in North America requires a significant investment of resources in a single exchange relationship, fraught with a high-risk burden for the smaller/weaker party.

In the absence of such investments in Type I processes, Type II governance marches on, in part because of its utility in asymmetrical exchange relationships. A plurality of exchange partners, limited and task-specific mandates, informality, temporary, or advisory versus binding, all mitigate asymmetrical power by equalizing the asset-specific investments contributed by each of the parties.

WHITHER NORTH AMERICA AT TWENTY?

This conclusion was drafted in the weeks after the North American Leaders Summit (NALS) in Toluca, Mexico, on February 19, 2014. In the typology of governance laid out in the introduction to this volume, official summitry like the NALS can be most readily categorized as traditional Type I governance: a limited number of actors (just three) atop traditional general-purpose, multifunction, and durable bureaucratic structures.[28] Yet, apart from the traditional Type I governance of the respective governments they head, the NALS fits awkwardly into this typology of Type I and Type II governance.

North America's citizenry would be right to assume that the leaders of the three countries see each other regularly. The presidents of the US and Mexico and prime minister of Canada meet regularly on the margins of meetings held under the auspices of a variety of international organizations. Much of the public also assumes trilateral "Leaders Summits" have long been institutionalized under the auspices of the North American Free Trade Agreement (NAFTA). But here, they are wrong. While the NAFTA negotiations themselves typified the kind of Type I governance described by Hooghe and Marks, formal, high-level summitry was never part of NAFTA's legacy. Indeed, NAFTA only went so far as to create and institutionalize annual meetings of the Free Trade Commission comprised of the three nations' respective trade ministers.[29] In terms of formal summitry, North America has, at first blush, instead been dominated by a kind of ad hoc governance that privileges traditional lines of communication and jurisdictions of control within and between governments. Robert Pastor, in particular, repeatedly pointed to some of the weaknesses of incomplete Type I governance in North America.[30] Yet, rather than fixing a problem, the NALS has reinforced this incompleteness by itself becoming ad hoc.

After its creation in 2005 alongside the Security and Prosperity Partnership (SPP), the NALS took place in each of the succeeding four years but became less and less important with each meeting. In fact, as the hosting duties rotated again to Canada in 2010, no meeting was held. Instead, bilateral meetings were held on the margins of the G20 Summit in Toronto that year. President Obama spent less than a day in Toluca, much of it focused on non–North American issues brewing elsewhere. Moreover, one reason for the decline in the importance of the NALS is that the SPP that spawned it was effectively gone as of 2009, replaced instead by two bilateral agendas anchored in Washington.

Angst and confusion over governance patterns in North America are at least as old as Governor Ronald Reagan's 1979 presidential campaign call for a "North America Accord." Considered by many at the time a throwaway line in his announcement for president, what Reagan meant by "Accord" was left undefined. However, as the first serious call for an explicitly trilateral form of governance, it foreshadowed the Type I governance projects embodied by the 1989 Canada-US Free Trade Agreement and NAFTA. Yet, the ink on NAFTA was barely dry when calls to finish what NAFTA started were heard. To the disappointment of many in government, the private sector, and academia, the years between 1994 and the early 2000s are often noted for the dearth of Type I governance activity. Multiple ideas were put forward, several processes launched, and frameworks put in place, none ever really coming to fruition.[31] Yet, the Type I integration projects of the late 1980s and early 1990s contributed to the construction of a kind of "variable geometry" of governance that has been constructing, and rewiring the latticework of Type I and Type II governance in North America for, arguably, hundreds of years.

NAFTA itself famously avoided the creation of supranational institutions that pooled sovereignty into traditional Type I governance structures. But NAFTA also created several new areas of quasi-Type II governance as well. The elimination of nearly all border measures, particularly tariffs, inherently began the well-documented rewiring of countless patterns of cross-border commercial interaction: everything flowing from increased trade volumes to changes in just-in-time supply chain management. Perhaps the most celebrated of formalized Type II structures are the Chapter 19 dispute settlement mechanisms covering the application of anti-dumping and countervailing duty laws. NAFTA left intact each country's trade remedy laws, but allowed ad hoc, quasi-judicial panels to sort through whether those laws had been applied as intended by administrative authorities, in a sense depoliticizing disagreements over those applications. Chapter 19 panels were task specific, limited in duration, flexible enough to consider different areas of expertise, and cases not intended to set trilateral precedents (although in practice they have); all characteristics of Type II governance. As Stephen Clarkson details in his contribution to this volume, the Chapter 11 investor-state rules, along with their binding arbitration measures, hived off investment issues from traditional Type I modes, shifting their governance into a new arena by moving the dispute to established arbitral bodies in the World Bank or United Nations, and conferring new obligations on the state in its relationship with foreign investors.

Moreover, NAFTA created more than twenty working groups comprised of experts and stakeholders to continue the substantive work advanced by NAFTA's requisite content areas. Like other Type II governance created by NAFTA, the working groups had task-specific jurisdictions, were flexible in how they pursued their work, and were limited only by the content of their work rather than the by jurisdictional boundaries. Some of these groups were charged only with very narrow and specific tasks, and were dissolved as soon as the work was done. For those with more open-ended agendas, network activity eventually faded with the absence of political support, and the processes became moribund. Thus a closer look at these examples of Type II governance reveals the way that they are enabled, sustained, and ultimately dependent on more conventional Type I priority setting and authority.[32]

Yet we can also readily identify instances in which Type II governance has been spawned by the perceived absence of robust Type I governance. The 2005 Security and Prosperity Partnership (SPP) is a case in point. On the surface, the SPP looked like a major Type I trilateral initiative, designed to deal with NAFTA's leftovers and other unresolved post-NAFT policy frictions. However, while Type I diplomacy gave political momentum to the working group process, it was clearly the subsequent Type II interactions that brought about the actual policy coordination that followed. This was particularly true with respect to border security and law enforcement coordination, as described in the chapter by Ackleson and Lapid. Moreover, as explained in the chapters by Hale and by Bow and Santa Cruz, the SPP was deliberately designed to avoid some of the core mechanisms of Type I governance, particularly oversight and ratification by national legislatures—especially the US Congress—and did not include any mechanisms for public input, apart from strictly limited, invitation-only engagement with selected private sector stakeholders.

One could argue that these efforts to short-circuit traditional mechanisms of Type I governance, and to constrain certain forms of Type II governance, were at least partly self-defeating because they stirred up resentment and suspicion from some excluded groups. Given the fanfare surrounding the SPP, with its initial list of more than three hundred issues under consideration, there was immediate demand for access from interested groups, from both the private sector and civil society. In early 2006, a group of private sector stakeholders led by United Parcel Service and the Council of the Americas formed the North American Competitiveness Council (NACC), in an effort to initiate dialogue with the intergovernmental process. A few months later, the NACC was formally "brought into the SPP process," and over the next few years issued two formal reports with specific proposals for moving the SPP agenda forward, including a recommendation to create a regulatory cooperation process.[33] The NACC continued to engage with the SPP intergovernmental process through the 2008 NALS meeting in New Orleans, but then disengaged and went dormant before the fatal 2009 NALS meeting in Guadalajara.

The story of the NACC—and of the SPP more generally—illustrates the importance of Type II governance structures based on "technical" collaboration among diverse network participants. Other recent examples include the role of regionally clustered subnational governments and cross-border stakeholder associations in pushing for the adoption of enhanced driver's licenses as acceptable documentation for border crossings.[34] The SPP featured the North American Energy Working Group as part of its agenda in 2005, but the NAEWG had actually been in existence for some time and was the spontaneous Type II outgrowth of the absence of trilateral energy governance.[35]

The NACC experience also reflects the way in which transnational and transgovernmental networks may be prevented from moving the regional agenda forward by Type I roadblocks.

Three other examples are raised in this volume. Hale's review of the roles played by Congress makes the case that the American legislative branch is the linchpin for regional governance in North America because it is the single biggest impediment to the initiation of any new Type I governance regimes. The extreme parochialism and partisanship of contemporary Congressional debate, ultimately driven by the electoral imperatives facing individual members, makes it virtually impossible for policy entrepreneurs to put together broad coalitions of legislators in support of new intergovernmental agreements. This virtual paralysis of Type I governance has pushed Canada and Mexico into a defensive posture, and encouraged them to focus on their respective bilateral relationships with the US, discouraging any further efforts at trilateral Type I coordination. Interestingly, Hale argues, these dynamics have actually raised the utility of Type II processes for making "progress" on North American governance, in part because narrower sets of issues can often be dealt with by Congress on their merits, avoiding the politicized nature of packaged Type I proposals.

Morales also picks up on the theme of formal state institutions as limits to Type II collaboration, in his chapter on Mexican energy policy reform. Whereas the North American energy market more generally is a complex mix of state, private sector, and nongovernmental stakeholder interaction—in other words, a mix of Type I and Type II governance—the energy sector in Mexico has been severely constrained by formal constitutional (i.e., Type I) constraints on market competition and foreign investment. Nevertheless, Morales makes clear, technological changes and broader market pressures in the region created powerful incentives for the Peña government to successfully pursue previously unthinkable reforms to open the door for limited foreign investment. This will also open the door for further transformation of the energy sector in Mexico over the next few decades, a process that will undoubtedly be guided by a mix of Type I diplomacy and Type II coordination.

Bow and Santa Cruz consider the role played by public attitudes and popular mobilization, arguing that this dimension has probably been much less important in circumscribing the regional agenda than observers have assumed. There was intense opposition to CUSFTA (in Canada) and NAFTA (in the US), and this reaction did discourage political leaders from pursuing further regional institution building after NAFTA came into effect. However, political leaders were inclined to informal coordination for other reasons, and public opposition is probably better understood as merely reinforcing that prior inclination. Bow and Santa Cruz argue that there is a fairly broad base of skepticism about regional integration in North America, but it has not been converted into meaningful politicization, partly because policymakers have deliberately chosen Type II governance initiatives as a way to avoid public criticism, and partly because the electoral system and party structure in the US and Canada tends to reinforce anti-regionalism's status as a marginalized, "outsider" view.

The embeddedness of Type II regional governance in North America comes out most clearly in the coordination of environmental policies, as described by VanNijnatten and Craik. The North American Agreement on Environmental Cooperation (NAEC), or the so-called environmental side agreement of NAFTA, was put in place by the three governments and, in most respects, represented a fairly weak form of Type I governance. Designed mainly as a forum for monitoring enforcement of environmental regulation and the exchange of research on shared issues, the Commission for Environmental Cooperation (CEC) was devoid of genuine enforcement power—in other words, it pooled no sovereignty nor did it establish any supranational institutions. One might therefore expect the weakness of Type I governance to have spawned some kind of spontaneous Type II alternative. VanNijnatten and Craik explain that indeed the absence of strong Type I institutions did create demand for Type II network engagement, but this activity has been firmly rooted in overarching state-led processes. The result is a set of "bundled" networks, orchestrated and sustained by central executives, but drawing ideas and initiative from technical experts and policy managers.

In contrast with the evolution of networked governance in environmental policy, the policy activism of substate governments in economic policy has not fostered significant engagement with civil society stakeholders. Throughout the 1990s, trade liberalization became a focal point for discussions about global governance, as trade rules were rewritten, patterns of economic activity shifted, and civil society was animated to action. Indeed, for a period in the late 1990s and early 2000s, international summitry was virtually overwhelmed by popular protests seeking to influence the reshaping of global economic governance.[36] Yet, as Kukucha argues in Chapter 6, institutional dynamics in all three North American states are having quite different effects on engagement between activist substate governments and civil society. He finds three different modes of governance across the three countries, with subfederal actors that remain highly embedded in Type I processes, in spite of the high degree of economic integration in North America. In Canada, trade policy is dominated by the Constitutional division of jurisdiction between Ottawa and the provinces. In the US, subfederal activity is much more ad hoc and driven by overwhelmingly by individual states' efforts to influence Washington. Lastly, Mexican states have historically taken virtually no interest in trade policy formulation, in part due to the legacy of strongly statist and centralized governance of the Partido Revolucionario Institucional (PRI). Interestingly, Kukucha argues that there are few transnational norms or institutions shaping subfederal trade policy activity, therefore serving as something of a corrective to the idea that integration is everywhere eroding the importance of national borders and leading to a "disaggregation" or "perforation" of the state.

Notwithstanding the urgency of the post-2008 economic crisis, the most pressing policy coordination challenges facing North America over the last ten or fifteen years have been border control and homeland security. Initial reactions to the post–9/11 terror attacks tended to focus on the search for intergovernmental agreements (e.g., the "Smart Border" accords) and, more commonly, the political leaderships' failure to reconcile their countries' divergent perceptions and priorities. Thus most observers were looking for Type I solutions and became pessimistic when little progress was made on this front. In retrospect, we can see now that some of the most interesting and important examples of transgovernmental network-led coordination have come in the security field. Ackleson and Lapid make it clear that the broad contours of the post–9/11 security agenda were shaped by Type I dynamics, and by the political leaderships' divergent priorities. However, they also find that these same political leaders have come to accept that traditional Type I governance models do not have the flexibility to respond effectively to the threat posed by more fluid transnational threats, and have decided to "fight fire with fire," by fostering the creation of transgovernmental networks to manage border control and homeland security. Zaiotti makes a supporting argument, through his comparison of the North American and European experiences with territorial security. He argues that while formal institution building on these issues is far more advanced in Europe—through the Schengen agreement and subsequent accords—these remain underspecified, and much of the policy coordination work is being done by transgovernmental networks. In that sense, Zaiotti argues, both the goals and the processes involved in regional security policy coordination in North America may be much more similar to those in Europe than most observers have recognized.

The Road Ahead

This concluding chapter has, somewhat unconventionally, tried to do more than summarize findings and synthesize them into suggestions for future investigation. The insights institutional economics introduced in this concluding chapter are less a reframing of this volume's analytical lens than they are an effort to explore the intersections between two broad approaches—in effect, an interdisciplinary conversation about governance.

The conceptual tools we put forward at the outset of this volume borrowed heavily from contemporary political science literatures on European and comparative regional integration. These approaches have proven useful in characterizing and explaining varying forms of governance within various relationships and issue-areas, both in the chapters that found extensive Type II governance (e.g., Ackleson and Lapid) and in those that did not (e.g., Clarkson). These approaches clearly also have their limitations, particularly when it comes to accounting for the patterns we observe *across* relationships and issue-areas. We have therefore proposed, here in this concluding chapter, an extension of these political science models of governance, through application of concepts and arguments from New Institutional Economics, with particular attention to the transactions cost economics pioneered by Ronald Coase, Oliver Williamson, and Douglass North.

As Blank reminds us in Chapter 10, with his call for an iterative approach to practical continentalism, those of us who study North America and are interested in its institutional future would do well to look at the organization of private activity up and down the scalar spectrum. How, for example, do changing forms of economic activity reflect the effects of technology and demographics on market pressures? How does pressure for government responsiveness on these issues translate into demand for policy coordination? Under what conditions does this policy coordination come about? And what are the causal dynamics and transmission mechanisms informing that coordination?

As is evident from the various contributions to this volume, these questions are relevant to a wide variety of policy areas, but the kinds of answers to these questions vary considerably. Should we look, for example, first to diplomatic processes and strategies, or to domestic political structures (e.g., division of powers between branches of government, electoral systems, etc.)? Where should we see these structural constraints as obstacles to policy coordination, and where should we see them as potential catalysts for more "targeted" policy coordination initiatives?

In 2003, David Lake weighed in on the debate over sovereignty by suggesting that "hierarchical" forms of sovereignty characterized the modern international system,[37] stating that "relationships between polities vary along a continuum defined by the degree of hierarchy between two or more polities. The degree of hierarchy, in turn, is defined by the locus of rights of residual control, or less formally, by the decision-making authority possessed by each polity."[38]

In other words, in different relationships and in different policy domains, there are degrees of policy sovereignty. Viewed through the typology of governance we have laid out here, we can recognize "hierarchies of governance," in which either Type I or Type II governance might be best suited to the unique, specialized, and profoundly asymmetrical policy circumstances of the North American experience. The varieties of governance, their sources, evolution, and function described throughout this volume suggest that different types of governance have greater utility than others. Moreover, the focus on hierarchies of governance can help avoid some of the dynamics of asymmetry that have arguably stood in the way of Type I governance projects.

This volume can therefore be read as a corrective to debates about North American integration focused on the false binary of the "big idea" and ad hoc incrementalism ("muddling through") as the only two options for the evolving architecture of North American governance. Instead of making general pronouncements about how the region works, our policy research ought to begin by trying to understand the distinctive dynamics of each issue-area (or each policy "problem"), with an eye to uncovering what parts of a given policy domain might lend themselves more readily to new forms of Type I or

Type II governance. Much has been written, for example, about the massive obstacles to a Type I breakthrough on immigration and labor mobility. But very little has been written on whether and how this policy area might be amenable to some kind of incremental, Type II process. The provision for the temporary entry of business professionals under Chapter 16 of NAFTA includes a "positive" list of professions for which temporary work visas can be obtained with relative ease. That list has been stubbornly difficult to amend, in part due to the resistance of state- and provincially based professional associations' desire to limit entry of foreign workers into local markets.[39] It may be possible, however, to make progress on these issues through informal coordination among federal and subfederal executives. Are there patterns that might reveal the circumstances under which subfederal governments have been successful in addressing their labor market needs through temporary foreign worker initiatives? Are there ad hoc exchanges that could be worked out, as reciprocal policy adjustments, between clusters of federal and/or subfederal agencies? And could these trade-offs be negotiated incrementally through some kind of "bundled" transgovernmental network process?

In other words, one important set of conclusions to be drawn from this volume is that we ought to be less concerned with the absence of architecture—i.e., of an overarching, region-building design—in trying to understand the dynamics of regional governance in North America. Neither the past nor the future of regional cooperation in North America has looked or will look like the European experience. Even in the absence of a regional architecture, however, there *is* a regional institutional structure—an enormously complex and varied compound structure, populated by numerous and varied relationship- and issue-specific substructures. Rather than following deductive arguments about what regional integration is supposed to look like, or measuring North America against the European model, we ought to be looking more inductively at the way that regional dynamics in North America actually play themselves out. In spite of the complexity of the overall structure, and the continuous evolution of the various component parts over time, we ought to be aiming to map out as much as possible of this broad and varied landscape, and to identify major (institutional) landmarks that can help guide both academic and policy debates.

NOTES

1. Hooghe and Marks 2003.
2. Posner 2005.
3. See Pastor 2001; Dobson 2002; Goldfarb 2003.
4. Ibid, 235.
5. North 1991, 97.
6. Williamson 1985, 1.

7. See Tversky and Kahneman 1974; 1981; Simon 1997.
8. North 1991, 99–100.
9. Coase 1937; Williamson 1981.
10. Coase 1937, 394–95.
11. Williamson 1979, 239.
12. Coase 1960, 15.
13. Williamson 1985, 52–56.
14. See Bolton and Scharfstein 1998. Bolton and Scharfstein recount the case of General Motor's 1926 acquisition of Fisher Auto Body in which asset-specificity played a major role in determining the dynamic of their contractual relationship and provided incentives for integration under one roof. See also Hart and Moore 1990.
15. Williamson 1979, 240–41.
16. Coase 1937, 394–95.
17. Bolton and Scharfstein 1988; Hart and Moore 1990; Holmstrom and Roberts 1998; see also Economist 2004.
18. See CNBC 2013.
19. See Kelly, Harbison, and Belz 1991, 467–86.
20. *The Wall Street Journal* 2013.
21. Walker 1969; Gardner 1996.
22. Williamson 1981, 1557. Williamson details the effects of changes to corporate governance structures in the 1960s, which led General Motors to "spin off" the Ethyl Corporation from its central operations, but retain a stake in the firm. Similarly, one of the key issues in contemporary labor relations with the Big Three automakers in the US is the outsourcing of parts manufacture to lower-cost input producers rather than production within the firm itself. In effect, this is a shift in governance structure in which transactions costs within the firm have allegedly become higher than those that can be obtained through market exchange.
23. Williamson 1979, 239.
24. Prashantham and Birkinshaw 2008; Callahan and Moeller 2009; Graebner 2009.
25. Krasner 1976; Keohane and Nye 1974; Keohane and Nye 1977.
26. See Anderson 2012.
27. See Hart 1994; Cameron and Tomlin 2000.
28. Hooghe and Marks 2003, 238.
29. NAFTA Article 2001, 5.
30. Pastor 2001; Pastor 2011; see also Clarkson 2008.
31. Anderson and Sands 2008.
32. Hooghe and Marks 2003, 238.
33. Anderson and Sands 2008, 21–24. There are actually now two regulatory cooperation processes: the US-Canada Regulatory Cooperation Council, formalized in February 2011, and the US-Mexico High-Level Regulatory Cooperation Council, formalized in March 2011.
34. See Gregoire and Campbell 2008.
35. Dukert 2007, 133–39.
36. See Scholte 2004.
37. Lake 2003.
38. Ibid, 311.
39. See NAFTA, Annex 1603.D.1 Professionals. Moreover, the "positive" list is limiting because of the rapidly changing nature of professional skill sets; for instance, "computer systems analyst" no longer captures the diversity of information technology professions that have proliferated since 1994 when the Internet was in its infancy.

REFERENCES

Anderson, Greg. 2012. "Securitization and Sovereignty in Post-9/11 North America," *Review of International Political Economy* 19 (5): 711–741.

Anderson, Greg, and Christopher Sands. 2008. "Negotiating North America: The Security and Prosperity Partnership," *Hudson Institute White Paper*, September.

Bolton, Patrick, and David S. Scharfstein. 1998. "Corporate Finance, the Theory of the Firm, and Organizations," *The Journal of Economic Perspectives* 12 (4): 95–114.

Callahan, Tyrone, and Thomas Moeller. 2009. "Who's Cheating Whom in Mergers and Acquisitions?" Unpublished Working Paper, University of Texas at Austin, July.

Cameron, Maxwell and Brian W. Tomlin. 2000. *The Making of the NAFTA: How the Deal Was Done*. Ithaca NY: Cornell University Press.

Clarkson, Stephen. 2008. *Does North America Exist?: Governing the Continent After NAFTA and 9/11*. Toronto: University of Toronto Press.

Coase, Ronald H. 1937. "The Nature of the Firm," *Economica* 4 (16): 398–401.

———. 1960. "The Problem of Social Cost," *The Journal of Law and Economics* 3 (October): 15.

CNBC. 2013. "Delta Jet-Fuel Gamble is Starting to Pay Off," CNBC News, December 6. www.cnbc.com/id/101253932

Dobson, Wendy. 2002. "Shaping the Future of the North American Economic Space," *The Border Papers: CD Howe Commentary* 162. Toronto: CD Howe Institute.

Dukert, Joe. 2007. "North America" (pp. 132–165), in Sidney Weintraub, ed., *Energy Cooperation in the Western Hemisphere*. Washington DC: Center for Strategic and International Studies.

Economist. 2004. "The Great Hollowing-out Myth," *The Economist*, February 19. www.economist.com/node/2446951

Gardner, James A. 1996. "The States-as-Laboratories Metaphor in State Constitutional Law," *Valparaiso University Law Review* 30 (Summer): 483–490.

Goldfarb, Danielle. 2003. "The Road to a Canada-US Customs Union: Step-by-Step or in a Single Bound?," *The Border Papers: CD Howe Commentary* 184.

Graebner, Melissa. 2009. "Caveat Venditor: Trust Asymmetries in Acquisitions of Entrepreneurial Firms," *Academy of Management Journal* 52 (3): 435–472.

Gregoire, Chris, and Gordon Campbell. 2008. "British Columbia/Washington State Partnership on Enhanced Driver's Licenses," *Canadian Parliamentary Review* (Spring): 1–5.

Hart, Michael. 1994. *Decision at Midnight: Inside the Canada-US Free Trade Negotiations*. Vancouver: University of British Columbia Press.

Hart, Oliver, and John Moore. 1990. "Property Rights and the Nature of the Firm," *The Journal of Political Economy* 98 (6): 1119–1158.

Holmstrom, Bengt, and John Roberts. 1998. "The Boundaries of the Firm Revisited," *The Journal of Economic Perspectives* 12 (4): 73–94.

Hooghe, Liesbet, and Gary Marks. 2003. "Unravelling the Central State, but How? Types of Multi-Level Governance," *American Political Science Review* 97 (2): 233–243.

Kelly, Alfred, Winfred Harbison, and Herman Belz. 1991. *The American Constitution: Its Origins and Development*. New York: WW Norton.

Keohane, Robert, and Joseph Nye, Jr. 1977. *Power and Interdependence: World Politics in Transition*. Boston: Little, Brown and Company.

Keohane, Robert, and Joseph Nye, Jr. 1974. "Transgovernmental Relations and International Organizations." *World Politics* 27 (1): 39–62.

Krasner, Stephen D. 1976. "State Power and the Structure of International Trade," *World Politics* 28 (3): 317–347.

Lake, David A. 2003. "The New Sovereignty in International Relations," *International Studies Review* 5: 303–323.

North, Douglas C. 1991. "Institutions," *Journal of Economic Perspectives* 5 (Winter): 97–112.

Pastor, Robert. 2011. *The North American Idea: A Vision of a Continental Future.* Oxford: Oxford University Press.

Pastor, Robert. 2001. *Toward a North American Community.* Washington DC: Institute for International Economics.

Posner, Eric. 2005. "International Law and the Disaggregated State," *Florida State University Law Review* 32: 797–842.

Prashantham, Shameen, and Julian Birkinshaw. 2008. "Dancing with Gorillas: How Small Companies Can Partner Effectively with MNCs," *California Management Review* 51 (1): 6–23.

Scholte, Jan Aart. 2004. "Civil Society and Democratically Accountable Global Governance," *Government and Opposition* 39 (2): 211–233.

Simon, Herbert. 1997. *Models of Bounded Rationality, Vol. 3: Empirically Grounded Economic Reason.* Cambridge MA: MIT Press.

Tversky, Amos, and Daniel Kahneman. 1974. "Judgement Under Uncertainty: Heuristics and Biases," *Science* 185 (September): 1124–1131.

Tversky, Amos, and Daniel Kahneman. 1981. "The Framing of Decisions and the Psychology of Choice," *Science* 211 (January): 453–458.

Walker, Jack. 1969. "The Diffusion of Innovations among the American States," *American Political Science Review* 63 (3): 880–899.

Wall Street Journal. 2013. "Facebook to Pay $19 Billion for WhatsApp," *Wall Street Journal*, February 19.

Williamson, Oliver. 1979. "Transaction-Cost Economics: The Governance of Contractual Relations," *Journal of Law and Economics* 22: 233–261.

———. 1981. "The Modern Corporation: Origins, Evolution, Attributes," *Journal of Economic Literature* 19 (4): 1537–1568.

———. 1985. *The Economic Institutions of Capitalism.* New York: The Free Press.

Contributors

Jason Ackleson is Associate Professor of Government at New Mexico State University. As a Truman and British Marshall Scholar, he earned his PhD in International Relations at the London School of Economics and Political Science. He has published over twenty-five articles, book chapters, reports, and other publications on questions of security, borders, immigration, and globalization.

Greg Anderson is Associate Professor of Political Science at the University of Alberta. He is the author of numerous articles on North American integration, international political economy, and US foreign economic policy. He was co-editor, with Christopher Sands of the Hudson Institute, of *Forgotten Partnership Redux: Canada-US Relations in the 21st Century* (Cambria 2012).

Stephen Blank's career spans the academic, business, and not-for-profit communities. For several decades, he has been known for work on North American integration—particularly cross-border production-distribution systems and physical infrastructure. He taught at Pace University in New York and held distinguished visiting appointments at other universities in the US and Canada.

Brian Bow is Associate Professor of Political Science and Director of the Centre for Foreign Policy Studies at Dalhousie University. He is the author of *The Politics of Linkage: Power, Interdependence and Ideas in Canada-US Relations* (UBC Press 2009), which was awarded the Donner Prize as the best public policy book published in Canada that year. He has also published a number of articles and chapters on US-Canada relations, Canadian foreign policy, and regional integration, and has co-edited volumes on North American security cooperation and Canadian foreign policy.

Stephen Clarkson is Professor of Political Economy at the University of Toronto. In the 2000s his trilogy on the dynamics of North America's integration and disintegration was published by the Woodrow Wilson Center and University of Toronto presses: *Dependent America? How Canada and Mexico Construct US Power* (2011, with Matto Mildenberger); *Does North America Exist? Governing the Continent after NAFTA and 9/11* (2008); *Uncle Sam and Us: Globalization, Neoconservatism, and the Canadian State* (2002).

Neil Craik is Director of the School of Environment, Enterprise, and Development at the University of Waterloo, where he is Associate Professor of Law. He is the co-editor of *Climate Change Policy in North America: Designing Integration in a Regional System* (University of Toronto Press 2013) and the author of *The International Law of Environmental Impact Assessment: Process, Substance and Integration* (Oxford 2008).

Geoffrey Hale is Professor of Political Science at the University of Lethbridge. He is the author of *So Near Yet So Far: The Public and Hidden Worlds of Canada-U.S. Relations* (UBC Press 2012), co-editor of a volume on Canada's policy relations in North America (*Borders and Bridges*, Oxford 2010), and author of numerous articles on various aspects of Canada-US relations, Canadian political economy, and North American integration.

Christopher J. Kukucha is a Professor of Political Science at the University of Lethbridge. He is the author of *The Provinces and Canadian Foreign Trade Policy* (UBC Press 2008) and the co-editor of *Readings in Canadian Foreign Policy: Classic Debates and New Ideas* (Oxford 2006, 2011, 2014). In 2007, he served as the William J. Fulbright Research Chair in Canadian Studies at the State University of New York (Plattsburgh).

Yosef Lapid is Regents Professor in the Department of Government at New Mexico State University. He has authored books and articles on nationalism and on international relations theory. He is also the lead editor of a book series on *Culture, Religion, and International Relations* at Palgrave Press.

Isidro Morales is Professor and Director of the Graduate School of Public Administration and Public Policy (EGAP) at ITESM-Monterrey. He has published numerous works on North America and Mexican politics, including *Post-NAFTA North America: Economic and Political Governance in a Changing Region* (Palgrave Macmillan 2008), and the edited volume *National Solutions to Trans-Border Problems?: The Governance of Security and Risk in Post-NAFTA North America* (Ashgate 2011).

Arturo Santa Cruz is Associate Professor of International Relations at the Department of Pacific Rim Studies and Director of the Center for North American Studies at the University of Guadalajara. His latest book is

Mexico-United States Relations: The Semantics of Sovereignty (Routledge 2012).

Debora VanNijnatten is Associate Professor of Political Science and North American Studies at Wilfrid Laurier University. She is co-editor of *Canadian Environmental Policy and Politics* (Oxford 2002, 2009); *North American Environmental Policy: Capacity, Approaches and Transboundary Issue Management* (University of Toronto Press 2013); and *North American Climate Change Policy: Designing Integration in a Regional System* (University of Toronto Press 2013). Her current research and publications focus on capacity building through transborder policy networks in North America.

Ruben Zaiotti is Director of the European Union Centre for Excellence and Assistant Professor of Political Science at Dalhousie University. He is the author of *Cultures of Border Control: Schengen and the Evolution of European Frontiers* (University of Chicago Press 2011). He is currently working on two research projects: the first looks at the transatlantic partnership over issues of homeland security; the second examines the challenges of European Union foreign policy after the signing of the Lisbon Treaty.

Index